Law Relating to
Banking Services

Law Relating to Banking Services

Andrew Laidlaw, LLB(Hons), Solicitor

Graham Roberts, BA(Hons), Barrister at law

First published 1990

Apart from any fair dealing for the purposes of research or private study, or criticism or review, as permitted under the Copyright, Designs and Patents Act 1988, this publication may only be reproduced, stored or transmitted, in any form or by any means, with the prior permission in writing of the publishers, or in the case of reprographic reproduction in accordance with the terms of licences issued by the Copyright Licensing Agency. Enquiries concerning reproduction outside those terms should be sent to the publishers at the undermentioned address:

BANKERS BOOKS LIMITED
c/o The Chartered Institute of Bankers
10 Lombard Street
London EC3V 9AS

Chartered Institute of Bankers (CIB) Publications are published by Bankers Books Limited under an exclusive licence and royalty agreement. Bankers Books Limited is a company owned by The Chartered Institute of Bankers.

© Laidlaw, A. and Roberts, G., 1990

 British Library Cataloguing in Publication Data

Laidlaw, Andrew
Law relating to banking services.
1. Great Britain. Banking. Law
I. Title II. Roberts, Graham
344.10682

ISBN 0 85297 277 6

Typeset 10/12pt Times, by Cotswold Typesetting Ltd, Cheltenham
Text printed on 80 gsm General Purpose, w'free; cover on 240 gsm matt coated art.
Printed by Commercial Colour Press Ltd, London E7

Contents

	Page
Table of Cases	xi
Table of Statutes	xix
Table of Rules and Regulations	xxiii
Preface	xxv

PART I—BANKING LAW AND THE CUSTOMER 1

1 The Banker–Customer Relationship 3
1.1 Introduction 3
1.2 Definition of a bank 4
1.3 Definition of a customer 4
1.4 The debtor–creditor relationship and other implied terms 5
1.5 Express terms 9
1.6 The bank's duty of care as agent 10
1.7 The bank's duty of care as trustee 12
1.8 The bank's right to interest and to charges 14
1.9 The bank's duty of confidentiality 15
1.10 The Data Protection Act 1984 19
1.11 Banker's opinions 21
1.12 Repayment on demand and limitation 24
1.13 Appropriation of payments 25
1.14 Combination of accounts and set-off 28
1.15 The banker's lien 31
1.16 Safe custody 33
1.17 Termination of the banker–customer contract 34

2 Types of Customer 37
2.1 Introduction 37
2.2 Individuals 37
2.3 Joint accounts 42
2.4 Minors 43
2.5 Trustee accounts 44

v

2.6	Partnership accounts	45
2.7	Companies	48

3 Consumer Credit Act Lending   55
3.1	Introduction	55
3.2	The definitions of regulated lending	56
3.3	Overdrafts	62
3.4	Credit-tokens	65
3.5	Connected lender liability	72
3.6	Secured lending	74
3.7	Exempt credit	77
3.8	The forms and formalities	81
3.9	Canvassing and circulars	89
3.10	Advertising and quotations	90
3.11	Credit brokerage	94

4 Financial Services Regulation   97
4.1	Introduction	97
4.2	Investments	98
4.3	Investment business	99
4.4	The regulatory bodies	99
4.5	Exempt bodies	102
4.6	Main 'rules' governing investment business conduct	103

PART II—CHEQUES AND PAYMENT SYSTEMS   109

5 Cheques   111
5.1	Introduction	111
5.2	Cheques and negotiable instruments	112
5.3	The Bills of Exchange Act 1882	113
5.4	Crossings on cheques	114
5.5	Indorsements on cheques	116
5.6	Holders of a cheque	117
5.7	Payment of cheques	119
5.8	The form of a cheque	120
5.9	Forgery of a drawer's signature	121
5.10	Fraudulent alteration	124
5.11	Countermand	126
5.12	Wrongful dishonour	129
5.13	Statutory protection for the paying bank	131

5.14	Other defences for the paying bank	134
5.15	The collecting bank	135
5.16	The collecting bank and its own customer	135
5.17	Statutory protection for the collecting bank	136
5.18	Negligence in opening the account	139
5.19	Negligence in collection of the cheque	141
5.20	Contributory negligence	147
5.21	The defence of *ex turpi causa non oritur actio*	147
5.22	The collecting bank's right to an indemnity	148
5.23	The defence of estoppel	148
5.24	The collecting bank as a holder in due course	148
5.25	Cheque cards	151
5.26	Recovery of money paid by mistake	153
5.27	Mistaken crediting of a customer's account	155
5.28	Practical examples of the law relating to cheques	156

6 Paper Payment Systems — 159
6.1	Introduction	159
6.2	Cheque clearing	160
6.3	Town clearing	162
6.4	Truncation of cheques	162
6.5	Credit clearing	165

7 Electronic Payment Systems — 171
7.1	Introduction	171
7.2	BACS	171
7.3	CHAPS	172
7.4	EFT clearing cycles	173
7.5	The legal aspects of EFT transactions: general	173
7.6	The payer and the payee	173
7.7	The payer and the paying bank	177
7.8	The paying bank and the payee bank	182
7.9	The paying bank and the payee	184
7.10	The payee bank and the payee	185
7.11	The payer and the payee bank	187

8 Cash Dispensing Machines — 189
8.1	Introduction	189
8.2	Cash cards as credit-tokens	189
8.3	Unsolicited credit-tokens	194

8.4	Machine failure or error	195
8.5	Unauthorised use of cash cards	199
8.6	Other ATM services	201

9 Electronic Funds Transfer at Point of Sale (EFTPOS) 203
9.1	Introduction	203
9.2	The EFTPOS payment process	204
9.3	The retailer	209
9.4	The cardholder	212

PART III—SECURITY 215

10 Insolvency 217
10.1	Introduction	217
10.2	Priority of claims in an insolvency	217
10.3	Voluntary arrangements and administration orders	220
10.4	Preferences and transactions at an undervalue	220
10.5	Transactions defrauding creditors	224
10.6	Extortionate credit transactions	224

11 Taking Security from Individuals 225
11.1	Introduction	225
11.2	Undue influence	225
11.3	Misrepresentation	228
11.4	Advice	230
11.5	*Non est factum*	230

12 Guarantees 233
12.1	Introduction	233
12.2	Guarantees and indemnities	233
12.3	Consideration	234
12.4	Duty to a guarantor before the guarantee is signed	235
12.5	Demand, determination and the Limitation Act	235
12.6	Joint guarantees	236
12.7	Standard bank guarantee terms	237
12.8	The guarantor's rights	241
12.9	Estoppel by convention	242
12.10	Letters of comfort	243

CONTENTS

13	**Land as Security**		245
	13.1	Introduction	245
	13.2	Legal estates and interests in land	245
	13.3	Registered and unregistered land	246
	13.4	Types of ownership of land	248
	13.5	Interests in registered land	250
	13.6	Interests in unregistered land	251
	13.7	The meaning of occupation	252
	13.8	The position of a purchaser or mortgagee	252
	13.9	The Matrimonial Homes Act 1983	254
	13.10	Types of mortgage over land	254
	13.11	Standard bank mortgage terms	257
	13.12	Realising the mortgage	258
	13.13	The mortgagee's power of sale	259
	13.14	Other remedies of the mortgagee	261
	13.15	Mortgages of leasehold property	264
	13.16	Discharge of a mortgage	265
	13.17	Risks for a lender	267

14	**Shares as Security**		269
	14.1	Introduction	269
	14.2	Type of mortgage	269
	14.3	The memorandum of deposit	270
	14.4	Realising the mortgage	271
	14.5	Risks for the lender	271

15	**Life Assurance Policies as Security**		275
	15.1	Introduction	275
	15.2	Types of mortgage on life policies	276
	15.3	Priorities between different assignees	277
	15.4	Standard terms	278
	15.5	Remedies of the assignee	278
	15.6	Potential risks for the lender	278

16	**Taking Security from Companies**		283
	16.1	Introduction	283
	16.2	Corporate capacity	283
	16.3	Execution of documents by a company	284
	16.4	The floating charge	284
	16.5	Standard debenture terms	286

16.6	Fixed and floating charges compared	287
16.7	Crystallisation of a floating charge	288
16.8	Administrative receivers	289
16.9	Retention of title or '*Romalpa*' clauses	292
16.10	Administration orders	293
16.11	Priority of charges and registration	295

17 Charges over Bank Balances 299
17.1	Introduction	299
17.2	Contractually extending the right of set-off	300
17.3	Taking a charge over the credit balance	301
17.4	The flawed asset	302

18 Charges over Book Debts 303
18.1	Introduction	303
18.2	Procedure for taking the charge	303

19 Agricultural Charges 307
19.1	Introduction	307
19.2	Fixed charges	307
19.3	Floating charges	308
19.4	Registration and priority	308

Appendix 1—Relevant Statutory Provisions 311

Appendix 2—Proposed Legislation: Extract from 'Banking Services: Law and Practice' White Paper 349

Index 351

Table of Cases

Abbey National Building Society v Cann [1990] 1 All ER 1085 . . 252, 253
Agra Bank v Barry (1874) LR 7 HL 135 257
Aluminium Industrie Vaasen B.V. v Romalpa Aluminium Ltd [1976]
   1 WLR 676 . . . . 292, 293
Amalgamated Investment and Property Co. Ltd v Texas Commerce
   International Bank [1981] 3 WLR 565 243
Arab Bank Ltd v Ross [1952] 2 QB 216 . . . . . . 117, 118
Avon County Council v Howlett [1983] 1 WLR 605 156
Avon Finance Co. Ltd v Bridger [1985] 2 All ER 281 227

Bache & Co. (London) Ltd v Banque Vernes et Commerciale de
   Paris S.A. [1973] 2 Lloyd's Rep. 437 241
Bacon (M.C.) Ltd, re [1990] 3 WLR 646 . . . . . 221, 222, 224
Baden, Delvaux and Lecuit v Société Général du Commerce S.A.
   [1983] BCLC 325 . . . . 12, 45
Baines v National Provincial Bank Ltd (1927) 96 LJKB 801 . . 127
Baker v Australian and New Zealand Bank Ltd [1958] NZLR 907 . 131
Baker v Barclays Bank Ltd [1955] 1 WLR 822 145
Bank of Credit and Commerce International S.A. v Aboody [1989]
   2 WLR 759 228
Banque Belge pour L'Etranger v Hambrouck [1921] 1 KB 321 . 184, 185, 187
Banque de l'Indochine et de Suez S.A. v Euroseas Group Finance
   Co. Ltd [1981] 3 All ER 198 50
Barclays Bank Ltd v Astley Industrial Trust Ltd [1970] 2 QB 527 . 118, 150
Barclays Bank Ltd v Simms (W J) Son and Cooke (Southern) Ltd
   [1980] QB 677 . . . . 128, 154, 184, 185
Barclays Bank plc v Taylor [1989] 1 WLR 1066 17
Barclays Bank plc v Quincecare Ltd and Unichem Ltd [1988]
   1 FTLR 507 11
Barclays Bank Ltd v Quistclose Investments Ltd [1970] AC 567 . 14, 168
Barclays Bank plc v Bank of England [1985] 1 All ER 385 . . . 136
Barney v Stubbs (Joshua) Ltd (1891) see Stubbs (Joshua) Ltd . . 290
Bartlett v Barclays Bank Trust Co. Ltd [1980] 2 WLR 430 . . 14
Bechervaise v Lewis (1872) 20 WR 726 242
Beckett v Addyman (1882) 9 QBD 783 238
Belmont Finance Corporation v Williams Furniture Ltd (No. 2)
   [1980] 1 All ER 393 12
Beresford v Royal Insurance Co. Ltd [1938] AC 586 280
Bevan v National Bank Ltd (1906) 23 TLR 65 . . . . . 115, 142
Bhogal v Punjab National Bank [1988] 2 All ER 296 29

xi

Bondina Ltd v Rollaway Shower Blinds Ltd [1986] 1 WLR 517 . . 50
Bourne, re; Bourne v Bourne [1906] 2 Ch 427 47
Bowes, re; Earl of Strathmore v Vane (1886) 33 ChD 586 . . 32
Box v Midland Bank Ltd [1979] 2 Lloyd's Rep. 391 11
Bradbury v Morgan (1862) 1 H & C 249; 31 LJ Ex 462 . . 238
Bradford Old Bank Ltd v Sutcliffe (1918) 2 KB 833 . . . 28, 236
Brandao v Barnett (1846) [1843–60] All ER Rep. 719 . . . 32, 33, 34
Brandon v Scott (1857) 7 E & B 234; 26 LJ QB 163 . . . 33
Brightlife Ltd, Re [1987] 2 WLR 197 . . . . . . 289, 304
Brimnes, The; Tenax Steamship Co. Ltd v The Brimnes (owners) [1974] 3 WLR 613 186
Bristol and West Building Society v Henning [1985] 1 WLR 778 . 254
British Eagle International Airlines Ltd v Compagnie Nationale Air France [1975] 1 WLR 758 . . . . 30, 31, 290
Brook v Hook (1871) LR 6 Ex 89 178
Brown v Westminster Bank Ltd [1964] 2 Lloyd's Rep. 187 . . 123
Buckingham v London and Midland Bank Ltd (1895) 12 TLR 70 . 300
Burnes v Trade Credits Ltd [1981] 1 WLR 805 239
Burnett v Westminster Bank Ltd [1966] 1 QB 742 128
Bute v Barclays Bank Ltd [1955] 1 QB 202 144

Carpenters Company v British Mutual Banking Co. Ltd [1938] 1 KB 511 . . . . 134, 135
Catlin v Cyprus Finance Corporation (London) Ltd [1983] QB 759 . 42, 120
Caunce v Caunce [1969] 1 WLR 286 252
Central Motors (Birmingham) v P.A. and S.N. Wadsworth [1983] CAT 82/231 46
Chambers v Miller (1862) 13 CBNS 125 130
Charge Card Services Ltd, re [1987] Ch 150 . . 30, 151, 210, 211, 300, 301
Charles v Blackwell (1877) 2 CPD 151; 46 LJ QB 368 . . . 132
Chase Manhattan Bank N.A. v Israel-British Bank (London) Ltd [1980] 2 WLR 202 . . . . 155, 184
China and South Sea Bank Ltd v Tan [1990] 1 AC 536 . . . 260
City of London Building Society v Flegg [1988] AC 54 . . . 251
Clayton's case, see Devaynes v Noble
Clutton v Attenborough [1897] AC 90 . . . . 116, 133
Cocks v Masterman (1829) All ER Rep. 431 154
Coldman v Hill [1919] 1 KB 443 34
Coldunell Ltd v Gallon [1986] 2 WLR 466 227
Coleman v London County and Westminster Bank Ltd [1916] 2 Ch 353 273
Commissioners of Taxation v English, Scottish and Australian Bank [1920] AC 683 5
Continental Illinois National Bank and Trust Co. of Chicago v Papanicolaou [1986] 2 Lloyd's Rep. 441 242
Cooper v National Provincial Bank Ltd [1946] KB 1 . . . 235
Cornish v Midland Bank plc [1985] 3 All ER 513 230

TABLE OF CASES

Coulthart v Clementson (1879) QBD 865 238
Coutts & Co. v Browne-Lecky [1947] KB 104 234
Cripps (R.A.) & Sons Ltd v Wickenden [1973] 1 WLR 944 . . . 290
Cuckmere Brick Co. Ltd v Mutual Finance Ltd [1971] Ch 949 . . 260
Curran v Newpark Cinemas [1951] 1 All ER 295 167
Curtice v London City and Midland Bank Ltd [1908] 1 KB 293 . . 127

Davidson v Barclays Bank Ltd [1940] 1 All ER 316 131
Dearle v Hall (1828) 3 Russ 1 277
Deeley v Lloyds Bank Ltd [1912] AC 756 . . . . . . 26, 258
Delbrueck & Co. v Manufacturers Hanover Trust Co. (DC NY 1979) 464 F Supp. 989 176
Destone Fabrics Ltd, re, [1941] Ch 319 288
Devaynes v Noble: Clayton's case (1816) 1 Mer 529, 572 . . . 26, 27, 43, 47, 52, 53, 238, 240, 256, 258, 270, 278, 288, 309
Drew v Nunn (1879) 4 QBD 661 129
Durham Fancy Goods Ltd v Michael Jackson (Fancy Goods) Ltd [1968] 2 QB 839 50

Ellesmere Brewery Co. v Cooper [1896] 1 QB 75 . . . . 236, 237
Elliot v Director-General of Fair Trading [1980] 1 WLR 977 . . 66
Emmadart Ltd, re [1979] 2 WLR 868 292
European Bank, *ex parte* (1871) 7 Ch App 99 239

Fedora, The, *see* Continental Illinois National Bank and Trust Co.
First National Finance Corporation v Goodman [1983] BCLC 203 . 237, 240
First National Securities Ltd v Hegarty [1984] 3 WLR 769 . . 267
Foley v Hill (1848) 2 HL Cas 28 5
Forman v Bank of England (1902) 18 TLR 339 135
Fullerton v Provincial Bank of Ireland [1903] AC 309 234

Garnett v McKewan (1872) LR 8 Exch 10 28
Gaunt v Taylor (1843) 2 Hare 413 47
Gibbons v Westminster Bank Ltd [1939] 2 KB 882 . . . . 130, 179
Gibson v Minet (1791) 2 Bing 7; 9 Moore CP 31 177
Governments Stock and other Securities Investment Co. Ltd v Manila Railway Co. Ltd [1879] AC 81 289
Graham (James) & Co. (Timber) Ltd v Southgate Sands [1985] 2 WLR 1044 236
Gray's Inn Construction Ltd, re [1980] 1 WLR 711 51
Great Western Railway Co. v London and County Banking Co. Ltd [1901] AC 414 5
Greenwood v Martins Bank Ltd [1933] AC 51 . . . 7, 122, 178, 200

Halesowen Presswork and Assemblies Ltd v Westminster Bank Ltd [1972] AC 785 . . . . 29, 30, 32–3
Hall (William) (Contractors) Ltd, re [1967] 1 WLR 948 . . . 53, 292

xiii

Hallett's Estate, re; Knatchbull v Hallett (1880) 13 ChD 696 . . 28
Hamilton v Watson (1845) 12 Cl & Fin 109 235
Hampstead Guardians v Barclays Bank Ltd (1923) 39 TLR 229 . 139
Harrold v Plenty [1901] 2 Ch 314 270
Hart, re, *ex parte* Caldicott (1884) 25 ChD 716 301
Hedley Byrne and Co. Ltd v Heller & Partners Ltd [1963] 3 WLR
101 . . . . 5, 11, 22
Hendon v Adelman (1973) 117 Sol Jo 631 50
Hibernian Bank Ltd v Gysin and Hanson [1939] 1 KB 483 . . . 115
Hichens, Harrison, Woolsten & Co. v Jackson & Sons [1943] AC
266 148
Hodson v Tea Company (1880) 14 ChD 859 289
Holland v Manchester and Liverpool District Banking Co. Ltd
(1909) 25 TLR 386 202
Hollins v Fowler (1875) LR 7, HL 757 34
House Property Company of London Ltd v London County and
Westminster Bank (1915) 84 LJ KB 1846 141
Hughes v Liverpool Victoria Legal Friendly Society [1916] 2 KB 482 279
Husband v Davis (1851) 10 CB 645 42

Jayson v Midland Bank Ltd [1968] 1 Lloyd's Rep. 409 . . . 131
Jeffery, re, *ex parte* Honey (1871) 7 Ch App 178 . . . 47
Jeffryes v Agra and Masterman's Bank (1866) LR 2 Eq 674 . . 28
Joachimson v Swiss Bank Corporation [1921] 3 KB 110 . . 6, 35
Jones (R.E.) v Waring and Gillow Ltd [1926] AC 670 . . . 118–19

Keever (a bankrupt), re [1966] 3 WLR 779 150
Ketley (A) Ltd v Scott [1981] ICR 241 224
Kings North Trust Ltd v Bell [1986] 1 WLR 119 229
Kingsnorth Finance Co. Ltd v Tizard [1986] 1 WLR 783 . . 252
Kleinwort Benson Ltd v Malaysian Mining Corporation Berhad
[1989] 1 WLR 379 243

Ladbroke and Co. v Todd (1914) 111 LT 43 . . . . . 137, 139, 141
Libyan Arab Foreign Bank v Bankers Trust Co. [1988] 1 Lloyd's
Rep. 259 . . . . 6, 18
Liggett (B) (Liverpool) Ltd v Barclays Bank Ltd [1928] 1 KB 48   42, 44, 46, 134
Limpgrange Ltd v Bank of Credit and Commerce International S.A.
[1986] FLR 36 35
Lipkin Gorman v Karpnale Ltd [1989] 1 WLR 1340   10, 12, 13, 38, 49, 129, 139
Lloyd's v Harper (1880) 16 ChD 290 238
Lloyds Bank and Co. v Savory (E. B.) and Co. [1933] AC 201   5, 37, 138, 141–2
Lloyds Bank Ltd v Brooks (1951) 6 Legal Decisions Affecting
Bankers 161 155
Lloyds Bank Ltd v Bundy [1974] 3 WLR 501 227
Lloyds Bank Ltd v Chartered Bank of India, Australia and China
[1929] 1 KB 40 142

TABLE OF CASES

Lloyds Bank Ltd v Marcan [1973] 1 WLR 1387 224
Lloyds Bank plc v Waterhouse, *The Independent*, 27 February 1990 229
Lombard Tricity Finance Limited v Paton [1989] 1 All ER 918 . . 83
London Association for Protection of Trade v Greenlands Ltd
[1916–17] All ER Rep. 452 23
London Intercontinental Trust Ltd v Barclays Bank Ltd [1980] 1
Lloyd's Rep. 241 123
London Joint Stock Bank Ltd v Macmillan and Arthur [1918] AC
777 . . . . 7, 124
London Provincial and South Western Bank Ltd v Buszard (1918)
35 TLR 142 128
Lumsden & Co. v London Trustee Savings Bank [1971] 1 Lloyd's
Rep. 114 . . . . 140, 147

M'Lean v Clydesdale Banking Co. (1883) 9 App Cas 95 . . . 149–50
Mardorf, Peach and Co. Ltd v Attica Sea Carriers Corporation of
Liberia [1977] AC 850 175
Marfani and Co. Ltd v Midland Bank Ltd [1968] 1 WLR
956 . . . . 138–9, 140–1, 145
Marzetti v Williams (1830) KB 150 130
McEvoy v Belfast Banking Co. Ltd [1935] AC 24 42
Metropolitan Police Commissioner v Charles [1977] AC 177 . . 151–2
Metsoja v Norman Pitt and Co. Ltd, *The Times*, 30 January 1989 . 91
Midland Bank Ltd v Harris (R.V.) [1963] 1 WLR 1021 . . . 150
Midland Bank Ltd v Reckitt [1933] AC 1 . . . . 119, 144, 149, 150
Midland Bank Ltd v Simpson (Charles) Motors (1960) CLY 217 . 156
Midland Bank plc v Perry, *The Times*, 28 May 1987 . . . 230
Momm v Barclays Bank International Ltd [1977] 2 WLR 407 . . 176
Montagu's Settlement Trusts, re [1987] 2 WLR 1192 . . . 13
Morel (E.J.) (1934) Ltd, re [1961] 3 WLR 57 53
Morison v London County and Westminster Bank Ltd [1914] 3 KB
356 . . . . 143, 148
Morris v Martin (C.W.) & Sons Ltd [1966] 1 QB 716 . . . 34
Motor Traders Guarantee Corporation Ltd v Midland Bank Ltd
[1937] 4 All ER 90 . . . . 144, 146

Nash v Inman [1908] 2 KB 1 43
National Bank of Commerce v National Westminster Bank plc,
Financial Times, 16 March 1990 24
National Bank of Greece S.A. v Pinios Shipping Co. (No. 1) [1989]
3 WLR 1330 . . . . 14, 65
National Provincial and Union Bank of England v Charnley [1924]
1 KB 431 296
National Provincial Bank Ltd v Brackenbury (1906) 22 TLR 797 . 236
National Westminster Bank Ltd v Barclays Bank International Ltd
[1975] QB 654 . . . . 154, 184

xv

National Westminster Bank Ltd v Halesowen Presswork &
Assemblies [1972] AC 785 . . . . 29, 30, 32–3
National Westminster Bank plc v Morgan [1985] AC 685 . . . 226, 228
National Westminster Bank plc v Oceancrest (No. 2), *The Times*,
3 May 1985 130
Nu-Stilo Footwear Ltd v Lloyds Bank Ltd (1956) 7 LDB 121 . . 140, 144
Nye (C. L.) Ltd, re [1970] 3 WLR 158 296

O'Hara v Allied Irish Banks Ltd [1985] BCLC 52 230
Opera Ltd, re (1891) 3 Ch 260 287
Orbit Mining and Trading Co. Ltd v Westminster Bank Ltd [1963]
1 QB 794 . . . . 37, 114, 138, 141, 143

Parker-Tweedale v Dunbar Bank plc, *Financial Times*, 20 December
1989 260
Parsons v Barclay and Co. Ltd (1910) 103 LT 196 22
Penmount Estates Ltd v National Provincial Bank Ltd (1945) 173
LT 344 145
Perry v National Provincial Bank of England Ltd [1910] 1 Ch 464 . 239
Polak v Everett (1876) 1 QBD 669 239
Pollard v Bank of England (1871) LR 6 QB 623 183
Port Swettenham Authority v Wu (T.W.) and Co. (M) Sdn Bhd [1979]
AC 580 33
Pound (Henry), Son & Hutchins Ltd, re (1889) 42 ChD 402 . . 292
Primrose Builders Ltd, re [1950] Ch 561 . . . . . . 27, 53
Prosperity Ltd v Lloyds Bank Ltd (1923) 39 TLR 372 . . . 35

R v Turner [1970] 2 All ER 281 31
Rae v Yorkshire Bank plc [1987] FLR 1 . . . . . . 178, 197
Redmond v Allied Irish Banks [1987] 2 FTLR 264 11
Robinson v Midland Bank Ltd (1925) 41 TLR 402 37
Rolin v Steward (1854) 14 CB 595; 2 CLR 959 178
Rouse v Bradford Banking Co. Ltd [1894] AC 586 130
Rowlandson v National Westminster Bank Ltd [1978] 1 WLR 798 . 45
Royal Bank of Scotland v Tottenham [1894] 2 QB 715 . . . 121
Royal Products Ltd v Midland Bank Ltd [1981] 2 Lloyd's Rep. 194 . 176
Rudd & Son Ltd, re; re Foster, Rudd Ltd, *The Times*, 22 January
1986 266

Sass, re [1896] 2 QB 12 239
Saunders v Anglia Building Society [1971] AC 1004 231
Saunders v Vautier (1841) [1835–42] All ER Rep. LCCt 58 . . . 45
Scholefield Goodman & Sons Ltd v Zyngier [1985] 3 WLR 953 . . 237
Selangor United Rubber Estates Ltd v Cradock (No. 3) [1968]
1 WLR 1555 49
Shamji v Johnson Matthey Bankers Ltd [1986] BCLC 278 . . . 290
Sheffield Corporation v Barclay [1905] AC 392 272

TABLE OF CASES

Shepard v Jones (1882) 21 ChD 469 262
Sherry, re; London and County Banking Co. v Terry (1884) 25 ChD
692 27
Siebe Gorman & Co. Ltd v Barclays Bank Ltd [1979] 2 Lloyd's Rep.
142 303
Sim v Stretch [1936] 2 All ER 1237 130
Slingsby v District Bank Ltd [1932] 1 KB 544 . . . . . 126, 132
Smith & Baldwin v Barclays Bank Ltd [1944] 65 Journal of Institute
of Bankers 171 145
Smith v Wood [1929] 1 Ch 14 236
Sowman v David Samuel Trust Ltd [1978] 1 WLR 22 . . . 292
Spencer v Clarke (1878) 9 ChD 137 277
Spencer v Wakefield (1887) 4 TLR 194 15
Standard Chartered Bank Ltd v Walker [1982] 1 WLR 1410 260, 261, 278, 291
Stubbs (Joshua) Ltd, re [1891] 1 Ch 475 290
Sunderland v Barclays Bank Ltd (1938) 5 LDB 163 . . . 18, 19
Swingcastle Ltd v Gibson, *The Independent*, 28 March 1990 . . 260
Swiss Bank Corporation v Lloyds Bank Ltd [1982] AC 584 . . . 301

Tai Hing Cotton Mill Ltd v Liu Chong Hing Bank Ltd [1986]
AC 80 . . . . 7, 9, 122, 178
Tailby v Official Receiver (1888) 13 App Cas 523 303
Thackwell v Barclays Bank plc [1986] 1 All ER 676 . . 139, 145, 147–8
Thomas v Nottingham Incorporated Football Club Ltd [1972]
2 WLR 1025 242
Titford Property Co. v Cannon Street Acceptances Ltd, unreported . 24
Tournier v National Provincial and Union Bank of England [1924]
1 KB 461 . . . . 15, 19, 21, 23, 202

UBAF Ltd v European American Banking Corporation [1984]
2 WLR 508 22
Underwood (A.L.) Ltd v Bank of Liverpool [1924] 1 KB 775 . . 143, 150
Unit Two Windows Ltd, re [1985] 3 All ER 647 . . . . 31, 53
United City Merchants (Investments) Ltd v Royal Bank of Canada
[1983] AC 168 178
United Dominion Trust Ltd v Kirkwood [1966] 2 WLR 1083 . . 4
United Overseas Bank v Jiwani [1976] 1 WLR 964 . . . 156
United Service Co., re; Johnstone's Claim (1870) 40 LJ Ch 286 . . 32
Uttamchandani v Central Bank of India [1989] NJLR 222 . . . 29

Westminster Bank Ltd v Cond (1940) 40 Com Cas 60 . . . 27, 240
Westminster Bank Ltd v Hilton (1926) 136 LT 315 127
Westminster Bank Ltd v Zang [1966] AC 182 . . . . . 149, 150
Wheatley v Silkstone and Haigh Moor Coal Co. (1885) 29 ChD 715 . 287
White Rose Cottage, re [1965] Ch 940 258
Williams v Everett (1811) 14 East, 582; 104 ER 725 . . . 167
Williams and Glyn's Bank v Barnes [1981] Com LR 205 . . . 24

xvii

Williams and Glyn's Bank v Boland [1981] AC 487 . . . . 229, 250
Windsor Refrigerator Co. Ltd v Branch Nominees Ltd [1961]
   2 WLR 196 290
Woodroffes (Musical Instruments) Ltd, re [1986] Ch 366 . . . 289
Woods v Martins Bank Ltd [1959] 1 QB 55 5
Wulff v Jay [1872] LR 7 QB 756 239

Yeovil Glove Co. Ltd, re [1965] Ch 148 . . . . . . 27, 288
Yorkshire Woolcombers Association Ltd, re [1903] 2 Ch 284 . . 285
Young v Grote (1827) 4 Bing 253; 12 Moore CP 484 124

Table of Statutes

Agricultural Credits Act	
1928 . . . . 4, 285, 307	
Bankers' Books Evidence Act	
1879 . . . . . 16, 198	
Banking Act 1979 . . . 63, 198	
s. 47 147	
Banking Act 1987 . . . 4, 212	
s. 89 . . . . . 67, 192, 194	
Bankruptcy Act 1914	
s. 31 300	
Bills of Exchange Act 1882 . 4, 112, 113–14, 120, 311–17	
s. 2 . . . . . . 117, 118	
s. 3(1) 113	
s. 3(4)(a) 120	
s. 7(3) 116, 133	
s. 9(2) 121	
s. 13(2) 121	
s. 20 125	
s. 20(1) 120	
s. 22 44	
s. 23(2) 46	
s. 24 . . . . . . 117, 122	
s. 26 50	
s. 27(2) 119	
s. 27(3) 118, 150	
s. 29 118	
s. 29(3) 119	
ss. 31–5 116	
s. 36(3) 118	
s. 45 . . . . . . 163, 164	
s. 45(2) 135	
s. 49(13) 136	
s. 50(2)(c) 154–5	
s. 53 167	
s. 59 . . . . 117, 133, 164	
s. 60 . . 132, 133, 136, 157, 164	
s. 64 125	
s. 64(1) 125, 126	
s. 73 113	
Bills of Exchange Act 1882—*continued*	
s. 74(3) 184	
s. 75 . . . . . 39, 43, 127	
s. 75(1) 126	
s. 75(2) 129	
s. 76 114	
s. 77 . . . . . . 114, 115	
s. 77(2) 158	
s. 77(4) 158	
s. 78 . . . . . . 114, 158	
s. 79 . . . . . . 114, 115	
s. 80 . . . 114, 133, 157, 164	
s. 81 . . . . . . 114, 115	
s. 82 139	
s. 90 . . . . . . 118, 133	
Charities Act 1960	
s. 34 45	
Cheques Act 1957 . . 4, 114, 117, 120, 132, 318	
s. 1 . . . . 132, 157, 164	
s. 2 . . . . . . 149, 150	
s. 4 . . . 5, 37, 137, 138, 147, 148, 157, 158, 160, 164, 169	
s. 4(1)–(2) 169	
s. 4(3) 146	
s. 5 . . . . . . 114, 133	
s. 5(2) 158	
Civil Evidence Act 1968 . . . 198	
Companies Act 1985 16, 283, 291, 293	
s. 35A 283–4	
s. 35B 284	
s. 36 284	
s. 37 49	
s. 151 49	
s. 322A 284	
s. 349 50	
s. 349(4) 50	
s. 395 . . . . . 295, 301	
s. 396 . . . . 295, 301, 303

xix

LAW RELATING TO BANKING SERVICES

Companies Act 1985—*continued*		Consumer Credit Act 1974—	
ss. 397-9	296	*continued*	
ss. 400-403	297	s. 17 .	. . . 61, 66, 69, 73
s. 410	289	s. 18 .	. . . . 59, 61, 68
s. 414	296	s. 19 .	 62
s. 415	295	s. 43 .	 90
s. 416	. . . 295, 296	s. 46 .	 91
s. 425	220	s. 47 .	 90
Companies Act 1989	. 49, 283,	s. 48(1)	 89
	295, 321-5	s. 49 .	 90
Part VII	 31	s. 49(1)	. . . . . 59, 89
Consumer Credit Act 1974	. 23, 55,	s. 49(3)	. . . . . 63, 89
	97, 105, 224, 233, 234,	s. 50(1)-(3)	 90
	255, 340-8	s. 51 .	. . . 69, 70, 192, 212
s. 8 .	. . . . . 56, 57	s. 51(1)	. . . 66, 69, 70, 194
s. 8(3)	 61	s. 51(2)	. . . . 69, 70, 194
s. 9(1)	 55	s. 51(3)	 70
s. 9(2)	 55	s. 52 .	 93
s. 10 .	 57	s. 58 .	 81
s. 10(1)(a)	. . . . 57, 193	s. 58(1)	 77
s. 10(1)(b)	 58	s. 58(2)	 76
s. 10(2)	 63	s. 60 .	 81
s. 10(3)(b)(i)-(iii)	 63	s. 61 .	 81
s. 11 .	 61	s. 61(2)	 77
s. 11(1)	 58	s. 61(3)	 77
s. 11(1)(a)	 79	s. 62 .	. . . . . 81, 85
s. 11(1)(b)	. . . 59, 68, 193	s. 63 .	. . . . . 81, 85
s. 11(2)	 58	s. 64 .	 81
s. 11(3)	 59	s. 65 .	. . . . . 56, 81
s. 12 .	. . . . 59, 61, 79	s. 65(1)	 77
s. 12(b)	. . 68, 72, 73, 193, 194	s. 67 .	. . . . . 76, 86
s. 12(c)	. . . . . 72, 73	s. 67(a)	 76
s. 13 .	. . . . 60, 61, 75	ss. 68-69	 86
s. 13(a)	. . . . . 76, 194	ss. 71-2	 58
s. 13(c)	. . . . . 76, 192	s. 74 .	191
s. 14 .	153	s. 74(1)(b)	 63
s. 14(1)	. . . 65, 67, 189	s. 74(2)	. . . 61, 66, 67
s. 14(1)(a)	. .67, 190, 191, 192	s. 74(3)	. . . . . 63, 76
s. 14(1)(b)	.66, 67, 190, 192, 212	s. 74(3A).	 63
s. 14(2)	. 66, 69, 72, 190, 193	s. 74(4)	. . . . . 63, 67
s. 14(3)	192	s. 75 .	. . 68, 69, 72-3, 212
s. 14(4)	. . . . 67, 190	s. 75(1)	. . . . . 72, 74
s. 16 .	. 55, 56, 61, 78, 193	s. 75(2)	 74
s. 16(1)	 75	s. 75(3)	 73
s. 16(2)	. . . . . 75, 78	s. 75(3)(a)-(b)	 73
s. 16(5)	. . . . . 68, 78	s. 75(4)	 73
s. 16(5)(a)	. . . .78-9, 94	s. 75(5)	 74
s. 16(5)(b)	 79-80	s. 76 .	. . . . 65, 77, 88

TABLE OF STATUTES

Consumer Credit Act 1974—
continued
s. 78(1) 64
s. 78(3)(b) 64
s. 78(5) 65
s. 82. 87
s. 83. . 72, 192, 200, 201, 212
s. 83(1) 71, 201
s. 84 69, 72, 192, 200, 201, 212
s. 84(1)–(2) 71
s. 84(4) 201
s. 87. . . . . 65, 77, 88
s. 88. 88
s. 94. 88
s. 97. 89
s. 98. . . . . 65, 87, 88
s. 126 . . . . . 77, 264
s. 127(1) 81
s. 127(3)–(4) 82
s. 145(2) 94
s. 145(2)(a)(ii) 94
s. 145(3)(a)–(c) 94
s. 145(8) 24
s. 149 95
s. 152 95
s. 168 90
s. 173 56
s. 181 . . . . . 57, 201
s. 187 194
s. 187(3) 191
s. 189 62
s. 189(1) 56, 69, 73
s. 810 63
s. 814(2) 61
Criminal Justice Act 1987 . . 16
Criminal Justice Act 1988 . . 17

Data Protection Act 1984 4, 19–21
Deeds of Arrangement Act 1914 220
Drug Trafficking Offences Act
  1986 . . . . . 16, 17

Enduring Power of Attorney Act
  1985 39
Evidence (Proceedings in Other
  Jurisdictions) Act 1975 . . 16

Family Law Reform Act 1969 . 43

Financial Services Act 1986 . 16, 97
  Sch. 1 98
Forgery and Counterfeiting Act 1981
  s. 5(5) 72
Friendly Societies Act . . . 102

Income and Corporation Taxes
  Act 1988 16
Insolvency Act 1986 .40, 217, 241,
  283, 286, 289, 291, 299, 326–39
ss. 1–7 220
s. 8 294
s. 9 . . . . . . 288, 294
s. 107 . . . . . 300, 302
s. 122 50
s. 123 51
s. 127 51
s. 214 51
s. 238 223
s. 239 . . . . . 221, 287
s. 244 224
s. 245 309
ss. 252–63 220
s. 284 . . . . . 40–1, 41
s. 284(4) 40–1
s. 284(5) 41
s. 307 41
s. 323 . . . . . 6, 30, 300
s. 339 223
s. 340 221
s. 343 224
s. 386 287
ss. 423–5 224
Sch. 1 292
Sch. 6 . . . . . 52, 287
Insurance Companies Acts . 98, 102

Land Charges Act 1972
  s. 4(5) 257
Land Registration Act 1925
  s. 70 250
Law of Property Act 1925 255, 289
  s. 1 245
  s. 27(1) 251
  s. 40 255
  s. 89(1) 265
  s. 91 263
  s. 93 . . . . . 257, 286

xxi

Law of Property Act 1925—
continued
s. 97. 257
s. 101 259
s. 103 . . . 257, 270, 286
s. 109(1) 290
s. 109(2) 261
s. 109(8) 261
s. 136 167
s. 172 224
s. 198 257
s. 199(1) 287
Law of Property Amendment Act 1926
s. 7 266
Law of Property (Miscellaneous Provisions) Act 1989 39, 319–20
s. 1 . . . . . 255, 259
s. 2 . . . . . 255, 258
Limitation Act 1980. . 24, 121, 236
Limited Partnership Act 1907 . 46

Matrimonial Homes Act 1983 250, 251, 259
Minors Contracts Act 1987 . . 234
s. 2 . . . . . . 44, 234
s. 3 44

Occupiers Liability Act 1957 . . . . 199, 262

Partnership Act 1890
s. 1(1) 45
s. 5 46
s. 9 46
s. 18 240
s. 35 47
s. 38 47
Police and Criminal Evidence Act 1984 . . . . . 16, 17
Power of Attorney Act 1971 . 38, 39
s. 10 38
Prevention of Terrorism (Temporary Provisions) Act 1989 . . 17

Protection from Eviction Act 1977 259

Registration of Business Names Act 1916 145

Sale of Goods Act 1979 . . .292
Stamp Act 1853
s. 19 . . . . . 132, 158
Statute of Frauds 1677
s. 4 234
Statute of Frauds Amendment Act 1828
s. 6 22
Supply of Goods and Services Act 1982
s. 13 3, 177, 181, 185, 195, 201
s. 15 15

Taxes Management Act 1970 . 16
Theft Act 1968
s. 16(1) 152
Torts (Interference with Goods) Act 1977 31
Trustee Act 1925
s. 16. 45
s. 17 251
s. 18 45
s. 23 44
s. 25 44
s. 36 45

Unfair Contract Terms Act 1977 . 3, 10, 23, 34, 71, 197
s. 2 74
s. 2(1) 198
s. 2(2) 198, 199
s. 3 . 74, 177, 182, 187, 212, 213
s. 3(2) 237
ss. 4–8 74
s. 11(1) 199
s. 11(4)–(5) 199
s. 83. . . . . 71, 198, 199

Table of Rules and Regulations

Consumer Credit Act (Total Charge
  for Credit) Regulations 1986   85
Consumer Credit (Advertisements)
  Regulations 1980 . . . 91
Consumer Credit (Advertisements)
  Regulations 1989 . . 90, 91
Consumer Credit (Agreements)
  Regulations 1983 . . . 82
Consumer Credit (Cancellation
  Notices and Copies of
  Documents) Regulations
  1983 86
Consumer Credit (Exempt
  Agreements) Order
  1989 . . 68, 75, 78, 193
para. 2 78
para. 2(2) 79
para. 3 . . . . 78, 192
para. 3(1)(a) 193
para. 3(1)(a)(ii) . . . 68

Consumer Credit (Exempt)
  Agreements Order
  1989—*continued*
para. 4 78
para. 4(1) 79
para. 4(5) . . . 79, 80
para. 5 . . . . 78, 90
Consumer Credit (Increase of
  Monetary Amounts) Order
  1983 . . . . 72, 201
Consumer Credit (Increase of
  Monetary Limits) Order
  1983 73
Consumer Credit (Quotations)
  Regulations 1989 . . 93, 95

Insolvency Rules 1986
  r. 4.90 . . . . 30, 300
Insolvent Partnerships Order
  1986 48

Preface

There is no shortage of law which is relevant to the business of banking and any textbook on banking law must be selective, both in terms of which matters to include and how much detail to provide on the chosen areas. The Chartered Institute of Bankers has recently sponsored a thoughtful review of the topics which the students of its Associateship examinations ought to be required to know, and this text is devoted to an explanation of the legal principles which the new syllabus for 'Law Relating to Banking Services' contains.

We have kept in mind the fact that students of this syllabus are not lawyers and, so far as is possible with sometimes complex legal issues, have tried to present the law in a form which a banker can hope to understand. Equally, we have tried not to assume too much knowledge of banking practice and we hope the text will be useful to lawyers and others not conversant with the esoterics of banking.

The general approach of the text is to provide detailed coverage of areas of law directly relevant to banking, such as the banker–customer relationship, the law on cheques and other payment systems, and outline coverage of areas of law which are not pure banking law but which are relevant to banking: for example, the Financial Services Act, the Consumer Credit Act, company law, partnership law, agency law and all the law relating to security. There is, however, no coverage of the law dealing with the regulation of banking, such as the Banking Act 1987.

The three parts to this book relate to the three sections of the CIB's syllabus for Law Relating to Banking Services and are of approximately equal length. It has been convenient, however, to divide the third part into a greater number of chapters, some of which are accordingly quite brief. CIB students should note that the final three chapters are not in the syllabus.

It is unfortunate, particularly when there are so many, much-needed women in the banking and legal professions, that there is no satisfactory alternative in the English language to the use of 'he' and 'him' when personalising illustrations of legal points in textbooks.

In setting out the legal principles relating to payment systems in the second part of this book, we are aware that, apart from the detailed law on cheques, the law is largely untested. Even where statutes clearly apply (e.g. the Consumer Credit Act 1974 and the Unfair Contract Terms Act 1977) they have seldom been the subject of judicial interpretation in relation to modern payment systems. There may, therefore, be valid alternatives to some of the principles set out in this book and we are sensitive to the fact that our views may require modification in the fullness of time.

Subject to this, the law is as stated at 31 October 1990 except that it has been assumed that the Companies Act 1989 is fully in force which, at the time of publication, is not yet the case but will be very soon hereafter. Some information is included on the Government's White Paper 'Banking Services: Law and Practice' which indicates forthcoming legislative changes to banking law, but at the time of writing this Preface there appears to be no immediate prospect of these being enacted. Neither is it possible to predict what effect, if any, the new Code of Banking Practice may have on banking law after the Code's introduction some time in 1991.

The letters HL, CA and PC, which appear after some cases in the text, indicate the court which heard the case, respectively House of Lords, Court of Appeal and Privy Council. Absence of letters normally means that the case was first instance before the High Court.

Graham Roberts
Andrew Laidlaw
London
October 1990

Part I—Banking Law and the Customer

1 The Banker-Customer Relationship

1.1 INTRODUCTION

Following general principles of law, the parties to the banker–customer contract are free at common law to negotiate whatever express terms they wish, subject to statute. For example, a term seeking to exclude liability for negligence may be rendered void by the Unfair Contract Terms Act 1977. When the customer is not entering into the contract in the course of a business and thus qualifies as a 'consumer', there will be an unexcludable implied term brought in by s. 13 of the Supply of Goods and Services Act 1982 that the bank will carry out its services for the customer with a reasonable degree of care and skill.

The traditional practice on the part of banks has been to avoid extensive express terms in their contracts with customers. However, there have been a number of decisions of the courts which establish what are the implied terms of the contract. It is remarkable that even today express terms are the exception rather than the rule.

In March 1990 the Government published a White Paper entitled 'Banking Services: Law and Practice'. A number of minor legislative changes are proposed but these relate mostly to cheques, to electronic funds transfers and to payment cards. Further details of these accordingly appear in Part II of this book.

The White Paper also proposes that a non-statutory statement of best practice should be set up, known as the Code of Practice. In matters relating to the banker–customer relationship, it is anticipated that this Code will oblige banks to:

(a) give customers clear information about the terms of the banker–customer contract, including the basis of charging for services, and reasonable notice of changes to the terms.

(b) establish clearly defined internal complaints procedures. The Banking Ombudsman will continue to adjudicate on disputes which cannot be resolved between the parties themselves but the Ombudsman scheme will remain voluntary in that banks are not compelled to join it.

Once in it, however, they are bound by the decisions. The Ombudsman will be able to make an award against a bank if it has breached the Code.

(c) give customers clear information about the bank's common law duty of confidentiality and the customers' rights of access to information under the Data Protection Act 1984. Customers are to have the opportunity to object to the use of information about them for marketing purposes or to it being passed to credit reference agencies.

1.2 DEFINITION OF A BANK

The first issue to consider is what in law constitutes a bank. This is relevant because certain rights and obligations attach to a bank at common law, e.g. a bank enjoys the right to exercise the banker's lien (see **1.15** below) and a bank is entitled to the protection of statute when paying and collecting cheques (see chapter 5). Similarly a bank is impliedly obliged to observe the duty of confidentiality (see **1.9** below).

The Banking Act 1987 establishes a framework whereby the Bank of England authorises institutions to refer to themselves as banks and under this Act, the definition of a bank for the purposes of certain specific statutes (such as the Agricultural Credits Act 1928) is simply an institution authorised under the Banking Act. For the far more important purposes of what constitutes a bank when applying the protective provisions of the Bills of Exchange Act 1882 and the Cheques Act 1957, the definition of a bank is not based upon authorisation under the Banking Act 1987 but upon common law.

This common law definition of a bank is provided by *United Dominion Trust Ltd* v *Kirkwood* (1966) CA. It was held that there are three essential characteristics of a banking business:

(a) collecting cheques for customers;
(b) paying cheques drawn by their customers;
(c) keeping current accounts for their customers.

It appears that all three must be satisfied in order for an institution to be considered a bank at common law.

1.3 DEFINITION OF A CUSTOMER

A person becomes a customer of a bank when an account is opened for him and at the same time a contract is formed (*Commissioners of Taxation* v *English, Scottish and Australian Bank* (1920) PC).

In one case it was held that the contract was formed well before an account was opened (*Woods* v *Martins Bank Ltd* (1959)). The branch manager of M Bank advised W to invest in a company customer of the same branch. This advice was held to be grossly negligent but as this case predated the decision in *Hedley Byrne* v *Heller* (1963) HL, there was no question of liability on the part of the bank unless a contract existed between W and the M Bank. It was held that W became a customer when the bank accepted his instructions to collect money from his account with another institution and to pay it to the company.

Since the *Hedley Byrne* decision it is open to the courts to find a bank liable for negligent advice to a non-customer. Indeed, as a matter of general law, a bank may be liable to any person against whom it commits a tort. A person may only become a customer, however, when a contract is formed with the bank.

The principal reason from a bank's point of view for determining when a person is a customer is for the purposes of s. 4 of the Cheques Act 1957 where a bank may be protected in collecting a cheque when it does so for a customer. It is thus protected whenever it collects a cheque for someone who has an account with it. Cashing a cheque for a person who does not have an account with the bank is not considered to be collecting a cheque for a customer (*Great Western Railway Co.* v *London and County Banking Co. Ltd* (1901) HL). It makes no difference if the person is asked to draw a counter cheque.

It was suggested by Lawrence LJ in the Court of Appeal in *Lloyds Bank Ltd* v *E.B. Savory & Co.* that a bank is not collecting a cheque for a customer when a person pays in a cheque at a different bank from the one where he has his account, and that this is so even where the cheque is paid in at a different branch of the same bank. If this is correct, the customer must be considered a customer of an individual branch, not of the whole bank.

1.4 THE DEBTOR–CREDITOR RELATIONSHIP AND OTHER IMPLIED TERMS

In *Foley* v *Hill* (1848) HL, it was held that when a customer pays money into his account, the bank becomes a debtor to the customer creditor. Therefore the money becomes the property of the bank. The bank has borrowed the money from its customer.

Certain important matters flow from this. First, the bank is free to do what it likes with the money and is not bound to account to its customer for what it does with it. The bank is merely liable to repay the money to the customer when he demands it. Second, if the bank fails to repay on demand, the customer ranks only as an unsecured creditor in any claim against an insolvent bank. In these circumstances, however, a customer may benefit from the statutory set-off provisions of s. 323 of the Insolvency Act 1986 so that, for example, if he owes a mortgage debt to the bank which exceeds his credit balance, his loss will be nil. Furthermore, the Bank of England underwrites 75% of the first £20,000 of all banks' liabilities to their customers.

Further implied terms of the contract were set out in *Joachimson* v *Swiss Bank Corporation* (1921). They include:

(a) the bank will receive the customer's deposits and collect his cheques;

(b) the bank will comply with written orders (i.e. cheques) issued by its customer, assuming there is sufficient credit in the account;

(c) the bank will repay the entire balance on the customer's demand at the account holding branch during banking hours;

(d) the bank will give reasonable notice before closing a customer's account, at least if it is in credit;

(e) the customer will take reasonable care when writing his cheques.

It was also stated that the relationship between bank and customer is contained in one contract which may encompass a variety of matters.

In *Libyan Arab Foreign Bank* v *Bankers Trust Co.* (1988), L had Eurodollar deposits amounting to over $300 million with the bank. There were two accounts, one was held in New York and one at a London branch. The bank refused to repay the deposit on L's demand as a US Presidential order had sought to freeze the accounts. It became important to decide whether the contract was subject to English or to New York law. It was held that there was one contract between the parties, although the New York account was subject to New York law and the London account was subject to English law. It was also decided that, in the absence of any express provision, L was entitled to demand the balance held on the London account in cash. This was despite evidence that it would involve seven plane journeys from New York to bring over the necessary dollar bills!

The implied terms of the banker–customer contract were examined in detail in *Tai Hing Cotton Mill Ltd* v *Liu Chong Hing Bank* (1986) PC. This important decision also considers the effect of certain express terms in the contract.

T Ltd had a current account with three different banks in Hong Kong. It had mandated the banks to pay cheques which were signed by its managing director. Leung, the accounts clerk of T Ltd, forged the managing director's signature on 300 cheques which totalled $HK 5.5 million and these were all paid by the banks. The forged cheques were payable to companies and Leung set up accounts into which these were paid. When Leung's fraud was exposed after five years, he fled to Taiwan and the money was not recovered from him. T Ltd therefore claimed recovery of the money from the banks.

Prima facie the banks were liable to T Ltd since the cheques were forged, T Ltd had given no authority to pay and no estoppel could arise since T Ltd as a company customer had no knowledge of the forgeries (see chapter 5). The banks raised a number of points in their defence, however:

(a) there should be an implied term to the effect that a customer has a duty to take reasonable precautions to prevent forged cheques being presented for payment on his account. It was clear that T Ltd's accounting system was lamentably negligent in allowing Leung to cover his tracks in perpetrating his fraud.

(b) there should be an implied term that a customer has a duty to check the statements of account which his bank sends him and where the unauthorised debits will appear. If the customer fails to raise queries, his claim against the bank should be prejudiced. Nobody in T Ltd apart from Leung had examined the bank statements for the five years that the fraud was going on.

(c) alternatively to the above, the customer should be under a duty in the tort of negligence to take care to prevent forgeries and check his statements.

All of the above submissions were dismissed by the Privy Council who reiterated the principles established in *London Joint Stock Bank Ltd* v *Macmillan and Arthur* (1918) HL and in *Greenwood* v *Martins Bank Ltd* (1933) HL, that a customer only has duties:

LAW RELATING TO BANKING SERVICES

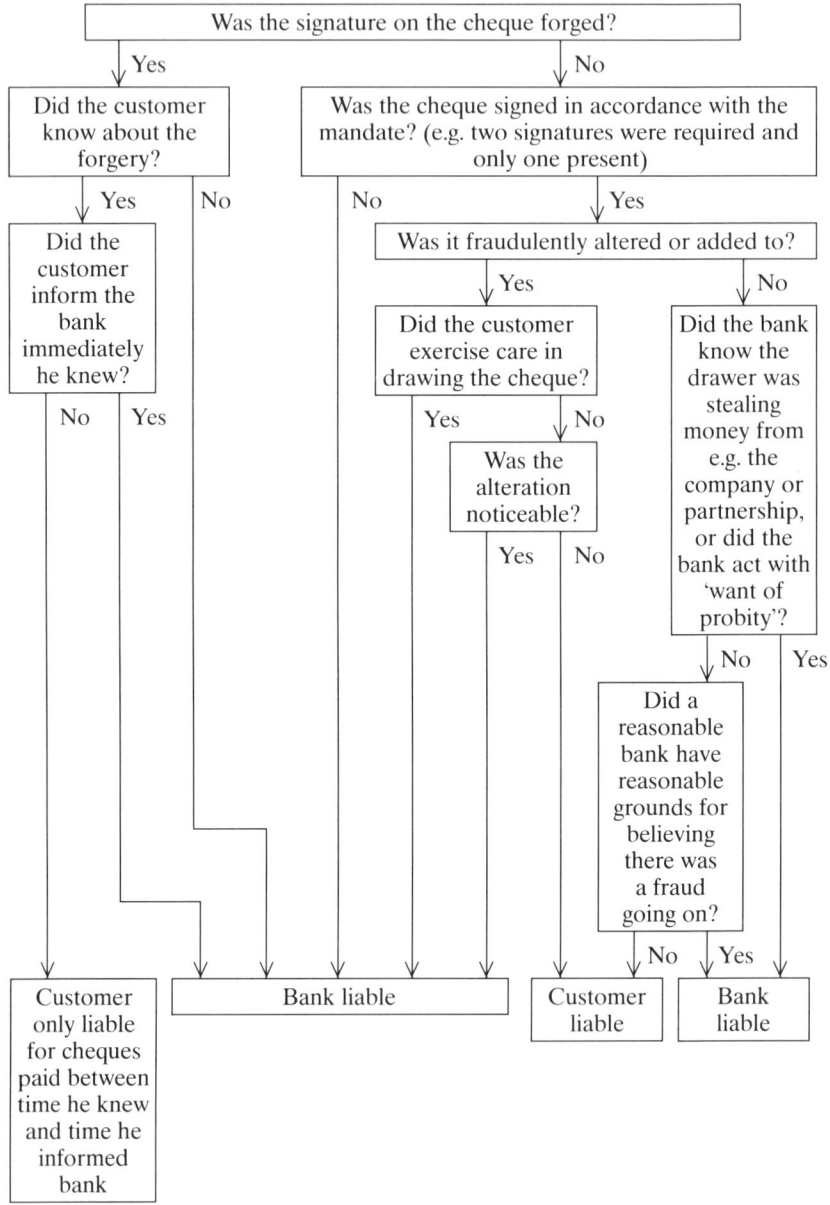

Figure 1

THE BANKER–CUSTOMER RELATIONSHIP

(a) to exercise reasonable care when drawing cheques to prevent forgery and alteration, and
(b) to notify the bank if he knows of forgeries on his account.

A customer therefore is not liable if he walks along the street tearing off unsigned cheques from his cheque book and scattering them around. However, if he sees someone pick up a cheque and start to complete it, he then has a duty to inform his bank forthwith. If he fails to do this, he will be liable for the forgery.

Equally a customer is not liable if he ignores all statements of account which he receives from his bank even when a cursory examination would reveal unauthorised debits. If he does look at his statement and notices unauthorised debits but does not inform the bank then he may be estopped from claiming on the basis that he then knows of the forgeries.

In the White Paper it is stated that the government considers this area of the law to be unfair to banks. It proposes legislative change to make the customer bear some of the loss where he has been negligent. This may occur through an adjustment to the general law of contributory negligence which was already under the scrutiny of the Law Commission. The suggestion is that contributory negligence becomes a defence to a claim in contract.

1.5 EXPRESS TERMS

The banks in the *Tai Hing* case in fact had incorporated express terms into their contracts with their customer which in various ways had sought to place an express duty on the customer to examine his statements of account and to raise queries within a given period, failing which the statements were to be deemed to be correct.

It was held in *Tai Hing* that at common law there is nothing to prevent such terms being effective (they may be referred to as 'conclusive evidence clauses'), but as terms which seek to exclude rights which the customer would otherwise enjoy, they can only be effective if the effect of them is clearly brought home to the customer; it was held that the banks in *Tai Hing* had not done so. It is suggested that banks would be unwise to incorporate such a term in any case, since it may happen that the account is wrongly credited with a large sum which would also be treated as conclusive. A better term from the bank's point of view would be one which obliges a customer specifically to inform the bank of unauthorised debits within a certain period.

As mentioned in 1.1 above, any express term which seeks to exclude liability on the part of one party to a contract, will be rendered void by the Unfair Contract Terms Act 1977 if it is considered to be an unreasonable exclusion of liability.

1.6 THE BANK'S DUTY OF CARE AS AGENT

When a bank pays a cheque it does so as agent for its customer. Also, when it collects a cheque it does so as agent (see chapter 5 for a bank's duties in this event). It has already been observed (in 1.5 above) that a bank may be liable to its customer if it pays a forged or altered cheque. There are also circumstances where a bank may be liable for paying a cheque which is drawn in accordance with the mandate from the customer and where there has been no alteration.

Illustrations

Lipkin Gorman v *Karpnale Ltd* (1989) CA. LG were a firm of solicitors who held a client account at a branch of Lloyds Bank. Any one partner of LG was mandated to operate the account. One of the partners, named Cass, also had a personal account at the same branch. Cass withdrew and used over £200,000 of client account money in gambling at the Playboy Club (then owned by Karpnale Ltd). He had removed the client account funds largely by signing cheques payable to cash and sending a clerk to the bank to cash the cheques. LG made a series of claims against Karpnale Ltd and Lloyds Bank for recovery of the money. The Court of Appeal found against LG on almost all of its claims but recognised that there can be circumstances which make a bank liable even if it has complied with the written mandate.

In this helpful decision for banks, May LJ declared:
'In the simple case of a current account in credit, the basic obligation on the banker is to pay his customer's cheques in accordance with his mandate. Having in mind the vast numbers of cheques which are presented for payment every day in this country ... it is my opinion only when the circumstances are such that any reasonable cashier would hesitate to pay a cheque at once ... that a cheque should not be paid immediately upon presentation.'

The court conceded that just one telephone call by the bank manager to the senior partner in Lipkin Gorman to inform him of Cass's gambling would have put a stop to the fraud but held that this would have been a flagrant breach of the bank's duty of secrecy to its customer Cass.

The test to be applied to determine whether a bank is in breach of its duty as agent was stated by Parker LJ as follows:
'If a reasonable banker would have had reasonable grounds for believing that Cass was operating the client account in fraud, then, in continuing to pay the cash cheques without enquiry the bank would, in my view, be negligent and thus liable for breach of contract, albeit neither Mr Fox (the bank manager) nor anyone else appreciated that the facts did afford reasonable grounds and was thus innocent of any sort of dishonesty.'

Later he stated:
'The question must be whether, if a reasonable and honest banker knew of the relevant facts, he would have considered that there was a serious or real possibility that Cass was drawing on the client account and using the funds so obtained for his own . . . purposes.'

Another recent case which was decided in favour of the bank is *Barclays Bank plc* v *Quincecare Ltd* (1988). S approached the bank for a loan of £400,000 in order to purchase some chemists shops. An account was opened in the name of Q Ltd and a guarantee for the loan was obtained from Unichem Ltd. S asked the bank to transfer a large sum of money from Q Ltd's account to the firm of solicitors which (he said) were acting in the purchase of the shops. This was done, whereupon S instructed the solicitors to transfer the money to the USA from where it was never recovered. The bank sued Q Ltd for the debt and Unichem Ltd on their guarantee. It was held that there had been no suspicious circumstances which should have alerted the bank before it transferred the money to the solicitors and that it was not liable.

There are two other cases of interest concerning a bank's liability to its customer:

Box v *Midland Bank Ltd* (1979). B approached the bank for a loan facility in order to finance an export contract. The bank manager explained that the Regional Head Office would have to approve the facility but that this would be a mere formality if an ECGD policy was obtained. B acted on this assurance and incurred expenses setting up the contract. In fact Regional Head Office would not have granted the facility under any circumstances and the facility was not granted. B sued for his loss and succeeded on the basis of the bank's liability for tortious negligent misstatement under the principle established in *Hedley Byrne* v *Heller* (1963) HL.

Redmond v *Allied Irish Banks* (1987). R was a customer of the bank.

G approached R, asking him to put two cheques through R's account; G said he did not want to put the cheques through his own account for tax reasons. The cheques were payable to individuals who appeared to have indorsed them in blank; they were crossed 'not negotiable' and 'account payee'. They had been obtained by fraud. R did pay them into his account, withdrew the funds when they cleared and paid G, whereupon G disappeared. R did not acquire good title to the cheques because of the fraud and the 'not negotiable' crossing. R contended that his bank owed him a duty to warn him of the risks of paying in indorsed cheques which were crossed 'not negotiable'. The court dismissed this argument and found in favour of the bank.

1.7 THE BANK'S DUTY OF CARE AS TRUSTEE

Constructive trusts

The constructive trust is a general principle which is not confined to banking law. It arises when a person who has not been appointed to act as a trustee becomes involved in the affairs of the trust and thus becomes liable to the beneficiaries of the trust in the same way as an appointed trustee who acts in breach of trust.

In the banking context, it has been seen that the bank is only liable to its customer as a debtor (see **1.4** above) and it is not liable as trustee unless it has been appointed as such. It might, however, become a constructive trustee if it permits an authorised signatory to withdraw funds from a company, partnership or joint account in circumstances where it knows that the funds are being misapplied. This was an alternative ground of claim in the *Lipkin Gorman* case.

It had been established in *Belmont Finance Corporation* v *Williams Furniture Ltd* (no. 2) (1980) CA that a bank may be liable as constructive trustee if it either:

(a) receives trust funds with actual or constructive notice that they are trust funds and that the transfer of the funds to the bank constitutes a breach of trust, or

(b) knowingly assists a trustee of the trust to dishonestly misapply trust funds.

With reference to (b) above, the term 'knowingly' was categorised in *Baden, Delvaux and Lecuit* v *Société Général* (1983) into five headings:

(a) actual knowledge;
(b) wilfully shutting one's eyes to the obvious;
(c) wilfully and recklessly failing to make such enquiries as an honest and reasonable man would make;
(d) knowledge of circumstances which would indicate the facts to an honest and reasonable man;
(e) knowledge of circumstances which would put an honest and reasonable man on inquiry.

It was held in *Lipkin Gorman* that only (a), (b) and (c) above constitute knowledge for the purposes of liability as constructive trustee.

As a simpler alternative to the above, in *Re Montagu's Settlement Trusts* (1987), it was suggested that a useful test of liability was to ask if the alleged constructive trustee acted with 'want of probity'.

In *Lipkin Gorman*, the Court of Appeal came to the conclusion that there is no possibility of a bank being liable as a constructive trustee of funds which have been fraudulently misapplied with the knowing assistance of the bank, without it also being liable in simple breach of contract for not conducting a customer's account with sufficient care. On the other hand, it might be liable in breach of contract for conducting the account negligently, in circumstances when it had insufficient knowledge to make it liable as a constructive trustee. In other words, liability in breach of contract is more extensive than liability as a constructive trustee. The effect of this dictum (Parker LJ) really amounts to rendering the entire issue of liability on the part of the bank, for knowing assistance in misapplication of trust funds, to be quite irrelevant.

Although the bank manager knew that Cass's personal account was being badly conducted and that he was gambling, there was held to be no knowledge, or even wilful or reckless turning of a blind eye, that Cass was using client account funds to finance his compulsive habit.

It is clear that the bank's liability in breach of contract is based upon the reasonable banker test and is thus objective in nature. The test for liability as a constructive trustee is more subjective in nature, so that a bank which is negligent but is not acting with 'want of probity' will be liable in contract, but not as a constructive trustee.

The law relating to unauthorised debits is summarised in **Figure 1**.

'Quistclose' trusts

Very much analogous to the constructive trust is the 'Quistclose' trust, which arises when money is paid to a bank which, to the bank's knowledge, is to be used for a special purpose.

Illustration

Barclays Bank Ltd v *Quistclose Investments Ltd* (1970) HL. Rolls Razor Ltd had a large overdraft with the bank. The company borrowed a sum of money from Q Ltd in order to meet a dividend it had declared. Q Ltd lent this money to RR Ltd on condition that it was used to pay the dividend. The money it lent was placed in a special account opened in RR Ltd's name with the bank. The bank was aware of the condition attached to the loan. RR Ltd went into liquidation before the dividend was paid; the bank claimed the money in the special account had belonged to RR Ltd and could therefore be set against the company's overdraft debt. It was held that as the bank knew of the purpose of the loan, the money was held on trust primarily to pay the dividend, but if that purpose failed, then secondarily for the benefit of the lender, Q Ltd.

A bank's liability under an express trust

Banks commonly act as trustees appointed as such under an express trust set up by a customer. In this event the bank is subject to all the general law on powers, duties and liabilities of trustees and this includes the duty to take care of the trust property to the standard of a prudent business person. It has been held, however, that a bank trustee is under a greater duty as it holds itself out as a trustee with a special degree of care and skill (*Bartlett* v *Barclays Bank Co. Ltd* (1980)).

1.8 THE BANK'S RIGHT TO INTEREST AND TO CHARGES

Interest

Where a customer has an overdrawn account, the right of the lending bank to interest on the debt may be expressed or may be implied from the customer's acquiescence in the debiting of interest.

Furthermore, a bank will compound interest on a longstanding debt, i.e. it will add the interest to the capital at intervals so that interest is charged on unpaid interest. The right to compound is also implied from the customer's acquiescence (*National Bank of Greece SA* v *Pinios Shipping Co.* (1989) CA).

This case went to the House of Lords in 1989 to decide the issue of whether the right to compound interest survives the making of demand by the bank and the closing of the overdrawn account. The House decided that it did.

Charges

It is nowadays common for banks to express the circumstances in which customers may be charged. In the absence of an express term, it was held in *Spencer v Wakefield* (1887) that acquiescence by a customer in the charging of commissions is sufficient to entitle the bank to charge. It is also likely that a bank may justify the practice by reference to custom and usage.

An implied term that a bank may make a reasonable charge for its services in the absence of any express term relating to charges is also established by s. 15 of the Supply of Goods and Services Act 1982.

1.9 THE BANK'S DUTY OF CONFIDENTIALITY

A bank owes an implied duty to its customer not to divulge information about its customers to third parties.

Illustration

Tournier v National Provincial and Union Bank of England (1924) CA. T had an overdrawn account with the bank. The branch manager spoke to T's employers in order to find out T's home address. In the process the manager revealed that T had defaulted on his obligation to the bank and was suspected of being a heavy gambler. T was dismissed from his job and successfully sued for his losses.

The *Tournier* case also lays down four exceptions to the duty of secrecy:

(a) where disclosure is under compulsion of law;
(b) where there is a duty to the public to disclose;
(c) where the interests of the bank require disclosure.
(d) where disclosure occurs with the express or implied consent of the customer.

Disclosure under compulsion of law

It is helpful to sub-divide this exception into three parts:

(a) where the compulsion takes the form of a court order to disclose. Examples of this include:

(i) an order under the Bankers' Books Evidence Act 1879 as part of the discovery process in advance of a civil or criminal trial;
(ii) an order under the Police and Criminal Evidence Act 1984 to assist police in the investigation of a criminal offence;
(iii) discovery orders made in aid of a party seeking a Mareva injunction;
(iv) an order for obtaining evidence in a foreign trial under the Evidence (Proceedings in Other Jurisdictions) Act 1975;
(v) a writ of subpoena or a witness order compelling a bank employee to give evidence in a civil or criminal trial;
(vi) an order by the court under the Drug Trafficking Offences Act 1986 to assist a police investigation into a suspected drug trafficking offence.

(b) where the compulsion takes the form of a valid request from an official. Examples include:

(i) information required by the Inland Revenue under the Taxes Management Act 1970 and the Income and Corporation Taxes Act 1988;
(ii) information required about a company by the Department of Trade and Industry acting under powers granted in the Companies Act 1985;
(iii) under the Criminal Justice Act 1987, the Director of the Serious Fraud Office may require a person to attend to answer questions;
(iv) under the Financial Services Act 1986, inspectors may require information in connection with suspected insider dealing in shares.

(c) where there is no direct compulsion to divulge information about a customer but an offence may be committed by the bank and there is specific statutory protection if information is divulged. Examples are:

(i) the Drug Trafficking Offences Act 1986. Disclosure to the police of a suspicion or belief relating to funds derived from illegal drug trafficking will not constitute a breach of the implied duty of secrecy. A degree of spice is provided by the provision that a serious offence is committed by a person who, knowing or suspecting the truth, facilitates the retention or control of funds derived from illegal drug trafficking. There is a defence available where the belief or suspicion is disclosed to the police as soon as it is reasonable to do so. The effect of this provision is of course to encourage banks to volunteer information about a customer.

(ii) the Criminal Justice Act 1988. Disclosure to the police of a suspicion or belief that any property has been obtained as a result of an indictable offence (e.g. burglary or robbery) will not be treated as a breach of contract. Unlike the Drug Trafficking Offences Act, however, there is no provision effectively rendering a person liable for non-disclosure.

(iii) the Prevention of Terrorism (Temporary Provisions) Act 1989. An offence is committed if a person gives, lends or otherwise makes available any money or other property, knowing or having reasonable cause to suspect that it will or may be applied or used for the commission of acts of terrorism. It is also an offence to assist in the control or retention of terrorist funds. As with the Drug Trafficking Offences Act, there is a provision that disclosure of information will not constitute a breach of contract.

Of the three categories of disclosure under compulsion of law, banks are likely to feel most comfortable with disclosure pursuant to a court order since there can be no question that there is a real compulsion.

Illustration

Barclays Bank plc v *Taylor* (1989) CA. Following the procedure set out in the Police and Criminal Evidence Act 1984, the police served notice to the bank of their intention to apply for a court order for disclosure. The bank did not resist the making of the order nor did it inform their customer that the order was being sought. When the order was made, the bank complied with it. The customer unsuccessfully argued that the bank was in breach of contract.

The second category of disclosure (that of following a valid request from an official) carries the danger that the official might claim to be entitled to the information when in truth he is not. In these circumstances the bank will be liable to its customer if it discloses. Legal advice may be necessary for the bank to determine whether it is obliged to disclose in any given situation.

The third category is potentially even more fraught. Here the bank may commit a serious offence by not disclosing, yet disclosure without sufficient suspicion or belief may amount to a breach of contract. In practice, banks use a centralised system for dealing with disclosure of information to the authorities.

Duty to the public to disclose

This has not been a well used exception to the duty of secrecy and its parameters are unclear. It has been suggested that it might apply to permit disclosure in wartime when a customer has dealings with the enemy. It was invoked by a bank in *Libyan Arab Foreign Bank* v *Bankers Trust Co.* (1988). Immediately prior to the making of a US Presidential Order freezing Libyan assets in the hands of US persons in 1986, the US authorities requested and obtained information about Libyan bank accounts with the bank. The court did not reach a conclusion on this point in the case, neither confirming nor denying that the bank was justified in disclosing in these circumstances.

Disclosure in the bank's interest

This exception was successfully invoked by a bank in *Sunderland* v *Barclays Bank Ltd* (1938). S telephoned her bank to complain about its dishonour of her cheques. The bank was justified in dishonouring the cheques as there were insufficient funds but it was also concerned about S's gambling. S's husband took the telephone from S to add his views whereupon the bank informed him of his wife's gambling. The court held the bank was entitled to disclose in its own interest and expressed the view that it would also be justified under this exception for disclosure in the common situation of it suing a customer for the balance of an overdrawn account. This is necessary as legal action in these circumstances will reveal to the public the balance on the customer's account.

Disclosure with the customer's consent

In *Tournier* it was stated that if a customer gives his bank as a reference, there is implied consent to disclosure of information. The court in

Sunderland also considered that the disclosure in that case was justified on the basis of implied consent as well as being in the bank's interest.

There is a well-established system of banker's opinions whereby one bank may make a status enquiry to another bank concerning the credit standing of a customer of the second bank. In some cases the customer will not be aware that the status enquiry has been made nor even that a system for giving information in this way exists. It is difficult to argue that a customer impliedly consents to something of which he is not aware.

It was stated in *Tournier* that the duty of secrecy commences when the banker–customer relationship (presumably the contract) is formed. The duty extends to information which the bank has obtained from other sources whilst acting as banker to the customer, e.g. information about its customer which it obtained from a reference on him provided by another bank. It was also stated that the duty does not cease on termination of the banker–customer contract.

Liability for breach of the duty of confidentiality will be based upon general principles of liability for breach of contract and therefore the customer will usually have to prove actual loss in order to obtain more than nominal damages. In both the *Sunderland* and *Libyan Arab Foreign Bank* cases, the court considered there had been no such loss. It would appear therefore that in the majority of situations where an unjustified disclosure occurs there will be no liability on the part of the bank.

The White Paper made recommendations concerning the duty of confidentiality. These were summarised in **1.1** above.

1.10　THE DATA PROTECTION ACT 1984

The Data Protection Act was introduced in order to control the collection, holding and use of personal information held in computerised form. The Act does not apply to information held on paper files (e.g. correspondence) nor does it apply to information about companies.

The Act established the Office of the Data Protection Registrar. The Registrar is charged with monitoring compliance with the Act. Any person who holds or processes data must register with the Registrar as a data user (for holding information) or a computer bureau (for processing information).

The register, which is open to public inspection, must show:

(a) the source of information obtained by a data user;
(b) the purpose for which it has been obtained; and
(c) the persons to whom it may be disclosed.

It will also show the country or countries to which data may be transferred and the address to which people can write for information held about themselves.

A data user may only obtain, hold, use and disclose information in accordance with his registration. Banks will register as data users and, possibly, as computer bureaux.

Individuals about whom information is held (data subjects) may ask a registered data user for a copy, in readable form, of the data held about them by the data user. There is a maximum statutory fee and a maximum frequency with which such requests may be made. A data subject may have incorrect information removed or corrected.

The Act is underpinned by the creation of statutory offences for breach. It must be construed in accordance with eight data protection principles (and guidance on their interpretation) set out in the First Schedule to the Act.

All eight principles apply to data users: only the last principle applies to computer bureaux.

As data users, banks will be concerned most with the first two data protection principles.

These are:

(1) Personal information must be obtained and processed fairly and lawfully.
(2) Personal data shall be held only for one or more specified and lawful purposes.

The guidance on interpretation of the first data protection principle, set out in the First Schedule to the Act, provides that information must not be obtained by deception. For instance, if a bank asks a personal customer for information in connection with the opening of a current account, but the bank actually wants that information in order to sell the customer life insurance, then the bank may be deemed to have deceived the customer if it did not advise him at the time of its true intentions.

As regards the second data protection principle, the guidance provides that a purpose for which personal information is held cannot be lawful unless that purpose has been registered by the data user. The onus is therefore squarely on banks to register all the possible purposes for which they may wish to use personal customer information.

Example

Suppose that a bank has a central computer system which holds details about all its customers; the bank's marketing department has access to the system and writes to personal customers who are shown by the system as owning property of a substantial value, suggesting that they take out insurance under one of the bank's policies. There may be a breach of the Data Protection Act if the bank has not registered the marketing of its insurance services as a registered purpose, or if the bank obtained the necessary information without telling its customers that it might use the information for marketing purposes.

It would seem that the definition in the Act of 'personal data' will include any personal information about a living individual, whether obtained from him or her directly, or from a third party or from the data user's own records. However, a data user can use information for a registered purpose if the data subject might reasonably expect that information to be used by that data user for that purpose.

Example

A bank may be deemed to be entitled to use information obtained from a customer's current account application form in order to inform the customer of the bank's savings accounts, because these are both common types of personal customer accounts which may be held by customers right across the financial spectrum.

In summary, it is important to appreciate that a bank's common law duty of confidentiality (i.e. the rule of *Tournier*'s case) applies only to the disclosure by a bank to a third party of information (held in whatever form) known by the bank about both its personal and corporate customers. In contrast, the Data Protection Act regulates the obtaining by and use within a bank, as well as the disclosure to third parties, of computer-held information about personal customers only.

1.11 BANKER'S OPINIONS

A banker's opinion is a reference which a bank provides about its customer. The reference is requested by and given to another bank but the ultimate recipient is normally a customer of the requesting bank. This customer of course has no contractual relationship with the bank giving the reference.

A banker must give a reference on the basis of facts actually known to him at the time; he is not obliged to make enquiries to ascertain new facts or other people's opinions (*Parsons* v *Barclay & Co.* (1910)). The bank giving the reference is concerned about potential liability to two different parties:

(a) the ultimate recipient of the reference; and
(b) its own customer.

Liability to the ultimate recipient

This may arise because the bank has given an unduly favourable reference about its customer, and the recipient, relying on this, extends credit to the customer who defaults. Liability may occur in fraudulent misrepresentation and in negligence.

Fraudulent misrepresentation

Liability under this head requires an intentional misrepresentation by the bank. This will always be difficult to prove in practice. In any case, by s. 6 of the Statute of Frauds Amendment Act 1828, no liability arises from a fraudulent misrepresentation as to someone's credit standing unless the statement is in writing and signed by the maker. By the simple expedient of not signing status opinions, therefore, banks are able to exclude any possibility of liability under this head. If the statement is signed by an employee of the bank acting within his authority, this will render the bank liable (*UBAF Ltd* v *European American Banking Corpn* (1984) CA). The Jack Report has recommended the repeal of the 1828 Act.

Negligence

Liability under this head was the issue in *Hedley Byrne & Co. Ltd* v *Heller & Partners Ltd* (1963) HL, where a negligent banker's opinion was given, causing loss to the recipient. The court opened up the possibility of liability for negligence in these circumstances, but it had to be established that the bank, when giving its opinion, was willing to accept responsibility for its statement. The bank had followed the usual practice of incorporating a disclaimer of liability in its opinion, which made it clear it was not prepared to assume responsibility for its statement.

The law would thus be clear were it not for the subsequent enactment of the Unfair Contract Terms Act 1977, which renders ineffective any attempt to exclude liability for negligence unless the exclusion can be justified as reasonable. A bank's liability therefore now depends on whether its exclusion of liability is deemed to be reasonable.

Liability to the customer

This may take the form of liability for breach of secrecy and for libel.

Breach of secrecy

The banker's duty of secrecy to its customer has been discussed in **1.9** above. The giving of information in the form of a banker's opinion has to be justified under one of the exceptions in *Tournier*, if it is not to amount to a breach of contract. The only possibility is that it is done with the customer's consent, express or implied. Where the customer is unaware that the opinion is being given or that the system of status enquiries exists, it is hard to argue that he impliedly consents. However, assuming there is a breach of contract, the customer will have to establish loss if he is to be entitled to more than nominal damages.

Libel

The customer would have to establish that his bank gave an unduly unfavourable reference which reduced his standing in the eyes of right-thinking people. It appears, however, that the bank can claim privileged statement as a defence if it gave the opinion bona fide (*London Association for Protection of Trade* v *Greenlands Ltd* (1916) HL). It may be that the customer could sue in breach of contract, on the basis of an implied term in the banker–customer contract that the bank will not give an erroneous banker's opinion about its customer.

Credit reference agencies

It may be suggested that, in giving references, a bank is acting as a credit reference agency. If this were the case, the bank would require a licence under the Consumer Credit Act 1974 and would also be obliged to disclose on request by a debtor under a regulated agreement any information held (in whatever form) by the bank about the debtor, and to correct or delete any inaccurate information about the debtor.

This would not only have the effect of extending the Data Protection Act to paper-based information held about individual borrowers, but it would also mean that the banks' internal files about those borrowers would no longer be private.

The definition of credit reference agencies (s. 145(8) Consumer Credit Act 1974) provides that an agency furnishes information relevant to the financial standing of individuals, 'being information collected by the agency for that purpose'. As banks do not collect information about any of their customers specifically for the purpose of giving status replies, they are not credit reference agencies.

1.12 REPAYMENT ON DEMAND AND LIMITATION

Where a bank permits a customer to borrow by overdrawing his current account, the bank is entitled to require repayment on demand (*Titford Property Co.* v *Cannon Street Acceptances Ltd* (1975)).

Where, however, the bank has expressed that the facility is available for a specific time period then the bank will not be able to demand repayment before this period has expired (*Williams and Glyn's Bank* v *Barnes* (1981)).

Where there are conflicting provisions in the facility letter, so that in one place it says that the overdraft is repayable on demand and in another that the facility is available for a certain period, then it is a question of construction of the true intention of the parties. On these facts in *Titford Property*, the repayment on demand clause was held to be subordinate to the term provision.

The Limitation Act 1980 statute-bars legal actions in simple contract when the cause of action arose more than six years previously. It is suggested that in the case of a bank overdraft which is repayable on demand, the cause of action does not arise until demand is made. The bank then has six years to bring legal action if it wishes to do so.

This is certainly established when a customer claims for a credit balance owed to him by the bank. In *National Bank of Commerce* v *National Westminster Bank plc* (1990), the defendant bank made some debit entries on the plaintiff bank's account with them between 1978 and 1980. These were disputed by the plaintiff bank in 1988 and the legal

THE BANKER-CUSTOMER RELATIONSHIP

action began in the same year. It was held that the claim was not statute-barred since, irrespective of the debiting of the accounts at an earlier stage, the demand was not made by the customer until 1988 and the six years started running then.

1.13 APPROPRIATION OF PAYMENTS

Appropriation of payments may arise in two distinct situations:

(a) Where a customer has two or more accounts with the same bank and he (for example) pays money in. The money will be appropriated to one of the accounts.

(b) where a customer has one account and he pays money into it as well as drawing cheques on it. Appropriation will settle the issue of which payment in relates to which payment out.

In the vast majority of situations it will not matter in the least what appropriation takes place. Where there are two or more accounts, the bank normally enjoys a right to combine the accounts, and the only relevant issue is the combined balance. In the case of a single account, the relevant matter will normally be the bottom line balance, and the issue of which debits relate to which credits will be quite academic.

There are a number of situations where the appropriation is crucial, however. For instance, where there are two accounts, one of which is a wages account and entitles the bank to claim as a preferential creditor, the bank will be keen that a payment in is appropriated to the general account. This will reduce the bank's unsecured claim without reducing its preferential claim.

In the case of a single account, there are a number of situations where the appropriation that takes place will have an impact.

First, a statement of the general law on appropriation. When a customer pays money in, he has the first right to appropriate the payment. It follows from this that a customer with an overdrawn account is entitled to pay in a cheque and appropriate it to a cheque he has drawn, and his bank will not be able to use the credit to reduce the overdraft.

If the customer does not appropriate, the bank may make an appropriation. In the case of appropriating between two accounts, the bank will normally make an appropriation simply because it has to make a credit entry somewhere.

If, in the single account case, the bank also does not appropriate, the rule in *Clayton*'s case is used to determine the issue. This rule essentially says that the first payment in relates to the first payment out.

Illustration

Devaynes v *Noble, Clayton*'s case (1816) CA. Devaynes was a banking partnership. One of the partners, D, died. The surviving partners continued the business for a year when it became bankrupt. D's estate, however, was solvent. Clayton had an account with the partnership which had always been in credit. Clayton was obviously keen to claim against the estate of D. As a matter of partnership law, the estate of a deceased partner is jointly liable for debts existing at the date of death but not for subsequent debts. The credit balance on Clayton's account at the date of D's death was £1,713. Subsequent to the death, Clayton had paid in and withdrawn sums exceeding £1,713, and the ultimate credit balance was greater than £1,713. Neither Clayton nor the banking partnership had expressed any appropriation when debits and credits occurred.

It was held that D's estate was not liable at all. This was because each debit was deemed to have been set against the earliest available credit. Thus on an active account, the credit items which predated D's death were extinguished by debits, and the ultimate credit balance was represented by the most recent credits, all of which postdated D's death, and for which D's estate was therefore not liable.

It can help to understand the rule if one thinks of its effect as simply moving forward the date of the debt, which is always represented by the most recent items on the relevant side of the account. Where the date of the debt does not matter, which will be the usual case, *Clayton*'s case will be quite irrelevant. Where a partner has died, however, and his estate is therefore not liable for debts incurred after his death, the date of the debt will be crucial.

Other examples of the operation of *Clayton*'s case

Deeley v *Lloyds Bank Ltd* (1912) HL. The bank had taken a second mortgage from a customer to secure an overdrawn current account. The bank subsequently received notice from D that she had taken a third mortgage over the same property. The current account continued to be operated, and by the time the bank sought to enforce its mortgage, the total credits on the account had exceeded the debit balance as at the date it received notice of second mortgage. The bank's mortgage covered the later debits since it contained a continuing security clause, but the sale of the property did not achieve sufficient funds to repay D. The issue therefore was, which had priority? Held D, because the payments into the running account had extinguished the debt owed at the time notice of third mortgage was given and the ultimate debt was represented by the latest debits, all of which arose after the notice was received. This was so even though the account had never moved into credit. In other words there is a notional repayment of the earlier debt.

The operation of the rule can also prejudice a bank's claim when a partner dies or retires and the bank continues the partnership account, and later it wishes to claim against the deceased or retired partner. Once again, even though the account has remained in debit, there is a notional repayment of the debt that existed at the relevant time. This situation is of course the reverse of the facts in *Clayton's* case itself. Instead of a bankrupt bank, there is a bankrupt customer.

The rule can improve a bank's claim in some circumstances where it is beneficial for the bank that the date of the debt is moved forward. These situations are explained in chapter 16 (see *Re Yeovil Glove Ltd*), and chapter 2 (see *Re Primrose Builders Ltd*).

Where, however, the bank wishes to prevent the date of the debt moving forward in time, it may freeze the debt in time by simply ruling off the account and continuing the account by starting with a nil balance. It is therefore standard practice to rule off a partnership account when a partner retires or dies, or a secured account when notice of second mortgage is received.

It is also possible for a bank to insert a clause in a security document, to the effect that there will be deemed to be a ruling off of the account when the relevant event occurs. For example, in a mortgage form, a clause may say that if notice of second mortgage is received, there will then occur an automatic ruling off of the account. Such a clause has not been tested in the courts, however. A somewhat similar clause in a guarantee form has been upheld (see *Westminster Bank v Cond* in chapter 12).

Limitations to the operation of the rule

(a) the rule only applies to a running account (*Re Sherry* (1884)).

(b) the rule does not apply when a customer mixes his personal funds and funds he holds on trust in the same account. In this event the rule in *Re Hallett's Estate* (1880) applies. The effect is that the personal funds are deemed to be withdrawn first.

1.14 COMBINATION OF ACCOUNTS AND SET-OFF

A banker's right to combine accounts

Where a customer has two different accounts with the same bank, the bank has a common law right to combine them without giving notice to the customer. This is so even if the accounts are with different branches of the bank (*Garnett* v *McKewan* (1872)).

To give an example, if the credit balance on a customer's account at branch A is £100 and his debit balance at branch B amounts to £90, branch A can refuse payment of more than £10. The first the customer need know is that his cheque has been dishonoured.

On the other hand, a customer has no such right to instantly combine accounts. Therefore a customer who has a credit balance at the A branch of a bank and nil balance at the B branch, has no right to demand payment at the B branch.

If there are three or more accounts, the bank is free to combine any accounts of its choice and to leave others intact. For example, where an employer customer has three accounts, one in credit, one overdrawn wages account and one overdrawn general account, the bank will choose to combine the credit account and the overdrawn general account, leaving the overdrawn wages account intact, as this enables the bank to claim as a preferential creditor.

Situations where the bank's right to combine accounts is limited

(a) Where the debit balance account is not yet a debt due and payable by the customer. Therefore a loan account which is repayable at a future date cannot be combined. Nor may a contingent liability, such as a customer's potential liability as a guarantor (*Jeffryes* v *Agra and Masterman's Bank* (1866)).

(b) Where the debit balance is on a loan account which is presently due and payable, there will still be no right to combine instantly due to an implied agreement to keep the accounts separate (*Bradford Old Bank Ltd* v *Sutcliffe* (1918) CA). The rationale behind this is that a customer in these circumstances should not have his cheques dishonoured without any warning. This implied agreement extends to the case of an overdrawn current account which has been frozen. In the usual case, however, the bank will still be able to combine after giving a short period of notice. This may of course defeat the object of the combination if, during the notice period, the customer quickly withdraws the balance of the account in credit. It has also been suggested that the customer has the right to withdraw, at any time, the credit balance as at the date he received notice to combine (*Halesowen Presswork and Assemblies Ltd* v *Westminster Bank Ltd* (1972) HL).

(c) Any express agreement not to combine the accounts will negate the bank's right to do so.

(d) Where one account represents funds held on trust by the customer. If the bank is aware that the funds are held on trust, it is unable to combine. This principle extends to the case where the funds have been lent to the customer for a special purpose—the Quistclose trust (see **1.7** above). Where the bank is unaware of facts which expressly or impliedly indicate that the funds are held on trust, however, it enjoys the right to combine.

The equitable right of set-off

Two recent cases have dealt with this issue: *Bhogal* v *Punjab National Bank* (1988) CA and *Uttamchandani* v *Central Bank of India* (1989) CA. They had similar facts which essentially were as follows:

The bank holds two accounts. One in the name of X which is in credit and one in the name of Y which is overdrawn. The bank believes that both accounts are nominee accounts operated on behalf of X or a third party, Z. The bank therefore seeks to combine X's and Y's accounts and refuses to honour X's cheques, whereupon X sues. In both cases the bank lost. The relevant general principles are:

(a) a bank has a duty to pay within a reasonable time all cheques properly drawn by its customer; and
(b) an equitable set-off is available only if there is clear and indisputable evidence of the nomineeship. An arguable case of nomineeship is insufficient as whilst the case is pending trial, the customer is denied his funds.

The banks in these cases could have protected their positions by having X sign a letter of set-off expressly permitting his account to be used as security for any debt owed to the bank by Y or Z.

Set-off following insolvency

All of the above comments are based on the assumption that neither the customer nor the bank has become subject to the insolvency regime. If one or other is insolvent then the following principles apply:

(a) At the relevant time there will be a statutory set-off under the provisions in s. 323 of the Insolvency Act 1986 (individuals) or rule 4.90 of the Insolvency Rules 1986 (companies).

(b) The statutory set-off is automatic and unexcludable so any express or implied agreement not to set-off or combine will become void (*Halesowen Presswork and Assemblies Ltd* v *Westminster Bank Ltd* (1972) HL).

(c) Any agreement to extend the right of set-off will also become void; the assets of the debtor must be distributed in accordance with insolvency law (*British Eagle International Airlines Ltd* v *Cie Nationale Air France* (1975) HL).

(d) Debts which were not yet due and payable become due and payable on the onset of insolvency and are therefore subject to statutory set-off. Contingent debts are also included (*Re Charge Card Services Ltd* (1987)).

(e) Where debits on a customer's account take place after the bank had notice of a petition for bankruptcy of an individual customer, or a petition for winding-up or the summoning of a meeting of creditors of a company customer, then these debits will not be set-off. Equally, where a customer has notice of a petition to wind-up the bank or of the summoning of a meeting of its creditors, any subsequent credits into his account will not be set-off when he proves against the bank's liquidator.

(f) Where the customer has three or more accounts, the statutory set-off will take place to effectively combine all the accounts. If there is one credit balance account and two debit balance accounts, one of which is a wages account, the credit balance will be allocated rateably to the two debit balances in proportion to their respective sizes (*Re Unit Two Windows Ltd* (1985)). For example, if the No. 1 account has a credit balance of £100, the No. 2 account a debit balance of £100 and the wages account a debit balance of £100, statutory set-off will apply so that the bank will claim in the insolvency of the customer for £100. It will claim £50 as a preferential creditor and £50 as an unsecured creditor. If the wages account balance had been £300, the bank would claim a total of £300, £225 as a preferential creditor and £75 as an unsecured creditor.

(g) Part VII of the Companies Act 1989 sets up a new set of insolvency rules which apply when a member of a 'recognised investment exchange', such as the Stock Exchange, becomes insolvent. The relevant exchanges are obliged to have default rules dealing with the insolvency of any member. In a complete reversal of the *British Eagle* principle (point (c) above) these default rules then take precedence over the general insolvency law. The effect is that when a member becomes insolvent, the first stage is a set-off exercise involving that member's debts to and credits from other members of the exchange. Any credit balance resulting can be used for the insolvent members liabilities to the outside world. Any debit balance resulting is provable by the liquidator. There are also provisions conferring special rights on an exchange holding a charge over a member's assets.

1.15 THE BANKER'S LIEN

A lien generally is a type of security which carries the right to retain property belonging to another pending satisfaction of a debt owed by the owner of the property. For example, when goods are put in for repair, the repairer has a lien over the goods until the repair is paid for. The goods remain the property of the original owner but the repairer has rights over them. In *R v Turner* (1970), it was held that the owner of a car who removed it from the repairer's workshop without paying the bill and without permission, was guilty of theft of his own car. The repairer's lien does not carry a power of sale at common law, although a statutory power does arise under the Torts (Interference with Goods) Act 1977.

A pledge is a different type of security which is more akin to a mortgage. For example, a pawnbroker has a pledge over goods deposited with him. The pledge carries a power of sale of the goods, which in the pawnbroking example will be deferred pending possible repayment of the debt.

The banker's lien is a special type of lien which is equivalent to an implied pledge. It therefore carries a power of sale (*Brandao* v *Barnett* (1846) HL).

Property which may be the subject of the banker's lien

In *Brandao* v *Barnett* it was stated that the lien could apply to 'securities' in the possession of a bank. Other cases restrict this to 'paper securities'. Share certificates are included (*Re United Service Co., Johnstone's Claim* (1870)), as, it seems, is an insurance policy (*Re Bowes, Earl of Strathmore* v *Vane* (1886)). A dearth of modern cases and a degree of contradiction in the older cases make it somewhat uncertain what other assets are capable of being subject to the lien. It would seem that government stock, Eurobonds, commercial paper and certificates of deposit would qualify. It seems doubtful that the lien can apply to documents of title to land.

Limitations on the operation of the banker's lien

(a) Cheques and bills paid in to the bank for collection. The bank may in fact have a lien over cheques paid in to an overdrawn account but it is also under a contractual duty to collect the cheque and credit the proceeds to the customer's account. It cannot therefore sell the cheque but this hardly matters as the proceeds of the cheque will reduce the overdrawn balance. If there are multiple accounts, the bank usually has the right both to appropriate the cheque to a specific account and to combine accounts. Where a bank has a lien over a cheque, it may be a holder for value and possibly a holder in due course of the cheque, see chapter 5.

(b) The lien does not apply to securities which are deposited with the bank for safe custody (*Brandao* v *Barnett*).

(c) The lien does not apply to an in-credit bank balance in the customer's name. This is because the money in question in fact belongs to the bank and it is not possible to have a lien over one's own property (*Halesowen Presswork and Assemblies Ltd* v *Westminster Bank Ltd*

(1972) HL). The bank may of course enjoy a right to combine the relevant accounts and there are other methods of taking a charge over a customer's bank balance (see chapter 17).

(d) The lien does not apply to securities which, to the bank's knowledge, are held in trust by the customer (*Brandao* v *Barnett*). If, however, the bank is not aware of the trust, the lien does not arise.

(e) The lien does not arise if there is any agreement to the contrary between bank and customer.

1.16 SAFE CUSTODY

It is a long established part of a bank's business to accept property from customers for the purposes of safe custody. When one party has possession of property belonging to another in this way, the law describes this as a voluntary bailment. The law further categorises this into a bailment for reward and a gratuitous bailment, depending on whether the bailee (the person accepting the property) is paid by the bailor. It is established, however, that a bank is always to be regarded as a bailee for reward when taking its customer's property for safe custody, whether or not it is specifically paid for this service (*Port Swettenham Authority* v *TW Wu and Co. (M) Sdn Bhd* (1979) PC). This is because the safe custody arrangement is seen as part of the broader contract between bank and customer.

Liability of a bank bailee

A bank accepting property for safe custody is under a duty to take proper care of it. A bank will be liable in breach of contract if it negligently allows the item to be stolen and it will be liable in conversion if it hands the item to the wrong person.

Other points in relation to safe custody

(a) Where an item has been deposited by two or more bailors jointly, delivery should be made only on the authority of all the bailors (*Brandon* v *Scott* (1857)). On the death of one bailor, a right of survivorship may accrue to the survivors. Otherwise the personal representative of the deceased should give a receipt.

(b) Where the bank is under some bona fide doubt as to who has title to the goods, it may refuse to hand them over on demand and may detain them for a reasonable time in order to clear up that doubt (*Hollins* v *Fowler* (1875)).

(c) Where the items are stolen by an employee of the bank, there are cases which suggest the bank will only be liable if the employee was acting in the course of his employment in the sense that he was performing his normal duties, albeit dishonestly. This is the test of vicarious liability in tort. The effect of this doctrine is that a bank will only be liable for a theft by an employee whose duties included looking after the property and not for a theft by an employee whose duties did not include supervision of it (*Morris* v *Martin &Sons Ltd* (1966) CA).

It is suggested, however, that a bank will in any case be liable in breach of contract for negligently permitting an unauthorised employee access to the property or for negligently employing a dishonest employee.

(d) A bank is free to take a mandate from joint bailors to the effect that any one may give a receipt for the property. Even so, by analogy with the cases on duty of care when making payment of cheques, a bank will presumably be liable if it hands over the property with knowledge that a breach of trust is being committed.

(e) A bank is free to disclaim liability for negligence and this was found to be effective in *Coldman* v *Hill* (1919). The Unfair Contract Terms Act 1977, however, requires that such an exclusion of liability has to be justified as reasonable. Liability for fraudulent conversion may not be excluded.

(f) Items deposited for safe custody are not subject to the banker's lien (*Brandao* v *Barnett* (1846) HL).

1.17 TERMINATION OF THE BANKER-CUSTOMER CONTRACT

It is considered that it is preferable to refer to termination of the banker-customer contract, rather than termination of the banker-customer relationship because the relationship may survive indefinitely, e.g. the bank's duty of secrecy.

Termination by customer

The customer may at any time demand full repayment of his credit balance (*Joachimson* v *Swiss Bank Corporation* (1921)). It is suggested that if the customer reduces the account to a nil balance, the account should not be closed without confirmation from the customer that this is his intention. It would seem that a customer with an overdrawn account may not terminate the banker–customer contract without repaying the debt.

Termination by bank

It was stated in *Joachimson* that a bank may only close an account after giving reasonable notice and making provision for outstanding cheques. In *Prosperity Ltd* v *Lloyds Bank Ltd* (1923), it was held that one month's notice was insufficient, but here the customer's banking arrangements were unusually complex. It was stated that a bank may close an overdrawn account at any time.

It has been observed that a bank's duty of secrecy survives the termination of the contract. Claims arising from unauthorised debits (such as forged cheques), which the customer raises for the first time after termination of the contract, may also be made (*Limpgrange Ltd* v *Bank of Credit and Commerce International SA* (1986)).

Termination by operation of law

The following events will terminate the contract:

(a) death of the customer;
(b) mental incapacity of a customer;
(c) bankruptcy or insolvency of bank or customer.

2 Types of Customer

2.1 INTRODUCTION

Chapter 1 dealt with the banker–customer contract in general terms. This chapter examines six different types of account–holder, each of which is commonly encountered in practice.

The law relating to the following matters is dealt with for each of the six types of customer, where relevant: the opening of the account, the general conduct of the account, operation of the account by an agent of the customer, insolvency of the customer, mental incapacity of the customer and death or dissolution of the customer.

2.2 INDIVIDUALS

A primary consideration for a bank when opening an account for an individual is to ensure that the person concerned gives his true name. If he does not, and the bank collects cheques which he has stolen, then the bank faces liability in conversion to the true owner of the cheques. It has a defence if it has acted without negligence (s. 4 of the Cheques Act 1957). The lengths to which a bank must go in taking references when opening a new account are discussed in chapter 5.

A bank should also ask a new customer for the identity of his employer (*Lloyds Bank Ltd* v *E.B. Savory & Co.* (1933) HL). There is no duty to keep track of changes of employer, however (*Orbit Mining and Trading Co. Ltd* v *Westminster Bank Ltd* (1963) CA).

In *Robinson* v *Midland Bank Ltd* (1925), an account was opened for an individual, without his permission, on the application of a third party. Not surprisingly, the practice was disapproved.

Where the new customer is a sole trader and an employer, the bank should consider opening a separate wages account so that it can make a claim as a preferential creditor in the event of the customer's insolvency. The law relating to wages accounts is considered in detail in **2.7** below.

Operation of the account by third parties

It may happen that an individual customer authorises another to operate his account. He may do this by specifically informing the bank, in which case he will be asked to sign a mandate form, or by executing a power of attorney. In either case an agency is set up.

Where a bank mandate form is signed by the customer, the powers conferred on the agent will be clearly set out and will normally be in broad terms. The bank must, however, operate the account strictly within the powers granted. Where the agent operates the account for his own benefit and the bank knows this, the bank will not be able to rely on the mandate form and will be liable in breach of contract to its customer and as a constructive trustee (*Lipkin Gorman* v *Karpnale Ltd* (1989) CA).

Powers of attorney

Similar considerations apply when the account is operated by the donee of a power of attorney. Under the Powers of Attorney Act 1971, a power must be executed under seal by the donor. If he is incapable of signing, it may be signed on his behalf in his presence. In this case, two witnesses must attest the deed. A bank may rely on a photocopy of the deed if it is certified by the donor or by a solicitor or stockbroker. A power may be expressed as a general power in accordance with s. 10 of the Act in which case the bank may assume that the donee has the widest possible powers. A bank which deals with the donee of a power, after the power has in fact been revoked, is protected by the Act, so long as it did not know of the revocation.

A mandate or a power of attorney will be revoked under general principles of agency law by:

(a) death of the principal or agent;
(b) mental incapacity of principal or agent;
(c) insolvency of principal;
(d) notice by principal or agent;
(e) fulfilment of the purpose of the agency;
(f) expiration of the term of the agency; or
(g) illegality or frustration of the agency.

If any of the above occurs, therefore, the authority of the agent is terminated whether or not the bank is aware of the event occurring. An exception to this is the revocation by the donor of a power of attorney, as stated above.

There are, however, two ways in which the agency will not necessarily be revoked by some of the above.

Enduring powers of attorney

A particular problem with powers of attorney is that where a donor becomes mentally incapable, the power is automatically revoked at a time when it is likely to be needed the most.

Under the Enduring Powers of Attorney Act 1985, an individual may grant a power which can survive his mental incapacity. The power must be in the precise form required by regulations made under the Act, executed by donor and by donee and witnessed. When the donor becomes mentally incapable, the donee must apply to the court for registration of the power. Meanwhile, pending the court hearing, the power enters a hiatus period during which time the donee has limited authority in order to maintain himself and the donor. If and when the power is registered by the court, the donee reassumes the power he had before the onset of incapacity.

Irrevocable power of attorney

An equitable mortgage under seal is discussed in chapter 13. The system relies upon a power of attorney being granted by the mortgagor in favour of the mortgagee, along with deposit of the title deeds to the asset being mortgaged. A full memorandum of deposit signed by both parties is now also required, in the case of a mortgage over land, in order to comply with the Law of Property (Miscellaneous Provisions) Act 1989. The mortgagee acquires a power of sale over the asset. Clearly the security would be vulnerable if the power could be revoked, and thus the Powers of Attorney Act 1971 recognises an irrevocable power when it is granted to secure the performance of an obligation owed to the donee. Until this obligation is performed, the power may not be revoked by notice from the donor, nor by his death, mental incapacity or insolvency.

Death or mental incapacity of an individual account-holder

It has been noted, in chapter 1, that either of these events will have the effect of terminating the banker–customer contract. By s. 75 of the Bills of Exchange Act 1882, however, a bank's authority to pay a customer's cheques is terminated when the bank receives notice of the customer's death. Presumably this statutory provision overrides the common law, and a bank is protected paying a customer's cheques until it knows of the death.

Bankruptcy of an individual account-holder

The bankruptcy regime set up by the Insolvency Act 1986 provides for the process to begin with a bankruptcy petition presented to the court. After a time, the court will consider the petition and may then make a bankruptcy order against the debtor. After another interlude, a trustee in bankruptcy will be appointed to supervise payment to the creditors. Finally, three years after the bankruptcy order (two years in the case of a 'small bankruptcy'), the debtor is discharged from bankruptcy.

The essential feature of the law is that on the making of the bankruptcy order, all property which at that time belongs to the debtor, automatically vests in the trustee in bankruptcy who holds it on behalf of the creditors. It matters not that the trustee is in fact appointed sometime after the making of the order, since his title relates back to the date of the order.

The bankrupt is allowed to retain the tools of his trade, clothing, household equipment etc. Also any assets he holds on trust do not pass to the trustee.

It follows from the above that where an individual has a bank account and he becomes bankrupt, on the date of the bankruptcy order any credit balance will cease to belong to the individual and will pass to the trustee. The bank should not therefore honour any cheques after the making of the bankruptcy order but should await the instructions of the trustee. Where the account is overdrawn the bank will make its claim as a creditor in the bankruptcy.

Where there is an overdrawn balance on the wages account of a sole trader customer, the bank may make a claim as a preferential creditor. The full legal position relating to wages accounts is discussed under company customers (**2.7** below).

Where the bank holds some form of mortgage from the bankrupt customer, it will be unable to claim in the bankruptcy except in as much as the security is insufficient. The law relating to the bank as secured creditor is discussed in chapter 13.

Conduct of the account after presentation of the bankruptcy petition but before the making of the bankruptcy order

Section 284 of the Insolvency Act states that payments and dispositions of property by the debtor that take place after the presentation of the bankruptcy petition and before the making of the bankruptcy order are void unless ratified by the court. Bankruptcy petitions are not published in the London Gazette so a bank may not be aware of the petition. If it is aware, however, it should not pay any cheque from an account in credit. Where it has paid in ignorance of the petition, it must hope that the court will ratify the payment.

Where an account is overdrawn when the bank hears of a bankruptcy petition, the bank should not pay any further cheques for obvious practical reasons but in addition, the bank will find it is unable to even claim for the debt. If a bank pays in ignorance of the petition, it is considered that it will be able to claim for the debt.

In respect of payments into the debtor's account between the presentation of the petition and the making of the order, in practical terms the bank will have no reason to refuse to accept these, so long as it declined to allow the debtor to withdraw the funds. However, the legal position is as follows. Payments into an overdrawn account will serve to reduce the sum owed to the bank if the bank is in ignorance of the petition and acts in good faith (s. 284(4)). Payments into an overdrawn account where the bank knows of the petition will have to be returned to the trustee unless the court ratifies this disposition of the debtor's property.

Operation of the account after the bankruptcy order is made

The Act permits a bankrupt to retain property which he acquires after the making of the bankruptcy order, unless the trustee serves notice under s. 307 to claim the property. On the other hand, s. 284 still applies to render void dispositions and payments that take place after the order. The safe course for a bank is therefore to refuse to allow the bankrupt to operate his account until a validation order is made by the court.

Where the court has ordered that the bankruptcy order should not be advertised, e.g. pending an appeal by the debtor, and the bank in ignorance of the order operates an account, some protection may be afforded by s. 284(5). This permits a bank to claim for a debit on the debtor's account which took place after the order if the bank was unaware of the bankruptcy and it is reasonably practicable to recover the money from the recipient (i.e. the payee of the cheque).

Once the bankrupt has been discharged from bankruptcy, all debts are permanently discharged. The debtor will remain liable, however, for debts which have arisen since the date of the bankruptcy order.

2.3 JOINT ACCOUNTS

When a bank opens an account in joint names, it will need to establish true identities and to find out the names of the new customers' employers in the same way as with an individual account.

A mandate will normally be taken, the chief purpose of which is to establish whether the account may be operated by either one on his own or only by both acting jointly. In the absence of an agreement to operate by either one, the presumption will be that both signatures are required (*Husband* v *Davis* (1851)). The mandate will in any event separately declare that a right of survivorship applies, so that on the death of one of them the bank may pay the whole balance to the survivor. Even without such a clause, the law would normally, but not always, assume that the survivor of a joint account would be beneficially entitled to the whole balance. In an exceptional case, the law may conclude that the whole balance accrues to the deceased, even when there is a survivorship agreement.

Illustration

In *McEvoy* v *Belfast Banking Co. Ltd* (1935) HL, a father opened a joint account in his name and that of his son. He deposited £10,000. Payment was mandated to either or to the survivor. The father died and over some years the bank paid the money away to his executors who were continuing the father's business and in which the son played a part. The son then sued for the money. In a case where the plaintiff's case had few merits in non-legal terms, the court managed to come to the conclusion that, in equity, the money had passed to the father's estate.

Where the mandate requires both signatures to operate the account, the bank will be liable to the non-signing party if it pays on the signature of only one. This liability will amount to half the sum that was withdrawn (*Catlin* v *Cyprus Finance Corpn (London) Ltd* (1983)). However, if payment of the cheque in question served to discharge a debt for which both of the account-holders were liable, the bank may rely on the subrogation principle to debit the account (*B. Liggett (Liverpool) Ltd* v *Barclays Bank Ltd* (1928)).

On the death of the first account-holder, assuming the normal survivorship agreement, it is considered that the bank will always be safe in paying the survivor, irrespective of the decision in *McEvoy*, unless it is restrained by court order.

If the account is overdrawn at the time of death, the bank may wish to rule off the account in order to preserve its claim against the estate of the deceased, as otherwise the rule in *Clayton*'s case will operate so that subsequent credits will extinguish the pre-death debt. This would appear to be a practical consideration only when there were three or more account-holders, as when there are two, the bank would necessarily have to close the joint account on the death of one.

Cheques signed by the deceased but presented after his death should not be paid, applying s. 75 of the Bills of Exchange Act 1882.

The mandate will authorise either account-holder to countermand payment of a cheque, even if cheques require both signatures.

If one account-holder becomes mentally incapable, the bank should not pay any further cheques until the Court of Protection has appointed a Receiver to manage his affairs. Payment can then be made on the joint instructions of the Receiver and the other account-holder. This is so even if the mandate permitted payment on either signature. Where the other account-holder holds an Enduring Power of Attorney, the position will differ, see **2.2** above.

If one account-holder is made bankrupt, no further cheques should be paid pending the appointment of a trustee in bankruptcy, and then the bank should act on the joint instructions of the solvent account holder and the trustee. This is so even if the mandate permitted payment on either signature. The considerations discussed in **2.2** above apply so payments after notice of the bankruptcy petition should not be made.

In the event of mental incapacity or bankruptcy occurring when the account is overdrawn, the account should be ruled off before fresh credits are entered on the account. This is to preserve the bank's claim against the trustee in bankruptcy or the Receiver.

2.4 MINORS

A minor is a person under the age of 18 years (Family Law Reform Act 1969). Special rules apply to a minor's ability to enter into contracts. Briefly, a minor's contracts will be enforceable only if they are for 'necessaries' as opposed to luxuries (*Nash* v *Inman* (1908)). As explained in chapter 1, the banker–customer relationship is not entirely concerned with contract. The position with respect to liability in other branches of the law is different. A minor can be liable for negligence and other torts and also may be prosecuted for crimes he has committed as young as the tender age of 10.

The contract between bank and a minor customer is thus enforceable if it is considered one for 'necessaries'. In the unlikely event that it is not considered to be for 'necessaries', the contract is still enforceable by the minor but not by the bank. If the account is in credit, the bank would in practice only need to sue for its charges.

If money is lent to a minor, the lender has no right to recovery even if the borrowing was intended for the purchase of 'necessaries'. However, if the loan is in fact spent on 'necessaries', the lender can recover the amount so spent under the subrogation principle, and where a cheque is drawn by a minor to pay for 'necessaries', the bank is entitled to debit the minor's account by operation of the rule of subrogation. This is analogous to the facts in *B. Liggett (Liverpool) Ltd* v *Barclays Bank Ltd* (1928). If the cheque was not for 'necessaries', the court has power to order that the money (or what has come to represent the money) be returned if it considers this just and equitable (s. 3 of the Minors Contracts Act 1987).

When money is lent to a minor and a guarantee is taken from an adult, the guarantee is enforceable notwithstanding that the minor may not be liable to repay (s. 2 of the Minors Contracts Act 1987). A guarantee taken from a minor, however, remains void.

A minor has no capacity to draw or indorse a cheque and can thus never be liable as party to a cheque even if it was drawn to pay for 'necessaries' (s. 22 of the Bills of Exchange Act 1882). However, for reasons explained above, a minor can still be liable to his bank for the debt the cheque creates and also to the payee under contract. The minor cannot be liable to remoter parties, however, such as an indorsee of the cheque. Section 22 makes it clear that when a cheque is drawn or indorsed by a minor, the holder is still entitled to payment from the other parties to the cheque.

2.5 TRUSTEE ACCOUNTS

Where two or more trustees are appointed under the terms of an express trust, the law generally requires them to act jointly. Delegation of the powers of a trustee is only permitted within the strict limits of ss. 23 and 25 of the Trustee Act 1925, or as permitted by the trust deed. It is considered that these powers to delegate do not extend to the signing of cheques, and that therefore a bank should always insist that all the trustees sign every cheque.

It is different in the case of a charitable trust. Statute permits the trustees to delegate the signing of cheques to any two or more of their number (s. 34 of the Charities Act 1960).

Where trustees have power under the trust to apply capital, they are also permitted to raise capital by mortgaging trust property (s. 16 of the Trustee Act 1925). Section 17 provides that a mortgagee of trust property is not concerned to see that the money so raised is wanted by the trust or as to the application of the money.

Under general principles of trust law, a bank is safe in permitting the trustees to breach the strict terms of the trust if this is done with full consent of all the possible beneficiaries, all of whom are over 18 and mentally capable (*Saunders* v *Vautier* (1841)).

Where a bank pays away money on the instructions of the trustee or trustees when he or they are acting in breach of trust, it faces liability towards the beneficiaries. The bank has a duty to make inquiry if it knows of the breach of trust. The principles of law discussed in **1.7** above in relation to constructive trusts are relevant here, in particular the concept of liability for 'want of probity' and the classification of knowledge that emerges from *Baden, Delvaux and Lecuit* v *Société Général* (1983).

Where the bank has not been specifically informed of the existence of the trust, it is nevertheless deemed to know that the account is a trust account if that is suggested by the name of the account or any other circumstances (*Rowlandson* v *National Westminster Bank Ltd* (1978)).

On the death of a trustee, the surviving trustee or trustees have power to operate the account (s. 18). On the death of the last surviving trustee, the account may be operated by his personal representatives.

A trustee who becomes bankrupt may continue as trustee and his trustee in bankruptcy does not take the property which he holds on trust.

A new trustee may be appointed in place of a retiring trustee under s. 36. The bank will wish to see the deed of appointment and to have him sign the mandate.

Where there are two or more executors then, unlike trustees, they do have power to act on their own. Like trustees, however, they have no power to delegate to third parties.

2.6 PARTNERSHIP ACCOUNTS

A partnership is defined by s. 1(1) of the Partnership Act 1890 as 'the relationship which subsists between persons carrying on a business in common with a view of profit'. No formal procedure is required to set up a partnership and one can be inferred from conduct. It can thus happen that the persons concerned are not even aware that they are considered in law to be partners.

Where the partnership is formalised it is common to find articles or a deed of partnership which sets out the rights of the partners and the extent of their authority. In the absence of express provision on any matter, however, the Partnership Act lays down implied rights, duties and powers.

As affects a third party, such as a bank maintaining a partnership account, the relevant rules in the Act are:

(1) Any partner has implied authority to bind the firm, as agent of it, when acting in the course of the usual business of the firm (s. 5). Any restriction on a partner's powers will not affect a third party unless he is aware of the restriction.

(2) More specifically, any partner has implied power to draw cheques.

(3) In a trading partnership (one whose main activity is buying and selling goods) any partner has implied power to borrow money and charge security on behalf of the firm. In a non-trading partnership these implied powers do not apply.

(4) There is no implied power to give guarantees on behalf of the firm. Any partner purporting to do so will only render himself liable under the guarantee.

(5) Partners are jointly liable for debts owed by the firm (s. 9).

(6) There is no concept of limited liability, except in the rare example of a Limited Partnership set up under the Limited Partnership Act 1907, where some but not all of the partners may have their liability limited to their initial contribution. General partners may therefore lose their personal assets if required to meet the debts of the business.

Some of the above law is modified by the standard bank mandate which expressly deals with operation of the account, borrowing money etc. It is common to find that at least two partners must authorise transactions and, if so, the bank is bound by this. However, if only one partner signs but does so using the firm's name, s. 23(2) of the Bills of Exchange Act 1882 has the effect of making all the partners liable on the cheque irrespective of any mandate requiring two or more signatures (*Central Motors (Birmingham)* v *P.A. & S.N. Wadsworth* (1983)). Furthermore, the subrogation principle exemplified in *B. Liggett (Liverpool)* v *Barclays Bank Ltd* (1928) entitles the bank to debit the partnership account if the payment discharged a legal liability of the partnership.

Invariably, the mandate will extend the joint liability of the partners into joint and several liability.

Joint liability permits the creditor to claim the full debt owed by the partnership from any one partner, assuming that partner is solvent and alive. The advantage of joint and several liability, from the bank's point of view, is that the bank is able to claim against the personal estate of a deceased partner (alongside that partner's personal creditors) as well as against the estate of the partnership (*Re Jeffery, ex parte Honey* (1871)). Additionally, the bank may prove against a bankrupt partner alongside his personal creditors. The ability to do these things can on occasions significantly improve the funds repayable to the bank.

Any one partner may countermand payment of a partnership cheque (*Gaunt* v *Taylor* (1843)).

When opening a partnership account, the bank will ensure that the mandate form is completed. The bank may prefer not to see a copy of the articles of partnership as, if it does, it will have notice of the contents, which may include a restriction on the powers of the partners.

If the partnership is an employer, the bank should consider opening a separate wages account (see **2.7** below for the law relating to wages accounts).

Dissolution of the partnership

If the articles do not provide to the contrary, dissolution will occur by operation of law when, inter alia, a partner retires, dies, is made bankrupt or when a new partner joins the firm.

Dissolution may also occur by court order under s. 35, e.g. on mental incapacity of one partner, or on just and equitable grounds.

On dissolution, the bank will wish to rule off the account if it is overdrawn, in order to prevent the operation of the rule in *Clayton*'s case.

The surviving partners will be under a duty to wind up the business of the old partnership, and in doing so, they have a residual power to deal with partnership property, including mortgaging it (s. 38 and *Re Bourne* (1906)). This permits the bank to continue the operation of the account and to accept mortgages from the members of the now dissolved partnership.

There is no residual power to continue the business, however, when the entire partnership is made bankrupt.

Where the dissolved partnership is reformed or where a new partner is admitted to the firm (even if this does not involve dissolution), the bank will wish to take a fresh mandate from the partners.

Insolvency of the partnership

The Insolvent Partnerships Order 1986 provides that a court may order a partnership to be made bankrupt, or wound up, or both. In any event there will be an automatic dissolution.

The effect of a bankruptcy order against the partnership is to make all the partners individually bankrupt. All of their personal assets are then available to pay both their personal debts and the firm's debts. The order provides that the partnership assets are used to pay the firm's debts, but that each partner's personal assets are firstly used to pay off his personal debts; only if there is a surplus remaining is the balance then used towards paying the firm's debts.

The result is that a partner's personal creditor is likely to receive a better payment than a creditor of the firm. As explained above, the bank mandate provides that partners will be severally as well as jointly liable for the firm's debts. This has the effect of entitling the bank to claim as a personal creditor of each partner, in addition to claiming as a creditor of the firm. The bank's prospects of debt recovery are thus vastly improved. A further benefit of several liability is that it permits the bank to set-off a credit balance on a partner's personal account with the bank, against the overdrawn partnership account.

Where a wages account has been operated, the bank may make a claim as a preferential creditor.

2.7 COMPANIES

It is a fundamental principle of English company law that a company is a separate legal entity from its shareholders and may sue and be sued in its own name. It can even be prosecuted for crimes it has committed.

The vast majority of companies in England and Wales are registered companies limited by shares. Such companies may be public or private; a public company must have 'plc' at the end of its name and a private company must have 'limited' (Welsh language equivalents are acceptable). The principles examined here are identical for public and private companies.

Until recently, banks had to be concerned about a company cus-

TYPES OF CUSTOMER

tomer's capacity to open an account, to borrow money, give security etc. and about the directors' powers to bind the company (the *ultra vires* rules). The Companies Act 1989, however, has effectively repealed these rules (see **16.2** below) and a bank need not be concerned about powers of the company or of its agents so long as it deals with the directors of the company. New rules also deal with company seals and the way that company documents may be executed (see **16.3** below).

Despite the new rules on corporate capacity, a bank still owes a duty of care to a company customer when paying its cheques (see **1.6** above). Thus if a bank has paid a company cheque (drawn by a director acting fraudulently), when a reasonable banker would have been suspicious in the circumstances, the bank is liable to the company, by analogy to *Lipkin Gorman* v *Karpnale* (1989) CA.

There are further possibilities with company accounts, however. The Companies Acts set out a number of criminal offences which only companies, or those associated with them, may commit. Thus it is a crime for a company to provide financial assistance for the purchase of its own shares (s. 151 Companies Act 1985)—this was the central charge in the Guinness trial in 1990. In *Selangor United Rubber Estates Ltd* v *Cradock (No. 3)* (1968), a bank was held to be unable to debit the account of a company customer in respect of a cheque to buy shares in the company in contravention of the rule in s. 151. It is submitted that, following *Lipkin Gorman*, a bank would now only be liable in these circumstances if it failed the 'reasonable banker' test.

General principles of agency law may also assist a bank. For instance, the managing director of a company has implied authority from the company to act on its behalf. Further, if the company (or its appointed agents) holds out a person as having authority to act for it, this will create an ostensible authority which overrides the true extent of the authority except if the bank is aware of the latter.

It is an offence for a company to lend money to its own directors (subject to numerous exceptions). A danger area would be when a bank lends money to a company customer, knowing that the company will onlend the funds to a director.

Company cheques

A cheque is deemed to have been made by a company if made in the company's name, or on its behalf, by a person acting under the company's authority (s. 37 Companies Act 1985). Further, every company must have its name on all cheques purporting to be signed by or on behalf of the company (s. 349).

Section 26 of the Bills of Exchange Act 1882 provides that a person who signs a cheque on behalf of a stated principal shall not be personally liable on the cheque. He may be liable, however, if the principal is not stated. Where a director signed a company cheque in his own name, but the cheque was printed with the company's name and account number, the company and not the director was liable on the cheque (*Bondina Ltd v Rollaway Shower Blinds Ltd* (1986) CA).

The company name must be printed in full and without any abbreviation, in order for the company to be liable on the cheque. Thus, 'L R Agencies Limited' will not suffice for 'L & R Agencies Limited' (*Hendon v Adelman* (1973)) and 'M. Jackson (Fancy Goods) Limited' will not suffice for 'Michael Jackson (Fancy Goods) Limited' (*Durham Fancy Goods Ltd v Michael Jackson (Fancy Goods) Ltd* (1968)). 'Co' and 'Ltd' are acceptable, however, as is any unambiguous abbreviation (*Banque de l'Indochine et de Suez SA v Euroseas Group Finance Co. Ltd* (1981)). Where the company is not liable on the cheque due to the misspelling, the signer of the cheque is personally liable on it (s. 349(4)).

Company insolvency

The insolvency regime now pertaining to companies extends to a number of possibilities. A company may set up a voluntary arrangement, it may go into liquidation, it may go into administration and administrative receivers may be appointed to manage its affairs.

The voluntary arrangement is briefly discussed in **10.3** below and administration orders are dealt with in **16.10** below. Administrative receivers may only be appointed by a holder of a floating charge and are discussed at length in chapter 16.

A company going into liquidation must be wound-up. The winding-up process may be voluntary or compulsory. A voluntary winding-up commences with the appropriate resolution at the company's general meeting of shareholders. The company must immediately cease to carry on its business, except for the purpose of a beneficial winding-up. A liquidator is usually appointed at the meeting and the powers of the directors cease on this appointment.

A compulsory winding-up consists of a court order to that effect. Seven different grounds for this are set out in s. 122 of the Insolvency Act 1986. The ground relating to insolvency states simply 'the company is unable to pay its debts'. This ground is established by four alternative routes (s. 123):

(a) a statutory demand is served on the company and no payment is received within three weeks;
(b) a judgment creditor attempts to enforce his judgment by having court officers seize the company's assets but insufficient assets are found;
(c) the company is unable to pay its debts as they fall due; or
(d) the company's liabilities exceed its assets.

The compulsory winding-up commences with a petition to the court. Sometime later the court hears the case. If the petition is dismissed, there is no winding-up. If the order is made, however, the winding-up is deemed to commence on the date the petition was presented.

By s. 127 any disposition of the company's property after the commencement of the winding-up is void, unless the court otherwise orders. It has been held that the effect of this is that payments by a company into its overdrawn bank account constitute a void disposition of the company's property, and also that payments out of a company's bank account constitute a void disposition of property (*Re Gray's Inn Construction Ltd* (1980) CA).

Petitions to wind-up a company are published in the London Gazette and it is important for a bank to search each issue for names of its corporate customers. Once the petition has been presented, the bank should not pay any more of the company's cheques. If it does so, the liquidator may later obtain a court order requiring the bank to repay the funds to him. The court is empowered, however, to sanction a disposition under s. 127. A bank is likely to obtain this sanction retrospectively in two situations:

(a) if it paid cheques after the petition was presented but before it was published, and
(b) if the disposition did not prejudice the position of the unsecured creditors of the company (*Re Gray's Inn Construction Ltd* (1980) CA).

The bank's liability as a shadow director

Section 214, dealing with 'wrongful trading', empowers the court to make an order rendering a director of a company personally liable for the company's debts if:

(a) the company has gone into insolvent liquidation, and
(b) at some time before the commencement of the winding-up, the director knew or ought to have concluded that there was no reasonable prospect that the company would avoid going into insolvent liquidation.

A director will not be liable, however, if he took every step with a view to minimising the potential loss to the company's creditors which he ought to have taken.

A shadow director is defined as a person in accordance with whose instructions the directors of the company are accustomed to act. The risk for a bank is that it will set out a rescue package for a financially troubled company customer. The company unsuccessfully follows the rescue plan, leaving the bank potentially liable for wrongful trading as a shadow director.

Wages accounts

The priority of creditors' claims in the event of a company's insolvency is set out in **10.2** below. The category of preferential creditor ranks higher than the unsecured creditor and also higher than the floating charge holder. A bank creditor is therefore pleased to rank as a preferential creditor, if only partially, unless it is fully secured with fixed charges.

Schedule 6 of the Insolvency Act 1986 declares that preferential claims include those who have lent money which has been used to pay:

(a) employees' wages in respect of any period of employment in the four months prior to the resolution to wind-up the company (if a voluntary winding-up) or prior to the winding-up order (if compulsory). There is an upper limit of £800 per employee.

(b) accrued holiday remuneration in respect of any period of employment at any time before the winding-up and without financial limit.

Where a company has a single bank account, the bank's ability to prove as a preferential creditor will depend on whether the most recently paid cheques include a cheque to pay wages. This is because the rule in *Clayton*'s case applies to apportion the debits. For example, if the overdrawn balance at winding-up stands at £5,000, and the last cheque was for £5,000 to pay general trade creditors, and the one before was for £5,000 to pay wages, the bank is not a preferential creditor. If the final cheque was the one to pay wages, however, the bank is a preferential creditor.

The advantage of opening a separate wages account is that any overdrawn balance on that account at the start of the winding-up constitutes a preferential claim, subject to the limits stated above, i.e. not more than £800 per employee and employment in the previous four months. The balance on the general account will indisputably constitute a non-preferential claim.

Clayton's case operates on the wages account, so that the relevant debits are always the most recent, and these will tend to be preferential because they represent employment in the previous four months.

A number of cases have decided some points on wages accounts. It is not essential that a wages account be opened in order for the bank to be a preferential creditor, it is just that it avoids the risk of the adverse operation of *Clayton*'s case as explained above (*Re Primrose (Builders) Ltd* (1950)). It is essential that the debits on the wages account constitute genuine loans to the customer. If the bank insists on credits to the general account before it permits a wages cheque to be drawn, there is no loan entitling the bank to claim preferentially (*Re E.J. Morel (1934) Ltd* (1961)).

The bank has a right of appropriation, so that if it holds fixed security, it may realise this and appropriate the proceeds to the general account, thus leaving it with a full preferential claim in respect of the wages account (*Re William Hall (Contractors) Ltd* (1967)).

It may also combine accounts as it wishes, and may choose to combine a credit balance account with an overdrawn general account, leaving a separate overdrawn wages account to constitute a preferential claim. This right of combination ceases on commencement of the winding-up, however, and on the above facts there would then have to be a rateable abatement of the preferential claim (*Re Unit Two Windows Ltd* (1985)), explained in **1.14** above.

As mentioned earlier in this chapter, the ability of a bank to claim as a preferential creditor, after lending money which the customer uses to pay wages, extends to any form of customer who is an employer, individuals and partnerships as well as companies.

3 Consumer Credit Act Lending

This chapter looks at the main aspects of bank lending to personal customers as it is regulated by the Consumer Credit Act 1974.
N.B. In this chapter, 'the Act' refers to the Consumer Credit Act 1974 and, unless otherwise stated, section numbers (e.g. s. 187) are sections of the Act.

3.1 INTRODUCTION

The Consumer Credit Act was passed following the report of the Crowther Committee in 1971 (Cmnd 4596), the main theme of which was that a new law was required to deal with the substance rather than the form of credit agreements. The new Act replaced a variety of Moneylenders, Pawnbrokers and Hire-Purchase Acts. It seeks to achieve three aims:

(a) to supervise those involved in granting credit by means of a licensing system;
(b) to place controls on the advertising and canvassing of credit; and
(c) to regulate individual credit agreements and to provide the debtor with certain rights, irrespective of express agreement between him and the creditor.

The Act defines credit widely, as 'a cash loan, and any other form of financial accommodation' (s. 9(1)). Credit provided in a foreign currency is within the Act (s. 9(2)), but credit granted abroad or with a foreign element is largely excluded. A wide variety of credit and ancillary arrangements are covered by the Act's subsequent definitions.
A credit arrangement which does not fall within those definitions will be unregulated. In addition, some specific credit arrangements which fall within those definitions are nevertheless expressly excluded from regulation by s. 16. These are exempt agreements.
The Act is underpinned by a system of licensing, by extensive powers for government officials (mainly Trading Standards Officers) to enter and inspect premises and to obtain information and documents, by

criminal sanctions for non-compliance and by s. 173, which prohibits in the widest terms any attempt to contract out of the Act's provisions.

3.2 THE DEFINITIONS OF REGULATED LENDING

Consumer credit agreements

The Act is concerned almost exclusively with 'regulated agreements', defined in s. 189(1) as a 'consumer credit agreement or consumer hire agreement other than an exempt agreement'. Consumer hire agreements are outside the scope of this book. By virtue of s. 8, a consumer credit agreement is an agreement under which a person, firm or company gives an individual credit of £15,000 or less, so long as the agreement is not an exempt agreement under s. 16.

The debtor: an individual

The debtor under a consumer credit agreement must be an individual.

Any loan agreement with a qualifying credit limit (and not exempt under s. 16) will be a consumer credit agreement if the debtor:

(a) is an individual; or
(b) is a partnership in which one or more of the partners is an individual; or
(c) consists of two or more individuals borrowing on joint account, (e.g. husband and wife, trustees or personal representatives); or
(d) is an unincorporated body of individuals (e.g. a club or association).

No loan to a limited company as sole borrower is regulated by the Act. The same applies to other corporations, such as foreign companies, unlimited companies, friendly societies, local authorities and government agencies.

Where a loan of £15,000 or less is advanced to an individual jointly with a company, the loan document will be a consumer credit agreement but only the individual will be entitled to the protection of the Act. For instance, s. 65 provides that an improperly executed regulated agreement is enforceable against the debtor on an order of the court only. As 'the debtor' only refers to an individual borrower, a company borrower cannot invoke the protection of s. 65 even if it is borrowing jointly with an individual.

The credit limit: £15,000 or less

The limit specified in s. 8 is £5,000, but this was increased with effect from 20 May 1985 to £15,000 by an Order made pursuant to s. 181. It can be changed again by similar Order approved by Parliament.

In the case of the loan of a single payment of money by the creditor to the debtor ('fixed-sum credit'—see below), the credit limit is easy to ascertain.

In the case of running-account credit, such as that provided by a bank overdraft facility or a credit card, the credit limit is deemed to be the maximum debit balance permitted, disregarding a term which permits temporary excesses (s. 10). Thus the overdraft facility is regulated if the credit limit is not more than £15,000, but it is also regulated if the credit limit does exceed £15,000 (or there is no limit) and the debtor does not in practice draw more than £15,000 at any time, or it is more expensive for him to do so.

The Act uses three important pairs of definitions to categorise consumer credit agreements:

(1) Running-account and fixed-sum credit—s. 10.
(2) Restricted-use and unrestricted-use agreements—s. 11.
(3) Debtor–creditor and debtor–creditor–supplier agreements—ss. 12 and 13.

Each of these categories will now be examined.

Running-account credit and fixed-sum credit

Running-account credit—s. 10(1)(a)

A rather tortuous definition in s. 10(1)(a) describes the situation where an individual (the debtor) can obtain cash, goods or services under a continuing credit arrangement, provided that their total value, taking account of payments made by the debtor, does not at any time exceed an agreed credit limit. The definition is complicated further by providing that there need not be a credit limit at all.

Where there is a credit limit, it must be £15,000 or less for the agreement to be regulated, but this is subject to the qualifications mentioned in **3.3** below. Where there is no credit limit (for instance, as with charge cards) the probability must be that, ignoring temporary excesses, the debtor will at no time borrow more than £15,000—otherwise the agreement will be outside the Act.

The most common forms of running-account credit are bank overdrafts and charge and credit card agreements, each of which receive special treatment under the Act and are individually discussed in **3.3** and **3.4** respectively.

Fixed-sum credit—s. 10(1)(b)

This is any form of credit other than running-account credit. Fixed-sum credit can be advanced in a single lump sum or by instalments.

Restricted-use and unrestricted-use credit

The main relevance of this pair of expressions is:

(a) to assist with the definitions of the next pair of expressions, namely, debtor–creditor and debtor–creditor–supplier agreements, and
(b) to establish different consequences of cancellation under ss. 71 and 72.

Restricted-use credit—s. 11(1)

Section 11(1) covers credit:

(a) to finance a transaction between the debtor and the creditor (sometimes called 'supplier credit'), e.g. goods bought on credit from a shop where the company running the shop is itself the creditor;
(b) to finance a transaction between the creditor and another person ('the supplier'), such as the example in (a), but where a finance company is the creditor; and
(c) to refinance any existing borrowing of the debtor to any person.

Unrestricted-use credit—s. 11(2)

Section 11(2) defines this as any regulated credit not falling under s. 11(1).

Essentially, the distinction is that restricted-use credit involves payment of the loan money by the creditor directly to a third party: the supplier under (a) and (b), and the refinanced lender under (c).

This is illustrated by a quirk which places two types of credit agreement into the opposite category to that which, at first sight, would appear to apply.

Firstly, when a credit card is used to buy goods, the credit is

CONSUMER CREDIT ACT LENDING

restricted-use even though it may be thought that the card holder can acquire goods and services from anywhere he likes (so long as the supplier accepts the credit card). But the credit is actually provided at the time of the transaction and can be used only for that transaction.

By contrast, if an individual enters into a credit agreement for the purchase of specific goods but is given a cash loan by the creditor to buy the goods, the credit agreement is for unrestricted-use credit even if the creditor has made specific prior arrangements with the supplier to provide the credit.

Section 11(3) expressly states that if the credit is in fact provided in such a way as to leave the debtor free to use it as he chooses, even though certain uses would contravene the credit agreement, the credit will not be restricted-use under s. 11(1)(b). In other words, once the money is handed directly to the debtor, he could spend it in breach of the purpose stipulated in the credit agreement but he would still be obliged to repay the loan in accordance with the other terms of the credit agreement.

As the drawing of cash by use of a credit card involves unrestricted-use credit, credit card agreements permitting cash withdrawal fall under both categories and are therefore 'multiple agreements', as defined in s. 18.

Debtor-creditor and debtor-creditor-supplier agreements

The main significance of this important pair of definitions is in two areas:

(1) Canvassing (see **3.9**)—it is an offence to canvass most debtor-creditor agreements: s. 49(1).
(2) Connected lender liability (see **3.5**)—in the case of a debtor-creditor-supplier agreement, the creditor will be equally liable with the supplier for any misrepresentation or breach of contract by the supplier in respect of the contract financed by the debtor-creditor-supplier agreement.

Debtor-creditor-supplier agreements—s. 12

(a) A restricted-use agreement to finance a transaction between the creditor and the debtor.

This will cover 'supplier finance', where a retailer operates its own instalment finance scheme: the retailer must be the creditor—contrast finance company schemes offered by retailers, which fall under (b) below.

(b) A restricted-use agreement made under pre-existing arrangements between the creditor and a third party supplier and made to finance a transaction between the supplier and the debtor.

As mentioned above, this covers the typical retailer scheme where the retailer completes, for a buyer's signature, a finance agreement under which the creditor is a third party finance house, thus enabling the buyer to purchase on deferred payment terms. Credit card schemes are also within this category. In both cases, the finance company or credit card issuer (or its agent) has to make arrangements in advance with the retailer for the latter to offer the deferred payment terms or to accept the credit card.

(c) An unrestricted-use agreement made under pre-existing arrangements between the creditor and a third party supplier, in the knowledge that the credit is to be used to finance a transaction between the debtor and the supplier.

This category applies where the creditor makes arrangements with, for instance, a retailer that the creditor will finance a purchase from the retailer by an individual (the debtor), but the creditor then makes a cash loan to the debtor to enable him to make the purchase. The cash loan is unrestricted-use credit but in all other respects, the scenario is the same as (b) above.

Debtor–creditor agreements: s. 13

These include:

(a) A restricted-use agreement where the lender provides the money directly to the supplier, but where there are no pre-existing arrangements between lender and supplier.

(b) A restricted-use agreement to refinance (wholly or partly) an existing loan advanced by the refinancing lender or any other person.

(c) An unrestricted-use agreement where there are no pre-existing arrangements between the creditor and the supplier. Examples: a bank overdraft facility or personal loan.

In addition to the above definitions, the Act defines a number of types of credit agreements.

Credit-token agreements: s. 14(2)

A credit-token agreement is a regulated agreement where the credit is provided by use of a credit-token—see **3.4** below.

Exempt agreements—s. 16

These have already been mentioned in the introduction to this chapter (**3.1** above) and will be looked at in detail in **3.7** below. As a general comment, the regulations made under s. 16 list various types of agreements as exempt from regulation under the Act, describing them by reference to the categories defined in ss. 11, 12 and 13. Those sections state that the categories they define are all 'regulated' agreements, but s. 8(3) correctly provides that a consumer credit agreement can only be a regulated agreement if it is *not* an exempt agreement. This has the effect of invalidating the whole of the Exempt Agreements Order!

This Gordian knot can only be untied if the word 'regulated' is deleted from ss. 11, 12 and 13, which can be done without altering their meaning. In the meantime, the Exempt Agreements Order is, in practice, construed as if 'regulated' were omitted from ss. 11, 12 and 13, so that the Order can have its intended effect.

Small agreements—s. 17

'Small agreements' are regulated consumer credit agreements for credit not exceeding £50 (other than hire-purchase and conditional sale). The figure of £30 stated in s. 17 was increased to £50, with effect from 1 January 1984, by Statutory Instrument. There are anti-avoidance rules relating to a series of small agreements. In the case of running-account credit, where the credit limit does not exceed £50, this is a small agreement. Small agreements are completely exempt from the documentation requirements of the Act (s. 74(2)). They also fall outside some of the other regulatory provisions of the Act, e.g. those relating to withdrawal and cancellation rights.

Multiple agreements—s. 18

In essence, s. 18 attempts to treat every purpose for which, and the way in which, the whole or any part of a loan is to be used as a separate credit agreement, attracting the appropriate documentary procedures and other formalities under the Act.

Example

A credit card with a cash withdrawal facility will constitute a regulated debtor–creditor–supplier agreement for the credit card use in retailers and a regulated debtor–creditor agreement for the cash withdrawal facility.

Linked transactions—s. 19

A 'linked transaction' is a sale of goods or supply of services which is associated with the granting of credit but which is a separate contract entered into with a different party. This may occur where the credit agreement is a debtor–creditor–supplier agreement which finances the purchase. For instance, goods paid for by a credit card or the purchase of a car financed by credit from a finance company. The sale of goods is then a linked transaction to the provision of credit.

There may be a right to withdraw from or cancel a linked transaction until the credit agreement is made, i.e. the borrower may cancel the purchase if the anticipated credit is not made available.

Non-commercial agreements—s. 189

Non-commercial agreements are loans made by a creditor not in the course of his business, e.g. season ticket loans to employees. Certain parts of the Act do not apply to these agreements, such as the documentation requirements and cancellation rights.

3.3 OVERDRAFTS

The essential fact to remember about bank overdrafts, in the context of the Consumer Credit Act, is that they are regulated by the Act: their exemption from the Act's documentation requirements should not distract one from this fact.

As we have seen, a bank overdraft is one of the most obvious examples of running-account credit and of unrestricted-use credit. Having said this, even the intricate drafting of the Act has been defeated by the transience and flexibility of bank overdraft facilities.

One illustration of this is that the 'credit limit' for running-account credit is defined as the maximum debit balance which is allowed 'as respects any period'. Since bank overdraft limits do not have to be set for a specified period, it would be easy to suggest that overdrafts could be taken out of the Act altogether. However, it has been generally accepted that s. 10 will be treated as covering overdrafts, if only because the worst regulatory effects of the Act do not in fact apply to them.

In order to prevent creditors avoiding the Act by fixing artificially high credit limits or no credit limit, an overdraft to an individual will be regulated if, despite there being no credit limit or a credit limit above £15,000, the borrower is not in practice likely, or enabled, to draw more than £15,000 at any time (s. 10(3)(b)(i) and (iii)).

Similarly, if a bank stipulates that the overdraft interest rate will increase when the debit balance exceeds a level which is less than £15,000, the overdraft will be regulated even if the credit limit is higher than £15,000 (s. 10(3)(b)(ii)).

Temporary excesses above a formal overdraft limit must be ignored in calculating the credit limit (for the purpose of determining whether or not the limit is £15,000 or less) (s. 10(2)).

So, overdrafts to individuals, with an actual or agreed credit limit of £15,000 or less, will be regulated debtor–creditor agreements for unrestricted-use, running-account credit.

A bank or its employees (but no-one else) can offer overdrafts to the bank's existing current account customers by approaching them personally away from the bank's premises, notwithstanding the prohibition on canvassing all other debtor–creditor agreements off trade premises (s. 49(3)).

The agreement regulations in Part V of the Act would make bank overdrafts inoperable in practice, and in recognition of this, there is provision for the Director General of Fair Trading to issue a Determination that Part V shall not apply to overdrafts on current accounts (s. 74(1)(b) and 74(3)).

By amendments to s. 74 introduced by the Banking Act 1979, the Director General became *obliged* to issue a Determination in respect of bank overdrafts (and, subsequently, building society overdrafts), unless he considered it against public interest to do so (s. 74(3A)).

The same amendments also excluded bank and building society overdrafts from s. 74(4). Accordingly, so long as such overdrafts comply with any documentary stipulations set out as conditions in the Director-General's Determination, there is no risk of bank overdraft agreements or letters being in breach of any other provision in the Act regarding the form and content of loan documentation.

A Determination was in force from 1985 until 1990, which enabled banks to grant overdraft facilities without anything having to be committed to writing. This was replaced, with effect from 1 February 1990, with a new Determination, which implemented European Economic Community proposals for the written disclosure to borrowers of certain minimum information.

The new Determination requires banks to give their customers certain details about both agreed and 'unagreed' overdrafts. An 'unagreed' overdraft only becomes subject to the Determination where an individual has a debit balance on current account, which is not agreed in advance by his bank but which continues for three months. It does not matter if the debit balance fluctuates, so long as the current account never moves into credit or shows a 'nil' balance during the three months. It is likely that an overdraft that lasts for three months will be deemed to be subject to the bank's tacit agreement, unless it can show it has made positive efforts to have the overdraft reduced or repaid.

Before or at the time of granting an agreed overdraft a bank must give the customer, in writing, the following details about the overdraft:

(a) the credit limit; and
(b) the annual interest rate and the charges, and the conditions under which they may be amended; and
(c) the procedure to terminate the overdraft (i.e. the fact that it is 'on demand').

In the case of an overdraft subject to tacit agreement, the written information must be given before, or within seven days after, the end of the three month period mentioned above.

A bank or building society must advise the Director-General of Fair Trading that it wishes to take advantage of the Determination—a single notification will suffice for all future overdrafts.

During the currency of an overdraft facility, the bank must give its customer on request a copy of any document embodying all or any of the terms of the facility, and a copy of any other document referred to in the facility agreement (s. 78(1)).

Section 78(1) only applies if the document embodying the terms of the facility is signed by both parties. This might, for instance, include an accepted facility letter. The bank can require payment of 15p. A bank can refuse to comply with its customer's request made under s. 78(1) if the last such request was made less than a month earlier (s. 78(3)(b)).

The bank must also provide a statement showing the state of the account, and must in addition give the debtor such statements at regular

CONSUMER CREDIT ACT LENDING

intervals not less frequently than annually: s. 78(5). In practice, most banks provide current account statements monthly or quarterly.

The provisions in ss. 76, 87 and 98 for termination and enforcement of regulated agreements will not usually apply to bank overdraft facilities. This is because those sections only apply to early termination or enforcement of agreements for a fixed period, or termination for breach by the debtor. Most overdraft facilities are not made for a specified period and they become repayable on demand, not on breach of condition.

However, if an overdraft facility is made for a fixed period, demand could not be made before the end of that period until seven days after the bank had given its customer notice of termination in the prescribed form under s. 98. It could be argued that a seven-day termination notice was not necessary because demand does not terminate the overdraft agreement: it merely requires repayment of the overdrawn balance on the current account, leaving other provisions (e.g. for the payment of interest) fully operative. This is unlikely to be the correct interpretation, since formal demand has a number of irreversible consequences (e.g. the termination of the right to draw cheques and the cessation of regular statements), even though demand does not terminate the banker–customer contract as a whole (*National Bank of Greece* v *Pinios Shipping Co.* (1989) HL).

3.4 CREDIT-TOKENS

Definition and scope

Section 14(1) of the Act defines a credit-token as follows:

'(1) A credit-token is a card, check, voucher, coupon, stamp, form, booklet or other document or thing given to an individual by a person carrying on a consumer credit business, who undertakes—
(a) that on production of it (whether or not some other action is also required) he will supply cash, goods and services (or any of them) on credit, or
(b) that where, on production of it to a third party (whether or not any other action is also required), the third party supplies cash, goods and services (or any of them), he will pay the third party for them (whether or not deducting any discount or commission), in return for payment to him by the individual.'

The phrase 'whether or not some [or, in (b), 'any'] other action is also required' covers the formalities which usually accompany the presentation of a credit-token to a creditor or third party supplier. For instance, the keying-in of 'commands' in an automated teller machine, the signature of a credit card voucher or the authorisation of a debit or credit card transaction by telephone. A claim that a credit card was not a credit-token (and, therefore, not issued unsolicited in contravention of s. 51(1)) because the cardholder had to sign a voucher and produce identification failed, because of the above interpretation of this phrase in s. 14(1)(b) (*Elliott* v *Director-General of Fair Trading* (1980)).

Many cards, tokens and vouchers fall within one or other of the two parts of the definition of credit-token: book tokens, meal vouchers, gift tokens, cheques, gift stamps and cash, debit, charge and credit cards.

The problem with book tokens and similar objects is that the financial accommodation, or implied credit, is paid for in advance. However, most agreements for the supply of book tokens and other credit-tokens of this nature will not be credit-token agreements despite s. 14(2): they will be for £50 or less and will therefore be 'small agreements' under s. 17, and thus exempt from the documentary requirements of Part V of the Act (s. 74(2)). Alternatively, an agreement between the supplier of meal vouchers and an individual employer will not be made with the intention of *the employer* presenting the vouchers to the suppliers of meals.

Payment cards as credit-tokens

Let us now look briefly at the five main types of plastic payment cards currently issued by banks in the United Kingdom.

Cheque guarantee cards

Cheque guarantee cards are not credit-tokens. These cards offer a guarantee to the payee of a cheque that, if the conditions of the guarantee are complied with, the bank issuing the card (and upon whom the cheque is drawn) will pay the cheque on due presentation. The bank does not, therefore, pay for the cash, goods or services supplied in return for the cheque: the bank pays the cheque itself.

Cash cards

A cash card enables the holder to obtain cash from an Automated Teller

CONSUMER CREDIT ACT LENDING

Machine (ATM). Banks not only have their own ATMs but also arrange for their customers to obtain cash from other banks' ATMs.

Insertion of a cash card into an ATM is deemed to constitute production of it to a person, within paras. (a) and (b) of s. 14(1) (s. 14(4)).

However, since an ATM cash withdrawal is debited electronically and immediately to the cardholder's current account, it is not obtained 'on credit' under para. (a) when obtained from the card-issuing bank's own ATM, and is exempt from regulation by virtue of s. 89 of the Banking Act 1987 when obtained from another bank's ATM. Indeed, if it can be shown that cash withdrawals from a third party bank's ATMs are supplied as agent for the card issuer bank, such withdrawals would also fall within (a) and the cash card would not be a credit-token at all.

Contrast the position when the cash card facility is combined in a charge card or credit card, with cash withdrawals being debited to the charge or credit card account. Here, cash is supplied 'on credit' within s. 14(1)(a) (whether the cash was obtained from the card issuer's own ATM or a third party's ATM), and the cash withdrawal facility will be subject to a regulated debtor–creditor (unrestricted-use) agreement. This is so unless the cash withdrawal facility is exempt by virtue of its credit limit exceeding £15,000.

A credit limit of £50 or less (unlikely as this is in practice) will not avoid the documentation requirements of Part V of the Act—by virtue of s. 74(2)—because the cash withdrawal facility will almost certainly be recorded in the charge card agreement and will thus be subject to Part V (s. 74(4)).

Further discussion of the relevant legal issues is contained in **8.1** on Cash Dispensing Machines.

Debit cards

A debit card (for example, the SWITCH card) enables a bank customer to pay, and a third party (typically a retailer) to receive payment, from and to their respective current accounts immediately upon them agreeing the sale of goods or provision of services by the third party to the customer. Payment is effected by electronic payment messages.

Although no credit by way of lending or deferred payment is involved in such a transaction, it clearly brings the debit card within s. 14(1)(b); it is equally clearly exempted from regulation by the Act by virtue of s. 89 of the Banking Act 1987. This exemption will still apply where the cardholder's account is debited up to three days after the transactions.

67

Debit cards are looked at in more detail in **9.2** on Electronic Funds Transfer at Point of Sale.

Charge cards

A charge card also involves payment for goods or services, but only upon receipt by the cardholder from the card issuer of a periodic (usually monthly) statement. Well-known examples are the banks' 'Gold' cards and the American Express card.

Charge cards are clearly credit-tokens and involve genuine credit. The card issuer's undertaking to the card holder is 'credit' used in respect of specific transactions between the cardholder and a third party supplier of goods or services. It is therefore restricted-use credit under s. 11(1)(b); the necessary existence of pre-existing arrangements between the card issuer and the supplier make the charge card agreement a debtor–creditor–supplier agreement under s. 12(b).

Although charge card accounts are generally subject to no credit limit, they seldom exceed £15,000 because they are repayable in full every month. At first sight, therefore, charge card agreements are regulated by the Act, as credit-token agreements providing running-account credit.

However, charge card agreements are excluded from regulation under the Act, by the following classification of exemption:

> a debtor–creditor–supplier agreement being ... an agreement for running-account credit which provides for the making of payments by the debtor in relation to specified periods and requires that the number of payments to be made by the debtor in repayment of the whole amount of the credit provided in each such period shall not exceed one (para. 3(1)(a)(ii) of the Consumer Credit (Exempt Agreements) Order 1989, made pursuant to s. 16(5) of the Act).

Because they are exempt, charge card agreements are also outside the scope of s. 75—see **3.5** below on Connected Lender Liability.

Where the charge card incorporated a cash withdrawal facility which was itself regulated (see 'Cash cards', above), the charge card agreement would be a 'multiple agreement' (s. 18). It would be partly regulated (i.e. as to the cash withdrawal facility only) but this would not make the charge card account either regulated or subject to s. 75.

Credit cards

Credit cards are identical to charge cards in all respects, save that they

CONSUMER CREDIT ACT LENDING

are subject to a credit limit and provide an extended credit option for the cardholder. This operates by the cardholder being entitled, instead of repaying his account in full when he receives his monthly statement, to repay a minimum amount—usually sufficient to ensure full repayment in two years, assuming no change in the debit balance. The cardholder can repay more than the minimum amount, and if he does elect to repay the whole debit balance within three weeks or so of the statement date, he will not be charged interest on new purchases.

By far the most common credit cards are the VISA and Mastercard (including Access) cards issued by the banks and building societies.

The legal incidents under the Act of credit cards are the same as for charge cards, save that the extended credit option has the major effect that credit cards are not exempt from regulation. They are fully regulated and within the ambit of s. 75.

Credit-token agreements

'A credit-token agreement is a regulated agreement for the provision of credit in connection with the use of a credit-token' (s. 14(2)).

Once it has been established that a bank payment card is a credit token, it is necessary to determine whether an agreement relating to its use is regulated or exempt.

As has been mentioned above, credit provided under debit, charge and credit cards is debtor–creditor–supplier credit, but debit and charge card agreements are exempt. Cash card agreements probably provide no credit, but even if they do, it is exempt credit. So, only credit card agreements are regulated. Apart from the application of the documentary requirements of Part V of the Act, this point is significant in relation to ss. 51 and 84 which will now be looked at.

Unsolicited credit-tokens

It is an offence for any person to give an individual a credit-token unless the individual has requested it (s. 51(1)).

However, the request must be in writing unless the credit-token provides credit under a debtor–creditor–supplier agreement which is a 'small agreement', as defined in s. 17 (credit limit £50 or less) (s. 51(2)).

'Give', in s. 51(1), means 'deliver or send by post to' (s. 189(1)).

Section 51(1) does not apply to the first, or to renewal or replacement, credit-tokens issued after a related credit-token agreement has already been executed (s. 51(3)).

The waiver in s. 51(3) is not as wide as it looks. It does not apply to a credit-token, such as a debit card or charge card, which does not provide regulated credit, or to the renewal or replacement of such a credit-token. In practice, the application form or agreement form for such cards may well be in sufficient terms to comply with ss. 51(1) and (2).

The distinction will become academic if legislation is introduced in accordance with the Jack Report White Paper. This has indicated (in para. 4.5) the Government's intention to extend s. 51 to all payment cards, and presumably 'credit-token' would be deleted from s. 51(3). Section 51 would also be applied to the issue of Personal Identification Numbers (PINs).

Use of credit-tokens by third parties

This issue is primarily one of the bank's mandate as card issuer. As with cheques, the bank can only act on its customer's mandate and a forged signature on a debit, charge or credit voucher will not entitle the bank, as card issuer, to debit the current, charge or credit card account of its customer, the cardholder. Nor will the bank be entitled, by an express contractual term, to make the cardholder liable for forgeries on his debit, charge or credit card account.

In cases where the cardholder's signature is not required, legal principles are different. In these cases, the person entering into a transaction as cardholder identifies himself and authorises the transaction—and, thus, his bank's right to debit his current account—by keying into a machine a Personal Identification Number (PIN).

This is typical of a cash withdrawal from an ATM; but it could also be extended to other payment card transactions, particularly debit cards. Where a PIN is used, the person using it will not usually be capable of identification in any other way, even when he or she is served in a shop. An ATM will not know if a man is using a cash card issued to a female customer. Having invested huge sums in secure systems and procedures, card issuers consider it reasonable to impose on cardholders the risk of improper third party use of their cards unless the cardholders have taken all reasonable care to safeguard both their cards and PINs. The mandate issue is still relevant, and a bank can only impose liability on a cardholder where third party use:

(a) occurs with the cardholder's consent or authority, whether express or implied; or

(b) is expressly made the cardholder's responsibility by a term of the card agreement between the bank and the cardholder.

To achieve this, cash card agreements may impose a duty of care on a cardholder to safeguard his card and PIN and not to keep them together, for instance, by writing the PIN on the card. It should be noted that such provisions, even if they are unreasonable, would not appear to be subject to the Unfair Contract Terms Act 1977: they do not seek to exclude or limit the bank's liability for its breach of contract, or to alter the bank's contractual duties or obligations.

However, it might be held that the bank's obligation was to debit a cardholder's account only in respect of card transactions undertaken by the authorised holder of the card, and that any additional right to debit third party transactions was a limitation on the bank's liability for breach of its obligation. As such, the limitation would fall within s. 3 and be subject to the 'reasonableness test' under UCTA.

As regards regulated credit-token agreements only, the Act limits a bank's ability to make its customers liable for third party use. A debtor cannot, save as provided below, be made liable for a third party's use of the debtor's regulated credit facility (s. 83(1)).

The exceptions are:

(a) Where the third party acts as the debtor's agent (s. 83(1)).

(b) Where the third party is authorised by the debtor to use the debtor's credit-token under a regulated agreement (s. 84(1)).

(c) Where the third party is in possession of the debtor's credit-token with the debtor's consent (s. 84(2)). In this case, it would seem that the debtor will be liable even if the third party is not authorised to use the credit-token, or if the debtor has not voluntarily disclosed his PIN to the third party.

(d) Where the creditor has not received notice (oral or in writing) from the debtor that the debtor or anyone authorised by him to use his credit-token has possession of it (s. 84(2)). However, the debtor cannot be made liable for more than £50 of 'use' of his credit-token by an unauthorised third party. (The figure of £30 stated in s. 84(2) was increased to £50, with effect from 20 May 1985, by the Consumer Credit (Increase of Monetary Amounts) Order 1983.)

To obtain the benefit of this last exception, the card issuer must ensure that its credit-token agreement gives a name, address and telephone number for the cardholder to give the necessary notice.

All the provisions of s. 84 apply separately to each credit-token, so that an additional card must be treated as being issued under a different credit-token agreement for these purposes.

It must be noted that the £50 limit under ss. 83 and 84 only applies to regulated agreements (see the definition in s. 14(2) of credit-token agreements) and the limit does not apply to cash cards or debit cards.

These statutory limitations may gain greater significance if legislation is introduced, in accordance with the Jack Report White Paper (para. 4.6), to extend ss. 83 and 84 to all payment cards.

The Jack Report White Paper also proposed legislation to combat the dishonest fabrication and duplication of payment cards by bringing such activities within the ambit of s. 5(5) of the Forgery and Counterfeiting Act 1981.

3.5 CONNECTED LENDER LIABILITY

'If a debtor under a debtor–creditor–supplier agreement falling within section 12(b) or (c) has, in relation to a transaction financed by the agreement, any claim against the supplier in respect of a misrepresentation or breach of contract, he shall have a like claim against the creditor who with the supplier shall accordingly be jointly and severally liable to the debtor' (s. 75(1)).

The rationale of section 75

The Crowther Committee Report, which gave birth to the Consumer Credit Act, justified the concept of connected lender liability on the grounds that the lender and the supplier both benefit from the provision of credit in connection with the sale of goods and services, and it is therefore in the nature of a 'joint venture'; they should both therefore share responsibility for the quality of the goods and services.

The concept of requiring damages payable by a supplier or manufacturer to be applied in repaying any purchase money finance is much fairer. Although this was attempted in the first version of the Consumer

Guarantees Bill sponsored in 1989/90 by the National Consumer Council, the way in which it was done in that Bill made it unworkable, and the Government felt unable to support it. Unfortunately, the Government also felt unable to support the Jack Report's recommendation that credit cards be excluded from s. 75 (see para. 8.4–5 of the Jack Report White Paper).

The scope of the section

Connected lender liability under s. 75 is limited to regulated debtor–creditor–supplier agreements falling within ss. 12(b) or (c). These agreements were discussed in **3.2** above. The two main examples of agreements carrying connected lender liability are:

(a) the major credit cards—Mastercard (Access) and Visa; and
(b) the finance house personal loan instalment finance agreements which are stocked by many high street retailers.

No claim can be brought in respect of a non-commercial agreement (s. 75(3)(a)). Non-commercial agreements are those which are not made by the creditor in the ordinary course of his business (s. 189(1)).

Neither can a claim be brought under a small agreement, financing £50 or less (s. 17). This is the result of a broader exemption which excludes all claims from s. 75 if they relate to goods or services, the cash price of which was less than £100 or more than £30,000 (s. 75(3)(b)).

(The figures of £30 and £10,000 stated in the Act were increased, with effect from 1 January 1984, to £100 and £30,000 respectively by the Consumer Credit (Increase of Monetary Limits) Order 1983.)

The limits under s. 75(3) are qualifying limits only. They do not prevent a claim being brought to recover damages of more than £30,000 in respect of the purchase of goods costing less than that amount.

The debtor can also claim under s. 75 even if he is in breach of the terms of his credit agreement (s. 75(4)).

The claim against the supplier

A claim may lie against the seller of goods for misrepresentation if some statement made or advertised about the goods was untrue. In addition, lack of title, defective quality or inadequate performance may give rise to a claim for breach of contract. Failure to provide a contracted service (either at all or in accordance with the agreement) or the provision of a service without due care and skill may also result in claims for misrepresentation or breach of contract.

Some contractual liabilities cannot be excluded by agreement. For instance, liabilities to a consumer under a contract entered into by the other party in the course of its business, cannot be limited or excluded unless it is reasonable to do so (ss. 2–8 Unfair Contract Terms Act 1977).

The claim under s. 75(1) lies against the supplier, not against, for instance, the manufacturer or the supplier's agent. Difficulties arise where the person with whom the individual debtor dealt, was in fact an agent of the true supplier, e.g. a travel agent. There are also legal problems where the transaction between the supplier and the debtor was only partly financed by the creditor, for instance, a deposit for a holiday, where the balance of the holiday price was paid by cheque or financed by a different creditor.

The creditor's indemnity

By virtue of s. 75, an individual can claim against either the supplier or the creditor or both of them, jointly or severally or both. In practice, the creditor is usually joined as a second defendant, unless the supplier is insolvent or obstructive, in which case the creditor alone is sued. Although pointless if the supplier is insolvent, the creditor can join the supplier as a co-defendant (s. 75(5)).

The creditor has a full indemnity against the supplier for all loss suffered in satisfying his (the creditor's) liability under s. 75(1). This indemnity extends to reasonable legal costs incurred in the proceedings (s. 75(2)).

The position regarding indemnity is less clear where the supplier's defence is successful, or where the supplier settles with the claimant on the basis that the supplier expressly does not admit liability. In these cases, the creditor may have expended money on legal costs without recourse under s. 75(2) to the supplier.

3.6 SECURED LENDING

Although the Consumer Credit Act includes provisions relating to all forms of security (e.g. land mortgages and pledges over chattels), this chapter is concerned only with the Act's treatment of mortgages over freehold and leasehold property in England and Wales.

Exempt transactions

Most property lending will be exempt from the Consumer Credit Act, if only because property values ensure that a majority of property-related loans will be for more than £15,000.

Even under that figure, many loans for the purchase or improvement of property are exempted from the Act by a complex network of provisions. As a preliminary observation, none of the exemptions described below requires the land mortgage to be given by the borrower.

Section 16(1) and (2) exempt certain land-secured lending by specified types of institutional lenders, including all local authorities. The Consumer Credit (Exempt Agreements) Order 1989 redefines s. 16 by extending the exemptions to all building societies, banks (including foreign banks), wholly-owned subsidiaries of banks, most insurance companies (175 are named in the First Schedule to the Order) and certain friendly societies and church charities. However, the loans exempted by the Order are not as widely described as in s. 16.

(a) The Exempt Agreements Order applies to any debtor–creditor agreement for a loan secured by a mortgage on any land, if the loan was advanced for the purchase of land or for the provision (i.e. erection or conversion) of residential or business premises.

(b) A debtor–creditor–supplier agreement for such a loan will only be exempt if it is secured on the land purchased with the loan.

(c) A lender under an existing debtor–creditor agreement for a loan which is itself exempt under (a) above may make a further loan for the alteration, enlargement, repair or improvement of a building on the land purchased or built on with the first loan, provided both loans are secured from drawdown by mortgages on that land.

(d) A debtor–creditor loan will be exempt if it is made to refinance another debtor–creditor loan which is itself exempt under one of the above categories, even where the refinanced loan was advanced by a different lender.

Recalling the definition in s. 13 of 'debtor–creditor agreements', it will be noted that, so long as there are no prior arrangements between the lender and the 'supplier' of the land, it does not matter whether the proceeds of the loan are paid directly to the 'supplier' (s. 13(a)) or to the borrower (s. 13(c)). The 'supplier' of the land will be the vendor, the borrower's new landlord if a new lease or sub-lease is being granted, or the owner, where a building or repair contract is entered into.

Having said this, a loan may not be exempt if the lender makes prior arrangements with an existing owner or creditor, in connection with financing the purchase or repair of the owner's property or refinancing the creditor's existing loan. In these cases, only the debtor–creditor–supplier exemption mentioned above can apply—for instance, refinancing loans would not be exempt.

There are some additional land-secured exemptions of less significance, but lending secured on land will generally still be regulated if the loan is not for a purpose related to the property.

Overdrafts

Once again, overdrafts are in a privileged position. Whereas a regulated agreement which is secured by a mortgage on land is subject to special procedures giving the borrower the right to withdraw (see **3.8** on The Forms and Formalities), these procedures are prescribed in Part V of the Act and, therefore, none of these procedures applies to overdrafts by virtue of the Determination made under s. 74(3).

Right of withdrawal

A regulated agreement which is not signed by the borrower on the lender's business premises is usually cancellable by the borrower during the seven days after he has signed the loan agreement (s. 67). But regulated agreements secured by land mortgages are not subject to cancellation, in order to avoid problems with the Land Registry (s. 67(a)).

Instead, special procedures apply to land-secured regulated loans. However, even these procedures do not apply to a restricted-use agreement to purchase the mortgaged land, or to a bridging loan in connection with the purchase of the mortgaged land (s. 58(2)).

In most residential property sales, the purchaser's mortgagee will usually remit the loan proceeds to his or the purchaser's solicitors, or against the solicitors' undertaking to apply the money towards the property purchase and to obtain the mortgage. The purchaser cannot get possession of the loan proceeds or procure them to be used for any purpose other than the purchase of the property to be mortgaged. Most such property purchase loans are therefore restricted-use.

In the case of unrestricted-use secured regulated agreements, the lender must give the borrower a copy of the agreement at least seven days before giving him the agreement itself for signing. The advance copy must contain a notice in a prescribed form informing the borrower of his right to withdraw and how to exercise it (s. 58(1)).

In addition, the lender must not communicate unsolicited (by letter, telephone or otherwise) with the borrower in connection with the loan, from the date of giving him the advance copy until seven days after giving him the agreement for signing or, if earlier, after the borrower has signed the agreement and returned it to the lender ('the consideration period') (s. 61(2) and (3)).

During the consideration period, the borrower may inform the lender (or the lender's agent or credit-broker) that he wishes to withdraw from the proposed credit agreement. The result is the same as if a cancellable agreement had been cancelled: the borrower is entitled to withdraw from or cancel any linked transaction (e.g. a purchase financed by the loan) and recover any money paid by him (e.g. for survey fees).

The lender's failure to comply with the procedural requirements relating to a land-secured regulated loan will render the agreement unenforceable by the lender without a court order (s. 65(1)).

The lender must give the borrower seven days' notice of the lender's intention to seek possession of mortgaged land (ss. 76 and 87). This will only apply to fixed term loan agreements where the right to possession is an express term of the agreement.

In any event, a land mortgage securing a regulated agreement cannot be enforced without a court order, and then only to the extent that the mortgage itself provides for its enforcement (s. 126).

3.7 EXEMPT CREDIT

Exempt agreements are mentioned several times in this book, because of their significance in relation to secured lending and payment cards. From the start, the Consumer Credit Act recognised that even within the various definitions of regulated agreements, some types of lending transactions should not be regulated by the Act.

For this purpose, the Act provides complete exemption from regulation for specified credit arrangements. These exempt agreements should be distinguished from:

(a) loans which are not regulated by the Act because they are outside the definition of regulated agreements, e.g. loans to companies and loans of more than £15,000.

(b) loans which are 'partially' regulated, by being excluded from the Act's documentary requirements, e.g. overdrafts, non-commercial loans and small agreements.

To be exempt from the Act, a loan must be exempted by s. 16 and the regulations made under that section. In effect, s. 16 only acts as the door to a room. The room is the Consumer Credit (Exempt Agreements) Order 1989 (SI 1989/869), and it is full of specifically defined types of loan agreements.

Section 16 empowers the Secretary of State for Trade and Industry to make regulations providing for exemption for certain descriptions of credit. Let us look at the principal ones.

Property lending

The exempted lenders and types of loan agreement are described initially in s. 16(2) and further refined in para. 2 of the Exempt Agreements Order. The important ones are described in **3.6** above on Secured Lending.

The remaining categories of exempt agreements are relatively straightforward. Section 16(5) lists three general heads of exemption, and paras. 3, 4 and 5 of the Exempt Agreements Order supply the detail, as follows:

Exemption by reference to the maximum number of repayments: s. 16(5)(a)

Paragraph 3 of the Order exempts the following agreements under this head:

(a) Debtor–creditor–supplier agreements:

(i) for fixed-sum credit which must be repaid in four or less instalments *and* within one year of the date of the agreement (e.g. trade credit where there is no running account, but not cash loans as these will be debtor-creditor agreements).

(ii) for running-account credit, where repayments are related to specified periods and the credit advanced in any period *must* be repaid in a single amount, although interest and charges can be subject to further payments (e.g. milkman's accounts and charge cards, but not credit cards which can be repaid in more than one amount if the cardholder chooses).

N.B. Credit advanced in a period need not be repaid at the end of that period, so that credit may be advanced on a running account by reference to monthly periods—perhaps with interest being debited monthly—but with a requirement that the borrower repays the entire debit balance quarterly. Also, the definition in (ii) covers the possibility that, on a running-account, there will not always be a debit balance at the end of each credit period.

(b) Debtor–creditor–supplier agreements financing the purchase of land and repayable in four or less instalments. In this case, the instalments must include all related interest and charges for the exemption to apply. The loan agreement need not be secured. As mentioned above, most property lending will be exempt under para. 2(2) of the Order, or simply because the amount advanced exceeds £15,000.

Example

A house-builder sells a property to an individual, leaving £15,000 or less of the purchase price outstanding unsecured, on terms that the purchaser will repay the outstanding purchase price, together with all accruing interest and associated charges, by four equal quarterly amounts.

The agreement will be restricted-use under s. 11(1)(a) and, therefore, debtor–creditor–supplier under s. 12(a). But it will also be exempt under head (b).

Heads (c) and (d) relate to debtor–creditor–supplier agreements for fixed-sum credit, to finance certain land-related insurance premiums.

Exemption by reference to the maximum rate of the total charge for credit: s. 16(5)(b)

Paragraph 4(1) of the Exempt Agreements Order exempts certain agreements under this head, the main one being debtor–creditor agreements under which the rate of the total charge for credit cannot exceed the specified maximum under para. 4(5)—see below. Many bank staff loans are exempt under this exemption.

The 'total charge for credit' includes interest and all other charges, and it is compiled in a certain way to produce a figure ('the annual percentage rate', or 'APR') which enables the true cost of credit charged by different lenders to be compared. This is discussed in more detail in **3.10** on Advertising.

Paragraph 4(5) of the Exempt Agreements Order specifies, as the maximum rate of the total charge for credit, 13% p.a. or, if higher, 1% above the highest annual base rate of certain banks either on the date 'or 28 days before the date' of the loan agreements. Where interest is the only item in the total charge for credit, the maximum rate cannot be exceeded at any time during the agreement.

The banks in question are the Bank of England and ten of the biggest English and Scottish clearing banks. An indexed interest rate, such as a bank's base rate, can be used so long as it applies throughout the duration of the agreement and there is provision limiting the interest rate to a figure which ensures that the maximum total charge for credit rate is not exceeded.

For instance, the Finance Houses Association Base Rate could be used but the loan would not be exempt unless either:

(a) the total charge for credit did not exceed the specified maximum rate under para. 4(5), as at the date 28 days before the date of the loan agreement; or

(b) interest was the only item in the total charge for credit, and the FHA Base Rate (plus any applicable margin) was subject to a maximum percentage of interest which was equal to or less than the specified maximum rate under para. 4(5) at any time during the loan agreement.

For the purposes of option (b), the contractual rate on any day must be compared to the specified maximum rate 28 days earlier.

Subject to this, the agreement cannot provide for the interest rate or other charges to increase either automatically or at the lender's option, save that the interest rate on staff loans can increase on termination of employment.

Exemption by reference to lending with a foreign element: s. 16(5)(c)

Paragraph 5 of the Exempt Agreements Order exempts certain trade finance and other agreements under this head.

3.8 THE FORMS AND FORMALITIES

Introduction

It is not the remit of this book to discuss in depth the many different forms and procedures prescribed by the Consumer Credit Act and the regulations made under it. Regulations dictate, in minute detail, the manner in which information must be displayed—what order, what size of print, what relative prominence, where, when, how it must be sent or advertised.

As has been seen (in **3.3** on Overdrafts) overdraft lending is largely excused from the bureaucratic plethora of the Act's documentation requirements.

This section will therefore look at the main areas in which the Act governs the contents, execution, variation and termination of a personal loan agreement for unsecured fixed-sum or running-account credit of £15,000 or less, by a bank to an individual.

Sections 60 to 64 inclusive (and s. 58, for land-secured agreements—see **3.6** above) set out the main requirements for the contents of regulated agreements and for the issue of copies and statutory notices. These requirements are amplified in detailed regulations. Before looking at these requirements, it is important to understand the consequence of a creditor's failure to comply with them. The Act provides that a regulated agreement which does not comply with the applicable requirements of ss. 58 and 60 to 64 will be unenforceable except with a court order (s. 65).

The court can usually exercise its discretion, taking account of

(a) any prejudice suffered by the debtor as a result of the creditor's non-compliance; and

(b) the extent to which the creditor was to blame for his non-compliance (s. 127(1)).

However, the court *cannot* order an agreement to be enforced in the following circumstances:

(a) if the debtor did not sign the agreement at all or in the prescribed manner; or

(b) if the agreement signed by the debtor, even though it was not in the prescribed form, did not contain all the prescribed terms; or

(c) if the agreement was cancellable and the required copies and statutory notices were not given to the debtor (s. 127(3) and (4)).

The contents of regulated agreements

To comply with the Act, a regulated agreement must:

(a) be in the prescribed form and be signed in the prescribed manner;
(b) embody all the terms of the agreement, other than implied terms; and
(c) be readily legible when presented to the debtor for signature (s. 61).

The form of agreement and manner of signature are prescribed in the Consumer Credit (Agreements) Regulations 1983. These Regulations comprise five main types of information to be given in regulated agreements:

(1) the heading, signifying the nature of the agreement;
(2) the name and address of each party;
(3) the financial details;
(4) a description of any direct security and default charges;
(5) specified notices, e.g. notice of cancellation rights.

These categories require further discussion.

(1) There are, in fact, only three statutory headings, the main one being a 'Credit Agreement regulated by the Consumer Credit Act 1974'. This book is not concerned with consumer hire and pawn agreements. So long as the statutory heading is shown prominently, other sub-headings can be used.

(2) The full name of a limited company, partnership or individual should be shown, correct as at the date of the agreement. A full postal address is required for each party.

(3) The main point about the financial details is that they must be shown 'together and as a whole'. This means that all the financial information, required by the Agreements Regulations to be set out in a particular agreement, must be set out in one part of the agreement, without

anything else being inserted in that part. This part of the regulated agreement form is, somewhat profanely, called 'the holy ground'. The main financial details required to be set out in the holy ground are:

(a) a description of any goods, services, land, etc. to be purchased with the loan if it is to be advanced under a restricted-use, debtor–creditor–supplier agreement for fixed-sum credit;
(b) the cash price of those goods, services, land, etc.;
(c) the amount of the credit or, for running-account credit, the credit limit (if any);
(d) the total charge for credit or, for running-account credit and variable rate fixed-sum credit, the interest rate and amount of charges;
(e) the timing and amounts of repayments;
(f) the Annual Percentage Rate (APR) and, for variable rate agreements, a statement:
  (i) that, in calculating the APR, no account has been taken of a variation in rate; and
  (ii) indicating the circumstances in which the rate might vary.

This last requirement is important for banks, most of whose lending is subject to a margin over base rate or a variable managed rate. It was thought that banks might need to describe the circumstances in which they change their base rates. However, this has been held to be an impracticable exercise which would be more likely to confuse a borrower than give him protection. It is therefore sufficient to state that the rate is subject to variation from time to time, in the absolute discretion of the creditor (*Lombard Tricity Finance Limited* v *Paton* (1989) CA).

The APR must be described as such (by its initials, or in full) and, along with the statutory notices, all of which must be both readily and easily legible, must be given no less prominence than any other financial details.

(4) Security to be given by the debtor, whether alone or jointly with another person, must be briefly described and the relevant security document referred to. Any security to be given by third parties only need not be mentioned in the agreement. Having said this, the execution of third party security may be a precondition of the loan, and it may therefore be mentioned as an express term of the agreement.

Any fees or other charges payable on default must also be described outside the holy ground. For instance, interest on the outstanding debt or the reimbursement of expenses incurred by the lender as a result of default might be specified.

(5) The only specified notices with which this book is concerned are the notices of cancellation rights. These are dealt with below. As already mentioned, the statutory notices must be given no less prominence than other terms of the agreement.

Apart from the five categories of information discussed above, other terms may also be included in a regulated credit agreement, provided that:

(a) they are not shown more prominently than the statutory heading of the agreement, the APR or the statutory notices; and
(b) they are not inserted in the holy ground.

Typically, a repayment covenant, a joint and several liability clause (where there are two or more borrowers) and a right of set-off may be included in a bank's regulated agreement forms. Such terms can be set out on the back of the agreement form, after the signature clause, so long as they are effectively incorporated by a suitable reference before the signature clause—e.g. 'This agreement is also subject to the terms set out overleaf'.

The APR and the total charge for credit

At the heart of the Consumer Credit Act is the concept of 'truth in lending'. While the tale of the Merchant of Venice may seem an extreme example of a money-lender's excesses, the law's ability to rectify every perceived wrong may be as naive as Portia's dramatic victory was romantic.

One of the main embodiments of the 'truth in lending' concept was the theory that one could provide a formula which would enable the cost of a credit agreement to be compared on an equal basis to the cost of every other credit agreement. By annualising the interest rate, taking account of compounding and repayments, adding in arrangement and other fees, and aggregating the cost of other arrangements (such as insurance) which the borrower was obliged to enter into as a condition of the credit, it is intended that the real annual cost of the credit can be calculated as an annual percentage. The Consumer Credit Act (Total Charge for Credit) Regulations 1986 set out how this must be done.

As just mentioned, the total charge for credit includes interest and certain other charges. Charges relating to the operation of a current account are excluded, even when those charges (e.g. money transmission fees) relate to the operation of the account in debit. The total charge for credit must then be annualised as a percentage of the total amount of the credit, taking account of the repayment requirements.

To arrive at the APR, it is necessary to make several assumptions, either because the data which would otherwise be fed into the APR calculation would be misleading, or because there is no relevant information at the time the calculation has to be performed. The most important assumption is that the credit will be drawn on the date of the credit agreement.

The assumptions are progressively more theoretical when APR has to be calculated for the purposes of the quotations and advertisements regulations.

Execution and cancellation procedures

The debtor must sign a regulated agreement in a signature box, the dimensions, location and contents of which are specified in regulations made under the Act.

Sections 62 and 63 of the Act provide for copies of a regulated agreement to be given to the borrower.

If the agreement is presented personally to the borrower for his signature, he must be given a copy immediately.

If the agreement is sent to the debtor for signature (e.g. by post), a copy must be sent at the same time and, where the creditor has not signed *before* sending the agreement, a second copy must be sent within seven days after the creditor signs. In the case of a credit-token agreement, the second copy can instead be sent at or before the time the credit-token is issued to the borrower.

A copy of a regulated agreement does not have to show the name and address of the debtor (unless the copy is delivered after the creditor has signed), the signatures or the date of signature. However, the date of the debtor's signature must be shown on a copy handed to him when he signs after the creditor *and* in the creditor's presence.

The copy of a cancellable agreement (see below) must contain a notice in statutory form, advising the debtor of his right to cancel the agreement, and how and when he can exercise the right. In addition, a statutory cancellation notice must be sent to the debtor within seven days after he or, if later, the creditor signs, unless a second copy agreement containing the notice is sent during that seven day period.

These and other matters are set out in the Consumer Credit (Cancellation Notices and Copies of Documents) Regulations 1983. Any regulated agreement may be cancelled by the debtor, unless:

(a) it is for the purchase of land and is secured on land (in which case, the debtor has certain pre-signature withdrawal rights—see **3.6** on Secured Lending);

(b) it is signed by the debtor on the creditor's trade premises (or, in the case of a restricted-use debtor–creditor–supplier agreement, on the supplier's trade premises); or

(c) the creditor does not discuss the agreement in the debtor's presence *before* the debtor signs—regulated agreements negotiated by post or telephone would not, therefore, be cancellable (s. 67).

The debtor does not have to give a reason for cancelling. He merely has to give the creditor written notice of his desire to cancel the agreement during the five days after receiving the statutory cancellation notice or the second copy of the agreement (see above). This is called the 'cooling-off period' (s. 68).

The effect of cancellation is to terminate the agreement and any linked transaction. The creditor must refund any interest and charges paid and the debtor must repay any monies borrowed and return any credit-token issued (s. 69).

Apart from the cost and waste of time and resources involved in negotiating and preparing an agreement which is then cancelled, a creditor must also give extra copies of statutory notices to debtors under a cancellable agreement, and take the risk of being unable to recover his loan if the debtor cancels after drawdown and is unable to repay, or if the creditor fails to issue the correct copies or notices (see Introduction above).

In practice, a lender will either try to avoid a regulated agreement being cancellable (e.g. by having it signed by the borrower in the lender's premises), or ensure that no borrowing is taken until the cooling-off period has expired.

Variation of a regulated agreement

An agreement may be varied in two ways. Most obviously, an agreement can be varied with the consent of both (or all) the parties to it. Secondly, one party can vary the agreement, or more likely a term of it, unilaterally by virtue of an express provision in the agreement permitting him to do so.

The second method is used in regulated agreements, as with other loan agreements, to vary a 'managed' or base rate-related interest rate.

As one might expect, the Act contains detailed and largely impracticable rules about varying agreements (s. 82).

In effect, these rules require variation of a regulated agreement to be by means of a 'modifying agreement', for which regulations prescribe the form and other requirements. The same applies to the variation of an unregulated agreement which results in it becoming regulated.

Fortunately, s. 82 preserves a creditor's ability to vary interest rates and repayment instalments (as a result of a prepayment or a change in interest rates) by written notice to the debtor, provided this is expressly permitted by a term in the agreement.

In particular, base rate changes can be notified by advertisement in three national newspapers and, if practicable, by notice in the lender's branches.

It is probable that forbearance to enforce the agreed repayment programme, for so long as the debtor complies with a less onerous repayment programme, will not constitute a modification of a regulated agreement. However, it is not always possible to avoid a full variation of the original agreement, thus necessitating a modifying agreement.

Termination

A regulated agreement can, like any other contract, be terminated on the occurrence of specified events, by operation of law (e.g. under the legal doctrine of frustration) or upon breach by either party.

The Act seeks to prevent a lender terminating a regulated agreement unless the borrower has been given at least seven days' notice and has, in the case of a breach by the borrower, been given the opportunity to make good his default.

Even if a regulated agreement contains a term stating that the agreement will terminate automatically at the end of a specified period, the lender must still give the borrower seven days' written notice of termination, expiring at the end of that period (s. 98).

CONSUMER CREDIT ACT LENDING

On request from the borrower, the lender must calculate and advise the borrower of the amount required to repay the loan, being the outstanding loan less the early settlement rebate (s. 97).

Naturally, there are detailed regulations describing how the early settlement rebate must be calculated.

3.9 CANVASSING AND CIRCULARS

It is an offence to canvass regulated debtor–creditor agreements off trade premises (s. 49(1)).

Canvassing is defined as soliciting the entry by an individual ('the consumer') into the regulated agreement by oral representations made to the consumer by the canvasser in person (i.e. not by telephone or in writing), provided that the criteria set out below are also fulfilled (s. 48(1)).

The additional criteria are:

(a) the canvasser (who may be a prospective lender or a credit-broker) must have visited the place where he canvassed specifically for the purpose of canvassing, but not at the prior written request of the consumer.

(b) the canvassing must have taken place on premises where none of the following carried on business at the time, either permanently or temporarily:

(i) the lender;
(ii) the supplier;
(iii) the canvasser, or the person for whom the canvasser was working as employee or agent;
(iv) the consumer.

Note that it is not unlawful to canvass debtor–creditor–supplier agreements, exempt agreements or agreements which are completely outside the Act.

Once again, overdrafts are in a privileged position because banks and their employees (but not others) may canvass overdrafts with their existing current account customers only (s. 49(3)), the necessary Determination having been made by the Director General of Fair Trading.

89

Although breach of s. 49 (including canvassing an overdraft agreement in breach of the conditions of the Director General's Determination) will not affect the validity of the unlawfully canvassed agreement, the company or individual in breach will be personally liable to prosecution unless it or he acted under a mistake or the action was beyond its or his control (s. 168).

It is also an offence for anyone to send a minor a document, inviting the minor to borrow money or to obtain goods or services on credit, or inviting him to apply for information or advice on any of these types of transaction (s. 50(1)).

A defence to an alleged breach of s. 50(1) will be that the sender of the document did not know, or have reasonable cause to suspect, that the addressee was a minor unless the document was sent to the minor at a school or other educational establishment for minors (s. 50(2) and (3)).

3.10 ADVERTISING AND QUOTATIONS

The advertiser and regulated advertisements

Regulations made under the Act apply to all advertisements indicating that credit may be provided by a person carrying on a consumer credit business or a business providing loans to individuals secured on land, unless the credit:

(a) is exclusively for business purposes; or
(b) can only be unsecured *and* for more than £15,000; or
(c) can only be borrowed by limited companies; or
(d) will be subject to a foreign law *and*, if subject to English law, would not be regulated (s. 43).

The regulations cover advertisements by credit-brokers and prospective lenders. If a credit-broker advertises, information required to be shown about the advertiser will include both the credit-broker and any specific prospective lender.

An offence under the Act for breach of the Advertisements Regulations will be committed by the credit-broker (if any), the prospective lender, the advertising agency and others who designed and procured the publication of the advertisement and the publisher, subject to certain 'equitable' defences specified in the Act (s. 47).

In this section, the 'advertiser' will usually refer to the prospective lender.

In essence, any advertisement of regulated or exempt lending will be governed by the Consumer Credit (Advertisements) Regulations 1989. These replaced, with no 'structural' changes, the 1980 Advertisements Regulations which had long been considered over-complicated.

The fundamental principle

Before looking at the 1989 Advertisements Regulations, it is important to note that the Act itself states as a fundamental principle, that an advertiser commits an offence if an advertisement governed by the regulations conveys information which is materially false or misleading, including by virtue of the advertiser's stated or implied intentions being untrue (s. 46).

This is, of course, in addition to any failure to comply with the regulations being an offence.

By way of example, a car dealer advertised a new car with '0% APR' credit available to finance its purchase. The dealer also offered a part exchange deal, but on the basis of valuing the second-hand car lower if the purchaser of the new car wanted the credit facility for the balance of the purchase price. The High Court held that the lower valuation of the second-hand car was a hidden charge for credit, and that the credit advertisement therefore appeared to infringe s. 46, as well as the regulations relating to the specifying of the total charge for credit (*Metsoja* v *Norman Pitt & Co. Limited* (1989)).

Form and contents

The Advertisements Regulations give detailed instructions on the form and contents of the advertisements they govern. For instance, such advertisements must be clear and easily legible, and the credit-related information must be shown together and as a whole. The APR, when required to be shown, must be given greater prominence than any other interest rate (e.g. a flat rate), and no less prominence than other credit-related information. 'Overdraft' may only be used in relation to overdrafts on current account.

The categories of regulated advertisements

The Advertisements Regulations divide credit advertisements into three categories: simple, intermediate and full.

Simple advertisements

Covering situations where, for lack of space or reader's time, the advertiser can only put over a brief message.

The only information which can be shown in a simple advertisement is the advertiser's name, logo, address, telephone number and occupation. Although other information may be shown, it must not indicate that the advertiser is willing to extend credit, and cannot therefore mention loans, interest rates, repayment instalments or periods or security. Neither must additional information state the cash price of any goods, services or land.

Intermediate advertisements

This is the most popular category of advertising governed by the regulations. Some basic loan-related information may be given and there is greater choice for the advertiser in what he can say.

Any intermediate advertisement *must* contain the following:

(a) the advertiser's name;
(b) the advertiser's address or telephone number;
(c) if applicable, a statement that security or insurance is required;
(d) if applicable, a statement that a sum of money must be deposited in an account;
(e) any credit-broker's fee payable by a prospective borrower;
(f) the APR;
(g) the cash price of any specific goods, services or land which is to be financed with the advertised credit; and
(h) a statement that written quotations are available.

In addition, an intermediate advertisement must contain one or two statutory 'warnings' if a mortgage is or may be required over a prospective borrower's home, or if the advertised credit is in foreign currency and is secured. These 'warnings' are:

'Your home is at risk if you do not keep up payments on a mortgage or other loan secured on it.'

'The sterling equivalent of your liability under a foreign currency mortgage may be increased by exchange rate movements.'

CONSUMER CREDIT ACT LENDING

Further information may, at the advertiser's option, be included in an intermediate advertisement, so long as it does not indicate either a willingness to extend credit or occupation, save by such means as the advertiser's logo, the APR and the amount of credit.

Full advertisements

If an advertiser wishes to include more, or different, information than is allowed for intermediate advertisements, he must publish a full advertisement.

The regulations governing full advertisements aim to ensure that a comprehensive and fair view is given of the advertised credit facilities.

There are provisions for the use of 'representative terms', designed to ensure that illustrative loans, credit limits, repayment tables and so on are likely to be typical in practice.

Where applicable, the statutory 'warnings' must be included—see 'Intermediate Advertisements', above.

It is worth making the point that even an advertisement of a specific loan facility cannot be as precise about such details as interest rates and repayment instalments as an actual loan agreement. The Advertisement Regulations recognise this and allow a limited amount of tolerance.

Quotations

As mentioned in connection with intermediate advertisements, a person carrying on a consumer credit business must, on request by an individual, supply that individual with a quotation (s. 52).

A quotation is intended to give an individual an indication of the financial terms of a specific credit facility in which he might be interested.

The inevitable regulations govern in detail the form and contents of a quotation. Unusually, the Consumer Credit (Quotations) Regulations 1989 also prescribe the circumstances in which a quotation may be sought—by whom, from whom, how, when and how often.

For instance, a second quotation for the same transaction cannot be requested within 28 days of the first request. Also, a quotation cannot be requested by a foreign resident or a minor.

The information which must be contained in a quotation is similar to that required for an intermediate advertisement (see above), plus the credit limit and the amounts, number and frequency of repayment instalments. Where applicable, the two statutory warnings required for certain intermediate and full advertisements must be included in a quotation.

3.11 CREDIT BROKERAGE

Credit brokerage consists of the introduction of individuals who require credit to other credit-brokers, or to persons who carry on business by providing certain kinds of credit (s. 145(2)).

The kinds of credit involved are:

(a) regulated credit (s. 145(3)(a));
(b) exempt credit, unless it is exempt under s. 16(5)(a) by virtue of the number of repayments (see **3.7** on exempt credit) (s. 145(3)(b));
(c) credit secured on land, but only where the relevant individual requires the credit for the acquisition or provision of a residential property for his own occupation or for occupation by a relative of his (s. 145(2)(a)(ii)); and
(d) credit the agreement for which is governed by foreign law (i.e. not English, Scottish or Northern Irish law), but which would be regulated by the Act if governed by English law (s. 145(3)(c)).

Section 145 also applies to regulated consumer hire agreements and hire agreements falling under the equivalent of (d) above.

A person who carries on business as a credit-broker must have a licence to do so. The licence will be granted under the Act by the Director General of Fair Trading to applicants who he thinks appropriate.

A single act, or even relatively infrequent acts of credit brokerage by a person will not constitute 'carrying on business', whether or not the person carries on any other business.

What constitutes an 'introduction' for the purpose of credit-broking? It is considered that the mere displaying or handing out of leaflets or other advertising material is insufficient. However, if a person helps an individual complete a loan application form and sends it to the prospective lender on behalf of the individual, that would be sufficient to constitute an introduction.

Example

A retailer who fills out a personal loan application form for a customer

CONSUMER CREDIT ACT LENDING

who wishes to buy the retailer's goods on credit, and who then sends the form to the finance company for approval, will require a credit brokerage licence. Contrast with this example retailers who advertise that they accept specified payment cards (e.g. Mastercard, Visa and Switch): they do not introduce shoppers to the banks which issue the payment cards. There is an important distinction between assisting someone to take credit under an existing agreement and introducing him to a prospective creditor.

A bank which arranges for a third party to market or sell its personal loan facilities must ensure that the third party holds a credit brokerage licence where necessary.

A regulated agreement entered into, pursuant to an introduction made by an unlicensed credit-broker, will only be enforceable if the Director General so directs. In considering his decision, the Director General must take account of all relevant factors, including:

(a) how far the debtor was prejudiced by the credit-broker's conduct; and

(b) the degree of culpability of the creditor in enabling the credit-broker to carry on business without a licence (s. 149).

Credit-brokers must, where appropriate, provide prospective borrowers with quotations, in accordance with the Consumer Credit (Quotations) Regulations 1989 (s. 152)—and see **3.10** on advertising and quotations.

Should the lender wish to terminate a regulated agreement because of the borrower's breach, he must again give the borrower seven days' written notice. The notice must specify the nature of the alleged breach and the amount of compensation payable by the borrower (and when it must be paid). Alternatively, if the breach is capable of remedy, the notice must, instead of requiring compensation, state what action the borrower must take to remedy the breach. The borrower must be given at least seven days to pay compensation or remedy his breach (s. 88).

A section 88 default notice must be issued before the lender can do any of the following things:

(a) terminate the agreement;
(b) demand early repayment;
(c) recover possession of goods or land;
(d) terminate, restrict or defer any of the borrower's rights;
(e) enforce security (s. 87).

Lastly, action of the kind described in (b), (c) or (d) above cannot be taken by the lender before the expiry of fixed-term regulated agreements where the borrower is not in default, unless the lender gives the borrower seven days' written notice (s. 76).

Regulations under the Act prescribe the form of the three notices under ss. 98, 88 and 76.

None of these provisions apply to overdrafts, because:

(a) they are not granted for a specified term, and
(b) formal demand for repayment does not amount to demand for early payment because until demand there is no obligation to repay on a specific date.

However, an overdraft to an individual of £15,000 or less and for a fixed term may fall within ss. 98 and 76 (and s. 88, if the overdraft agreement contains 'events of default').

Voluntary early repayment

The borrower may at any time pay off the whole, *but not part only*, of his regulated loan ahead of schedule. If he does so, he is entitled to a refund of that proportion of the total charge for credit as is equal to the proportion of the unexpired period of the loan (s. 94).

4 Financial Services Regulation

4.1 INTRODUCTION

Despite good parentage and a well-planned gestation period, the Financial Services Act has had a turbulent infancy. Professor L.C.B. Gower, a highly-respected 'elder statesman' among legal academics, prepared a Green Paper for the Government on the regulation of investment business; his recommendations were largely adopted in the form of the Financial Services Act 1986. That is when the problems started. Many investment advisers, brokers and securities dealers had operated in an almost unregulated environment, and the extremely detailed 'rule books' that the regulatory bodies proceeded to draw up after the Act came into force, upset many of them. The main 'rule book' had to be re-written, but it is clear that businesses regulated by the Act are subject to comprehensive supervision.

There are similarities between the Financial Services Act and the Consumer Credit Act. Both Acts were aimed at protecting the public. Both seek to do so by establishing a licensing system for professional bodies. Both Acts underpin detailed secondary rules. Both were brought into full effect a long time after receiving the Royal Assent.

There are, however, major differences. The CCA provides protection only for individuals, whereas the FSA protects companies as well. There are financial limits in the CCA, none in the FSA. The regulatory apparatus of the CCA is based on direct licensing and control by the Department of Trade and Industry: responsibility for ensuring compliance with most of the FSA has been delegated to the Securities and Investment Board, and by it to Self-Regulatory Organisations and Recognised Professional Bodies. Lastly, the CCA sets out most of the main rules affecting the lending it regulates, whereas the FSA is concerned almost exclusively with the regulatory framework.

In the remainder of this Chapter, the Financial Services Act 1986 is referred to as 'the Act' or 'the FSA'.

4.2 INVESTMENTS

'Investment' is widely defined in Schedule 1 to the Act, and includes:

(a) securities;
(b) options;
(c) futures;
(d) long term insurance contracts; and
(e) contracts for differences.

Examples of these investments are:

(a) Securities: stocks and shares, bonds, debentures, certificates of deposit, government and local authority bonds and units in unit trusts. The statutory definition of 'securities' is so wide that it was considered appropriate to make an express exemption for cheques and other bills of exchange, bank drafts, letters of credit and bank notes.

(b) Options: options to buy or sell an investment, sterling and foreign currency, gold, silver and platinum or an option to buy or sell any such option.

(c) Futures: contracts for the sale of commodities and land, where the price is agreed at the contract date and the subject matter of the contract is to be delivered at a future date. Contracts made for commercial purposes, not investment, are excluded.

(d) Long term insurance contracts: long term insurance business, as defined by the Insurance Companies Acts, but not personal health and injury insurance or term assurance (i.e. life insurance which terminates on the expiry of ten years or earlier death).

(e) Contracts for differences: these are contracts under which a profit (or loss) arises by reason of currency exchange rates or price fluctuations in property of any kind—for instance, currency and interest rate swaps and index-linked National Savings Certificates.

It is interesting to note that such commonly traded assets as stamps, coins, works of art and land are not 'investments' for the purposes of the Act.

4.3 INVESTMENT BUSINESS

The Act seeks to regulate all types of investment business. Schedule 1 to the Act covers five categories of business in relation to investments:

(a) dealing in investments,
(b) arranging deals in investments,
(c) managing investments,
(d) advising on investments, and
(e) operating collective investment schemes, such as unit trusts.

Subject to the exemptions in **4.5** below, a person who carries out one of the above activities as a business within the UK commits an offence under the Act if he is not authorised to do so by one of the regulatory bodies set up or approved under the Act.

4.4 THE REGULATORY BODIES

There are four categories of regulatory bodies:

(1) The Securities and Investments Board;
(2) The Self-Regulatory Organisations;
(3) The Recognised Professional Bodies; and
(4) Insurance companies and friendly societies.

We will look at each category in turn.

The Securities and Investments Board
Better known by its initials, the SIB was set up by the Department of Trade and Industry so that the Secretary of State could delegate to the SIB most of his supervisory powers under the Act. This was both envisaged by the Act and recommended by the Green Paper produced by Professor Gower. The Secretary of State can withdraw his delegated functions if they are not being properly discharged by the SIB.

The SIB has three main roles:

(a) to publish conduct of business rules for those persons it regulates directly (see (c) below), and for certain other bodies;

(b) to recognise and regulate the Self-Regulating Organisations and the Recognised Professional Bodies; and
(c) to grant authorisation to persons to carry on investment business.

The SIB and the Self-Regulating Organisations have extensive investigative and enforcement powers, backed by effective sanctions. They can, for instance, order a member's bank accounts and assets to be frozen. Not many investment businesses are directly authorised by the SIB—mainly building societies—because the SIB has made it known that it would far prefer that authorisation be obtained from one of the subsidiary bodies.

The Self-Regulating Organisations (SRO's)

The Financial Intermediaries, Managers and Brokers Regulatory Association (FIMBRA)

FIMBRA is responsible for regulating a vast majority of the independent financial advisors, the small firms throughout the country who give insurance and other financial advice to members of the public.

FIMBRA's specific remit is to regulate anyone whose investment business consists of:

(a) advising on and arranging the acquisition of life insurance and authorised unit trusts;
(b) providing investment and management services to retail customers; or
(c) advising on and arranging deals in securities (but only where such advice or arrangements are incidental to either of the first two classes of activity).

The Life Assurance and Unit Trust Regulatory Organisation (LAUTRO)

LAUTRO regulates life assurance companies, friendly societies and some unit trust managers.

As is clear from its name, LAUTRO's members are in life assurance and unit trust business, on the retail marketing side; life insurance companies and friendly societies are regulated by the Act itself for their main business—see below.

The Investment Management Regulatory Organisation (IMRO)

IMRO regulates banks (for their investment management business only), pension scheme managers, unit trust managers and trust fund managers and trustees.

IMRO's regulatory gamut extends only to investment management, and this must be its members' sole or major FSA-regulated activity.

The Securities Association (TSA)

The Securities Association was formed by a 'partnership' of The Stock Exchange and another SRO, the International Securities Regulatory Organisation. As a result, TSA regulates all the securities houses operating in England, and the range of activities covered by TSA is therefore wider than that of any of the other SROs. These activities include:

(a) dealing in and arranging deals in all manner of securities;
(b) dealing in financial futures and options, but only where this is not a member's main business;
(c) corporate finance advice and resulting transactions; and
(d) investment management, as part of a traditional stockbroker's service for private clients.

The Association of Futures Brokers and Dealers (AFBD)

The AFBD regulates all brokers, dealers, advisers and managers in futures contracts, contracts for differences (swaps) and related options.

The Recognised Professional Bodies (RPBs)

The Act permits the Secretary of State to grant RPB status to a body, thus enabling it to authorise its members to carry out investment business. The Secretary of State's authority having been delegated, SIB has prescribed that not more than 20% of an RPBs member's turnover can be investment business and all of that business must be incidental to the member's main business.

Among RPBs so far granted recognition are:

The Law Society of England and Wales
The Law Society of Scotland

The Institute of Chartered Accountants in England and Wales
The Institute of Actuaries.

Each RPB must regulate its members to SIB's satisfaction in their conduct of investment business.

The insurance companies and friendly societies

An insurance company authorised by the Insurance Companies Acts to carry out long term business need not be additionally authorised for that purpose under the FSA. This is because the insurance legislation provides for the appropriate controls. Such an insurance company can also carry on related investment business (e.g. advice), although it will require separate SRO membership for unrelated investment activities—see LAUTRO above.

Friendly societies are similarly covered by the Friendly Societies Act.

4.5 EXEMPT BODIES

Some bodies which conduct investment business are exempt, wholly or partly, from having to be authorised.

The Bank of England

The Bank of England is exempt in respect of all kinds of investment business.

Lloyd's and Lloyd's underwriters

Lloyd's of London and its underwriters are exempt for investment business related to its own insurance.

Recognised Investment Exchanges (RIEs)

RIEs must obtain recognition from the SIB. Once recognised, they are exempt from investment business carried out in the normal course of their operations.

Miscellaneous bodies

Various other bodies, including recognised clearing houses and 'listed money market institutions', and certain public officers (e.g. the Public Trustee), have exemption for general or specific purposes.

FINANCIAL SERVICES REGULATION

Appointed representatives

Perhaps better known as 'tied agents', appointed representatives are individuals who are tied by contract to advise on and sell the investment services and products of only one company. They do not have to be employees of that company. Having said this, bank employees are frequently appointed representatives of their employer for the purpose of selling its life insurance and other investment products.

An appointed representative must disclose his 'tied' status to a prospective or actual customer, and the company he is 'tied' to is bound by all his representations, acts and omissions in respect of a particular investment deal, and is also responsible for his conduct to the company's SRO or other regulatory body.

4.6 MAIN 'RULES' GOVERNING INVESTMENT BUSINESS CONDUCT

Many of the operating rules for firms regulated by the FSA are detailed or relate to specific types of business. Some are subject to review and will no doubt change from time to time. This section attempts to summarise the main regulatory requirements designed to protect customers who invest or seek investment advice. These requirements are, for the most part, set out in the SIB and SRO rule books, although some are contained in the FSA itself.

Solvency

To qualify for and retain membership of an SRO, a firm must satisfy the SRO that the firm is solvent. This will normally be a balance sheet test, with 'external' guarantees being acceptable in some cases to make good a shortfall in the capital base. However, a guarantor will not be entitled to have recourse to the firm's assets. Regular accounts must be produced and certain other information reported periodically.

Complaints procedures

Both the SRO (or RPB) and its members will have a formal complaints handling procedure which must be advised to members' customers and followed whenever appropriate.

Compensation fund

Every SRO member must pay a levy towards the SIB's compensation fund, which will, in prescribed circumstances, pay out up to £48,000 to an investor as a result of the insolvency of an authorised investment firm. Each RPB has its own compensation fund.

Independence

Every firm must be independent, so that it can give independent financial advice. This fundamental principle is at the heart of many of the important rules that follow.

Maintenance of 'Chinese walls'

A financial services company will usually have several departments whose combined interests are not necessarily synonymous with a client's. For example, a banking group may have departments for stockbroking, market-making (buying shares for its own account) and research. Suppose that a client wishing to sell shares approaches one of the stockbrokers for advice. If the broker talks to the market-makers, they may wish to buy the stock themselves for their own reasons and encourage the broker to advise an immediate sale, even though that may not be right for the client. Equally, a research analyst may modify his advice to his corporate clients if he hears of a major share sale being handled by his bank's broking department.

To avoid this (and to reduce 'insider dealing'—see below), firms conducting investment business must maintain a strict separation, known as a 'Chinese wall', between different parts of their business.

Employee investment dealing rules

To ensure independence, an investment business must establish, and monitor compliance with, staff dealing rules. These rules must restrict staff from buying, selling investments or from acquiring or disposing of any option or other interest in investments on the basis of confidential customer information. There are related criminal offences for which prosecutions have successfully been brought.

Control of advertising

No advertisement of investment business may be published except by or with the express approval of an authorised investment firm.

As with the Consumer Credit Act 1974, regulations have been issued under the FSA controlling the form and contents of advertisements for investments. For instance, the phrase 'investments may go down as well as up in value' must be shown in certain advertising, and the use of past bonus declarations or profit performance (as an implied assurance for the future) are strictly proscribed.

'Cold calling' prohibited

Unsolicited approaches to a potential customer, away from the investment company's premises, to solicit investment business are generally prohibited. There are some exceptions: for example, for life insurance business, for professional or business investors or for soliciting new business under an extant customer agreement. Contracts entered into as a consequence of a prohibited approach will be unenforceable save with a court order or at the instance of the investor.

The 'know your customer' rule

In order to enable them to give their customers what is called 'best advice', investment firms must find out sufficient relevant information about customers before giving advice.

The information obtained from a customer will enable the investment adviser to decide which category his customer falls into and, therefore, what the adviser's duties are.

However, the 'know your customer' rule does not apply to one category of customer, the 'execution only' customers—see below.

Full disclosure required

An investment firm must disclose to a customer details of any material interest the firm may have in any 'product' it is advising the customer to buy or sell, or not to buy or sell. In particular, any commission the firm may earn will have to be disclosed unless the customer agreement says otherwise.

Written customer agreements

An investment firm must have written customer agreements. These must contain certain information. The agreements for professional and business investors are less regulated and mere 'market counterparties' and 'execution only' customers need not sign any customer agreement. No customer agreement is necessary for a life insurance contract.

A 'market counterparty' is a firm in the same business as the investment firm and for whom the contact between them is in the ordinary course of business.

An 'execution only' customer is one who the investment firm can reasonably assume is not relying on the investment firm's judgment or advice as to the merit or suitability of the relevant investment transaction.

Fair charges

Remuneration must be fair and reasonable. As mentioned above, commissions must be disclosed unless the customer agreement provides otherwise.

'Best advice' rule

A 'product' must be appropriate to the needs and budget of the investor—advice must ensure this, regardless of any benefit (or lack of benefit) for the adviser.

'Cooling off' period

An investor must be allowed a short period after entering into a life insurance contract or purchasing units in a unit trust during which he can withdraw from the transaction without loss.

'Best execution' rule

When requested to buy or sell investments, an investment firm must do so at the best price reasonably obtainable by the firm within an appropriate time, or at the time required by the customer.

Fair allocation of stock

When an investment firm has purchased stock for itself and for its customers but has been unable to purchase sufficient to satisfy all their requirements, the firm must allocate the stock fairly between itself and its customers.

Safe custody of investments

An investment firm must provide safe custody for its customers' investments—custodian trusteeship, safe deposit, etc.

Segregation of clients' money

It is fundamental to the proper conduct of any investment business that clients' money held by the investment firm should be kept separate from the firm's own funds. The firm may receive the client's money from the client to purchase investments, or from the sale of the client's investments. In either case, all SRO and RPB 'rule books' must make specific provisions on this point, including as to the issue of statements and, where appropriate, the payment of interest.

As bankers will know, neither an investment firm nor its bank can set off the firm's clients' accounts against its 'office' accounts, the former being trust accounts. Banks are usually asked to sign an acknowledgement to this effect, to enable investment firms to comply with their SRO's rules. Being trust accounts, clients' accounts must also be kept in credit, any debit balance being a borrowing liability of the firm, not of its clients.

Maintenance and retention of records

Proper records of transactions must be kept; accounts must be kept for customers and the investment firm. These records and accounts must be retained for an appropriate period, and are subject to inspection by the firm's SRO or RPB.

Finally, it is important to emphasise that the above rules are in addition to the common law duties of good faith and confidentiality, fiduciary duties and duties of care and skill, to which all professional advisers, agents and trustees are subject in the conduct of their business. Indeed, many of the rules do no more than reiterate or amplify specific common law requirements.

Part II—Cheques and Payment Systems

5 Cheques

5.1 INTRODUCTION

We are concerned here with cheques and other paper-based money transmission instruments. These can be said to include:

(a) cheques;
(b) bankers' drafts;
(c) dividend and interest warrants;
(d) orders and warrants payable by government departments;
(e) instruments drawn on a bank which, in legal terms, do not qualify as cheques; and
(f) bills of exchange other than cheques.

The legal principles concerning a bank's dealing with the above will be examined, with the exception of bills of exchange. In particular, the rights and obligations of the parties involved, both in the normal transaction and in the event of some irregularity such as forgery, fraudulent alteration, loss or theft.

The law relating to these matters consists of a blend of common law contract and a variety of statutory provisions. It will be apparent that much of the law has developed in a piecemeal fashion and little attempt has been made, since 1882 at least, to render it coherent. Some of the more difficult areas, such as the holder for value, appear to have been almost deliberately fudged in the relevant statutes and cases. In spite of these drawbacks, there is a remarkable degree of common understanding throughout most of this area of the law, and in practice it appears to function well, at least as regards cheques.

Anyone approaching this area of the law for the first time, however, may be forgiven if he finds it somewhat confusing. An attempt has been made here to place the various principles in a logical order but in many instances there is an interdependence, and a proper understanding of any part is likely only to emerge at the conclusion.

It should be noted that in March 1990 a White Paper entitled 'Banking Services: Law and Practice' was published. A summary of the proposed legislative changes appears in Appendix 2. The proposed changes to the law relating to cheques concern crossings on cheques, negotiability of cheques, statutory protection of the bank paying a cheque and truncation of cheques. Further details of the proposals are contained in the relevant places in this chapter. A Review Committee reported (the 'Jack Report') prior to the White Paper. This Report recommended more widespread changes in banking law and specifically the law relating to cheques. Most of the Report's recommendations were, however, not adopted in the White Paper.

5.2 CHEQUES AND NEGOTIABLE INSTRUMENTS

A negotiable instrument enjoys a special status in English law whereby it is not only transferable but also is negotiable, which means that a good faith taker for value of the instrument can acquire a good title to it, irrespective of the quality of the title of the giver. This is in contrast to the position with goods generally, where a good faith purchaser will not ordinarily acquire a good title from a thief, and will have to return the property to the owner from whom it was stolen.

Negotiable instruments include:

(a) bank notes (currency of the realm);
(b) other promissory notes;
(c) bills of exchange;
(d) cheques (other than those crossed 'not negotiable');
(e) banker's drafts;
(f) bearer bonds;
(g) certificates of deposit;
(h) commercial paper; and
(i) eurobonds.

This book is only concerned in detail with (d) and (e) above, and with instruments analogous to cheques. Cheques are negotiable instruments because the Bills of Exchange Act 1882 declares them so to be. Heads (e) to (i) are either covered by this Act or are considered to be negotiable instruments by virtue of the common law doctrine of the 'law merchant'.

Illustration of negotiability

Suppose A sells a stolen car to B, who purchases it in good faith and pays a full market price. The true owner of the car may at any time reclaim it from B, as A did not have good title to it and B cannot acquire good title through A, however honest B is. Suppose now that A sells a genuine car to B and that B pays A with stolen bank notes. The original owner of the bank notes cannot reclaim them from A (assuming A acts in good faith) because they have been negotiated to him and he thereby acquires a good title even if B's title to them was bad. Obviously the original owner could have recovered the notes from B before they were negotiated to A.

Thus it can be seen that negotiation must involve transfer but that transfer will not necessarily involve negotiation. Put another way, negotiation is a special form of transfer.

The law relating to the use of cheques and other instruments dealt with by banks through the clearing system, includes a study of the principles of negotiability and of the Bills of Exchange Act 1882, as these will frequently have an impact on the rights and duties of the parties. It should be clearly noted, however, that the law relating to the bank which pays cheques, and its customer who draws them, is also very much a matter of the terms of the contract between bank and customer. It is also a matter of general principles of law, such as constructive trusteeship. These matters have been dealt with in chapter 1.

5.3 THE BILLS OF EXCHANGE ACT 1882

By s. 73 of this Act a cheque is defined as:

'A bill of exchange drawn on a banker payable on demand.'

And applying s. 3(1), which defines a bill of exchange, it must be an unconditional order in writing, addressed by the drawer to the bank, requiring the bank to pay on demand a sum certain in money to or to the order of a specified person, or to bearer.

It follows that, in legal terms, a cheque is a special form of bill of exchange. Also, there must be at least three parties to a cheque:

(a) the drawer (or customer of the bank);
(b) the drawee (the bank); and
(c) the payee or bearer.

This is because a cheque must be addressed by one person to a bank and must be payable to a specified person or to bearer.

Most of the Bills of Exchange Act consists of provisions which concern bills of exchange generally and many, but not all, of these apply to cheques. Examples are the rules on indorsement, holders for value and holders in due course. Some sections are devoted specifically to cheques, such as those dealing with crossings. The Cheques Act 1957 contains further provisions specific to cheques. A selection of these sections is contained in Appendix 1.

It should be noted that whilst the drawer of a cheque will be liable to the payee (or subsequent holder) assuming valid consideration has been given, a drawee bank is never liable to the payee or holder, as it does not in practice accept a cheque (although it can in law do so). Special arrangements are made for cheques backed by a cheque card. Bills of exchange other than cheques are frequently accepted by banks which thereby do become liable on them.

A banker's draft does not come within the definition of a cheque, nor of a bill of exchange, because it is not addressed by one person to another (the bank is addressing itself). Nor is a cheque drawn 'pay cash' or 'pay wages' since this is not payable to a specified person or to bearer (*Orbit Mining and Trading Co. Ltd* v *Westminster Bank Ltd* (1963) CA).

Some provisions of the Cheques Act and even some of the Bills of Exchange Act do apply to these instruments, however.

References hereafter to 'cheques' are intended to include these analogous instruments unless otherwise stated and references to 'the Act' are to the Bills of Exchange Act 1882.

All cheques must have a drawee or paying bank, and in the majority of instances there will also be a collecting bank involved. This is because the payee of the cheque pays it into his account with his own bank and this bank then obtains payment from the paying bank.

5.4 CROSSINGS ON CHEQUES

The provisions in the Act which deal with crossings on cheques (ss. 76 to 81) apply not only to cheques but also banker's drafts, government warrants and to 'cheques' drawn 'pay cash' (s. 5 of the Cheques Act).

In practice, most of these cheques and analogous instruments are crossed and the effect of the crossing is well understood, i.e. from the point of view of the payee, the cheque must be paid into a bank account, cash cannot be obtained over the counter at the paying bank. The Act, however, expresses this as a duty of the paying bank who is obliged to pay another bank only. In fact two types of crossing are recognised:

(a) general—this consists of two parallel lines, with or without the words '& Co.' or 'not negotiable';
(b) special—which consists of the name of one bank written on the face of the cheque, with or without the parallel lines and any accompanying words.

Specially crossed cheques are rarely issued in this form but it is common practice for a collecting bank to stamp its name on a cheque paid in by its customer. The Act recognises this as a crossing and also the right of a holder to put on and to add certain crossings (s. 77).

By s. 81, a generally or specially crossed cheque may have the words 'not negotiable' added, in which case the cheque is not a negotiable instrument. It is, however, still a cheque and remains transferable.

Uncrossed cheques which have 'not negotiable' written across their face are considered to be not transferable by analogy to the crossing having this effect on a bill of exchange (*Hibernian Bank* v *Gysin and Hanson* (1939) CA).

The 'A/C Payee' crossing is not recognised by the Act, but case law establishes that it has no effect on the paying bank whilst putting the collecting bank on enquiry if the cheque has been transferred (*Bevan* v *National Bank Ltd* (1906)). A 'Not Transferable' crossing is not recognised by the Act nor by any reported case.

The Act does not permit the removal of any crossing on a cheque, even by the drawer. In practice, as cheque forms are commonly issued by banks ready crossed, customers often wish to delete the crossing. This practice is recognised by a statement of the Committee of London Clearing Banks made in 1912, although the full signature of the customer should accompany the 'opening' of the cheque and he, or his known agent, should be presenting the cheque for cash. In any event, if the customer himself is presenting the cheque, there is unlikely to be another person to object to him receiving his own money, whatever the position under the strict terms of the Act. Cheques opened in this way, however, should not be paid to a third party payee who is not a known agent, as the bank would then be in clear breach of s. 79.

The White Paper proposes:

(a) that a crossing on a cheque will make it not negotiable, whether or not those words are written;
(b) the special crossing will be discontinued;
(c) the account payee crossing will make a cheque not transferable; and
(d) an open cheque will, as at present, be a negotiable instrument and one which can be presented for cash.

5.5 INDORSEMENTS ON CHEQUES

Section 31 of the Act provides that cheques payable to bearer may be negotiated by delivery but that those payable to order require indorsement of the holder. Negotiation is complete when the transferee becomes the holder.

Cheques which are drawn payable to a fictitious or non-existent person are by s. 7(3) treated as payable to bearer.

Illustration

Clutton v *Attenborough* (1897) HL. A cheque was drawn by a fraudulent employee in favour of 'Mr Brett' and the employer signed, believing he owed money to this person. In fact the employee had made the name up, he indorsed the cheque and obtained payment. Held, the cheque was payable to bearer and therefore required no indorsement in order to be transferred.

Sections 32 to 35 of the Act set out the rules relating to different types of indorsement. In practice the most common is the indorsement in blank, which consists of just the signature of the holder. An order cheque indorsed in this way becomes payable to bearer and therefore may then be negotiated by delivery any number of times without any further indorsement.

A special indorsement consists of the signature of the holder in addition to the name of the indorsee, e.g. 'Pay X, signed Y'. An order cheque so indorsed remains an order cheque and therefore may be negotiated again but only by further indorsement.

The Act also provides for restrictive indorsements, e.g. 'pay X only, signed Y'. Further negotiation of such a cheque is not then possible. A conditional indorsement places some condition on the negotiation. A drawee bank is entitled to ignore the condition, however.

Indorsements must be valid and regular in order for the indorsee to obtain the benefit of the negotiability of the cheque. A forged indorsement will have no effect (s. 24 of the Act) whilst an irregular one, e.g. a signature which does not correspond fully with the name of the transferor, may transfer his title but is not negotiated, so the transferee will not obtain a good title if the transferor's was defective (*Arab Bank Ltd* v *Ross* (1952) CA).

Prior to the passing of the Cheques Act 1957, all cheques paid into a bank account had to be indorsed by the person paying in, and the collecting bank had the responsibility of ensuring that the indorsements of their customers were valid and regular.

The Cheques Act set up a framework whereby indorsements on cheques would no longer be required, so far as the paying and collecting banks are concerned, although an order cheque which is transferred to a non-bank will still need to be indorsed if the transferee is to acquire the transferor's title, let alone obtain the benefit of negotiation.

The effect of the Cheques Act has been qualified, however, by a practice agreement made by the clearing banks in 1957. This is discussed below in the context of the statutory protection that exists for paying and collecting banks.

It should be noted that a cheque, which is not a negotiable instrument because it is crossed 'not negotiable', is subject to the same rules on indorsements in the Act. It cannot of course be negotiated.

5.6 HOLDERS OF A CHEQUE

A holder is defined in s. 2 of the Act as the 'payee or indorsee [of a cheque] who is in possession of it, or the bearer thereof'. Thus a thief is the holder of a bearer cheque he possesses, and the recipient of a gift is the holder of an order cheque payable to him.

Mere holders have few rights, but the term is significant because a bank which pays a holder can be protected by s. 59 of the Act.

A holder in due course is the personification of the principle of negotiability. This type of holder enjoys the following privileges:

(a) he acquires good title to a cheque even if he acquires it from a thief or fraudster; and

(b) he can claim against all other parties to the cheque, i.e. the drawer and indorsers.

To be a holder in due course, the conditions contained in s. 29 of the Act must be satisfied. These are:

(a) He must be a holder of a cheque which is complete and regular.

Thus the drawer's and indorser's signatures must be valid, regular and authorised. All necessary indorsements must be present. We have seen that an irregular indorsement will lead to the transferee not being a holder in due course (*Arab Bank Ltd* v *Ross* (1952) CA). An unauthorised alteration on the cheque will lead to it not being regular.

(b) He became the holder of it before it was overdue.

By s. 36(3) the cheque becomes overdue when a more than reasonable time has passed since it was issued. There are no modern reported cases to enlighten this point. It is tentatively suggested that a cheque would become overdue well before banks (for other reasons) ordinarily treat them as stale, i.e. after six months.

(c) He took it without notice that it was previously dishonoured (if such was the case).

Previous dishonour would be evident to a transferee, by words written on the cheque.

(d) He took the cheque in good faith.

This is defined in s. 90 as something done honestly, whether or not it is done negligently.

(e) He took it for value.

This is defined in s. 2 as 'valuable consideration'. By s. 27(3) of the Act, the holder of a cheque who has a lien on it, is deemed to be a holder for value, and this has been interpreted to mean that value has been given for the purposes of s. 29, thus making the holder a holder in due course (*Barclays Bank Ltd* v *Astley Industrial Trust* (1970)). Where a customer pays a cheque into his overdrawn account, the bank has a lien on the cheque; it therefore gives value and can qualify as a holder in due course.

(f) The cheque was negotiated to him.

Since other sections of the Act imply that negotiation involves transfer to a remoter party than the payee, it has been held that the original payee may not be a holder in due course (*Jones* v *Waring and Gillow* (1926)

HL). The original bearer may, however, be a holder in due course, as well as any indorsee.

(g) He had no notice of defect in the title of the transferor.

The notice may be of a general or of a particular nature. A bank receiving cheques drawn by a customer in favour of himself, using his power of attorney to operate another's account, was held to have had notice (*Midland Bank Ltd* v *Reckitt* (1933) HL).

A holder, whether or not he gives value, who takes a cheque from a holder in due course, acquires all the rights of that holder in due course (s. 29(3)). Even notice of fraud will not defeat that holder's title, unless he was a party to the fraud.

Such a holder will constitute a holder for value under s. 27(2), as will a holder who has a lien over the cheque he takes but who cannot be a holder in due course, as he fails to satisfy one of the conditions, e.g. *Midland Bank* v *Reckitt*, above.

The Act does not state what are the precise rights of a holder for value and the reported cases do not assist greatly.

Illustration of a holder in due course of a cheque

Suppose A draws a cheque payable to B. B cannot be a holder in due course as he is the original payee. B indorses the cheque and transfers it for value to C. C is a holder in due course. C can enforce the cheque against A and against B. This is so even if A gave the cheque to B purely as a gift or if B obtained the cheque from A by some fraud. If A orders his bank to stop the cheque, C may enforce payment from A. This would not be possible in these circumstances if the cheque was crossed 'not negotiable'.

Sometimes the bank which collects the cheque qualifies as a holder in due course and, if so, it is in the same position as C.

5.7 PAYMENT OF CHEQUES

The legal position of a bank paying a cheque may be considered in two separate parts:

(a) the contract it has with its customer (the drawer); and
(b) the impact of the Bills of Exchange Act and the Cheques Act.

LAW RELATING TO BANKING SERVICES

The legal relationships involving the paying bank may include:

(a) that with its customer;
(b) that with some remote true owner of a cheque;
(c) that with the collecting bank.

The impact of the banker/customer contract is limited to (a) above. Heads (a) and (b) are much affected by statutory provision, whilst (c) is concerned mainly with the doctrine of the recovery of money paid by mistake.

The paying bank and its customer

The banker/customer contract has been fully explored in chapter 1. It will be recalled that a bank must pay within its authority (also called mandate) from its customer, otherwise it will not be entitled to debit the account. It is also liable as a constructive trustee where it acts with 'want of probity'. It must exercise a reasonable degree of care and skill when conducting its customer's account.

5.8 THE FORM OF A CHEQUE

Signature

The cheque must be validly signed in order for the bank to have evidence of its customer's authority to pay, and in order for it to be covered by the Bills of Exchange Act and the Cheques Act. A forged signature is no authority (see below) and the cheque does not qualify as such legally. Where it is agreed that two or more signatures are required, there is no authority to pay on one only (*Catlin* v *Cyprus Finance Corporation (London) Ltd* (1983)). Likewise if one of the joint signatures is forged. In these cases it is still legally a cheque.

Date

By s. 3(4)(a) of the Act, a cheque need not be dated at all. It is arguable that the paying bank has authority to insert a date under s. 20(1) but it is safer for the paying bank to return it unpaid, stating 'not dated'.

A post-dated cheque should not be paid before the date stated as the bank has no authority to do so and may be liable:

(a) for wrongful dishonour of other cheques issued later but before the relevant date, and returned for lack of funds; and

(b) the customer may countermand payment (or die, or become insolvent) before the relevant date. It seems from s. 13(2) that a post-dated cheque is within the legal definition of a cheque as there is no contradiction with it being payable on demand (*Royal Bank of Scotland* v *Tottenham* (1894) CA).

A drawer remains liable on a cheque to the holder for six years under the Limitation Act 1980. It is normal bank practice, however, to return cheques as 'stale' which are dated more than six months in the past. There appear to be some risks in this practice, as a customer may claim that his instruction was dishonoured. The bank's only defence would appear to be that it is an implied term of the banker/customer contract not to pay six months after date.

Another interesting practice is that of paying those cheques, in the early days of each year, which are dated the previous year, and thus appear to be 12 months old and would otherwise be returned as stale. Where the customer's mistake is genuine, however, it can easily be established from the cheque number that it was recently issued.

Amount of money

In order to come within the definition, a cheque must be payable for a sum certain in money. Beyond this, it is purely a matter of practice not to pay when the amount is stated in figures only. This may amount to a breach of contract. A discrepancy between the amount stated in words and figures can be dealt with in two ways:

(a) return the cheque as an ambiguous order, 'words and figures differ'; or
(b) pay according to the words, relying on s. 9(2) of the Act.

The practice of paying the smaller of the differing amounts is unsound.

5.9 FORGERY OF A DRAWER'S SIGNATURE

If the customer's signature on a cheque is forged, the bank has no authority to pay and, if it does so, cannot debit the customer's account. It makes no difference that the forgery could not be detected; as a matter of the banker/customer contract the bank is in breach if it pays such a cheque.

By s. 24 of the Act, a forged drawer's signature is inoperative; therefore the cheque is invalid and no one can become a holder of it.

Illustration

Tai Hing Cotton Mill Ltd v *Liu Chong Hing Bank* (1986) PC. A fraudulent employee forged the signature of his employer's managing director and thereby obtained payment of $HK 5.5 million, representing 300 forged cheques over six years. It was clear that the company had an inadequate accounting system which had facilitated the fraud. No one in the company, other than the fraudulent employee himself, had reconciled the bank statements. It was argued that the customer owed a duty to the bank to take care of its cheque-books and to inspect its bank statements, but these points were rejected. The cheques were forged and the bank had no authority to pay.

There are circumstances, however, when the law considers it inequitable for a customer to rely on the above rule. In these cases, an estoppel is said to arise to deny the customer the right to assert what would normally be his right.

Illustrations

Greenwood v *Martins Bank* (1933) HL. Mr G had an account with the bank. Mrs G, without his authority or his knowledge, forged his signature on a number of cheques. Eventually Mr G became aware of this, but agreed not to inform the bank if Mrs G agreed to desist. Some eight months later, Mr G did inform the bank and reclaimed the relevant debits. Meanwhile, Mrs G committed suicide. It was held that a customer has a duty to inform his bank at once, if he is aware of forgeries on his account. As the bank in this case had no right of action against Mrs G's estate, the bank suffered loss as a result of Mr G failing in this duty, and accordingly an estoppel prevented Mr G from succeeding. Since the Law Reform (Miscellaneous Provisions) Act 1934, a plaintiff has been able to take an action in tort (except for libel) against a deceased's estate. Therefore, on the same facts today, the case would be decided differently.

The court defined an estoppel in this context as requiring:

(a) a representation, or conduct amounting to a representation, which was intended to induce a particular course of conduct by the other person to whom it was made;
(b) the other person, as a result of (a), acts (or omits to act) in a particular way; and
(c) detriment to the other person is caused.

Applying the test to the facts in Greenwood:

(a) Mr G knew about the forgeries but, by his silence for eight months, he intended to induce the bank not to claim against Mrs G;
(b) as a result the bank did not realise the truth and did not claim against Mrs G; and
(c) the bank consequently suffered loss, because she killed herself and there was no right of action against her estate.

It seems Mr G's best argument (not reported as raised) would have been that Mrs G would have shot herself as soon as he went to the bank, even if he had done so eight months earlier and the bank would therefore have had no claim against her estate in any case. If this was accepted, the bank would not have established the third part of the estoppel.

Brown v Westminster Bank (1964). B's employee had forged many of her cheques. The bank were suspicious of the cheques and queried them with B, who answered that they were genuine. B later claimed recrediting of her account but it was held she was estopped from doing so, as from the date of her representation that the cheques were genuine. She was able to recover those cheques which were paid before she made the representation to the bank.

London Intercontinental Trust Ltd v Barclays Bank Ltd (1980). It was agreed that L Ltd's account would be operated by two signatures but the bank inadvertently operated it with only one. The customer noticed the consequent debits on its statements but said nothing. It was therefore held to be estopped from claiming recrediting of its account, as it had failed to notify the bank of the wrongful debits. There was no forgery in this case but the principle appears to be identical.

5.10 FRAUDULENT ALTERATION

We are concerned here with a cheque which is genuinely signed by the customer but which is altered or added to. A payee, for instance, may seek to increase the amount for which the cheque is payable. As he lacks the authority to do so, this also is a forgery, not of the signature but of the details on the cheque. Once again, the starting point is to examine the banker/customer contract and, as the customer's authority to his bank is to pay the amount he stated, the bank is not able to debit the account for the increased amount.

Again, however, an estoppel may arise to prevent the customer from asserting his right. This estoppel is based on the customer's duty to take usual and reasonable precautions to prevent forgery when he draws cheques.

Illustrations

London Joint Stock Bank v *Macmillan and Arthur* (1918) HL. M & A's employee had the task of filling in cheque forms for signature by M or A. The employee drew a cheque payable to the firm or bearer in the sum of £2, written in figures, no words being written at this stage. It was signed and the employee later wrote 'one hundred and twenty pounds' in words and added the necessary figures. The bank was held to be entitled to debit the account for £120, as an estoppel operated when the customer failed in his duty, by signing a cheque with the amount in words left blank and space in the figures section for the addition of more numerals.

Young v *Grote* (1827). Mr Y signed some blank cheques and left them with Mrs Y to be used in his absence for paying business debts. Mrs Y asked an employee to complete a cheque for £50. The employee wrote the word 'fifty' in the middle of the line used for figures and without using a capital 'F'. The amount in figures was inserted with a gap remaining after the £ sign. The cheque was shown to Mrs Y and she asked the employee to get it cashed. Before doing so, he inserted 'three hundred' in words and the figure '3' and obtained payment for £350. It was paid by the bank and Y sued. Held in favour of the bank due to gross negligence on the part of Y and his agent, Mrs Y.

Whether or not the customer has drawn the cheque with reasonable care, the bank should not pay if there is an obvious alteration. It is normal practice not to pay unless the drawer signs next to the alteration, sometimes initials are accepted. Presumably if this signature or initialling is forged, the bank is liable. For this reason, it must be better practice to require a full signature by the alteration.

To summarise the position, on fraudulently altered cheques as between the bank and the customer:

(a) Did the customer exercise reasonable care in drawing the cheque?
(b) Was the alteration detectable by the bank?

If the answer to both questions is 'no', the customer must bear the loss. If the answer to either is 'yes', the loss falls on the bank.

The Act contains provisions dealing with inchoate cheques (s. 20) and with material alterations (s. 64).

The effect of s. 20 is that a signed but incomplete cheque may be completed by anyone in possession of it. It should be completed within a reasonable time and in accordance with the drawer's wishes. However, a holder in due course acquires a good title to the cheque even if it was completed for a larger sum than the drawer authorised.

A prudent drawer who wishes to leave the payee to complete the precise amount will, of course, write an amount across the top of the cheque which is not to be exceeded. It would then be clear to a holder in due course that the cheque has not been completed within the drawer's authority.

Section 64(1) renders a cheque which has been altered in some material way (such as the amount being increased) unenforceable against the drawer. There is a proviso to this, to the effect that if the cheque has come into the hands of a holder in due course and the alteration is not apparent, it is enforceable against the drawer for the original amount. The cheque is enforceable against the person who altered it (and subsequent parties) for the new, altered, amount.

These provisions in the Act do not have any direct effect on the paying bank but merely on the position of some holder in due course of the cheque, which may include a collecting bank.

Illustrations

(a) Suppose A writes an open cheque drawn on the X Bank for £2 which is fraudulently altered by B to read £2,000. If B presents this for cash to the X Bank and obtains payment, the issue is simply whether A exercised reasonable care in drawing the cheque. If he did not, then he must bear the loss. If he did, the X Bank must bear the loss. Whoever loses may sue B if he can be found.

(b) Suppose that B negotiated the cheque to C, who is a holder in due course, and that he obtains payment from X Bank. The issue between X Bank and A is the same (did A exercise reasonable care) but, by s. 64, C is not entitled to more than £2 and presumably the excess may be recovered from him as a payment made under a mistake, see **5.26** below. Therefore it may not matter whether A or the X Bank must bear the loss.

(c) Suppose A writes an open cheque payable to B and leaves the amount (in both figures and words) blank. B, fraudulently, completes it for £2,000 and negotiates it to C who obtains payment from the X Bank. Once again, the issue between A and the X Bank is whether A exercised reasonable care but this time (by s. 20), C as a holder in due course is entitled to the full £2,000 and the money cannot be recovered from him as a mistaken payment. The position of a collecting bank which qualifies as a holder in due course will be identical to that of C.

In *Slingsby* v *District Bank Ltd* (1932) CA, a fraudulent solicitor drew cheques for the signature of the plaintiffs. After a cheque drawn payable to JP & Co. was signed, the solicitor added 'per C and P', which was the name of his firm. The bank had no means of knowing that an alteration had been made to the cheque after it was signed, as the whole cheque (apart from the signature) was in the solicitor's handwriting. In an action against the paying bank, it was held that the drawer of a cheque was under no obligation to draw a line after the payee's name. Furthermore, the alteration had the effect of 'avoiding' the cheque under s. 64(1) of the Act; the proviso to this did not apply in this case, since no one was a holder in due course of this cheque. Consequently, the cheque was a worthless piece of paper when presented to the bank, and it should therefore not have been paid.

5.11 COUNTERMAND

Section 75(1) of the Act states that a bank's duty and authority to pay a cheque are determined by countermand of payment. In other words a customer may 'stop' a cheque by giving notice to his bank.

Obviously the customer must give notice before the cheque has been paid.

Illustration

Baines v *National Provincial Bank Ltd* (1927). B issued a cheque to X shortly before the bank's closing time. X obtained payment from B's bank five minutes after its closing time. B attempted to stop the cheque the next morning but was unable to do so.

The stop order must be clear and unambiguous; special importance is attached to the number of the cheque, as this is the one detail which is unique to it (*Westminster Bank Ltd* v *Hilton* (1926) HL).

The stop order is only effective when it comes to the actual notice of the bank. In *Curtice* v *London City and Midland Bank Ltd* (1908) CA, the notice was sent by telegram which was placed in the bank's letter-box. When the box was emptied, the telegram was left behind. Rather incredibly, it was held that the bank was justified in paying the cheque, as it had not actually received notice of countermand at the time it paid the cheque, because it had not read the telegram. It is considered, however, that the bank is liable in negligence in these circumstances, for failing to empty its letter-box.

There is no requirement in the Act that the stop notice be in writing. Naturally, for reasons of haste, the initial order is often telephoned; banks ordinarily act on this and later seek written confirmation in order to have evidence of the stop. It is considered that a bank which ignored a telephoned stop would be in breach of s. 75.

In practice stop orders seem to give rise to a number of problems including:

(a) mishearing the details of the cheque over the telephone and therefore stopping the wrong cheque;

(b) agreeing to stop a cheque which is backed by a cheque card. The customer agrees not to do this by the terms of the issue of the card, and a bank may be within its rights not to stop the cheque even where it had 'accepted' the stop order. It seems a bank would be within its rights to agree a term with its customer that no cheques may be stopped. Meanwhile the practice is to charge the customer for stopping cheques;

(c) the bank pays a stopped cheque and as a result wrongfully dishonours another cheque;

(d) the bank receives notice from the payee of the cheque that it has been lost. The bank is unable to treat this as grounds for not paying, and can only advise the payee to contact the customer who may or may not choose to countermand. If the bank pays the cheque meanwhile, it may not do so in the ordinary course of business and thus may lose its statutory protection. If it fails to pay it risks a breach of contract action from its customer;

(e) the bank receives notice of stop, which is later cancelled. The bank fails to pay the cheque and is liable for breach of contract.

The customer must give notice of stop to the account holding branch (*London Provincial and South Western Bank Ltd* v *Buszard* (1918)). The exemption in *Burnett* v *Westminster Bank Ltd* (1966) is based on special facts which were a product of its time, now long past.

Where a bank ignores a valid stop notice, it is unable to debit the customer's account. This will often be advantageous for the payee of the cheque, and the law provides two remedies for the bank:

(a) to recover the money as a payment made by mistake (*Barclays Bank Ltd* v *W J Simms, Son and Cooke (Southern) Ltd* (1980)). This is discussed in **5.26** below.

(b) to claim from the payee any goods which have been paid for by the stopped cheque. This is an example of the principle of subrogation. There are no reported cases on this precise point but it has been resorted to in practice and with success.

In any joint account or account which requires the signature of more than one person, a stop may be accepted from any one party. It is practice, however, only to lift a stop on the orders of all parties concerned.

From the point of view of the customer or drawer of the cheque, he is entitled to order his bank to stop payment but this does not negate any liability he has on the cheque itself. Where the cheque was given as a gift or for consideration which has totally failed, his liability to the payee will be nil. However, if the payee has negotiated it to a holder in due course, the customer will be liable to that person.

Summary of matters obliging a bank not to pay a cheque:

(a) Notice of countermand by its customer.
(b) Notice of the customer's death, s. 75(2). Actual notice is required and payment after death but before notice is valid.
(c) Notice of mental incapacity of customer, on the basis that the bank's agency to pay cheques is terminated (*Drew* v *Nunn* (1879)).
(d) Notice of a bankruptcy petition having been presented against a customer or against one of joint account holders.
(e) Notice of winding-up petition against a company customer (this notice may be constructive as the petition is 'gazetted'), or notice that a resolution to that effect has been made.
(f) Service of a garnishee order on the bank. This has the effect of freezing the account up to the amount stated in the order.
(g) Service of a 'Mareva' injunction on the bank.
(h) Service of a sequestration order on the bank.
(i) Closure of the customer's account.
(j) Adequate notice of facts which give rise either to a constructive trust or to a suspicion in the mind of a reasonable banker that the account is being conducted fraudulently (*Lipkin Gorman* v *Karpnale Ltd* (1989) CA).

The above are in addition to matters appearing on the face of the cheque discussed under 'Proper Form', e.g. cheque not signed, forged signature, undated etc.

5.12 WRONGFUL DISHONOUR

It may happen that a bank declines payment of a cheque when it does not have valid grounds for doing so. The reason might be:

(a) failing to realise the customer had removed a stop order;
(b) wrongly believing there were insufficient funds, or where there would be sufficient funds if the bank had not already paid a post-dated or stopped cheque;
(c) forgetting that an overdraft facility had been agreed;
(d) believing the customer had closed the account when he had not.

In all of these cases the bank will be in breach of contract to its customer and may also have libelled him. The bank must pay if there is an agreed overdraft facility (*Rouse* v *Bradford Banking Co. Ltd* (1894) HL).

First, however, there is authority to the effect that a bank is entitled to a reasonable time after the receipt of funds to the credit of an account, in order to carry out the appropriate book-keeping (*Marzetti* v *Williams* (1830)). In this case, however, sufficient cash was paid in at 1 p.m. and payment of a cheque was refused at 3 p.m. the same day. This was held to be beyond a reasonable time and the bank was liable for breach of contract. Presumably a longer time is reasonable if cash is paid in at another branch or if a cheque is paid in which requires clearing. Established clearing custom and statements made about how many days a cheque takes to clear will have a strong influence on what is reasonable time.

We have seen in chapter 1 that a bank is usually entitled to combine two accounts and thereby validly dishonour a cheque drawn on one account which was in credit.

We have also seen (chapter 1) that a customer is entitled to appropriate a particular payment into his account to a particular payment out, and in this case the bank must honour the chosen cheque, whatever the general balance of the account.

If the bank does pay cash for an open cheque it cannot change its mind once it discovers there are insufficient funds. In *Chambers* v *Miller* (1862), the payee had obtained payment and was counting the money when the cashier asked for it back. The payee declined to return it and the cashier took it from him by force. The bank was liable for assault and false imprisonment.

Under general principles, damages for breach of contract are normally limited to the actual loss suffered by the customer. Some cases suggest that if the cheque is paid on a second presentation, the customer may suffer no actual loss and only nominal damages are then awarded. Nominal damages are fixed at £2. (*Gibbons* v *Westminster Bank Ltd* (1939) and *National Westminster Bank plc* v *Oceancrest (No. 2)* (1985) CA.) A trader may be able to prove consequential loss of credit or custom.

A libel consists of the publication to a third party of an untrue imputation against the reputation of another, ordinarily in writing. The test to be applied is:

Would the words tend to lower the plaintiff in the estimation of right-thinking members of society generally? (*Sim* v *Stretch* (1936) HL.)

It has been held that by writing 'not sufficient' on a cheque and by returning this cheque to the collecting bank or the payee, the drawee bank commits a libel on its customer's reputation (*Davidson v Barclays Bank Ltd* (1940)). This is assuming there truly are sufficient funds or an agreed facility. In *Jayson v Midland Bank Ltd* (1968) CA, the words 'refer to drawer' were held to be defamatory.

In *Baker v Australian and New Zealand Bank Ltd* (1958), a New Zealand court case based on similar law, it was said that whatever euphemistic form of words is used on the cheque, if the clear intimation is that the bank is dishonouring the cheque because of insufficient funds, the bank is liable.

The award of damages for libel is not limited, as is that for breach of contract, to the proof of real loss resulting from the bank's actions. Thus a non-trader may recover substantial damages in libel.

Damages for libel may be reduced if the defendant made an apology to the plaintiff (the Libel Act 1843). In *Baker* it was said that the lack of any apology and of any explanation to the payees of the cheques, were factors in fixing the level of damages.

5.13 STATUTORY PROTECTION FOR THE PAYING BANK

The matters discussed so far have largely been limited to the legal relationship between a paying bank and its customer. The provisions of the Act which are now to be examined are relevant to a paying bank because they may give it protection against two possibilities:

(a) an action for breach of contract from its customer; and
(b) an action in conversion from some third party true owner of a cheque.

Conversion is a tort which is actionable when the defendant deals with the plaintiff's goods without authority and thereby deprives the plaintiff of his property. The goods in this context consist of the piece of paper which is the cheque.

Illustration of paying bank converting a cheque

Suppose A draws a cheque on the X Bank payable to B. C steals the cheque and forges B's indorsement and obtains payment from the X Bank. C had no title to the cheque and B remained the true owner of it.

By paying C, the X Bank has converted B's property and is liable to him at common law.

Furthermore, conversion is an absolute tort, i.e. no intention to convert or negligence need be established; if the property was in fact converted the tort is complete.

In the above example, it is clear that in practice the X Bank would have no means of knowing whether B's signature on the back is genuine, because B is not its customer. There has long been a need, therefore, for some protection for a bank in these circumstances, and this is now contained in s. 60 of the Act. The section deals only with order cheques— not with bearer cheques or analogous instruments. It protects when there is a forged or unauthorised indorsement on the cheque, and the conditions for that protection are that the bank pays in good faith and in the ordinary course of business.

The section protects when an agent places an indorsement on the cheque without authority (*Charles* v *Blackwell* (1877)) but not when there is no indorsement or the indorsement is irregular, i.e. does not correspond properly with the payee's details (*Slingsby* v *District Bank Ltd* (1932) CA).

A similar provision, s. 19 of the Stamp Act 1853, protects a bank paying a banker's draft which purports to be indorsed by the payee but which is not made by him or by his authority. Expressed in a different way, this deals with the same situations as s. 60, i.e. forged and unauthorised indorsements. In s. 19, however, there is no requirement that the bank act in good faith and in the ordinary course of business.

It will be recalled that prior to 1957, all cheques had to be indorsed and that the Cheques Act 1957 was passed to enable indorsements to be dispensed with. Thus s. 1 of that Act provides protection when a bank pays a cheque which is not indorsed or has an irregular indorsement. The section applies to all cheques and to analogous instruments, i.e. drafts and 'cheques' drawn pay cash. The conditions for this protection are identical to s. 60: the bank should pay in good faith and in the ordinary course of business.

The Committee of London Clearing Banks Circular to Branches of September 1957 contains a practice direction to the effect that paying banks should still require indorsements before paying the following:

(a) combined cheque and receipt forms marked with the letter 'R';
(b) travellers' cheques;

(c) bills of exchange other than cheques;
(d) promissory notes;
(e) cheques and other instruments cashed at the counter.

This statement of practice is relevant to the law, if it amounts to a definition of what is payment in the ordinary course of business.

Illustration

Suppose A draws an open cheque payable to B. C steals it and obtains payment but is not asked to indorse it. Section 1 protects when there is no indorsement but only when the bank pays in the ordinary course of business, and the bank in this case has not followed the practice statement. Suppose C forges B's indorsement and the bank pays. It will now be protected by s. 60.

Further protection is provided by s. 80 of the Act. This applies to crossed cheques and is extended to crossed analogous instruments and drafts by s. 5 of the Cheques Act. The bank must pay another bank or, if the instrument is crossed specially, it must pay the other bank named. The conditions for protection are that the bank pays in good faith and without negligence.

Finally, it should be added that by s. 59 of the Act, a bank is protected if it pays a cheque to the holder thereof in good faith and without notice that his title is defective. It has already been seen that a thief is the holder of a bearer cheque simply by having it in his possession. A bank paying a bearer cheque is protected if it satisfies the conditions of doing so in good faith and without notice of defect of title.

It will be recalled (see **5.5** above) that a cheque drawn payable to fictitious or non-existent persons is a bearer cheque by virtue of s. 7(3) of the Act, and therefore a bank paying in the circumstances which occurred in *Clutton* v *Attenborough* can be protected:

(a) if the indorsement is forged but it does not pay in the ordinary course of business, so long as it is in good faith and has no notice of defect of title; and

(b) if there is no indorsement when normally the ordinary course of business would require one.

'Good faith' is defined in s. 90 of the Act as something done honestly, whether or not it is done negligently.

In *Carpenters Company* v *British Mutual Banking Co. Ltd* (1938) CA, the majority of the court considered that, 'in the ordinary course of business' had a different quality to that of being without negligence and, in effect, that it was an easier condition to satisfy.

This case also establishes that when a cheque is paid into the same branch as that upon which it is drawn (known in practice as a 'house' cheque) and the bank involved is therefore both paying and collecting, the bank in order to be protected must satisfy the conditions, both as a paying bank and as a collecting bank.

It will be clear that there is a considerable degree of overlap between the sections protecting the paying bank.

Illustration

Suppose A draws a crossed cheque on X Bank payable to B. C forges B's indorsement and obtains payment. The X Bank may be protected by ss. 60, 80 and arguably also by s. 1. It only requires the protection of one section, however.

It should be noted that nothing in these sections protects a bank which pays a cheque where the drawer's signature is forged or some addition or alteration has been made to it. The proviso to s. 79(2) of the Act does protect where a crossing is altered or obliterated.

The White Paper proposes that ss. 60 and 80 of the Bills of Exchange Act, s. 1 of the Cheques Act and s. 19 of the Stamp Act all be repealed and be replaced by a single protective section. The condition for protection in the new section will be that the paying bank acted 'in good faith and without negligence'.

5.14 OTHER DEFENCES FOR THE PAYING BANK

It has already been seen that a bank which pays, without authority, a stopped cheque, is entitled by subrogation to any goods which were thus paid for. It may be that this right extends to being able to debit the customer's account if the goods have passed into the customer's possession, or if payment of the cheque has discharged a debt of the drawer.

Illustration

B. Liggett (Liverpool) Ltd v *Barclays Bank Ltd* (1928). It was agreed that B Ltd's account would be operated by the signatures of at least two directors. The bank operated it with only one, and thereby paid creditors of B Ltd who had a genuine claim against the company. It was held the bank was entitled to debit the account, provided it appeared that the one director who signed did have authority as between himself and B Ltd to pay its debts.

5.15 THE COLLECTING BANK

There will not necessarily be a collecting bank involved in the life of a cheque but this will only occur when an open cheque is presented for cash at the drawee bank. In the great majority of cases, therefore, a collecting bank is involved. This includes house credits (where a cheque is paid into the same bank where it is payable). This bank is considered to be both a paying and collecting bank (*Carpenters Company* v *British Mutual Banking Co. Ltd* (1938) CA).

5.16 THE COLLECTING BANK AND ITS OWN CUSTOMER

As regards its own customer, the collecting bank has a duty to exercise reasonable care and skill in collecting his cheque.

Thus the collecting bank appears to have the following specific duties to its customer:

(a) To present a cheque for payment within a reasonable time. In *Foreman* v *Bank of England* (1902), the bank was liable to its customer when it dishonoured a cheque for insufficient funds, two days after another cheque to cover this had been paid in. Under the practice operating at that time, the second cheque (drawn on a London bank) could have been drawn against the next day, but it was treated as a country cheque and consequently there were insufficient funds at the time the first cheque was presented for payment.

It is considered that a collecting bank has a duty to adhere to the current practice relating to clearing of cheques, and that the *Foreman* case does not lay down firm rules for the time which should be taken to collect a cheque. Except for house credits, all banks are reliant on the clearing system to collect cheques, and it would be most harsh if one was liable when it had simply used this system.

Section 45(2) of the Act declares that a cheque must be presented for payment within a reasonable time of it being issued, if the drawer is to be liable on it. A reasonable time is to be interpreted according (inter alia) to the 'usage of trade'.

(b) If a cheque is dishonoured, the collecting bank (as agent of its customer) should send notice of dishonour to him by post on the same day it becomes aware of the dishonour (s. 49(13) of the Act). Posting on the following day is permitted in some circumstances.

(c) The collecting bank's responsibility, for a cheque which it is presenting for payment, is not fully discharged until the cheque in favour of its customer has been delivered to the branch on which it is drawn (*Barclays Bank plc v Bank of England* (1985)). This case settled that the Bank of England must contribute towards the costs of operating the clearing system, which it uses when it acts as a collecting bank for its customers. It also presumably establishes that a collecting bank is liable to its customer if a cheque is delayed in the clearing system. The bank may in turn be able to claim from the clearing system.

The White Paper proposes that truncation of cheques be permitted. Banks will be permitted to obtain payment by presentation of electronic information rather than the paper cheque itself (see Chapter 6 for a review of truncation).

5.17 STATUTORY PROTECTION FOR THE COLLECTING BANK

Apart from the contractual relationship it has with its own customer, the collecting bank may have a liability to, and occasionally rights against, third parties. Namely, other parties to the cheque it collects. Suppose that A draws a cheque payable to B, from whom C steals it and forges B's indorsement. C pays it into his bank account, possibly one he has opened in a false name, and when the cheque clears, he withdraws the funds and disappears. The true owner of the cheque is B but C obtained payment. B may sue C in conversion but this is rarely practicable. The paying bank is protected by s. 60 of the Act if it paid in good faith and in the ordinary course of business. B has a claim against the collecting bank which has assisted C in his fraud. This claim is in conversion since the collecting bank has wrongfully dealt with B's property. In some older cases, the true owner sued the collecting bank for 'money had and received' and it appears this remains valid as an alternative remedy to conversion, although it adds nothing to the level of damages.

A collecting bank will have no means of knowing whether the indorsement on the cheque in the above example is genuine, because B is not its customer. For this and other reasons, the collecting bank has long needed statutory protection from an action in conversion by the true owner of a cheque. This protection is now contained in s. 4 of the Cheques Act 1957. Unlike the variety of statutes which protect the paying bank, there is only one that does so for the collecting bank, and it also deals with the abolition of the need for indorsements—which occurred with the passing of the Cheques Act.

Section 4 protects a bank when it:

(a) receives payment for a customer; or
(b) having credited a customer's account, receives payment for itself.

The section applies to:

(a) all cheques;
(b) 'cheques' drawn 'pay cash';
(c) most warrants issued by government departments; and
(d) bankers' drafts.

The conditions of the protection being available are that the collecting bank:

(a) collects the cheque for a customer;
(b) does so in good faith; and
(c) does so without negligence.

The spirit of the change in indorsement practice that occurred in 1957 is reflected in sub-s. (3), which declares that a banker will not be considered to be negligent by reason only of his failure to concern himself with the absence of, or irregularity in, an indorsement.

The matter of who constitutes a customer of a bank was addressed fully in chapter 1. So long as the bank is collecting the cheque for someone who holds an account with it, it will satisfy this condition. This is so even if the account is opened with the very cheque which is in dispute (*Ladbroke* v *Todd* (1914)).

Sometimes, however, a cheque is paid into a different bank than the account holding branch. In the judgment of Lawrence LJ in the Court of

Appeal in *Lloyds Bank Ltd* v *Savory* (1933), a bank cannot claim the protection when the cheque is paid into and collected by a different branch of the same bank, since the collecting bank is not receiving payment for a customer. The case went to the House of Lords but this point was not considered there. The same circumstances did not prevent the Court of Appeal from granting the bank protection in *Orbit Mining and Trading Co. Ltd* v *Westminster Bank* (1962), although the issue was not addressed.

It may be that the customer is considered to be a customer of the whole bank for these purposes and not just of the account holding branch.

It seems most unlikely, however, that a bank which collects a cheque for a customer of a different bank would come within s. 4, at least if the normal procedure is followed, whereby the bank puts the cheque into clearing directly and only a credit slip is sent to the account holding bank.

In the majority of instances the collecting bank will have no difficulty in satisfying the first two conditions above. Lack of negligence is a stiffer test. There is no shortage of case law to illustrate what is negligence in this context and what is not, yet the cases are not always a model of consistency. At least part of the reason for this is that the matter of negligence turns to a large extent on the contemporary context of banking practice, and it has been said that some of the older cases may not be an accurate guide in modern conditions (*Marfani & Co. Ltd* v *Midland Bank Ltd* (1968) CA).

First, it should be noted that when the collecting bank is negligent, it is not liable in the tort of negligence. It is liable in conversion, but will be protected from such liability if it has not been negligent. This may seem pedantic but it does have an impact on the burden of proof. The true owner does not have to prove that the collecting bank was negligent; it is for the latter to prove it was not negligent, on a balance of probabilities.

The collecting bank is not expected to be infallible. A constant thread running through the cases is that the collecting bank is expected to make appropriate enquiries and, having done so, is not to be fobbed off with a weak reply. There will be occasions when there has been a fraud but the collecting bank has acted sufficiently carefully to absolve itself from liability. By and large, therefore, the cleverer the fraud perpetrated, or the more plausible the false explanations given in response to inquiries, the less likely the collecting bank is to be liable.

The test to be applied may be summarised thus:

Did the bank take reasonable care, taking into account antecedent and present circumstances?

Further relevant guidelines which emerge from *Marfani* are:

(a) when a cheque is presented by a customer who appears to be a holder, the bank is entitled to assume the customer is the true owner, unless there are facts which are known, or ought to be known, which would cause a reasonable banker to be suspicious.

(b) the facts which ought to be known, the inquiries which ought to be made and what will cause a reasonable banker to be suspicious will depend upon current banking practice. This point was recently cited with approval by the Court of Appeal in *Lipkin Gorman v Karpnale Ltd* (1989) CA.

(c) such current practice will not conclusively define what the law expects of a reasonable banker but the courts will hesitate before condemning a generally adopted practice.

(d) inquiries which would probably not have prevented the fraud and would therefore only have risked offending the customer had he been honest, need not be made. This point was recently doubted by the High Court in *Thackwell v Barclays Bank* (1986).

Cases decided on facts which occurred before 1957 are based on the now repealed s. 82 of the Bills of Exchange Act. This applied a similar test, also based on the bank being without negligence. Therefore these cases are relevant.

It is probably helpful to divide the cases into two categories:

(a) where it is alleged the bank was negligent when it opened the account, usually because this later turned out to be in a false name;

(b) where it is alleged the bank was negligent when it accepted a specific cheque or cheques for collection.

5.18 NEGLIGENCE IN OPENING THE ACCOUNT

It has long been established that a bank has a duty to obtain references before opening a new account (*Ladbroke v Todd* (1914)).

Illustrations

Hampstead Guardians v Barclays Bank Ltd (1923). An account was opened in a false name. The reference was asked for and obtained but it was forged. The court held that some further check on identity was necessary.

Nu-Stilo Footwear Ltd v *Lloyds Bank Ltd* (1956). An account was opened in a false name, the customer giving his real name as a reference. The bank obtained a satisfactory reference from the bankers of the 'reference'. Held, the bank had acted without negligence in opening the account.

Marfani & Co. Ltd v *Midland Bank Ltd* (1968) CA. A false name account was opened by an employee of M Ltd. He used the name E, which was the name of a supplier to M Ltd and to whom, therefore, cheques were made payable. The new customer explained that he had no job but intended to open a restaurant. Two references were given. A sum of cash and a stolen cheque for £3,000 were paid into the account. The bank specially cleared the cheque (without being asked to do so). The account was credited but the bank awaited a reply from the references before allowing withdrawal of the funds. One of the references, who had had an account with the branch for some years, recommended the new customer to the bank, saying that the customer had been known to him for some time. In fact this was not so. The customer had, in preparation of the fraud, introduced himself as E to this reference one month earlier. Nothing was heard from the second reference. The bank then allowed the funds to be withdrawn. Held, the bank was not negligent. Further evidence of identity was unnecessary in view of the bank having obtained a good reference from an apparently reliable source.

Lumsden & Co. v *London Trustee Savings Bank* (1971). A false name account was opened by an employee of L. Once again, the name chosen was the same as one of the persons to whom the employer often made cheques payable. The new customer explained that he was a self-employed chemist and gave his real name as a reference, falsely giving himself the title of Doctor and also saying he was newly arrived from Australia. This 'reference' did not respond to the bank's request for the name of his bank. The bank had not adhered to its internal rules and whilst the court did not consider that conclusive, it held the bank should have done more to establish identity.

It may be concluded from the above cases that identity is of paramount importance and that perhaps a bank, when opening a new account, would be better advised to obtain solid evidence of identity such as a passport, rather than seeking references from persons who may be spurious. Such a procedure is also likely to be less time-consuming for the bank. Following *Marfani*, however, a reference may still be the best method when it comes from another (satisfactory) customer of the same bank.

Whether or not a reference is taken, certain inquiries must be made of the new customer, such as whether he is employed and, if so, the nature of his job and the name of his employer, so that the bank may notice if he starts paying in cheques drawn by or payable to that employer (*Lloyds Bank & Co. v Savory* (1933) HL), where it was also held that the bank should have requested the same details concerning the customer's spouse.

In *Orbit Mining and Trading Co. Ltd v Westminster Bank Ltd* (1963) CA, it was stated that a bank has no obligation to keep itself up to date with the identity of a customer's employer.

It is suggested that where a customer receives his pay through the BACS system, or even by cheque, his bank may be deemed to have such up to date knowledge.

5.19 NEGLIGENCE IN COLLECTION OF THE CHEQUE

This category may be sub-divided into:

(a) suspicious matters which are obvious, or ought to be obvious, from the face of the cheque, possibly coupled with the information the bank has about its customer; and

(b) purely contextual matters which should arouse suspicion, in the absence of which the cheque could have been safely accepted without inquiry.

Suspicious matters and existing information

A clear example of this sub-category is the cheque crossed 'account payee' which is not originally payable to the customer. There can be no doubt that where a bank collects such a cheque without making inquiry, it will be negligent (*Ladbroke v Todd* (1914)). This is so even if the cheque is payable to 'X or to Bearer' and Y is paying in the cheque (*House Property Company of London Ltd v London County and Westminster Bank* (1915)).

Where the bank does make inquiry of the customer and a reasonable explanation is forthcoming as to why the cheque is being paid into a different account than that of the payee, the bank is not negligent (*Bevan v National Bank Ltd* (1906)). Here cheques payable to W & Co. were paid into W's personal account. W explained that he was trading under the name of W & Co. In fact it was not his business; he was only the manager but it was held to be a reasonable explanation.

In practice banks accept many cheques crossed 'account payee' for collection because many cheques so crossed are made payable to persons without bank accounts.

The White Paper proposes that the account payee crossing be given statutory force, and that it will make a cheque truly not transferable. A defence will still be available to the collecting bank if it acted in good faith and without negligence, where, for example, the account name was indistinguishable from that of the payee on the cheque and it had taken steps to establish the identity of the customer whose account had been credited. A second example is where, on the basis that the bank does know or may be deemed to know the name of the customer's employer, it collects cheques without inquiry which are drawn by or payable to that employer.

Illustrations

Lloyds Bank Ltd v *Savory* (1933) HL. P and S were employees of stockbrokers, which drew many cheques payable to bearer. They stole a number of these cheques; P paid some into his bank account while S paid some into Mrs S's account. All the payments in were made at other branches of the bank, i.e. not at the account holding branch. The cheques were sent to the Clearing House and the accounts credited with the appropriate amounts. The cheques never went to the account holding branches and thus, even if the latter had the relevant information about the employers, they would have been unable to connect this to the drawer's name on the cheques. Held, it was a negligent practice to not send cheques, or details of them, to the account holding branch.

Lloyds Bank Ltd v *Chartered Bank of India, Australia and China* (1929) CA. L had power to draw cheques on his employer's (Lloyds Bank) account, but those for large amounts had to be co-signed by another official. L persuaded, by fraud, another to co-sign some cheques which were made payable to the C Bank, where L had a personal account. L asked the C bank to collect payment of the cheques and to credit his account with them with the proceeds. The C Bank knew that L worked for Lloyds Bank. Over two years L embezzled £17,000. Lloyds Bank sued the C Bank in conversion and succeeded, as the latter had been negligent in failing to make inquiries about the cheques.

Orbit Mining and Trading Co. Ltd v *Westminster Bank Ltd* (1963) CA. E and W were directors of O Ltd and were authorised to operate its bank account by joint signatures. W went abroad and signed some blank cheques so that E could carry on the business alone. E co-signed some cheques which he drew 'pay cash' and paid them into his personal account with the W Bank. The W Bank had asked for the name of E's employer when he opened the account and this was truthfully given, but he had changed his employment meanwhile. Held, the bank was not obliged to keep up to date with E's employment details and, as the signatures on the cheques were illegible (E's normal signature), it was not immediately obvious that E was one of the signers of the cheque, and the bank was not negligent.

A.L. Underwood Ltd v *Bank of Liverpool and Martins* (1924) CA. U had had a business account at the L Bank for some years when he incorporated his business into U Ltd. He maintained a personal account with the bank but opened a company account at another bank. He paid into his personal account a number of cheques which were payable to U Ltd, which he had indorsed. Held, notwithstanding that U Ltd was a 'one person company', it had to be regarded as a separate entity even if both U and the L Bank had not done so. Some inquiry should therefore have been made as to why a director was indorsing his company's cheques and paying them into his personal account.

Morison v *London County and Westminster Bank Ltd* (1914) CA. A was an employee of M and he had authority to draw M's cheques. Over $4\frac{1}{2}$ years, A drew a large number of cheques payable to himself, which he paid into his account with the L Bank. Held, the L Bank was negligent in collecting the cheques but that it had been 'lulled to sleep' after about two years, by the absence of any complaint from M. Thus L Bank was not liable for the later cheques. This doctrine of lulling to sleep was, however, disapproved by the House of Lords in *Savory*.

Thirdly, and similar in principle to the cases in the second category, there are those where it should be obvious to the collecting bank that its customer is paying in cheques which he has in his capacity as agent of the drawer or payee.

Illustrations

Midland Bank Ltd v *Reckitt* (1933) HL. A solicitor (T) had power of attorney from R, which authorised him to operate R's account. T's account with the M Bank was overdrawn and he drew cheques on R's account, paying them into his own account. M Bank accepted these without any inquiry. Held, it was negligent.

Bute (Marquess of) v *Barclays Bank Ltd* (1955). M was an employee of B. After he left this employment he received some government warrants, payable to M but also stating 'for B'. Held, it was clear from the face of the warrant that M was entitled to payment only as agent for B, and the collecting bank was negligent in not making any inquiries.

Purely contextual matters

These are cases where negligence arose, not because of something that was clear from the cheque itself, but because the collecting bank did not take into account other information which should have aroused its suspicions. These are probably the harshest decisions from the bank's point of view.

Illustrations

Nu-Stilo Footwear Ltd v *Lloyds Bank Ltd* (1956). A false name account had been opened but the L Bank had acted without negligence in this respect, see **5.18** above. The customer then paid in a series of cheques stolen from his employer, of whom the bank knew nothing. Held, the collection of the first cheque (for £172) was not negligent but that collection of the second (for £550) without inquiry did amount to negligence, as it was inconsistent with the details the customer had given of his business.

Motor Traders Guarantee Corporation Ltd v *Midland Bank Ltd* (1937). T forged an indorsement on a cheque payable to W & Co. and paid it into his account. This was collected after some superficial inquiries. Held, the duty to make further inquiry arose in this case because T's account had a history of cheques dishonoured for lack of funds.

Thackwell v *Barclays Bank plc* (1986). S simultaneously paid two cheques into different accounts with B Bank. One was payable to himself, which he had indorsed, and the other (for £44,000) was payable to T and appeared to be indorsed by T. It was obvious from a comparison of the indorsements on the two cheques that they were written by the same person (although of course the names were different) and S had indeed forged T's indorsement on the second cheque. Held, that the circumstances of the situation were out of the ordinary and inquiries should have been made. It made no difference that S need not have put his indorsement on one of the cheques and that it would not then have been obvious that the other indorsement was forged. Also it made no difference that if the bank had asked S some questions, he would have replied convincingly. The court was unhappy with the *Marfani* principle on this latter issue.

Finally, there are cases where the collecting bank succeeded because, although it had been put on inquiry, it had asked questions and received a reasonably plausible explanation.

Illustrations

Smith & Baldwin v *Barclays Bank Ltd* (1944). B paid cheques payable to a business name into his personal account. The bank asked why he was doing so and B produced a certificate under the Registration of Business Names Act 1916 (since repealed), which showed him as the sole proprietor of the business. B had obtained this certificate by fraud but it was held the bank had acted without negligence.

Penmount Estates Ltd v *National Provincial Bank Ltd* (1945). A solicitor paid a stolen cheque (drawn payable to P Ltd and indorsed) into an account he maintained at the N Bank. Inquiries were made and the solicitor explained that the cheque represented payment to a client on a matter where he had been acting, and he was paying the cheque into his own account, whereupon he would draw a cheque in favour of the client for the balance after deduction of his fees. The court held this was a plausible explanation from a solicitor and the N Bank had therefore acted without negligence.

In *Baker* v *Barclays Bank Ltd* (1955), however, inquiries were made and an explanation given which the court held to be inadequate. The bank was therefore negligent.

It is clearly very hard indeed for a banker to know exactly when the law demands that he should make inquiry before accepting a cheque, and when an explanation given in reply to an inquiry is sufficiently plausible. Each situation will vary on its facts. Sadly, there are dicta from some of the decided cases which appear to be unrealistic. For instance, it was said in *Motor Traders Guarantee Corporation* that there was something untoward in a trader indorsing a cheque to a third party, and in *Baker* that, when indorsed cheques are paid in regularly and for large sums, the bank is put on inquiry. As Byles comments (at page 327, *Byles on Bills of Exchange*) 'one would think that some regard should be had to the fact that a cheque is a negotiable instrument, although in the great majority of cases it is not negotiated'.

The Committee of London Clearing Banks Circular of September 1957 is considered to be relevant in defining when a collecting bank is negligent in collecting a cheque and when it is not. This provides that the following instruments presented for collection will require indorsement:

(a) instruments tendered for the credit of an account other than that of the payee. Where the payee's name is misspelt or he is incorrectly designated, no indorsement is required unless there are circumstances to suggest that the customer is not the person to whom payment is intended to be made;
(b) combined cheque and receipt forms, marked 'R';
(c) bills of exchange, other than cheques;
(d) promissory notes;
(e) drafts drawn on the Crown Agents and other paying agents;
(f) travellers' cheques;
(g) instruments payable by banks abroad;
(h) instruments payable to joint payees which are tendered for the credit of an account to which all are not parties, e.g. a cheque payable to A and B which is paid into A's account.

Having set out these rules, banks will presumably be negligent in law if they fail to adhere to them. Therefore, if a cheque is accepted which, according to the Circular, requires indorsement, and no indorsement is present or it is irregular, the collecting bank will be liable to a true owner. However, s. 4(3) declares that the collecting bank will not be negligent by reason only of the absence of, or irregularity in, indorsement.

5.20 CONTRIBUTORY NEGLIGENCE

This is a statutory defence, which for the purposes of a collecting bank is contained in s. 47 of the Banking Act 1979. In any action against a bank where s. 4 of the Cheques Act 1957 is used as a defence, the bank may also set up the defence that the plaintiff was contributorily negligent. The defence is only partial, and serves only to reduce the amount of damages which the bank is liable to pay. This is quantified on a percentage basis, so if the plaintiff is considered to be 10% contributorily negligent, his award will be reduced accordingly.

There is only one reported case of contributory negligence being successfully raised by a collecting bank; this is *Lumsden* v *London Trustee Savings Bank*, already discussed in **5.18** above. The contributory negligence in this case consisted of the employer plaintiff's practice of drawing the cheques payable to 'Brown', leaving a gap before the word 'Brown'. The intended payee was 'Brown, Mills & Co'. The fraudster inserted initials before the name Brown and opened an account in this name. The court held the employer had been contributorily negligent in the manner in which he drew the cheques. The damages were reduced by 10%.

5.21 THE DEFENCE OF *EX TURPI CAUSA NON ORITUR ACTIO*

This translates as 'out of an immoral situation, an action does not arise'. The only reported banking case in which it arose is *Thackwell* v *Barclays Bank plc* (1986), already discussed in **5.19** above for the relevance it has to negligence for the purposes of s. 4. T and some others set up a fraud on a finance company and one result of this was that a cheque for £44,000 was made payable to T. A forged indorsement was placed on this cheque and it was paid into another account. The collecting bank was held to have been negligent due to the unusual circumstances of the cheque being paid in, but it succeeded in its defence of '*ex turpi*'.

The defence is based on it being contrary to public policy to enforce a claim which indirectly arises from a criminal act. The test is:

(a) has there been a crime which the court should take notice of (i.e. how serious is the crime?); and
(b) how proximate is the crime to the claim; if the claim is upheld

would the court be seen to be indirectly assisting or encouraging the plaintiff in his criminal actions?

It was held in *Thackwell* that the underlying crime was serious and that the cheque represented the very proceeds of it. It is interesting to observe, however, that the victim of the crime was not assisted by the application of the doctrine.

It was suggested, obiter, that even if T had been a totally innocent party to the crime, an action in conversion would not lie to recover the very proceeds of a crime.

5.22 THE COLLECTING BANK'S RIGHT TO AN INDEMNITY

Where the bank is liable in conversion to the true owner of a cheque, it is entitled to a full indemnity from its customer, on the basis that it collected the cheque as the customer's agent and an agent is entitled to be indemnified against losses incurred in the reasonable performance of his duties (*Hichens, Harrison, Woolston & Co.* v *Jackson & Sons* (1943) HL).

In practice this will generally mean that the collecting bank will redebit its customer's account for the amount of the cheque, but the bank is presumably also entitled to reasonable expenses. The remedy is unlikely to be of practical assistance in the majority of cases where the customer is fraudulent.

5.23 THE DEFENCE OF ESTOPPEL

Such a defence would be based on some representation made by the plaintiff (and true owner) of a cheque to the collecting bank, which leads the latter to assume that the customer is the true owner of the cheque. The plaintiff would then be estopped from claiming. This is close to the decision in *Morison* (already discussed in **5.19** above), where a failure on the part of the drawer of the cheques to notify the collecting bank that a fraud was occurring, was considered to be sufficient.

5.24 THE COLLECTING BANK AS A HOLDER IN DUE COURSE

The collecting bank will not need the protection provided by s. 4 from an action in conversion by the true owner of a cheque, if it is itself the true owner. This will arise if it qualifies as a holder in due course (see **5.6** above).

It will be recalled that two of the conditions which must be satisfied before a holder can be a holder in due course are:

(a) the holder gives value; and
(b) the cheque was negotiated to him.

The condition in (b) above requires the indorsement of the payee unless the cheque is payable to bearer. In 1957 the practice of all cheques being indorsed by customers before being paid into their accounts was discontinued. In order to preserve the collecting bank's rights in this situation, s. 2 of the Cheques Act provides that where a bank gives value for, or has a lien on, a cheque payable to order which the holder delivers to him for collection without indorsing it, he has such rights as he would have had if the holder had indorsed it in blank. Section 2 only applies to a cheque, other instruments not being covered. Cheques payable to bearer do not require indorsement.

Thus the condition in (b) above will automatically be satisfied if the condition in (a) is satisfied.

Situations where the collecting bank gives value

It is submitted that this area of the law is in a state of lamentable confusion, due to many of the cases failing to distinguish between a holder for value and a holder in due course, compounded by the fact that there is no common understanding generally of what constitutes a holder for value.

It was decided in *Midland Bank Ltd* v *Reckitt* (1933) HL that the collecting bank did qualify as a holder for value, as it had given value for the cheque, but not as a holder in due course because it did not satisfy the condition of taking the cheque without notice of any defect of title of the transferor. If this is correct then there can be no doubt that the collecting bank must be a holder in due course in order to be protected against a claim from some other party to the cheque. Being a holder for value is insufficient.

It has been decided that a collecting bank can be a holder in due course when it allows funds to be withdrawn against an uncleared cheque (*Westminster Bank Ltd* v *Zang* (1966) HL), and when a cheque is accepted in permanent reduction of the customer's overdraft (*M'Lean* v

Clydesdale Banking Co. (1883) HL). These matters may be academic, however, in view of the following.

A bank automatically has a lien on cheques which a customer pays into his overdrawn account, so long as there is no agreement to the contrary (*Re Keever* (1966)).

Under s. 27(3) of the Act, the bank thus becomes a holder for value of any cheque paid into an overdrawn account, but in *Reckitt* this was considered to be insufficient to defeat a claim from a true owner. However, some of the cases declare that the bank is also a holder in due course in these circumstances, as it has given value by virtue of having the lien on the cheque (*Barclays Bank Ltd* v *Astley Industrial Trust Ltd* (1970)), citing dicta from *Reckitt*.

The confusion arises from the fact that in *A.L. Underwood Ltd* v *Bank of Liverpool*, cheques were paid into an overdrawn account, but the Court of Appeal held that the bank was not a holder in due course, in the absence of any agreement between bank and customer that the latter could draw against the cheques before clearance. This principle was cited with approval in *Zang*, where it was also held that the bank had not given value as it had charged interest on the amount of the cheque pending clearance. In *Zang* also, the account was overdrawn but the bank was held not to be a holder in due course. In *Midland Bank Ltd* v *Harris* (1963), the bank did qualify as a holder in due course of a cheque issued to its customer by H and paid into an overdrawn account, but there was an agreement that the customer could draw against uncleared effects.

The lien will be irretrievably lost if the cheque is returned to the customer (*Westminster Bank Ltd* v *Zang*).

The collecting bank cannot be a holder in due course when:

(a) the cheque is crossed 'not negotiable', as the collecting bank cannot then acquire a better title than its customer. If the White Paper's proposals are put into effect, all crossed cheques will automatically be not negotiable.

(b) drafts, 'cheques' drawn 'pay cash' and government warrants are collected, as these are not covered by s. 2 of the Cheques Act; thus there will be no deemed indorsement on them and the bank cannot therefore be a holder in due course unless the instrument has been actually negotiated to it. If the instrument happens to be indorsed by the customer, or if the customer is paying in an instrument which has been indorsed in blank by some other who is the payee, the bank may become a holder in due course if the instrument is considered to be negotiable by custom. The same applies to such an instrument drawn payable to bearer. The White Paper proposes that these instruments will be treated fully as cheques.

5.25 CHEQUE CARDS

The first cheque card was issued in 1965 in order to satisfy customers' needs to draw cash elsewhere than at the account holding branch, and to use cheques for the payment of goods where the trader would not otherwise accept a cheque, due to the risk that it might be dishonoured.

The card has proved to be an effective vehicle for fraud, however, when it is stolen with the customer's cheque book. Banks therefore now limit withdrawals of cash to one per day. The standard conditions applicable to the use of the card, to back a cheque drawn to pay for goods or services, state that the bank guarantees payment if:

(a) the cheque is signed in the presence of the payee in the UK and the signature agrees with that on the card;

(b) the name, sort code number and account number on the card agree with that on the cheque book;

(c) the payee writes the card number on the back of the cheque;

(d) the cheque is issued and dated before the card's expiry date;

(e) the card has not been altered or defaced;

(f) the cheque is drawn for an amount within the limit stated on the card and in settlement of one transaction only.

The final condition is clearly breached if the card is used to back two cheques drawn to pay for one item. This is so even if the cheques bear different dates.

The effect of the use of the card is to set up a legal relationship between drawee bank and payee, which would not otherwise exist, since normally, a bank is not liable to the payee of a cheque. This relationship is created by the customer, acting as the bank's agent (*Re Charge Card Services Ltd* (1987)). It may be analysed either as a collateral contract between bank and payee or as a representation by the bank which is intended to be acted upon. In either event the payee has a direct right in contract to claim payment from the bank (*Metropolitan Police Commissioner* v *Charles* (1977) HL).

A bank will set out certain conditions of use of the card when it is issued to the customer, and these will form part of the banker/customer contract. Included will be a promise by the customer not to use the card to create an unauthorised overdraft, and that the customer is unable to countermand payment of a cheque backed by the card.

Because the bank is obliged to the payee to honour the cheque, it is therefore also obliged to grant its customer an unauthorised overdraft, if the card is used when there are insufficient funds and no agreed facility. The customer will of course be liable to his bank to repay such an overdraft.

However, if the customer does use the card in this manner, he may commit an offence of obtaining a pecuniary advantage by deception under s. 16(1) of the Theft Act 1968; the pecuniary advantage being the overdraft facility which his bank might not otherwise have granted him. This offence is punishable by imprisonment for up to 5 years and an unlimited fine.

Illustration

Metropolitan Police Commissioner v *Charles* (1977) HL. C visited a casino where, in order to fund his gambling, he issued an entire book of 25 cheques in one evening, backed by a cheque card, each drawn for the then maximum of £30. It was held that an implied representation to the payee is made each time a customer issues a cheque backed by the card. This is that he will have sufficient funds in his account when the cheque is presented for payment. It was also held that payees in general would refuse to accept the cheque if they know there will be insufficient funds to meet payment when the cheque is presented. Thus the deception occurs, not of the bank which grants the overdraft, but of the payee. It is submitted that the House of Lords credits payees of cheques with a degree of sympathy with banks which goes far beyond the reality of most such transactions, where perhaps the payee is solely concerned with whether the cheque will be honoured, which it will be if the conditions of its use are satisfied. This is so whether or not the customer has funds in his account. However, in *Charles* the deception was established by this implied representation and, as the jury had considered the defendant had acted dishonestly, the offence was complete.

In the light of this decision, a bank customer who is not certain that there will be sufficient funds to meet a cheque which he is drawing with the backing of a cheque card, should express this doubt to the retailer.

This practice would negate any possibility of a criminal deception based on an implied representation.

Finally it should be noted that a cheque card, unlike a credit card, is not governed by the Consumer Credit Act 1974. This is because it is not a 'credit token' within the meaning of s. 14 of that Act. When the bank pays the payee, it is not paying for the goods or services on behalf of its customer, it is merely honouring his cheque, and this pertains whether or not an overdraft results from payment of the cheque.

5.26 RECOVERY OF MONEY PAID BY MISTAKE

The doctrine of the recovery of money paid by mistake may be relevant in the following circumstances:

(1) A bank pays a forged cheque;
(2) A bank pays a stopped cheque;
(3) A bank pays a cheque with insufficient signatures;
(4) A bank pays an altered cheque; or
(5) A bank makes the same payment twice.

This area of the law is not a model of clarity and consistency but the following propositions are advanced.

The conditions which must be satisfied for the operation of the doctrine and to enable a mistaken payment to be recovered are:

(a) The bank pays the money to another person, doing so under a mistake of fact, e.g. it believed the signature was genuine when in fact it was forged or it believed payment had not been countermanded when in fact it had been. It does not matter if the bank was negligent in paying, it must simply have been mistaken in doing so.

(b) The bank has no authority from its customer to pay. It has no authority in the five circumstances described above, but it does have authority if it pays when there are insufficient funds, and thus would not be able to recover if this is the reason for the mistaken payment.

The bank will not be able to recover if any of the following apply:

(a) It would have paid the cheque even if it had realised the truth (most unlikely in the above examples).

(b) The bank made a representation to the payee that it was making the payment (for instance, following a special presentation) and the payee has changed his position in good faith and to his detriment as a result of receiving the payment. This would set up an estoppel preventing the bank from recovering. Some of the later cases hold that the payee must also establish that he was not at fault.

(c) The bank has paid another bank as collecting agent for the payee and the latter has withdrawn the funds. The paying bank cannot then recover from the collecting bank, only from the payee. The collecting bank must have no notice of the mistake before the funds are withdrawn and have acted in good faith.

The above principles emerge from:
Barclays Bank Ltd v *W J Simms, Son and Cooke (Southern) Ltd* (1980) where the bank paid a stopped cheque and succeeded in recovering the funds; and
National Westminster Bank Ltd v *Barclays Bank International Ltd* (1975). Here a thief removed a cheque form from an unused book of cheques, taking care to remove the stub as well. Consequently the owner had no knowledge of the theft. The cheque next appeared in Nigeria where, drawn for £8,000, it was sold to I, who bought it on the basis that if it was dishonoured, the deal was off. The cheque was specially presented and was paid. Naturally the truth began to emerge when the customer was next told his balance. It was clear that NatWest had no authority to debit its customer's account and the bank sought to recover the funds which remained in I's account with Barclays. It succeeded, as I's good faith was questionable.

A fourth principle which may prevent a bank from recovering its funds emerges from *Cocks* v *Masterman* (1829). Where a bank pays a cheque and later attempts to recover the funds, it may be prevented from doing so unless it acts with great speed.

This will only be so, however, if thereby the holder has lost his right to claim against other parties to the cheque as a result of his not having been given notice of dishonour.

Cocks v *Masterman* concerned a bill of exchange with a forged acceptance, so a parallel situation could not arise with a cheque. In relation to cheques, the principle would apply in the example of an indorsed cheque, payment of which had been countermanded by the drawer. Notice of dishonour need not be given to the drawer (s. 50(2)(c)

Bills of Exchange Act 1882) but would need to be given to the indorser on the day of, or the day following, dishonour. The principle does not apply if the cheque either bears a forged drawer's signature, as it would not then be a valid bill of exchange, or if it bears a forged indorsement as notice of dishonour to the indorser is not then relevant.

If the paying bank is unable to recover the payment as one made by mistake, it may be able to exercise a proprietary right to 'trace' the funds (*Chase Manhattan Bank NA* v *Israel-British Bank (London) Ltd* (1980)). This remedy is based on the premise that the funds still belong in equity to the paying bank. Tracing is not available from a good faith purchaser for value, however, and this would presumably prevent recovery of funds which had been paid into an overdrawn bank account, as the collecting bank would rank as such.

Tracing would be successful, however, in recovering from the credit account of an insolvent payee, as the funds constitute trust funds. A claim based on mistaken payment would only entitle the bank to prove as an unsecured creditor in these circumstances. Furthermore, a mistaken payment claim is statute-barred after six years, whereas a tracing claim may be made at any time.

5.27 MISTAKEN CREDITING OF A CUSTOMER'S ACCOUNT

This interesting area of the law deals with a situation which is not uncommon in practice.

The applicable legal principles are similar to those discussed in **5.26** above on recovery of payments made by mistake. The bank may prima facie redebit the account or reclaim any funds which the customer has withdrawn from the account.

An estoppel will arise, however, preventing the bank from recovering if the customer changes his position in good faith as a result of the credits.

Once again, the cases are not a model of consistency.

Illustrations

Lloyds Bank Ltd v *Brooks* (1951). The bank was administering a trust and paying income from it to various beneficiaries, one of whom was B. The trust department of the bank, in error, decided that B was entitled to income from two holdings of shares, whereas in fact she was only entitled to income from one holding. The relevant income was transferred to B's account regularly for some years. The bank was unable to recover because B had altered her position as a result of her good faith belief that she was entitled to the money.

United Overseas Bank v *Jiwani* (1976). The bank mistakenly credited J's account twice with the same credit of $11,000. On being told of the additional credit, J immediately issued a cheque for $11,000. The bank succeeded in recovering the funds. It was held that in order to keep the money J had to establish:

(a) the bank misrepresented the state of the account;
(b) J was misled and, in the belief that he had more money, he spent the surplus; and
(c) as a result, the customer changed his position in a way which would make it inequitable to require him to return the money.

It was held that J satisfied the first part but not the others.

Avon County Council v *Howlett* (1983) CA. An employer mistakenly credited H's account. The estoppel was here defined slightly differently:

(a) a representation of fact which led H to believe the money was his;
(b) H, bona fide and without notice of the employer's claim, changed his position; and
(c) the payment was not primarily caused by the fault of H.

5.28 PRACTICAL EXAMPLES OF THE LAW RELATING TO THE USE OF CHEQUES

(1) Suppose A draws a cheque payable to B. B indorses it in blank and loses it. C finds it and asks D to cash it. Assuming D satisfies all the other conditions of being a holder in due course, he has given value and has perfect title. B cannot recover from him. If a bank cashes a cheque in a similar way, whether or not for a customer, it also is protected (*Midland Bank Ltd* v *Charles Simpson Motors* (1960)).

(2) Suppose the same facts as in (1) but that either B's indorsement is forged or that the cheque is crossed 'not negotiable', D then is not a holder in due course. B can recover from D.

Section 80 of the Act provides that where a crossed cheque is issued by a customer, which comes into the hands of the payee then, assuming the customer's bank fulfils its duty to pay a bank rather than cash to the payee, the drawer is protected. The section says that the drawer can assume that the true owner of the cheque received payment, whoever in fact did.

(3) Suppose A gives B a crossed cheque. A is conclusively considered to have paid B and B bears the loss. However, if the cheque is stolen in the post and payment obtained, A must bear the loss.

(4) Suppose the cheque is crossed 'not negotiable' and 'account payee'. If the cheque is stolen after B indorses it in blank, B can claim from the collecting bank, since it has collected a cheque crossed 'account payee' for another's account (or opened an account in a false name). The bank may be protected by s. 4 if it made inquiries and received a reasonable explanation. The bank cannot be a holder in due course, even if the cheque was paid into an overdrawn account, because of the 'not negotiable' crossing.

(5) Suppose B perpetrates a fraud on A, obtains a cheque from him and pays it into an overdrawn bank account. A quickly realises the truth and manages to stop the cheque. B's bank have a lien on the cheque, and therefore may qualify as a holder in due course and sue other parties to it, including A. If A had crossed the cheque 'not negotiable', this would not be possible.

(6) In all the above examples, the bank paying the cheque will be protected by one or more of ss. 60 and 80 of the Bills of Exchange Act and s. 1 of the Cheques Act. This is assuming it acted in good faith and in the ordinary course of business or without negligence (for s. 80).

It can be seen that from the drawer's point of view it is wise to:

(a) cross the cheque;
(b) cross it 'not negotiable', to maintain his right to effectively stop the cheque if the consideration on it fails (as in (5) above) and to maintain his right to claim from some ultimate holder (as in (2) above);

(c) cross it 'account payee' in case it is stolen before it reaches the hands of the payee.

From the payee's point of view it is prudent to have cheques:

(a) crossed 'not negotiable', in case it is stolen from him and a collecting bank or some other holder qualifies as a holder in due course. This can only happen, however, if the payee has indorsed the cheque.

(b) crossed 'account payee' in case it is stolen from him, so that he should then have a claim in conversion against the collecting bank.

As a holder of the cheque (or analogous instrument) the payee is entitled to put a crossing on it and to add 'not negotiable' (s. 77(2) and (4) of the Act). There is no statutory provision authorising the addition of 'account payee' by the payee, and indeed this would be unlawful by s. 78.

In purely practical terms, however, it will benefit the payee to write 'account payee' on a cheque which he might lose. The reason is that, whilst if it came to litigation against the collecting bank he would presumably fail because of s. 78, any collecting bank would in practice be reluctant to accept the cheque.

(7) A crossed banker's draft is requested by A from the X Bank, drawn payable to B. It is lost by A. A asks his bank to stop the draft. This will not be agreed to because the instrument is not drawn on A's account and the bank will not dishonour its own paper. C pays the draft into his account with the Y Bank. B's indorsement has been forged. If X Bank pay the draft they appear to be protected by s. 19 of the Stamp Act 1853. The X Bank may choose, however, to return the draft stating 'payee's indorsement requires verification'. The Y Bank is protected by s. 4.

(8) Suppose the Y Bank cashed the draft for C, or that it was simply paid into Y's overdrawn account. Drafts may be treated by the holder at his option, either as a bill of exchange or as a promissory note by s. 5(2) of the Act. The Y Bank therefore has good title as a holder in due course (assuming it satisfies all the other conditions), and thus has a good defence even if it was negligent in collecting the draft.

6 Paper Payment Systems

6.1 INTRODUCTION

All high-volume payment systems are highly automated—handling sorting, distribution and effecting account entries by machine. Electronic payment systems are those in which the payment (or, more accurately, the payment message) is transmitted in electronic form, e.g. disk or from computer terminal to computer terminal. Paper payment systems are those in which the payment (e.g. a cheque) or payment details (e.g. credit transfer slip) is transmitted on paper.

Although truncation is a hybrid, it is dealt with in this chapter because it follows on from, and still involves, the handling of (and rights and obligations under) cheques.

A bank is, essentially, the operator of a payment system. It is true that banks started life as the holders of deposits for their customers, but the offering of a money transmission service is certainly one of the most important functions of every major bank in the world today. A bank can act on its customers' instructions to make payments to third parties to whom those customers owe money or wish to make a gift; or a bank can make a payment from one customer to another. However, it is when several banks collaborate in offering a joint payment service to all their customers, that a payment system is established.

The banks participating in a payment system must agree their own rules and operate their own procedures for effecting, revoking, verifying and settling payments within the system. The operation of a payment system is largely unaffected by the participating banks' customers and, therefore, the courts.

Since a payment system is operated by banks primarily as a means of enabling their customers to transfer funds to each other, it follows that, in any single transfer of funds, a bank would not wish to undertake obligations to anyone other than:

(a) its own customer; and
(b) the other clearing bank involved in the transfer.

In any transfer of funds, each bank should accept an obligation:

(a) to its customer, to act as paying bank on his valid instructions to transfer funds, to the debit of his account, or as collecting bank to receive funds for the credit of his account; and

(b) to the other bank, to which or from which payment is made, to operate the clearing system in accordance with the contractual agreements and operational rules and procedures of the clearing.

Customers need to know the legal position on these and several other issues affecting their use of a payment system, such as:

(a) Fraud or forgery by a person purporting to be the payer.
(b) Want of authority by the payer's agent.
(c) Mistake, whether by the payer, the recipient or their respective banks.
(d) Revocation of payment by the payer.
(e) Time of completion of payment.

First, it is necessary to describe briefly the process whereby payments are made in the payment systems with which we are concerned.

6.2 CHEQUE CLEARING

A cheque must be presented to the branch of the bank on which it is drawn. Presentation for payment is the essence of the cheque system of payment, and only presentation to the drawee branch will give the collecting bank the protection of s. 4 of the Cheques Act 1957: see the report in *Banking World,* January 1985, p. 49 on the Bank of England arbitration. The law relating to cheques will require amendment to permit widescale truncation (see **6.4**). Each bank which participates in the daily clearing of cheques is called a Clearing Bank.

Three situations are possible:

(a) a cheque drawn on a clearing bank may be paid in to that bank;
(b) a cheque may be paid in to a bank or other organisation (e.g. a building society) which is not itself a member of the clearing);
(c) a cheque drawn on one clearing bank may be paid in to another clearing bank.

Cheques falling under (a) do not go through the clearing. They are paid into the branch on which they are drawn. The branch can deal with them itself. Otherwise, the collecting branch sends the cheques to its central clearing department, which sorts them and sends them to the drawee branches for payment.

Cheques falling under (b) must first be delivered to a clearing member as agent for collection. The agent bank then follows the same procedure as for cheques falling under (c). The sequence of presentation and payment ('the clearing cycle') is set out briefly below.

DAY ONE Cheques paid in to a clearing bank which are drawn on another bank are sent up to the collecting bank's central clearing department for sorting into batches, a separate batch (or bundle of batches) for each drawee bank.

DAY TWO The batches of sorted cheques are delivered to the Bankers' Clearing House by 11.30 a.m. on the day after being paid in to the clearing bank for collection.

Each clearing bank then collects all batches of cheques drawn on it or on a bank for which it acts as clearing agent. Each batch will be marked with the collecting bank's name.

DAY THREE The drawee (paying) banks sort their cheques by drawee branch and then agree the value of all their batches with each collecting bank by 10.30 a.m. on the day after delivery at the Clearing House. This agreement of values is the settlement. It is a daily striking of balances between the clearing members. The net position between any two clearing banks is actually paid by an appropriate adjustment in their respective accounts at the Bank of England at 4.30 p.m. on the day of settlement.

On the day of settlement each paying bank sends its cheques to the drawee branches, which must pay them or return them unpaid on the day of receipt. Allowance is made for a cheque to be returned by noon the next day if the drawee branch has, through inadvertence, failed to return it the previous day. Payment by the drawee bank is effected by debiting the account of its customer, the drawer.

LAW RELATING TO BANKING SERVICES

Since the account of the payee or indorsee of a cheque will be credited on Day 1 of the clearing cycle, it follows that the amount of the cheque will normally be uncleared until Day 4. Unlike most electronic payment systems, the drawer can also 'stop' his cheque until actual payment by the drawee branch.

The legal rights and obligations of the various parties to a cheque are discussed in detail in chapter 5.

6.3 TOWN CLEARING

Large value cheques (currently, at least £100,000) drawn on one City of London branch of a clearing bank and paid in for collection at another are cleared separately from the general clearing.

These cheques are walked round to the central clearing departments and can be presented for payment up to 3.30 p.m. on that day, if they have been sorted in time. The sorted batches are settled by 3.45 p.m. and payment made at the same time as payment of the general clearing.

Dishonoured cheques must be returned by 4.30 p.m. on the day of delivery, although they are not charged back until the following day. It follows that such a cheque cannot be 'stopped' by the drawer after 4 p.m. on the day it is paid in for collection at a City branch of a clearing bank.

The Town Clearing is merely an accelerated form of the general Cheque Clearing, and the legal rights and liabilities of the parties to cheques in both clearings are the same.

6.4 TRUNCATION OF CHEQUES

It is actually the clearing process which is truncated or shortened. The collecting bank sorts, by machine, cheques payable to its customers. Magnetic tapes produce details of the drawers and amounts, each tape comprising cheque details for the same drawee bank. The tapes are then distributed to the drawee banks who sort their tapes by machine into batches of cheque details for each of their branches.

The drawee branches decide, on receiving the information relating to cheques drawn by their customers, whether or not to pay. In respect of each cheque a drawee branch either returns (by electronic means) notice of dishonour or its head office pays the cheque in the normal daily clearing settlement.

The advantage to the banks of truncation is the saving in not having to transfer so much paper around the country.

Truncation gives rise to some significant risks for the paying and collecting bankers. The Jack Report recommended (in paras. 7.38–45 and Recommendation 7(8)), and the Jack Report White Paper accepted (in paras. 5.11–13) the need for amending legislation to facilitate truncation. However, such legislation may not resolve all the legal risks, the most important of which are described below.

(1) Section 45 of the Bills of Exchange Act requires a cheque to be presented for payment to the drawee branch of the paying bank. Failure to do so discharges the drawer (and any indorsers) from liability on the cheque. If a truncated cheque is not paid, neither the payee (or indorsee) nor the collecting bank will have any rights on it against the drawer (or any indorser).

The collecting bank will not have discharged its contractual duty to its customer, and will therefore be liable to the payee (or indorsee) if the cheque is not paid. Having said this, the collecting bank's customer will usually have to show that the cheque would have been paid if it had been properly presented.

(2) The paying bank will be at risk of paying a cheque without mandate, since it cannot know whether its customer's signature was genuine or, in the case of a business customer's cheque or a cheque signed by a third party, whether the signatory was the duly authorised agent. For instance, a company will often give authority for its cheques to be signed by *one* director for amounts of up to £X and by *two* directors for larger amounts. The drawee branch will not be told whose, or how many, signatures appear on a truncated cheque. The risk of forgery will also be greater.

It is doubtful that there could be an implied representation given by the collecting bank to the paying bank. The former will have no knowledge of the latter's mandate, nor will it be able to recognise even a poor forgery of the drawer's signature. For these reasons, the presenting bank is unlikely to be willing to indemnify the paying bank against the risks of truncation. At most, the collecting bank could only be liable for breach of contractual duty if a truncated cheque bore an obviously incorrect signature, e.g. a cheque with the drawer's name printed as 'J. Smith' but clearly signed 'A. Jones'. Equally, the collecting bank would be liable for requiring payment of the wrong amount or on the wrong date.

No duty, whether in contract or tort (i.e. negligence), would apply to a company cheque where the signatories had signed within mandate but not expressly in a representative capacity: in such a case, the paying bank has an option to pay the cheque to the debit of its corporate customer's account, and cannot therefore attribute any loss to the truncation process.

(3) The paying bank will not have the protection of ss. 60 or 80 of the Bills of Exchange Act, or of s. 1 of the Cheques Act (see **5.13** above).

Section 60 protects the paying banker who pays a cheque bearing a forged or unauthorised endorsement. Section 1 is similar, but covers an irregular or missing endorsement. However, these protections only apply to a cheque if it is paid in good faith and in the ordinary course of business. It is doubtful that truncation, however well established, can lead to payment in the ordinary course of business, because of the effect of s. 45.

Section 80 protects the paying banker against a claim of conversion where he has paid a crossed cheque to a banker in good faith and without negligence, notwithstanding that it contains a forged endorsement. It is doubtful that the paying bank can discharge its duty of care to pay the true owner if it has not even seen the cheque.

Contrast the position of the collecting banker under s. 4 of the Cheques Act, which protects him against a conversion claim if he collects a cheque in good faith and without negligence. Truncation will not affect the collecting banker's right to such protection, since it is his own customer—the payee or indorsee of the cheque—who must be accused of not being the true owner of the cheque, for the collecting banker to be liable in conversion. No requirement to collect in the ordinary course of business is therefore imposed by s. 4.

(4) The paying banker is at risk of a truncated cheque being 'properly' presented for payment a second time. This could happen if the collecting bank makes a mistake, or if the cheque is lost by or stolen from the collecting bank before the latter has cancelled the cheque on behalf of the paying bank. Although a paid cheque could be lost by or stolen from the *paying* banker, the latter could, on a later presentation, refuse payment. It is arguable that the paying banker could not refuse payment if the earlier payment was made on a truncated presentation, because the paying banker will not have paid the cheque in the ordinary course of business and thus has not discharged all obligations on the cheque under s. 59.

(5) Lack of possession of a paid cheque will also hamper the paying

PAPER PAYMENT SYSTEMS

bank in the event of a dispute arising in respect of the payment of the cheque. If, for instance, the paying bank's customer claims that he did not sign the paid cheque, the first thing the paying bank would normally do is obtain the original or a copy of the paid cheque, in order to verify the drawer's signature.

The absence of the primary evidence will in many cases force the paying bank to concede its customer's claim. This problem was particularly noted by the Jack Committee and the Jack Report White Paper, which both recommended that the paying bank should re-credit its customer's account within three days of a truncated cheque payment being disputed, unless the dispute had been satisfactorily resolved by then.

It will therefore be important, in any established truncation system, for the collecting banks to be required to store the truncated cheques for a specified period or to send them to the paying banks within an agreed time.

6.5 CREDIT CLEARING

Credit transfers

Credit transfers, or Bank Giro Payments, enable a bank customer to transfer funds to a person who is a customer of the same or another bank, simply by giving his bank a written instruction on a printed standard form supplied by the banks.

The paper-based clearing of credit transfers is similar to the Cheque Clearing.

DAY 1 The payer's bank delivers the credit slips for its credit transfers to the Bankers' Clearing House. In the case of an individual transfer (as opposed to a standing order), this will be the day after the payer's written instruction has been given to the bank. The payers' accounts will be debited on Day 1 or, for individual transfers, the day before (i.e. the day the credit transfer instruction is given).

Day 2 The day after delivery to the Bankers' Clearing House, the credit slips, sorted by recipients' bank and each batch marked with the payees' bank's name, are agreed by the clearing banks (settlement), and net payments are made at 4.30 p.m. across the clearing banks' accounts at the Bank of England.

DAY 3 The next day the recipients' accounts are credited.

Direct debits

Paper-based Direct Debits are no more than a variant of Credit Transfers, and are effected through the Credit Clearing but in reverse.

Only a company can originate a direct debit. It must first secure the sponsorship of its bank, completing the required agreement form, the terms of which are fixed by the clearing banks. This agreement contains an indemnity which enables the payer's bank to re-debit the originating company's account through the clearing, immediately in the event of the payer's bank advising that a direct debit payment has been made for the wrong amount, or after the direct debit arrangement has been terminated by notice from the payer.

This is important for a number of reasons. Firstly, it characterises the direct debit arrangement as a purely contractual matter. Secondly, it shows that reversal of a direct debit payment can effectively be achieved after the payment has been completed, but only by prior and express written agreement between all the parties—in other words, in accordance with the terms of the contract. Both these issues are dealt with in the discussion of legal principles below.

Each direct debit payment is effected by the originating company (the payee) submitting a credit transfer slip, completed by it as agent for the payer, to the payee's bank which immediately credits the payee's account. The clearing cycle then proceeds as follows:

DAY 1   The day after receipt of the credit transfer slip, the payee's bank submits the slip to the payer's bank.

DAY 2   The payer's bank delivers the slip to the Bankers' Clearing House.

DAY 3   All the credit transfer slips are agreed and the clearing banks make the appropriate net payments across their Bank of England accounts.

DAY 4   The payer's bank will then distribute the credit transfer slips to its branches, who will debit the payer's accounts.

DAY 5   A payer may have already given his bank notice to terminate the direct debit arrangement or the amount may be incorrect or the payer may have insufficient funds. If the payer's bank is unable to pay for any of these reasons, it must return the credit transfer slip unpaid to the payee's bank the next day. The latter bank will then re-debit the payee's account.

Credit and debit transfers: the legal principles

Two hundred years of case law and statutes have determined the detailed rights and duties in respect of cheques. Established in 1967, the Credit Clearing is relatively new. What, then, are the rights and duties of the parties to a credit transfer or a direct debit?

Assignment

The drawing of a cheque does not constitute an assignment, to the payee, either of funds in the drawee bank's hands, or of the credit balance (debt) owed by the drawee bank to its customer, the drawer (s. 53 Bills of Exchange Act 1882). This section was necessary because an assignment of a debt can be effected by agreement between the creditor and the assignee. The agreement will be a legal assignment if it is in writing, signed by the assignor (the creditor), and notified to the debtor (the bank) (s. 136 Law of Property Act 1925). This definition would be satisfied every time a cheque was presented to the drawee bank for payment.

By contrast, a credit transfer does not normally constitute a legal or equitable assignment, since there is no agreement between the payer and the payee that payment be made from a credit balance on the payer's bank account. Where the payer requests his bank to transfer money to the payee's bank account, it is not intended that the payee or his bank should have any claim for the money against the payer's bank (*Williams* v *Everett* (1811)).

Even when there is agreement between payer and payee for payment directly between their accounts, this usually relates to method of payment: it does not constitute payment by discharging the payer's liability to the payee and giving the payee an assignment of the bank's debt to the payer (*Curran* v *New Park Cinemas* (1951)).

Trust

Similarly, the payer's bank does not hold the payer's funds or debt on trust for the payee. A bank would not casually change the debtor–creditor relationship into a trust situation. Clear evidence of intention is necessary to create a trust, and the trust fund must usually be separated and expressly appropriated to the beneficiary (*Barclays Bank Ltd v Quistclose Investments Ltd* (1970) HL).

Contractual duty

It has already been seen that a bank has an implied contractual duty to collect cheques for its customers' accounts. It cannot be doubted that a bank which participates in the Credit Clearing also has an implied contractual duty to collect credit transfer payments for its customers' accounts. Such a duty can be implied by custom, resulting from the very high volumes of payments made by credit and debit transfer over recent decades. A bank receiving funds paid by credit transfer for the credit of its customer's account has a contractual obligation to the paying bank through the credit clearing rules to receive and pay for such transfer, and cannot therefore refuse to accept it unless the payee account details are incorrect or the payee has previously instructed it to refuse the payment.

Agency

The legal status of the bank to which a person pays funds for credit transfer (the paying bank), may fall into one of three possible categories.

Agent for the payer

If the paying bank were the payer's agent, this would imply that a banker–customer relationship had to exist between them. However, the credit transfer system is available to customers and non-customers alike, and is frequently used by people to pay in funds at one bank for the credit of their own account at another bank. Credit transfer slips are not addressed to the paying bank, whose name is not even mentioned on them. The credit transfer system does not, therefore, contemplate an account or agency relationship between the payer and the paying bank.

Independent contractor

It is arguable that the paying bank could act independently of either the payer or the payee. However, although a bank holds funds as creditor (not trustee or assignee), it acts in the transfer of funds as an agent, not as principal. It could not, therefore, be an independent contractor.

Agent for the payee bank

The paying bank must therefore receive funds for credit transfer as agent for the payee or, more accurately, as agent for the payee bank.

The paying bank is under a duty to the payee bank to remit the funds to the latter. If the payer has an account with the paying bank, he may ask the bank to transfer the funds from his account, but this initial mandate instruction is separate and distinct from the bank's position, once it has debited its customer's account and holds the funds.

Similarly, a bank asked to pay funds from its customer's account in response to a direct debit request will act as the requesting bank's agent, subject only to compliance with its (the paying bank's) mandate from its customer. Although a direct debit can only operate between two persons with bank accounts, it is the use of the credit transfer system which must determine the legal relationship of the parties to a direct debit.

It may be that an important legal consequence of this analysis is that both the paying bank and the payee's bank will be entitled to the benefit of s. 4 of the Cheques Act 1957. Section 4(2) provides that the protection of s. 4(1) extends to 'any document issued by a customer of a banker, which though not a bill of exchange, is intended to enable a person to obtain payment from that banker of the sum mentioned in that document'.

However, s. 4(1) refers to 'the owner of the instrument', ownership being the essential element of conversion: there are no payment rights inherent in a credit slip, which is merely a record of the remitter's payment instructions (similar to a receipt). Section 4 cannot, therefore, apply.

Forgery and fraudulent alteration

It is unlikely that a credit transfer slip would be forged or fraudulently altered, since cash or a cheque for the correct amount would have to be handed in. However, if an unauthorised direct debit request is paid, the paying bank will have paid contrary to mandate. It will have to re-credit its customer's account (at least with any unauthorised excess) and will be able to recover from the originator under the standard indemnity, or under the doctrine of payment by mistake (see **5.26** above).

Completion of payment

As with cheque clearing, the rules of the credit clearing permit a credit transfer or direct debit to be reversed up to the point at which the payee bank credits the payee's account or, if earlier, the point at which the payee bank properly commits itself to the payee to credit the latter's account.

Payment by mistake

The principles of recovery of a payment made by mistake are the same as for cheques and have been discussed in chapter 5.

7 Electronic Payment Systems

7.1 INTRODUCTION

Electronic Funds Transfer ('EFT') refers to electronic payment systems, such as BACS and CHAPS (discussed in this chapter), as well as SWIFT (the Society for Worldwide Interbank Financial Telecommunication) which is outside the scope of this book.

Electronic cash dispensing machines (ATMs) and electronic payment for goods ('EFTPOS') are dealt with in chapters 8 and 9 respectively. 'Home banking', whether by telephone or computer terminal, is not specifically dealt with in this book. However, it has many of the same practical features as CHAPS, ATMs and EFTPOS; to that extent, the same legal principles and consequences will apply.

Electronic Funds Transfer is a misnomer: no funds are transferred. The various systems comprise the transfer by electronic means of payment messages and consequent adjustment, also by electronic means, of various debtor-creditor relationships. A brief description of BACS and CHAPS will show how this happens; the legal basis of the relationships and the legal rights and obligations of the parties to those relationships will then be discussed.

7.2 BACS

Bankers Automated Clearings Services Limited ('BACS') is owned and operated by the Royal Bank of Scotland and the four major English clearing banks. BACS is a clearing house through which credit or debit payments may be made electronically.

BACS credit transfers

Details of credit transfers are transmitted to BACS in electronic form, by tape, disk or by computer terminal connected by telephone directly to BACS.

Banks transfer funds through BACS for themselves and their customers. Some major customers are sponsored by their banks to send transfer details directly to BACS.

171

Transfer details received by BACS up to 9 p.m. on any clearing day (Day 1) are processed by BACS overnight. The processing operation sorts the transfers into tapes for each payee bank, which receives its tapes from BACS by 6 a.m. on Day 2. The payee banks credit their customers' accounts at 9.30 a.m. the next day, Day 3.

BACS debit transfers

Debit transfers can also be made through BACS. For instance, some insurance companies collect their premiums this way when they hold a direct debit. The originator of the debit sends a tape to BACS, which sends a tape of the credits to the originator's bank: the debit items are included in the debit tapes sent to the bankers for the various customers who have completed direct debit forms. The first time a customer's account is to be debited through BACS under a direct debit arrangement, a code in the debit tape against his debit item alerts his bank to check that it has received his direct debit mandate from the originator.

7.3 CHAPS

The Clearing House Automated Payment System ('CHAPS') is operated by a company—CHAPS and Town Clearing Company Limited—which, like the BACS company, is owned by the major clearing banks.

CHAPS can only be used for 'irrevocable guaranteed unconditional sterling payment for same day settlement' in amounts of £5,000 or more. Each bank or customer who wishes to make payments through CHAPS makes its payments through its electronic terminal (called a 'gateway') to the gateway of the recipient or, if the recipient is not itself a CHAPS settlement member, the recipient's settlement bank.

Payments are time-stamped by the payer's gateway. Payments made before 3 p.m. on a clearing day are settled shortly after that time, although payments which the receiving gateway rejects as wrongly delivered or addressed can be returned by noon the following clearing day, with a consequent adjustment in that day's settlement. Settlement is effected by each settlement bank transmitting to the Bank of England's CHAPS gateway the details of its end of day net position with every other settlement bank. The Bank of England then makes the appropriate payments across the settlement banks' accounts with it.

Because payment through CHAPS is unconditional, it is effectively immediate. The payer cannot impose conditions on its payment—any conditions must be subject to an agreement between payer and payee, and CHAPS and its settlement banks are not concerned with any such agreement.

7.4 EFT CLEARING CYCLES

The main differences between the BACS and CHAPS clearing are twofold. Firstly, at the centre of BACS is a processing operation, whereas CHAPS only has an electronic switching system which directs payment messages straight to the payee's bank.

Secondly, and as a consequence of the first difference, BACS involves payment—both debiting the payer and crediting the payee—on the third day of its clearing cycle, whereas CHAPS involves immediate payment.

These differences are illustrated in Figure 2 on page 174.

7.5 THE LEGAL ASPECTS OF EFT TRANSACTIONS: GENERAL

The legal aspects of EFT transactions will be examined by reference to the relationship which each party to a transaction has to each other party.

7.6 THE PAYER AND THE PAYEE

Discharge of a debt by EFT

Whether a payment is a gift of money or made pursuant to a contractual obligation is usually irrelevant in the context of the rights and obligations arising out of the payer's use of any particular payment system. Also, the validity or terms of any contract between the payer and payee seldom concern their respective banks or affect the operation of the payment system. Having said this, some aspects of the payment process may affect or be affected by the legal relationship between the payer and the payee.

If the payer and payee agree that payment must or may be made through a specified payment system, then the payee cannot object to payment by that method, and completion of payment through that system discharges the payer from his debt to the payee.

The payee's agreement would normally be implied for an EFT payment, because he will have given his account number and bank details to the payer.

However, if no particular payment method is agreed or required, the

BACS Clearing Cycle

```
DAY 1            PAYER 1 ──────▶ PAYING BANK         PAYER 2
                                      │
        9 P.M.                      BACS ◀───────────┘
                                      │
DAY 2                                 ▼ ▼
                                 PAYEE BANKS
        6 A.M.
                                      │ │
DAY 3                                 ▼ ▼
                                   PAYEES
        9.30 A.M.
```

CHAPS Clearing Cycle

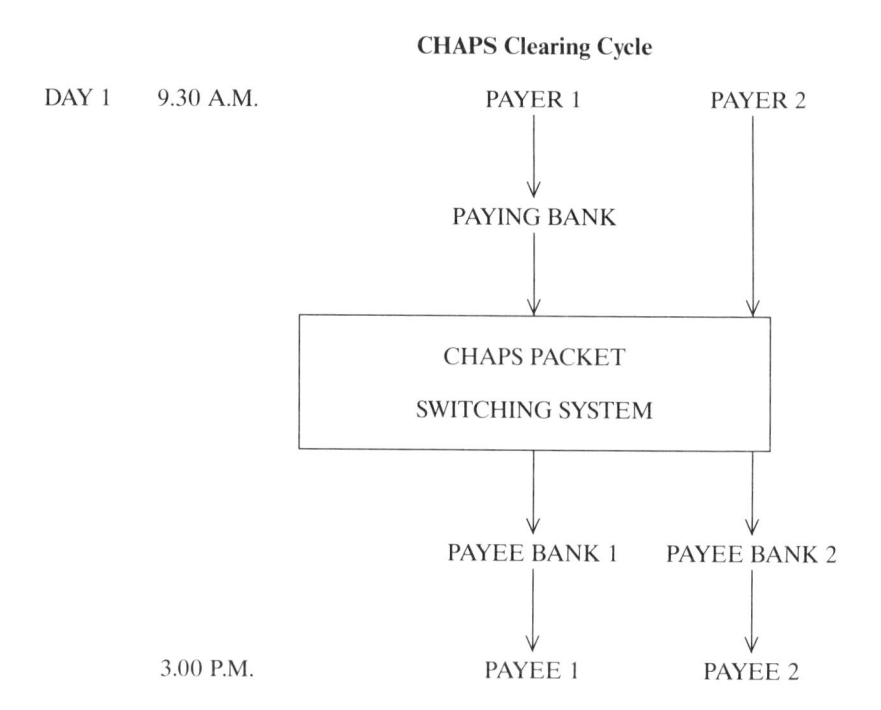

```
DAY 1   9.30 A.M.         PAYER 1              PAYER 2
                             │                    │
                             ▼                    │
                         PAYING BANK              │
                             │                    │
                             ▼                    ▼
                    ┌─────────────────────────────────┐
                    │       CHAPS PACKET              │
                    │     SWITCHING SYSTEM            │
                    └─────────────────────────────────┘
                             │                    │
                             ▼                    ▼
                        PAYEE BANK 1         PAYEE BANK 2
                             │                    │
        3.00 P.M.            ▼                    ▼
                          PAYEE 1              PAYEE 2
```

Figure 2   Comparison of BACS and CHAPS Clearing Cycles

N.B. (1) PAYERS and PAYEES could all be non-settlement banks.
(2) PAYING BANK and PAYEE BANK can make or receive payments for their own account or for the account of their customers or other banks. (If payments are made or received for other banks, they could be making or receiving payments for their own account or for the account of their customers.)

payee of a debtor could object to payment otherwise than by cash. For instance, the payee's account may already be overdrawn and he may not wish to reduce his bank borrowing; or the payee's bank may become insolvent *after* completion of payment (see below). It is unlikely that a payee would accept a proof in his bank's insolvency in preference to full payment from his original debtor.

Failure by the payer to discharge a contractual debt on the due date could give rise to a damages claim against him for breach of contract, particularly if time of payment were of the essence. The measure of damages would be the payee's reasonably foreseeable loss. The payer may have known the likely loss to the payee of not receiving payment on time, and damages could substantially exceed the amount of the payment and interest on it.

By contrast, the paying bank and the payee bank are seldom going to incur a liability beyond the face value of the payment and interest. Their liability is discussed below.

Completion of payment

Apart from any legal issues concerning the contract which gives rise to the EFT payment, the most important legal question for consideration as between the payer and payee is the time for completion of payment.

Once the payee has an accrued right of action against the payee bank, payment is complete as between the payer and the payee, and the payer has discharged any legal obligation he may have had to pay the payee. After completion of payment, the payee's only rights in respect of payment are against the payee bank (*Mardorf Peach & Co. Ltd* v *Attica Sea Carriers Corporation of Liberia* (1977) HL).

In the CHAPS payment system, the payee bank's issue of a Logical Acknowledgement (LAK) to the paying bank completes payment, even though the payment may remain on a suspense account of the payee bank and the payee bank will credit its customer's account later in the day (*Delbrueck & Co.* v *Manufacturers Hanover Trust Co.* (1979), an American case on the SWIFT payment system, which is similar to CHAPS in this respect).

In this case, the crediting of the payee's account is not necessary to complete payment. The fact that the payee bank may not have credited the payee's account in an EFT transaction is considered a purely administrative step, which has no bearing on completion of payment as between payer and payee (*Royal Products Ltd* v *Midland Bank Ltd* (1981)).

This should be contrasted with the position with the cheque clearing, where the payment can be reversed until the payee's account has been credited. Similarly, where the paying bank and the payee bank are one and the same and the payment does not pass through a payment system, the payment can obviously only be complete when the payee's account is actually credited, even with a payment by cheque (*Gibson* v *Minet* (1791)).

In no case is it necessary, in order to complete payment, for the payee to be advised of receipt by his bank of the payment (*Momm* v *Barclays Bank International Ltd* (1977)).

The significance of completion of payment is illustrated by the effect where either the paying bank or the payee bank becomes insolvent during the payment process.

If either bank should become insolvent *before* completion of payment, the payer will not have paid his debt and must pay the payee by another means. If the payee bank has already received funds, they can be recalled by the paying bank's liquidator, leaving the payer to claim in his bank's insolvency.

If the payee bank should become insolvent *after* completion of payment but before the payee has drawn the funds, the payee's rights are against its own bank and it must prove as a creditor in the bank's insolvency.

Payment by mistake

As in any other situation, a payment made under a mistake of fact can be recovered unless the payer has made a representation to the payee (other than by making the payment), which the payee has relied on to his detriment.

ELECTRONIC PAYMENT SYSTEMS

The position regarding payment of cheques by mistake has been examined in some detail in chapter 5. Where the payer of an EFT payment makes the payment by mistake, then, subject to the same common law principles as apply to any mistake, the payer can recover from the payee after completion of payment.

7.7 THE PAYER AND THE PAYING BANK

The paying bank's mandate

As with cheques, a customer's instruction to his bank is a mandate to pay which the bank is impliedly obliged to honour (subject to availability of funds). In the case of cheques, the implied obligation derives from the banker–customer contract. The obligation to pay by EFT derives from the bank's acceptance of the payment instruction, but not before, unless the bank has a general agreement with its customer to make payments on request by BACS or CHAPS. Such an agreement will probably exist with corporate customers who are regular (but not direct) users of BACS or CHAPS.

The paying bank is the payer's agent in transmitting the payment instruction; but it does not transfer the payer's funds, nor can it refuse to pay the payee bank if the latter acts on the paying bank's instruction to credit the payee's account.

The paying bank is providing a service to the payer and must act with due skill and care (s. 13 of the Supply of Goods and Services Act 1982).

Electronic 'signatures' (such as entry codes and Personal Identification Numbers) are more susceptible to unauthorised use than manuscript signatures, and the paying bank may seek an indemnity from the payer against the bank acting on unauthorised instructions, purportedly given in the payer's name. Such an indemnity should not infringe s. 3 of the Unfair Contract Terms Act 1977, since it will not reduce or eliminate a liability of the bank: it will impose a duty on the customer. In any event, a bank is only likely to seek indemnity from a regular corporate user of BACS or CHAPS. In these cases, the customer is able to arrange its own internal security and insure against loss, and the amounts being transferred could be extremely high in relation to the fee charged by the bank for the service.

In the absence of an enforceable indemnity, the payer may ratify an insufficiency of authority on the part of its employee or other agent. A total lack of authority, like a forgery, cannot be ratified (*Brook* v *Hook* (1871)).

In the case of forgery or an instruction given by an unauthorised person, the paying bank may be able to rely on estoppel if:

(a) the payee knew that the unauthorised instruction had been, or might be, given and failed to tell the bank (*Greenwood* v *Martins Bank Ltd* (1933) HL); or

(b) the payer affirmed the authenticity of a payment instruction *before* it had been implemented by the paying bank.

Carelessness by the payer will not avail the paying bank; neither will the payer's failure to check his bank statements (*Tai Hing Cotton Mill Ltd* v *Liu Chong Hing Bank Ltd* (1986) PC).

The Law Commission are considering whether to recommend a change on this point—see their Working Paper No. 114 on Contributory Negligence.

Subject as above, the paying bank may debit the payer's account with any EFT payment made on the payer's instructions. The only exception is if the underlying transaction were known to the paying bank to be illegal or a fraud. The documentary credits cases are analogous, e.g. *United City Merchants (Investments) Ltd* v *Royal Bank of Canada* (1983) HL.

The paying bank should not, therefore, be affected by any other matters arising from the contract or other arrangement between the payer and payee, pursuant to which the payment is made.

If the paying bank fails to give effect to its customer's proper payment instructions, the payer can sue the bank for breach of contract. The measure of damages will be sufficient to compensate for the loss which was a reasonably foreseeable consequence of the breach.

In practice, only nominal damages—the traditional amount is £2—is payable unless special damage is proved or the claimant is a trader (*Gibbons* v *Westminster Bank Ltd* (1939)).

Special damage, or actual loss, is unlikely to be provable in most cases, since the paying bank will not know the purpose of its customer's payment and, thus, the consequence of non-payment. This may not always be so (*Rae* v *Yorkshire Bank plc* (1987)).

A trader will be entitled to substantial (but not excessive) damages for injury to his commercial credit (*Rolin* v *Steward* (1854)).

The distinction between personal and business customers, in terms of damages entitlement, is largely nullified in the case of wrongful dishonour of cheques, by the fact that either may claim for libel. A trader's damages claim in libel will be the same as in breach of contract, whereas a non-trading individual can obtain much more by claiming for libel.

However, this possibility does not arise with EFT payments, since the paying bank would not usually have reason to tell anyone that it is not making a payment requested by its customer (contrast a dishonoured cheque sent back to the payee or indorsee, marked 'Refer to Drawer').

The payer's right to countermand an EFT payment

The basic principle is that a payer can revoke his payment instruction at any time, until the payee bank becomes obliged to pay the payee.

Only when the payee's account has actually been credited, can the payee bank truly say that it would be in breach of its duty to its customer if it returned the payment to the paying bank, unless at some earlier time in the payment process:

(a) the paying bank had authorised the payee bank to commit itself to the payee to make the payment *and* the payee bank had so committed itself; or

(b) the paying bank had, by virtue of the express or implied rules of the payment system, lost its right to countermand payment.

Having said this, it is always open to the paying bank to agree expressly with the payer an earlier time or event in the EFT process as the last moment at which it will act on the payer's order to 'stop' payment.

A CHAPS payment is irrevocable, by the rules of the payment system, so that a payer cannot countermand a payment instruction given to his bank if the bank has properly initiated the payment by CHAPS and the payment message has left the bank's CHAPS gateway. This will be so, even though the payee bank may not confirm the payment, by issuing a Logical Acknowledgement (LAK), until later that day.

A payment made through the BACS clearing could be recovered from the payee bank up to the time it credits the payee's account. The payee bank does not receive a payment; it receives a unilateral payment instruction from the paying bank, who can revoke it at any time until the payee bank has acted on that instruction.

Debit transfers through BACS are unlikely to be revoked by the originator. The customer whose account is to be debited can only prevent the transfer being completed by terminating his direct debit mandate to his bank before the bank debits his account.

In practice, most paying banks discourage their customers from stopping payment. It diminishes the reputation of the payment system, especially if a payer is guilty of bad faith towards the payee. Also, there is a considerable amount of administrative work involved which could, if 'stop' instructions were issued excessively, clog up the system.

The last moment for valid countermand by the payer should be contrasted with the time of completion of payment as between paying bank and payee bank (see below). If the banks complete payment and a valid revocation is then made by the payer, the banks can give effect to the revocation and adjust their respective positions in a later settlement. The payer and payee are not concerned with, or directly affected by, payment between their respective banks.

The payer as direct remitter

Where the payer is a major corporate customer (including banks which are not settlement members), it may have direct access, as a remitter of funds, to BACS or CHAPS. However, if it is not a settlement member, it will have to be sponsored by a settlement bank with which it maintains an account. The sponsor will receive, electronically, details of every payment made by the direct remitter and will debit its account for the remitter and settle the payment with the payee bank. The sponsor bank is responsible only for settling the payer's payment obligations. If a payer is also a bank making an electronic payment on behalf of one of its own customers, the payer will be acting as agent of that customer, as discussed above.

Payment by mistake

The question of payment by mistake does not arise between the payer and his bank. The payer can countermand his payment instruction until a certain point in the payment process. After that time, the paying bank will have parted with, or become irrevocably committed to part with, funds on behalf of the payer, and will be entitled to debit the payer's account. The payer's recourse, if any, is against the payee, although he may also be able to claim against the payee's bank—see **7.6** and **7.11** respectively.

Equipment and systems failure

If a validly requested EFT transfer is not completed (as between the payer and the payee—see **7.6** above) because of equipment or systems failure, will the paying bank be liable to its customer, the payer?

Three alternatives appear to be possible:

(1) If the paying bank's contractual obligation to obey its customer's mandate is absolute, then the bank will not only be liable for the performance of its own systems and equipment, but also for those of the payee bank, to the extent that the latter is the paying bank's agent. In neither case would reasonable excuse (such as national power grid failure) assist the paying bank at law.

(2) The paying bank's mandate could be to make a validly requested payment on behalf of its customer, subject only to the necessary systems and equipment operating correctly. This alternative would absolve the paying bank from all responsibility for its own equipment and systems, and for the performance of the payee bank and its equipment and systems.

(3) The paying bank could be treated as providing a service, through the medium of which it will effect payments in accordance with its customer's mandate.

This would import the statutory duty of care and skill imposed on all providers of services by s. 13 of the Supply of Goods and Services Act 1982.

It seems reasonable for a paying bank, in order to discharge such a duty of care:

(a) to maintain in working order the equipment it needs to effect payments which it holds itself out as being able to make; and

(b) to operate such equipment properly; and

(c) to carry out each procedure in the payment process in the time required by, and otherwise in accordance with, the rules of the payment system; and

(d) to use appropriate agents where necessary, being agents selected and known for their authorisation and competence as well as the efficiency of their equipment and systems; compliance with these criteria should be verified by the paying bank regularly, not just when the paying bank or, if later, the payee bank joins the payment system.

Such a duty of care and skill would be quite strict (for instance, it would require a bank to maintain emergency generators and 'duplicate' computer processing equipment), but it would allow:

(a) for faults by the paying bank and its systems and equipment, which the paying bank could not reasonably be expected to foresee or prevent; and

(b) for faults of any kind by the payee bank and its systems and equipment, provided the payee bank had been reasonably selected as the paying bank's agent in the first place (on the basis mentioned above).

This last alternative view of the paying bank's liability seems the most appropriate, subject to two additional considerations.

Firstly, the paying bank may seek to exclude or limit its liability for the failure of its (and its agents') systems and equipment by an express contract term. This would be subject to the statutory requirement of reasonableness (s. 3 of the Unfair Contract Terms Act 1977). This is discussed more fully in relation to ATM failure—see 'Limitation of Liability' in **8.4** below.

Secondly, the Jack Report White Paper has announced the Government's intention to enact a statutory liability on banks for 'customer-activated EFT equipment' and a statutory prohibition on contracting out of that liability. If such legislation were to extend to corporate direct users of BACS and CHAPS, banks might well have to reconsider their willingness to provide such direct user facilities, unless they could be adequately insured at the users' expense.

However, it seems more likely that such legislation, if enacted, would be aimed solely at electronic banking transactions effected by individuals, e.g. ATM cash withdrawals.

7.8 THE PAYING BANK AND THE PAYEE BANK

The payee bank's duty

In the same way as the paying bank acts on the payer's mandate, so the payee bank acts on the paying bank's instruction.

The payee bank must exercise due skill and care in applying payment to the credit of the correct account and in accordance with the timetable of the EFT payment system, through which it received the payment instruction. A BACS payment instruction should refer to a particular payee account number. In a CHAPS payment instruction, the payee's name must be shown and is given priority over the account number. In neither case is it the payee bank's duty to ascertain that the quoted account number is that of the intended beneficiary of a BACS payment (or vice versa for CHAPS), unless other details in the payment instruction put the payee bank on enquiry.

This is more likely to happen in CHAPS than BACS, because a CHAPS payee bank will usually credit payments to a suspense account while checking the payment instruction details. BACS payment instructions do not always advise the payee's name, and the BACS banks, by custom, simply apply payments they receive to the account number quoted by the paying bank.

If appropriate, whether by virtue of a valid countermand, an irreconcilable discrepancy or a lack of necessary information, the payee bank must send back to the paying bank, within the time required by the payment system, any payment it cannot apply.

Completion of payment

The paying bank is obliged to settle (agree) payments with the payee bank at the time required by the payment system (usually just after 3 p.m. every working day). At that moment, each bank becomes obliged to pay each other bank the *net* debit between them, and must therefore give instructions to the Bank of England to this effect.

The speed of, and lack of paper in, the CHAPS system may result in a discrepancy in the net positions submitted by two banks in their respective EFT payment instructions to the Bank of England. In such a case, the Bank of England will adjust their accounts in accordance with the payee bank's instruction, thus emphasising the guaranteed nature of the CHAPS system.

Although the paying bank may be committed to pay earlier, an EFT payment is complete, as between the two banks, only when the payment has been included in the aggregate amount and agreed between the paying and payee banks *and* their accounts at the Bank of England have been appropriately adjusted in respect of that payment. This is also the normal rule in the paper clearings (*Pollard* v *Bank of England* (1871)).

Payment by mistake

If an EFT payment is completed as between the payer and the payee but the payment was made in error, the question may arise as to whether the paying bank can recover the payment from the payee bank. For instance, the paying bank may have transmitted the payment instruction through BACS despite having received a valid countermand instruction from the payer, or a payment instruction transmitted by CHAPS may not have been given to the paying bank by an authorised 'signatory' of the payer.

The legal principles are the same as for cheques (see chapter 5), so that the payee bank can be sued to the extent that it still holds the payment or assets acquired with the proceeds of the payment (*Chase Manhattan Bank N.A.* v *Israel–British Bank Ltd* (1980)).

The payee bank would only retain the proceeds of an EFT payment to the extent of any credit balance on the account of its customer the payee. Once the payee had drawn against that credit balance, the paying bank's right to claim against the payee bank would be lost (*National Westminster Bank Ltd* v *Barclays Bank International Ltd* (1975)).

The paying bank's claim would then have to be made against the payee (*Barclays Bank Ltd* v *W J Simms Son & Cooke (Southern) Ltd* (1980)).

If the proceeds of the payment have passed to a third party, they can be traced by the paying bank, under the equitable doctrine of tracing (*Banque Belge pour L'Etranger* v *Hambrouck* (1921)).

7.9 THE PAYING BANK AND THE PAYEE

The paying bank's duty

In the case of a cheque, the paying bank's duties are clearly owed to its customer, the drawer. Although it is possible for a payee or endorsee to sue the paying bank for conversion, the circumstances are unlikely to arise often. Claims against the paying bank under s. 74(3) of the Bills of Exchange Act 1882 are by way of subrogation to the drawer's rights.

As only goods can be converted—this was extended by case law to cover paper instruments such as cheques—it follows that an EFT payment cannot be converted.

It seems unlikely that the paying bank could be liable to the payee in negligence, since the nature of any payment system is to transmit funds between banks without the direct involvement of their customers.

The payee has contractual rights against his own bank and, where the payment is made pursuant to a binding promise, against the payer. It is submitted that there will be no duty owed by the paying bank to the payee, who is not in sufficient proximity to the paying bank. The latter will usually know little of the payee or why he is receiving the payment, and will have no direct contractual or other relationship with the payee in respect of the payment.

Payment by mistake

The legal principles have already been explained in chapter 5. It has also been mentioned, in relation to the paying bank and the payee bank, that the paying bank can look to the payee, or even beyond him, for recovery of funds representing a payment by mistake (*Barclays Bank Ltd* v *W J Simms Son & Cooke (Southern) Ltd* (1980) and *Banque Belge pour L'Etranger* v *Hambrouck* (1921)).

7.10 THE PAYEE BANK AND THE PAYEE

The payee bank's mandate

The payee bank's authority for collecting payments through BACS and CHAPS is implied, since the payee will have given his account number and bank details to the payer to enable the BACS or CHAPS payment to be made.

It may also be argued that BACS and CHAPS payments have become a sufficiently common method of payment that banks have authority, by virtue of bankers' usage or custom, to receive EFT payment instructions.

Should the payee revoke his authority for his bank to receive a future EFT payment, the bank would have to return the payment to the paying bank in the same way as if it had been wrongly addressed. (In practice, a bank may be unwilling to undertake the administrative work and legal risk of attempting to distinguish between different incoming payments or between payments received through different payment systems.)

The payee bank's duty

Once again, the payee bank is providing a service to its customer, the payee, and must exercise due skill and care in crediting the payee's account with any payment received for his benefit (s. 13 Supply of Goods and Services Act 1982). As mentioned above, the paying bank may require the return of a payment up to a certain point in the payment cycle. After that point, the payee bank must credit the payee's account within the time required by the payment system.

The payee bank must also take care to resolve any apparent ambiguity in the payment instructions it receives, so that the right account is credited. Although the payee bank owes duties of care and skill, the bank cannot be sued in conversion. Conversion only applies to goods, having been extended to cheques by the judicial fiction that the paper (not its proceeds or the legal rights it evidences) is converted.

Accordingly, the payee bank's liability to its customer for failing to credit the latter's account, at the right time or at all, with an EFT payment will be a simple debtor–creditor action, or in damages for breach of contractual duty. However, this is unlikely to result in a valid claim for more than the face value of the payment, plus interest. Even a claim for interest may be rejected if the payee's account is non-interest-bearing and the payee cannot prove that, to the bank's knowledge, the payment would have been transferred on receipt to an interest-bearing account.

The practical consequence for the payee bank is more likely to be that, having failed to credit its customer's account with an incoming EFT payment, the bank may then dishonour its customer's subsequent payment instructions for apparent lack of funds. The payee's claim would then be that of a *payer* whose bank was in breach of mandate—see 'The paying bank's mandate' in **7.7** above.

The payee's right to payment

The payee has an accrued right to payment, once its bank has accepted a payment instruction to credit the payee's account and the payer has lost his right to countermand the payment instruction (*The Brimnes* (1974)).

This will usually occur only when the payee bank has processed the payment instruction and decided to credit the payee's account (*The Brimnes* (1974)). However, it might occur earlier if the payee bank has advised the payee that his account will be credited *and* the payee has acted on that advice to his detriment, or if the rules of the payment system so provide, or if it has been so agreed by the payee bank and the payee, so long as any such agreement is not inconsistent with the rules or practice of the payment system. Once he is entitled to payment, the payee can sue the payee bank if it fails to credit his account in the time required by the payment system; indeed the payee must look to his bank,

ELECTRONIC PAYMENT SYSTEMS

not the payer, even if his bank becomes insolvent. This would not be so in the unlikely event that the payee is entitled to reject payment by that payment system because it is not a valid discharge of the payer's contractual obligations to him.

7.11 THE PAYER AND THE PAYEE BANK

Privity of contract

There is no direct contractual relationship between the payer and the payee bank. The payer must look only to the paying bank to ensure compliance by the payee bank with the latter's duty (owed only to the paying bank), to credit the payee's account in accordance with the paying bank's instruction and the rules of the payment system.

The common law doctrine of privity of contract bars any contractual claim by the payer against the payee bank, and it is unlikely that the courts would, in effect, interfere with the way in which payment systems work by establishing that a duty of care (in tort) is owed by the payee bank to the payer. The paying bank is responsible to the payer, its customer, for the actions of its independent contractor, the payee bank.

Any attempt by the paying bank to exempt itself from responsibility for the payee bank's default by express contractual exclusion of liability would be at risk of invalidity under s. 3 of the Unfair Contract Terms Act 1977. The payee bank would not be willing to accept direct liability to the payer by express agreement, since this would undermine the fundamental object of a payment system.

Payment by mistake

The legal principles relating to the recovery of an EFT payment made by mistake are the same as for payment by cheque and are dealt with in chapter 5.

If the payer made his payment in error (perhaps thinking he owed the payee money when he did not), the payer would have no recourse to the payee bank, save by way of a tracing action against the payee bank's assets, to the extent of any credit balance on the payee's account with the payee bank. There seems no reason why the principle applied in *Banque Belge pour L'Etranger* v *Hambrouck and others* (1921) should not also apply for the payer's benefit.

187

8 Cash Dispensing Machines

8.1 INTRODUCTION

All the main banks and building societies with branch networks in England and Wales issue their personal customers with plastic cards ('cash cards') which can be used to withdraw cash from cash dispensing machines, or automated teller machines (ATMs), situated within and on the outside of bank branches and in other places such as shopping precincts and supermarkets. The amounts withdrawn from ATMs are debited automatically to the account of the customers whose cash cards were used for the withdrawals.

8.2 CASH CARDS AS CREDIT-TOKENS

Definition of 'credit-token'

Section 14(1) of the Consumer Credit Act 1974 defines a credit-token as 'a card, check, voucher, coupon, stamp, form, booklet or other document or other thing given to an individual by a person carrying on a consumer credit business, who undertakes:

(a) that on production of it (whether or not some other action is also required) he will supply cash, goods and services (or any of them) on credit, or

(b) that where, on production of it to a third party (whether or not any other action is also required), the third party supplies cash, goods and services (or any of them), he will pay the third party for them (whether or not deducting any discount or commission), in return for payment to him by the individual.'

The phrase 'whether or not ... other action is also required' covers the fact that, in addition to production of the cash card, a series of 'commands' must be keyed into an ATM before the cardholder can actually obtain cash.

189

Sub-section (4) adds that 'use of an object to operate a machine provided by the person or a third party shall be treated as the production of the object to him'. This clearly gets over the possible objection to sub-s. (1) applying to cash cards because they are not produced to a person.

To be a credit-token, a cash card must provide cash 'on credit' (s. 14(1)(a)) or through a third party (s. 14(1)(b)). In essence, a cash card will not normally be a credit-token or give rise to credit. At most, implied credit (under s. 14(1)(b)) can only be granted when a cash card is used in a third party's ATM, but this can be avoided by express agency arrangements between the banks and, even if it is not, the credit would be exempt from regulation. Therefore, no cash card agreement or conditions of use would be a credit-token agreement under s. 14(2) (save to the extent that the card performed other functions which gave rise to regulated credit).

Typically of the Consumer Credit Act, the way in which this conclusion is reached is tortuous and by no means free from doubt. The following analysis serves to demonstrate both these points.

Cash cards used in card issuers' own ATMs

Paragraph (a) of s. 14(1) only applies if cash is supplied 'on credit'. Subject to the points made below, a cash card should only be used to draw credit monies available to the cardholder on his current account. Even if a bank's own ATMs are 'off line', they are likely to debit their customers' accounts within 24 hours of ATM cash withdrawals, and this can hardly be described as a credit transaction.

Agreed overdraft

A cash card may be issued on the basis that an overdraft facility is available with it, and the terms of the facility may be set out in the cash card agreement. However, it is submitted that the overdraft facility is a separate agreement from the cash card agreement, and the cash card does not of itself provide credit.

In support of this, the customer can overdraw his current account by payment of cheques, standing orders, direct debits and so on, not just by use of his cash card. Also, if credit is provided, by virtue of s. 14(1)(b), on the use of a cash card in another bank's ATM (see below), that credit will not consist of the overdrawing of the cardholder's current account.

While it might be conceded that a right to overdraw on current account only by use of a cash card (and not by cheque, etc.) could bring the card within s. 14(1)(a), this is never likely to occur in reality.

By contrast, a cash card facility within a charge card or credit card may result in cash withdrawals appearing on the monthly charge card or credit card account. This really would be credit, whether cash were withdrawn from the card issuer's ATM or a third party's ATM. It would have no significant effect on a regulated credit card agreement (except to make it a multiple agreement), but it would make the charge card agreement partly regulated unless the cash withdrawal facility carried a credit limit higher than £15,000.

As a 'footnote' on this point, the overdraft agreement forms or letters which are now required by the Office of Fair Trading under s. 74 of the Act (see **3.3** on Consumer Credit Act Lending) will make it less easy to incorporate overdraft terms within a cash card agreement, because of the problems of dealing with variations to those terms.

Overdraft without bank's agreement

If the use of a cash card enables the cardholder to overdraw his current account without a prior agreement, does this make the cash card a credit-token? Most contracts, or standard terms of use, under which cash cards are issued expressly or impliedly prevent the card being used to obtain credit, and require the cardholder to agree in advance separate overdraft arrangements before overdrawing by use of his cash card. If such an arrangement is made, it will be the overdraft agreement, not the cash card agreement, which gives rise to the credit.

However, if the card issuer's systems cannot prevent the card being used to obtain credit on overdraft, is the contractual condition sufficient? The cash card situation is not analogous to the position where a cheque is drawn when there are insufficient funds on the account. Here, the bank has the opportunity to refuse payment; payment of the cheque will be treated as the bank's positive agreement to its customer's request for an overdraft. Contrast the drawing of a cheque in conjunction with a cheque guarantee card when there are insufficient funds: s. 187(3) of the Consumer Credit Act ensures that the cheque card does not become a credit-token.

It must be inferred in the Act generally that 'credit' means credit agreed by the creditor. It is therefore considered that credit which is taken in breach of contract and in reliance on a limitation in the card issuer's systems cannot have been contemplated as falling within the Consumer Credit Act's regulatory framework.

If this is not so, and credit is granted by use of a cash card in the card issuer's ATM, the credit would be given under a debtor–creditor agreement (s. 13(c)). Because the agreement would involve no pre-existing negotiations, it would not be exempt under para. 3 of the Consumer Credit (Exempt Agreements) Order 1989 or s. 89 of the Banking Act— see below. The agreement would therefore be fully regulated by the Consumer Credit Act. For the reasons stated above, this is not thought to be the correct legal position.

Cash cards used in a third party's ATMs

Most banks have links with other banks, enabling the customers of one bank to withdraw cash from the ATMs of other banks. It is not clear whether a cash card issued by one bank and used by its customers in another bank's ATMs is covered by para. (a) or (b) of s. 14(1).

It could be argued that the third party bank is acting solely as agent of the card issuer bank, and that there is no true third party supplier, unlike the situation where the creditor and supplier are in different businesses. Such an agency arrangement would have to be expressly constituted between the two banks. It would result in the use of a third party bank's ATMs being treated, for legal purposes, in the same way as if the cash had been withdrawn from the card issuing bank's ATM.

If this argument is correct, there is no question of credit and the cash card would not be a credit-token at all. It would be entirely excluded from the Consumer Credit Act, and ss. 51, 83 and 84 would not apply to the card (see **8.3** and **8.5** below).

If an express agency arrangement does not exist between the two banks, s. 14(1)(b) may apply. To fall within para. (b), the card issuing bank must undertake that it will pay the other bank for the cash supplied by the latter to the card issuer's customers.

Section 14(3) states that 'the person who gives to an individual an undertaking falling within s. 14(1)(b) shall be taken to provide him with credit drawn on whenever a third party supplies him with cash, goods or services'. This implies that the credit consists of that undertaking.

In practice, such an undertaking is seldom given expressly. At best, it is implied in the cash card conditions of use. The same is true of credit card conditions of use, so unless the cash card conditions are exempt under s. 16 of the Consumer Credit Act, they will form a regulated credit-token agreement (s. 14(2)).

Because the use of the credit (i.e. the card issuer's undertaking, not the cash) is limited to reimbursing the particular cash withdrawal from the third party bank's ATM, the credit is restricted use under s. 11(1)(b) of the Consumer Credit Act. The card issuer makes arrangements with the third party bank whose ATM is to be used by the cardholder. This brings the agreement within s. 12(b) as a debtor–creditor–supplier agreement. Whether it is an exempt agreement depends on whether it is a debtor–creditor–supplier agreement for fixed sum credit or running account credit.

The agreement for issue and use of a cash card will usually provide for a limit on the maximum amount which can be drawn with the card during any one day or week; but this does not fulfil the definition of 'running-account credit' in s. 10(1)(a) of the Consumer Credit Act because the cash card limit is a 'gross' limit: it is not affected by payments into his current account made by the cardholder. A cash card agreement must therefore be an agreement for a series of fixed sum credits, each of which may be drawn on in sums of the cardholder's choice up to his daily or weekly limit.

Alternatively, it might be argued that there is a true credit limit, being the credit balance or agreed overdraft limit from time to time on the cardholder's current account. If this is the correct view, the cash card agreement would be for running-account credit. However, since this 'limit' varies from day to day, according to the cardholder's use of his current account, and in any case this 'limit' is still affected by the actual daily or weekly limit, it is unlikely to be correctly viewed as running account credit.

The Consumer Credit (Exempt Agreements) Order 1989, introduced under s. 16 of the 1974 Act, specifies a number of arrangements which are completely excluded from regulation by the Act. Paragraph 3(1)(a) of the Order covers a debtor–creditor–supplier agreement:

(a) for fixed-sum credit under which the total credit must be repaid in four or less instalments within 12 months of the agreement; or

(b) for running-account credit during successive periods, so long as the total credit outstanding at the end of each period must be repaid in a single amount.

In the case of fixed-sum credit, it must be assumed that sub-para. (a) means that each ATM cash withdrawal is a credit which must be repaid in four or less instalments. The card issuing bank's undertaking to reimburse cash drawn from a third party bank's ATM is 'repaid' by a single debit to the cardholder's current account. But unless each cash withdrawal gives rise to a new fixed sum credit agreement, repayment will not necessarily be completed within 12 months of the issue of the cash card and its conditions of use. The exemption in sub-para. (a) may not, therefore, apply. (Note that since no specific availability periods or regular repayment dates apply to a current account, sub-para. (b) could not apply.)

Fortunately, banks can claim exemption under s. 89 of the Banking Act 1987 from debtor–creditor–supplier agreements, whether for fixed sum or running-account credit. Section 89 introduces a new provision into s. 187 of the Act, the effect of which is to take out from s. 12(b) (see above) 'arrangements for the electronic transfer of funds from a current account at a bank'. Since there still are arrangements with the third party bank, the cash card agreement does not then fall within s. 13(a): those arrangements are simply 'ignored' for the purpose of s. 12(b). Under s. 89, 'bank' includes building society.

The Banking Act exemption is badly drafted; for example, as mentioned in chapter 7, electronic funds transfer is a misnomer and does not actually involve the transfer of any funds.

However, s. 89 of the Banking Act was introduced specifically to take EFT transactions out of the Consumer Credit Act. It is therefore generally accepted that s. 89 is effective to exempt transactions which might otherwise fall within para. (b) of s. 12.

8.3 UNSOLICITED CREDIT-TOKENS

A credit-token cannot be given to a person unless he has asked for it in writing (s. 51(1) and (2)).

This section only applies to cash cards as credit-tokens, i.e. where the cards are issued by a bank for use not only in its own ATM's but also in another bank's ATMs, otherwise than under agency arrangements—see **8.2** above.

The Jack Report White Paper heralds the Government's intention to extend s. 51 to all payment cards, including cash cards. A detailed discussion of s. 51 is contained in **3.4** on Credit-Tokens.

8.4 MACHINE FAILURE OR ERROR

The bank's duties

In permitting customers to make ATM cash withdrawals, a bank is providing a service. As with any other service, the bank must perform the service with due care and skill (s. 13 Supply of Goods and Services Act 1982).

The bank must ensure that its ATMs:

(1) are designed and programmed to respond accurately to the proper commands of cardholders authorised to use the ATMs;
(2) are, as far as is reasonable, maintained in working order; and
(3) provide sufficient information to the bank of completed cash withdrawals to enable cardholders' current accounts to be debited with the right amount on the right date.

These three duties bear further examination.

(1) The bank's duty to ensure that its ATMs perform cash withdrawal transactions properly must be absolute. If a valid card is inserted in an apparently operating ATM, and the right Personal Identification Number (PIN) and a permissible amount of cash are correctly keyed in, then the ATM should dispense the requested amount of cash. This is no more than a question of the bank obeying its customer's mandate.

An ATMs failure, despite accepting a cardholder's valid cash card, PIN and payment instruction, to dispense the correct amount of cash raises two possibilities.

Firstly, the machine could dispense more than the customer has requested. The customer holds the excess on trust for the bank. He should return it to the bank at the earliest reasonable opportunity. The bank should not debit the customer's account with the excess. If it does so, the bank cannot demand that the excess be returned. Conversely, if the customer keeps the excess, he cannot complain if it is debited to his account.

If the bank does not debit the excess payment to its customer's account, it can sue the customer for money had and received, since the bank (through its ATM) will have made a mistake of fact. Such an action could only be contemplated if the bank had adequate records of the cash withdrawal transaction, as to which see (3) below.

Secondly, an ATM may dispense no cash at all or less cash than the customer properly requested. The position regarding mitigation of loss and contributory negligence will apply as for machine failure (see (2) below). If the customer's account is debited with the full amount originally requested, he will be entitled to have the debit entry corrected and any consequential interest adjusted.

The ATM could retain the customer's card, thus preventing him from mitigating his loss and, indeed, from making any other cash withdrawals. In practice, it is difficult to see how a customer can properly claim any more from his bank than if his card had been returned without the requested cash. The inconvenience the cardholder suffers is not likely to entitle him to much by way of damages under the courts' current interpretation of rules on measure of damages.

(2) The requirement of reasonableness will only apply to the second of the above duties. A bank cannot be expected to guarantee that all ATMs are operational and loaded with sufficient cash twenty-four hours a day and seven days a week. If a bank advertises, generally or to its cardholders, the locations of its ATMs, it must reload and repair them within a reasonable time. If it simply provides cash cards for use at its ATMs wherever its cardholders may find them, it is arguable that the bank is not offering to provide an ATM service at specific sites and that the bank should only take reasonable steps to ensure that empty or faulty machines do not accept cards and thereby cause their holders loss, e.g. by debiting a cardholder's account without giving him any cash.

The Jack Report White Paper has indicated that new legislation will make banks liable for the failure of their ATMs to complete a transaction and they will not be able to contract out of that liability. The liability would be for 'foreseeable and specifically contemplated losses'. This proposal appears to involve no liability arising on a bank unless the ATM accepts a customer's card.

Most ATMs automatically display a 'Not in use' or similar notice when there is a power failure, or they are being repaired or re-loaded, or they are empty. This should reduce the risk of claims against banks.

It seems unlikely that the proposed legislation will change existing law a great deal: a cardholder's provable loss for his bank's breach of its contractual duties and obligations in respect of its ATMs cannot, on the analogy of cheques, extend to consequential losses and will therefore remain limited to the amount of the cash withdrawal and related charges, unless the new legislation specifies the exact types of loss and measure of compensation payable (*Rae* v *Yorkshire Bank plc* (1987)).

The main effect of new legislation on the lines mentioned above is that banks would be prevented from contracting out of their liability, even where it might otherwise have been considered reasonable for them to do so. This would close an already small hole left by the Unfair Contract Terms Act 1977—see 'Limitation of Liability' below.

As with EFT payments, no claim for defamation can be made if an ATM cash withdrawal is refused. To be defamatory, a statement must be broadcast to someone other than the defamed person. Even if a person other than the cardholder witnesses his rejected cash withdrawal attempt, no reason is displayed on the machine's screen which could justify a defamation claim and the machine's refusal could obviously result from many reasons which have nothing to do with the cardholder's creditworthiness.

In any of the above cases, a cardholder must mitigate his loss. The cardholder must therefore use another ATM if he knows of one within reasonable proximity to the defective machine.

A cardholder must not be guilty of contributory negligence. If the machine failure results from the customer's unreasonably incorrect operation of the machine, or if he inflicts damage on it, the cardholder's claim against his bank will be reduced.

In the case of machine failure affecting another bank's ATM, the cardholder's bank would not be liable unless the other bank's ATMs regularly broke down or remained in disrepair or empty for long periods. The liability would be for failure to select a reasonably appropriate third party bank. However, the measure of damages for loss would be no greater than for failure of the card issuer bank's own ATMs.

Presumably, the proposed legislation (see above) would not prevent the two banks from contracting with each other that, whichever of them is liable to the cardholder, the third party bank would be liable for the failure of its own ATMs.

(3) A bank's duty to ensure that the correct entry relating to an ATM transaction is made on its customer's account, is simply part of the bank's wider duty to account.

Many ATMs are 'on-line' and send an electronic message, immediately a transaction is completed, to the bank's main computer, so that the cash withdrawal may be taken account of immediately in determining the customer's available balance on current account. This will enable the bank to assess more accurately whether to give electronic or telephoned authorisation for future cash withdrawals or EFTPOS transactions by the cardholder, even if the cash withdrawal will not actually be debited to his account until after close of business on the day of withdrawal.

The bank must also be able to verify the details of an ATM transaction. For this purpose, ATMs incorporate a tally-roll which records details of each transaction and attempted transaction undertaken by the machine.

This record is in an acceptable form for the purpose of the legal rules on admissibility of evidence. The Bankers' Books Evidence Act 1879 (as amended by the Banking Act 1979) and the Civil Evidence Act 1968 both provide for microfilmed, machine readable and electronically held information to be admissible in evidence.

While the infallibility of this record can be disputed, its general accuracy will, in effect, place a heavy burden of proof on the cardholder to show that the ATM had dispensed no cash or less cash than he had been debited with. The question of fraudulent third party use is dealt with in **8.5** below.

Limitation of liability

The question may arise as to whether a bank can exclude or limit its responsibilities to its customers in respect of ATMs. As has already been mentioned, a bank will usually set out, in a standard printed agreement with each cardholder, the conditions of use of the bank's cash cards and ATMs. The bank thus has the opportunity to limit or completely exclude its legal liability to its cardholders by an express clause in those conditions. However, the Unfair Contract Terms Act 1977 ('UCTA') severely restricts a bank's ability to do this.

Liability for death or personal injury cannot be excluded by notice or by a contract term (s. 2(1) UCTA).

Nor can liability for any other loss be excluded or limited by notice or contract term, unless the exclusion or limitation is reasonable (s. 2(2) UCTA).

Where one party to a contract is a consumer and the other party contracts in the course of business, the latter party cannot exclude or restrict the performance of his contractual obligations or exclude or limit his liability for breach of those obligations, unless in any such case it is reasonable to do so (s. 3 UCTA).

CASH DISPENSING MACHINES

Sections 2(2) and 3 will always apply in a bank's contracts with its non-bank personal customers. Section 2(2) will also be relevant to a situation where a bank owes a duty of care outside its contractual duties, for example, under the Occupiers' Liability Act 1957.

To be reasonable for the purposes of ss. 2(2) and 3, a contract term excluding or limiting liability must have been fair and reasonable, having regard to the circumstances which were, or ought reasonably to have been, known to or in the contemplation of the parties when the contract was made (s. 11(1) UCTA).

The customer's resources and the availability to him of insurance against his loss will also be relevant if the bank limits its liability to a specified sum (s. 11(4) UCTA).

The onus will be on the bank to prove the reasonableness of an exemption clause intended to benefit it (s. 11(5) UCTA).

If enacted, the proposed legislation to prevent banks from contracting out of liability for an ATM's failure to complete a cash withdrawal transaction (once it has accepted a customer's card), will limit the bank's ability to rely on exemption clauses—even when reasonable—still further.

8.5 UNAUTHORISED USE OF CASH CARDS

As with cheques, a bank can only debit its customer's account with cash card withdrawals made by the customer. However, where a customer consents to, or requests, the use of his cash card by another person, the customer will be liable to his bank for that use.

If a customer questions a debit to his account resulting from an ATM transaction, his bank must be able to substantiate from the machine's tally-roll that it acted on the customer's authority. If the bank shows that its records indicate that the customer's card was used, the customer may be able to show:

(a) either that he could not have used the card because he and his card were somewhere else at the time; or

(b) that he had lost the card or left it somewhere else at the time.

In the first case, it is possible that the bank may, in error, have issued a second card with the same Personal Identification Number (PIN) or that someone had fraudulently duplicated the customer's card and PIN.

There is certainly a risk of fraud although the instances of erroneously duplicated PINs issued by banks are thought to be rare. In neither case can the bank debit its customer's account. However, once the customer learns of the fraudulent use of a duplicate of his card, his failure to inform his bank of the fraud may render him liable for further fraudulent withdrawals with the duplicate card (*Greenwood* v *Martins Bank Ltd* (1933) HL).

A person who uses someone else's cash card without authority or a fraudulently manufactured card will be guilty of a number of criminal offences including, possibly, theft. Although the actual manufacture of a duplicate cash card does not constitute forgery, it is to be made a new criminal offence by amendment of the Forgery and Counterfeiting Act 1981: this is recommended in the Jack Report White Paper.

As regards the second case—where the cardholder had lost the card or left it somewhere else—the legal consequences are entirely different.

In order to reduce fraud, banks normally require, in their cash card agreements, that customers retain their cash cards in a safe place, keep their cash cards and PINs separate and keep their PINs secret. A customer's failure to observe these requirements will render the customer liable for any resulting loss.

It is often difficult to determine whether a customer has in fact been careless. An obvious example is where the customer writes his PIN on his card and leaves it lying around where others can find it. But is the customer at fault if he carelessly discloses his PIN to someone who later steals the card?

It may be that the customer has acted in such a way as to give the user of his cash card implied authority to use it. In this case, the customer will be liable to his bank as if he had given express authority.

Even where the customer has not given express or implied authority to a third party to use the customer's cash card, the bank's conditions of use may still make the customer liable for the third party's cash withdrawals. Sometimes, the customer's liability will extend only to third party cash withdrawals effected prior to the customer notifying the bank of the loss or theft of his card.

As the cash card is probably not a credit-token and is certainly not subject to a credit-token agreement (see **8.2** above), ss. 83 and 84 of the Consumer Credit Act will not apply to limit a bank's right to make its customer liable for cash withdrawn by third parties. However, the Jack Report White Paper has suggested that these two sections should be extended to all payment cards, whether or not they are credit-tokens.

If such legislation were enacted, it would prevent a bank from making its customer liable for a third party's use of the customer's cash card unless the third party was authorised, or treated as authorised, by the customer to make a withdrawal as his agent. Implied authority, as mentioned above, may still be relevant (s. 83(1)).

Notwithstanding s. 83, a bank may still, by an express contract term, make a cardholder liable for up to £50 of all withdrawals by third parties with the customer's card (but without the customer's consent) during any period when the card was not in the possession of the bank, the customer or anyone authorised by the customer to use the card (s. 84).

(The £30 limit specified in s. 83 was increased, with effect from 20 May 1985, to £50 by the Consumer Credit (Increase of Monetary Amounts) Order 1983, introduced under s. 181.)

Again, a third party's use with the express or implied consent of the customer will not be subject to the £50 limit.

The bank must give its customer, in his cash card agreement, a name, address and telephone number so that the customer can report the loss or theft of his card (s. 84(4)). There is further discussion of ss. 83 and 84 in **3.4** on Credit-Tokens.

8.6 OTHER ATM SERVICES

Most ATM's can provide services in addition to cash withdrawal.
Typical services are:

(a) Cheque book ordering
(b) Statement ordering
(c) Balance enquiries
(d) Depositing cash and other payments
(e) Instructions for transfers between the cardholder's accounts.

As with all services, banks must act in accordance with their mandate and with due skill and care in providing these services (s. 13 Supply of Goods and Services Act 1982).

Apart from the above points, the only legal issues of significance arise with balance enquiries. Firstly, the giving of a balance to a customer on an ATM constitutes a representation by the bank. The customer is entitled to rely on that representation, and may resist the bank's attempt to recover money withdrawn thereafter, if the funds shown by the ATM as standing to the customer's account never stood to the customer's account or were credited in error by the bank, provided that it was not inequitable for the customer to rely on the representation (*Holland* v *Manchester and Liverpool District Banking Co.* (1909)).

Secondly, the bank owes its customer a duty of confidentiality (*Tournier* v *National Provincial and Union Bank of England* (1924) CA). The bank must, therefore, take reasonable precautions to ensure that its ATMs are designed in such a way that, when its ATM displays a customer's balance, the amount cannot easily be seen by other people.

9 Electronic Funds Transfer at Point of Sale (EFTPOS)

9.1 INTRODUCTION

EFTPOS is a consumer payment system which enables a bank customer to pay for goods and services by direct and immediate transfer of funds electronically from his bank account to the bank account of the party supplying the goods or services ('the retailer').

In practice, this definition is inaccurate in every detail except as to the parties! The payment is not direct or immediate, funds are not 'transferred' and the whole transaction is not usually electronic. However, these inaccuracies are largely due to practical, rather than conceptual, considerations as will be seen. In any event, the legal principles are discussed in this chapter on the basis of a 'pure' EFTPOS debit card scheme, as defined above, but taking into account the more common variations in current practice.

The same principles will apply to charge and credit card schemes, save as regards the timing of payment by the cardholder and the consequent credit and related statutory regulation. In order to avoid these aspects distracting from the essential legal point relevant to EFTPOS as a payment system, charge and credit card schemes are not referred to in this chapter. (There is some discussion of them in chapter 3.)

It must also be borne in mind that electronic banking is in its infancy. As technology progresses and as the economics of banking change, so existing payment schemes will change and new schemes will be developed: different legal principles may then become applicable. Similarly, the terminology of EFTPOS transactions may change. In this chapter, use is made of expressions which are currently prevalent.

Although EFTPOS currently consists, legally, of a chain of contractual relationships with little statute or case law of direct relevance, legislation may be brought into effect to regulate all or some aspects of electronic banking. For instance, the Jack Report White Paper contains recommendations for new laws on liability for some electronic equipment and for payment cards. These recommendations are referred to below.

9.2 THE EFTPOS PAYMENT PROCESS

As with credit and charge cards, a debit card can be used to pay for most goods or services, whether obtained in a shop, garage, restaurant, solicitor's or insurance broker's office, or almost anywhere else. For the sake of simplicity, the principal parties to a debit card transaction will, in this chapter, be called 'the cardholder' and 'the retailer'; the bank or building society which has issued the debit card will be called 'the card issuer', and the bank which has undertaken responsibility to the retailer for his debit card transactions will be called 'the retailer acquirer'.

A cardholder, wishing to pay for goods or services at the retailer's premises, will present his card to the retailer, who will key the transaction details into his electronic till in the usual way, as well as into a separate terminal. Alternatively, a terminal may be connected to the till, and the transaction details are transferred into the terminal automatically. The cardholder's card is then 'swiped' through a slot in the terminal so that the terminal can 'read' the electronic information stored in the black 'magnetic stripe' on the back of the card.

The retailer will have a 'floor limit' of an amount specified by the retailer acquirer. The floor limit is set by the retailer acquirer in the light of the normal highest level of transactions likely to pass through the retailer's till. It acts as a fraud control mechanism on both the retailer and the cardholder, because the card issuer may be asked to authorise a transaction above the floor limit. Authorisation is obtained by telephone, and an authorisation number, or 'code', is given as evidence that the transaction has been approved. This is marked on the transaction receipt. Some terminals can make the authorisation call automatically, recording the authorisation code on the terminal receipt.

The retailer acquirer initially receives and considers requests for authorisation. If the transaction amount also exceeds a figure agreed between the retailer acquirer and the card issuer ('the interchange limit'), the retailer acquirer will telephone the card issuer for authorisation. As the cardholder is only permitted to use his debit card in the same way as a cheque (i.e. not to obtain credit when none has already been expressly agreed by the card issuer), the card issuer will be obliged to authorise the transaction if it would have been obliged to pay a cheque for the same amount; the card issuer may, in its discretion, authorise the transaction if there are insufficient funds or facilities on the cardholder's account.

The cardholder himself must then signify his authority for the transaction, since his account will be debited. This can be achieved by electronic signature, or 'PIN' (Personal Identification Number). In fact, most EFTPOS systems in England still involve the cardholder signing a paper voucher, and the retailer should check his signature against that on the debit card.

The retailer completes his part of the transaction by entering the final instruction in the terminal and giving the cardholder his normal till receipt and his copy of the debit card voucher (or a copy of the section of the terminal's tally roll which contains the transaction details).

At this point, in a 'pure' debit card scheme, the payment process will be completed by the retailer's terminal transmitting the transaction details to a remote processing unit, or the retailer acquirer collects the transaction details from a disk. At the processing unit, transaction information is separated out and a credit instruction is sent to the retailer's bank, and a debit instruction to the cardholder's bank. These instructions are sent electronically, and the computerised account management systems of the respective banks automatically credit and debit the relevant customer accounts.

The remote processing unit may be owned by the retailer acquirer, the retailer or a specialist processing company employed by one of them.

In practice, even when the terminal is 'on line' and the transaction details are transmitted immediately to the remote processing unit, accounts will not be credited and debited instantly. Where the terminal is 'off line', the transaction information is taken electronically ('polled') from the terminal at the end of each day, and transmitted electronically or sent by magnetic tape or disk to the remote processing unit. This is done overnight and processing is carried out the next day.

Whether they receive credit and debit instructions immediately or the day following the related transaction, the card issuer and the retailer acquirer can effect payment immediately, or they can defer the process. In practice, neither the retailer's account nor the cardholder's account will be credited until between one and four days after the transaction date, depending on the card scheme and the individual agreements made by the retailer acquirer and the card issuer.

If the retailer acquirer is not the retailer's bank, it will send the retailer's bank (sometimes by BACS) a credit for the retailer's account. The card issuer will always maintain a current account for the cardholder. A separate charge or credit card account may be maintained if no current account has been opened, but debit cards are only operated from a cheque book current account.

205

The last step in the payment process is settlement and payment between the card issuer and the retailer acquirer. The net position is established once each day through a centralised automated system, and payment is effected through BACS or CHAPS.

Figure 3 shows how the EFTPOS payment process may be represented in diagrammatic form.

Settlement and payment may take effect through an intermediary clearing system. Also there may be more, or less, third parties involved: for instance, the retailer acquirer may be the processor and will usually issue its own cards, so that it will sometimes be the card issuer in particular transactions; alternatively, a card issuer may not be a direct settlement member of the card scheme but may prefer to be 'sponsored' by and settle through another card issuer. Another variation would arise where a full card scheme member was not a settlement member of the payment system (e.g. BACS or CHAPS) and had to settle through an agent settlement member.

As an alternative to a multi-party scheme, a bank may operate its own debit card scheme for its own personal customers and retailer customers. In such a case, all the above procedures will be followed but customer accounts will be credited and debited without inter-bank settlement and payment being necessary. This is more likely to occur with charge and credit cards.

The role of the polling company is to direct the transaction 'traffic'. The retailer's terminal will be used for all electronic payment cards accepted by the retailer, provided they adhere to certain common technical and physical standards, and have an appropriately programmed magnetic stripe. The polling company polls all the card transactions retained by the terminal, sorts them and sends to the processor for each card scheme the polled transaction details for that processor's scheme.

By way of example, a garage may accept a specialist charge card processed by the petrol company's own processing subsidiary, a major credit card processed by one of the independent processors and a debit card processed by the garage company's bank. At the end of each day, the polling company will collect from the garage's terminal the transaction details for all charge, credit and debit card transactions retained in the terminal during the day. It will sort them overnight, together with the transaction information it has collected from all the other terminals it polls. In the morning, the polling company will transmit to the petrol

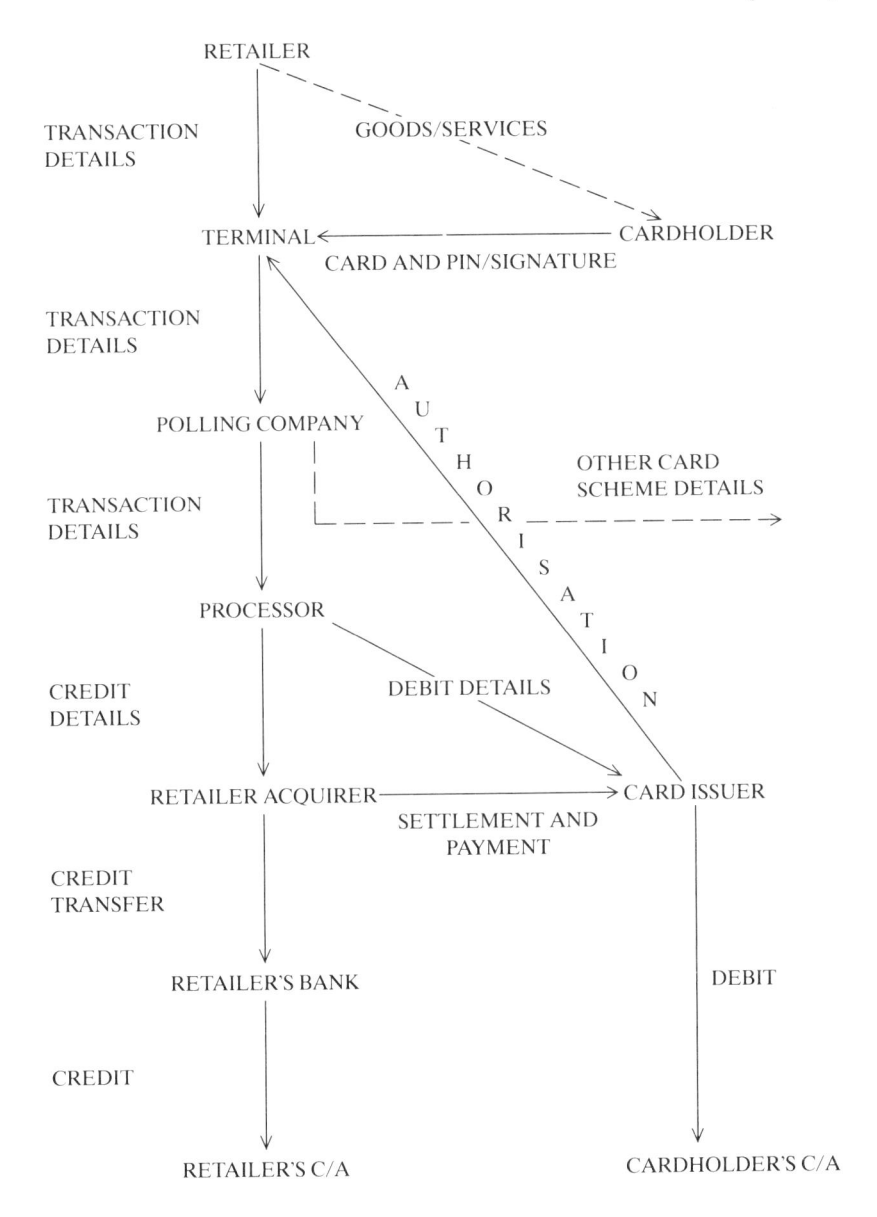

ELECTRONIC FUNDS TRANSFER AT POINT OF SALE (EFTPOS)

Figure 3   The EFTPOS Payment Process

LAW RELATING TO BANKING SERVICES

company's processing subsidiary all the charge card transaction details, to the independent processor all the credit card transaction details, and to the processing unit of the garage company's bank all the debit card transaction details.

Thus it will be observed that the only difference between debit, charge and credit cards schemes is in the cardholder's payment obligations (immediate for debit card, deferred for charge and credit cards). The Consumer Credit Act imposes some additional distinctions, in terms of whether or not a card is a credit-token and whether or not a regulated agreement is required, and the statutory consequences of those distinctions. These are discussed in **3.4** and **3.5** above.

The legal implications of an EFTPOS system revolve around the contractual relationships of the parties. **Figure 4** shows between which parties the contracts are usually made.

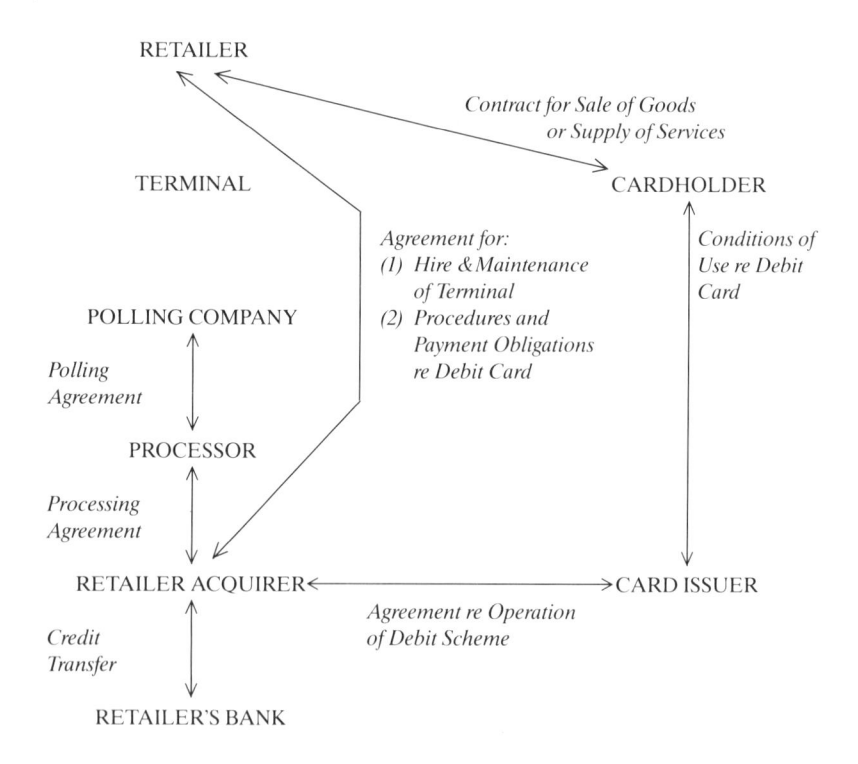

```
                RETAILER
              ↙   ↖
            ↙       ←─────────
          ↙                   ─────
        ↙         Contract for Sale of Goods
      ↙              or Supply of Services
                                        ↘
   TERMINAL                           CARDHOLDER
                                          ↑
              Agreement for:         Conditions of
              (1) Hire & Maintenance  Use re Debit
                  of Terminal         Card
  POLLING COMPANY
        ↑     (2) Procedures and
  Polling       Payment Obligations
  Agreement     re Debit Card
        ↓
   PROCESSOR
        ↑
  Processing
  Agreement
        ↓
   RETAILER ACQUIRER ←──────────────→ CARD ISSUER
        ↑            Agreement re Operation
  Credit             of Debit Scheme
  Transfer
        ↓
   RETAILER'S BANK
```

Figure 4   **EFTPOS Contractual Relationships**

208

ELECTRONIC FUNDS TRANSFER AT POINT OF SALE (EFTPOS)

As with any payment system, there must be a contractual link between the paying and payee banks: in a payment card scheme, they are the card issuer and the retailer acquirer. In the case of the cheque clearing, there is no formal contract, but the Clearing House Rules, supported by agreement on clearing fees and over one hundred years of cheque law, ensure that the clearing banks' obligations are well understood. More recent schemes have followed the same path of setting up clearing rules, although some schemes have required formal agreements to be signed by each clearing member.

As mentioned above, it is possible for a single bank to operate a card scheme by itself, issuing payment cards to its personal customers for use in retailers with which the bank has contracted directly as retailer acquirer. The legal issues discussed in **9.3** and **9.4** below will still apply in such a situation.

Payment card schemes depend for their success primarily on the cards being accepted in as large a number of outlets as possible. The issue of cards is the secondary factor, since banks and building societies have the necessary number of personal customers to ensure adequate use of the payment cards, provided the scheme is attractive to those customers. (However, the obvious link is that a retailer must be satisfied that enough cards will indeed be issued to ensure an acceptable level of usage in his premises.) One result of this is that the retailer acquirer will often organise the polling and processing facilities for its retailers and hire a terminal to them.

In theory, however, there is no reason why the retailer should not contract directly with third parties for these facilities.

9.3 THE RETAILER

Once he has contracted with the retailer acquirer in respect of an EFTPOS scheme, the retailer must accept payment from his customers by means of the scheme's debit card, if it is tendered. So long as the retailer keys into his terminal the correct transaction information and follows the required procedures for authorisation and submission of transaction details, he will be entitled to payment by his retailer acquirer in respect of the transaction. Payment will be by direct credit to his account with the retailer acquirer or, if applicable, by credit transfer (for instance, through BACS) to the retailer's bank.

The legal effect, as between the retailer and his customer (the cardholder), of 'payment' by debit card is to discharge the cardholder's obligations as to payment for the goods or services he obtains from the retailer (*Re Charge Card Services Limited* (1987)).

The facts of the case

A petrol station charge card scheme was operated by a company called Charge Card Services Limited. It sold its debts to a factoring company under a standard invoice discounting agreement. Its debts consisted mostly of the sums payable by the scheme's cardholders, people who had paid for fuel or other supplies at the petrol stations participating in the scheme.

Charge Card Services Limited went into liquidation, owing nearly £2,000,000, mostly to petrol stations in respect of scheme card transactions. The petrol stations claimed that:

(a) their acceptance of cards was only a conditional payment (as for cheques);

(b) on the company's insolvency, the petrol stations were entitled to direct payment from cardholders; and

(c) the liquidator was therefore obliged to pay the petrol stations the whole of any money he received from cardholders (as they paid their charge card accounts). These claims were disputed by the factoring company, which said it had bought the cardholders' debts.

Held (Millett J):

(1) by the contracts between them, the charge card company promised the petrol stations unconditional payment in respect of the supply of goods by the petrol stations if they accepted the scheme's charge cards; and the cardholders promised to pay the charge card company, on receipt of monthly statements, for their purchases from petrol stations.

(2) The legal effect of these agreements was to substitute the charge card company for the cardholders as the debtors of the petrol stations. A petrol station accepted the scheme's charge cards as a method of payment in place of payment by cash or cheque, and the cardholder's payment obligation was therefore completely discharged by the petrol station's acceptance of his card.

ELECTRONIC FUNDS TRANSFER AT POINT OF SALE (EFTPOS)

(3) The petrol stations had to claim in the charge card company's liquidation. The debts payable by the cardholders were still due to the company—but because the debts had been sold to and were owned by the factoring company, the cardholders' payments had to be passed on to the factoring company, which could also sue cardholders directly for outstanding card scheme debts.

One result of the decision in *Re Charge Card Services Limited* is that, if the retailer fails to obtain authorisation for a debit card transaction over his floor limit, and the card issuer rejects liability for payment under the 'chargeback' provisions of the card scheme, the retailer will not be legally entitled to pursue the cardholder for payment.

Chargeback is the process whereby the retailer acquirer can refuse to credit, or can re-debit the retailer's account for transactions which have not been properly submitted, e.g. with the correct information or within the procedural rules of the card scheme. In addition to errors attributable to the retailer or to the transaction processing, the retailer must bear the risk, through the chargeback process, of fraud or forgery by the cardholder (or the person purporting to be the cardholder). This is the same as if a customer's cheque in favour of the retailer had been returned unpaid by reason of forgery: the retailer could not sue for payment on the cheque, either against the drawee bank or against the named drawer.

The decision in *Charge Card Services* means that the retailer has no recourse in contract to the cardholder, either for the retailer's own processing or other errors, or for the cardholder's fraud. However, the retailer could pursue a customer in tort for fraud (whether by reason of forgery or otherwise), or simply for restitution of the goods or their value—it is only the contractual payment obligation which is lost.

As between the retailer and the retailer acquirer, who is liable for equipment failure? As with all payment card scheme questions, the answer depends on who is contractually responsible for the equipment.

If the retailer owns his terminal, or rents one from a third party, he will have no claim against the retailer acquirer if the terminal breaks down or transmits the wrong information through an electronic fault. Such a fault might render the retailer liable to the retailer aquirer if the latter suffered loss. If the breakdown or defect results in the retailer acquirer not receiving information about a card transaction, the retailer acquirer will not be liable to pay for the transaction.

The same principles will apply if the retailer carries out his own processing, or makes himself responsible to the retailer acquirer for having the polling or the processing carried out by third parties.

Where the retailer acquirer is responsible for providing the terminal, the polling or the processing, it will also be responsible to the retailer for any failure or defect in the terminal or in the polling or processing services. If the retailer acquirer provides these services under a standard term contract, it will be unable to exclude or limit its liability to the retailer for breach of contract, unless it is reasonable for the retailer acquirer to do so (s. 3 of the Unfair Contract Terms Act 1977).

The chargeback process effectively places on the retailer responsibility for the terminal, polling and processing. It may be that the retailer acquirer's reliance on third parties to supply the terminal maintenance, polling and processing will be sufficient to justify its exemption of liability to the retailer for those services, save to the extent that the retailer acquirer itself has recourse to the third party suppliers.

EFTPOS card schemes may require participants to have back-up equipment or a fall-back system in case their terminals or processing hardware or software becomes inoperative. For instance, if the retailer knows his terminal is not working, he can use payment card vouchers and pay them in over the retailer acquirer's branch counters or by post. The existence of back-up equipment or fall-back facilities will reduce the likelihood of legal claims arising, not only because the system will be more likely to remain operative, but also because the very existence of an alternative system will help to discharge a party's legal liability for equipment or processing failure.

9.4 THE CARDHOLDER

Most of the cardholder's rights and obligations have already been discussed.

A debit card is a credit-token, under s. 14(1)(b) of the Consumer Credit Act 1974. A full discussion of this, and of its consequences, is set out in **3.4, 8.2** and **8.3** above.

In summary, a debit card cannot be issued unsolicited (s. 51 of the 1974 Act), debit card agreements are exempt from regulation by the Consumer Credit Act (s. 89, Banking Act 1987), and debit card transactions are not, therefore, subject to s. 75 claims.

As with cash cards, the holder of a debit card can be made liable to the card issuer for the whole of a third party's use of the card without the holder's consent, since ss. 83 and 84 only apply to regulated agreements.

Contrast the £50 limit applicable to credit and charge cards (see **3.4** above). However, the imposition on a cardholder of liability for third party usage of his card may be subject to reasonableness under s. 3 of the Unfair Contract Terms Act 1977.

By transferring liability to the retailer the card issuer avoids a potential difficulty.

If the card issuer mistakenly refuses authorisation for a debit card transaction above the interchange limit, when the cardholder has sufficient funds on his current account, this would be both breach of contract by the card issuer and defamation of the cardholder in the same way as if the card issuer had dishonoured the cardholder's cheque wrongfully.

What is the legal position of the cardholder if the EFTPOS equipment or software fails in any way?

It seems doubtful that the retailer can be liable to the cardholder if, for any reason, the retailer's terminal is defective or the retailer cannot obtain authorisation. Although by displaying an EFTPOS scheme logo in his premises the retailer holds himself out as willing to accept payment by a particular debit card, the retailer cannot reasonably be expected to allow the cardholder to take away goods simply by leaving his card details. Nor can the retailer be faulted for having no 'fallback' process if the scheme does not provide for one.

Could the card issuer be liable? The card issuer may not be the supplier (directly or through third parties) of the retailer's terminal or his polling or processing. The card issuer will therefore have no control over defects in these.

It could be said that the card issuer represents to its cardholders, in giving them debit cards, that presentation of the cards in payment for goods or services to retailers who advertise acceptance of the cards, will result in a correctly completed, polled and processed EFTPOS transaction.

If this is correct, the cardholder's claim will be the same as if he were the holder of a cash card, who could not withdraw cash because of a failure in a cash dispensing machine—as to which, see **8.4** above.

In EFTPOS schemes where the cardholders authenticate debit card transactions by keying in a PIN, the retailer's terminal would appear to fall within the expression 'customer-activated EFT equipment'. This expression is used in the Jack Report, and the Jack Report White Paper recommends legislation to make a bank liable to a cardholder for the bank's customer-activated EFT equipment.

This could pose problems if the card issuer were made liable for a retailer's terminal, since this is a risk over which the card issuer would have no control, except through the retailer acquirer. Having said this, the Jack Report references were undoubtedly aimed at cash dispensing machines and the protection of personal customers, and it may be that any legislation will be limited to ATMs.

However, once a transaction has entered the retailer's terminal correctly, the cardholder can only be made liable to his card issuer for the correct amount of the transaction—any overcharge by the card issuer must be recouped from the retailer acquirer.

Where the retailer acquirer has no direct contractual relationship with the cardholder, it will not be liable to him for a failure in the EFTPOS system.

In the event of the retailer acquirer also being the card issuer, the legal position would again seem to be the same as for cash dispensing machines—see above.

Part III—Security

10 Insolvency

10.1 INTRODUCTION

It is salutary to note that in 1988, 7,286 companies went into insolvent liquidation. In 1989 the total rose to 7,966. The prospect of a customer borrower becoming insolvent is one of the driving forces behind a bank's decision to secure its loan. It is therefore vital to understand the impact that an insolvency would have in any particular case.

Many aspects of insolvency which do not directly affect a security are discussed in chapter 2 and many aspects are discussed under the specific securities. In this chapter the intention is to examine some general principles which will be relevant when security is taken, whatever the asset charged, and whether the chargor is an individual or corporate entity.

The first principle to grasp is that there are two quite separate insolvency regimes. One applies to individuals and the other to companies. There are, however, many similarities between them and some rules apply to both regimes.

The governing law is the Insolvency Act 1986 and the Insolvency Rules made pursuant thereto. Individuals are made bankrupt after the making of a 'bankruptcy order', and companies are 'wound up' after a resolution in general meeting or a court order to that effect. 'Insolvency' is a useful umbrella term which can be used to refer to either or both procedures.

10.2 PRIORITY OF CLAIMS IN AN INSOLVENCY

The law begins by asserting the principle of *pari passu* or equal treatment of creditors. A 'dividend' is declared of x pence in £, depending on the amount of money available, and the creditors paid accordingly. When a creditor makes a claim against an insolvent debtor, this process is known as 'proving' for his debt.

Insolvency law is very much a matter of some being more equal than others, however, as there are categories of claimant and, by and large, each category must be paid in full before any is paid to the next in order.

The categories for a company are:

(a) Creditors with fixed charges must be paid first from the proceeds of sale of the asset they have a charge over. Thus a bank with a charge over the company's land will receive the proceeds of sale of that land (after the costs of sale have been deducted). If there is insufficient from this source to pay off the bank, it must take what there is and prove in a lower category for the balance.

(b) The expenses of the liquidation.

(c) The preferential creditors. Section 386 and Schedule 6 defines these. They include:

(i) the Inland Revenue for the net amount of PAYE deductions which the company employer was liable to make from employee's wages over the previous 12 months but which have not yet been paid over to the Revenue.
(ii) the Department of Social Security for the equivalent Class 1 Social Security deductions and also for the company's own Class 1 liability, also over the previous 12 months.
(iii) the Customs and Excise for unpaid Value Added Tax over the previous 6 months and Betting Duties and Car Tax over the previous 12 months.
(iv) Occupational Pension Scheme trustees for sums owed under pension contribution obligations.
(v) employees for unpaid wages and salaries, limited to the previous 4 months and to £800 per person.
(vi) lenders who have lent money which has been used to pay employees who would otherwise be proving as preferential creditors. This is an example of the subrogation principle. Thus the bank practice of operating a wages account for customers who are employers.

The above time limits on the debts which may be proved as preferential are calculated backwards from the date of the resolution to wind up the company or from the date of the court order winding it up or from the date of the appointment of administrative receivers, as the case may be. If the creditor has a claim which is outside the time limit, he may still prove for this debt, but not as a preferential creditor.

(d) The floating chargeholders. If more than one, then in order of priority.

(e) The unsecured creditors, usually the trade creditors.

(f) For preferential and unsecured creditors, interest on the debt arising since the winding-up commenced. (Secured creditors are entitled to claim interest alongside their debt.)

(g) The shareholders can recover the nominal value of their shares and divide any surplus assets among themselves, in the order provided in the company's Memorandum and Articles of Association (preference, ordinary and deferred shares usually rank one after the other). This is only relevant in a member's voluntary winding up, when the company must be solvent.

The categories for an individual debtor are:

(a) Secured creditors. These must of course have fixed charges, as only companies can grant a floating charge.
(b) The expenses of the bankruptcy.
(c) Preferential creditors. These are the same as for company debtors above, *mutatis mutandis*. Social Security liability extends to include Class 2 and Class 4 contributions. The time limits run back from the date of the bankruptcy order. Again, a bank may be subrogated to an employee's claim if it has advanced money for wages.
(d) Unsecured creditors.
(e) Interest on debts for preferential and unsecured creditors. (Once again, secured creditors are entitled to their interest alongside their debt.)
(f) The bankrupt's spouse for debts owed to him or her.

It should be noted that if there is insufficient to pay a category of preferential or unsecured creditors, a dividend is declared, and each creditor in that category will receive x pence in the pound.

Secured creditors are unable to prove in the bankruptcy unless they release their charge. If the security is inadequate, the asset in question must be sold and proof made as unsecured (or preferential) creditor for the balance. If sale is not convenient, the asset can be valued for this purpose.

Third party security, such as a guarantee, is not affected by this rule. Thus the chargeholder may prove fully in the debtor's bankruptcy at the same time as calling on the guarantor to pay (see chapter 12).

10.3 VOLUNTARY ARRANGEMENTS AND ADMINISTRATION ORDERS

Certain 'schemes of arrangement' and 'compositions' specific to companies may be made under s. 425 of the Companies Act 1985. Individuals may execute a 'Deed of Arrangement' under the Deeds of Arrangement Act 1914. All of these, however, are little used in practice and are not discussed here.

A voluntary arrangement under the Insolvency Act 1986 (ss. 1–7 and 252–263) involves either a company or an individual making a proposal to creditors, whereby the creditors may agree to accept something less than full payment on their claims. They may do so as a voluntary arrangement, which avoids the considerable expense of a full bankruptcy or liquidation, and therefore there will be more funds available to pay the creditors.

The creditors will meet to consider the proposal and a decision is taken on a majority vote, so that some minority creditors may have the scheme forced on them. However, the salient point for present purposes is that this is not true of secured and preferential creditors, who must either be paid in full or individually agree to the scheme.

If the scheme is approved, it is implemented by a 'nominee' who must be an insolvency practitioner.

The important matters arising from the Administration Order procedure are discussed in chapter 16.

10.4 PREFERENCES AND TRANSACTIONS AT AN UNDERVALUE

When a company is wound up or an individual is made bankrupt, the liquidator or trustee in bankruptcy has a duty to realise the available assets and to distribute them according to the law. Some implications of the law dealing with exactly what assets are available have been discussed in chapter 2. Some others arise here. For instance, the assets may be swelled by the reclaiming of a preference, or of a transaction at an undervalue. If so, a secured creditor may be adversely affected. Note, however, that any adjustment to the debtor's assets in this way can only be made by court order, and in practice a liquidator or trustee in bankruptcy will be reluctant to incur the expense of seeking the order.

The Insolvency Act refers to 'associates' of company and individual debtors and to those 'connected' with a company. 'Associates' include employees and relatives. 'Connected persons' include directors and shadow directors of companies as well as associates of such persons. Companies in a group and their directors and associates are likely to be caught by these provisions.

Preferences

The law on preferences is contained in ss. 239 and 340. A preference is an example of the principle of *pari passu* treatment of creditors. It may consist of the debtor paying off a perfectly genuine debt shortly before he becomes insolvent, so that the recipient is better off than other creditors who have not been paid. It occurs when the debtor:

(a) does anything which has the effect of putting a person, who is a creditor or guarantor of the debtor's liabilities, into a position which, in the event of the debtor's bankruptcy or insolvent liquidation, will be better than the position of the creditor or guarantor would otherwise have been; and

(b) was influenced by a desire to produce the effect mentioned in (a) above. This motive is rebuttably presumed if the debtor and creditor were connected persons or associates; and

(c) the preference occurred when the debtor was unable to pay his debts and within the 'relevant time'. This is a six months' period prior to the commencement of the insolvency unless the debtor and creditor were connected persons or associates, in which case it is 24 months.

In *Re M.C. Bacon Ltd* (1990), these definitions were judicially considered for the first time. It was emphasised that the cases based on the old law were no longer pertinent. A preference under the new rules would only occur when the debtor positively and subjectively wished to improve the creditor's position in the event of the debtor's insolvency. In addition, this desire must have influenced the debtor's decision to enter into the transaction in question (in this case, granting a charge to a bank). However, it need not have been the decisive factor, merely one of the factors. It was also held that the relevant time (for considering whether there had been a preference) was the time when the decision was made to grant the charge, not the time when the charge was granted.

Illustrations

The preference rules may affect a bank in the following situations:

(a) A customer repays his unsecured debt to the bank. He later becomes insolvent, the repayment is declared a preference of the bank and the court orders it to be repaid to the liquidator.

(b) A debt secured by a guarantee is repaid and the guarantor is released. The principal debtor becomes insolvent, the repayment is declared a preference of the bank and the court orders it to be returned to the liquidator. This is dealt with by a suitable clause in the guarantee form to preserve the guarantor's liability (see chapter 12).

(c) The same circumstances as in (b), except that the intention is held to be to prefer the guarantor. Where the debtor and the guarantor are connected persons, such as companies in a group, this intention is presumed. The court may order the guarantor to pay or it may order the bank to do so, in which case it may also order that the guarantor's obligation to the bank be revived. However, a bank may be protected from an order by the proviso that the court cannot make an order against a recipient who took in good faith, for value and without notice of the relevant circumstances, unless he was a party to the transaction, or the repayment was in respect of a preference given to the recipient at a time when he was a creditor of the debtor. Once again, a suitably drafted clause will preserve the bank's claim against the guarantor.

(d) An unsecured debt is secured by a charge taken directly from the debtor, who later becomes insolvent. The bank is now in a better position in the insolvency than it otherwise would have been, and the court may declare the giving of the security to be a preference and has power to void the charge.

A question which is of interest to bankers is this. By putting pressure on a customer to pay or secure an unsecured debt, and by the customer reluctantly then making payment or granting security, is the customer influenced by a desire to produce the effect of the preference? The Cork Committee Report, which led to the Insolvency Act, considered that putting pressure on a debtor should provide a defence, and the decision in *Re M.C. Bacon Ltd* (1990) affirms that 'a man can choose the lesser of two evils without desiring either'.

Floating charges granted by companies to secure pre-existing debts are subject to a related, but quite different, rule contained in s. 245 and are discussed in chapter 16.

Transactions at an undervalue

The rules in ss. 238 and 339 are designed to enable the court to order the return of assets given away by the debtor over a fairly long period before the insolvency begins. The definition is:

(a) the debtor makes a gift or enters into a transaction whereby he (or some other person) receives significantly less value than he gives; and
(b) this takes place:

    (i) for companies, within two years before the winding-up commences, and at a time when the company was unable to pay its debts, or it became so as a result of the transaction (this is rebuttably presumed if the persons are connected);
    (ii) for individuals, within five years before the bankruptcy petition. Inability to pay debts need not be proved if it occurred in the two years before the petition. Otherwise this must be proved, although it is rebuttably presumed if the parties were associates.

No order may be made in respect of a company debtor if it entered into the transaction in good faith and for the purpose of carrying on its business, if at the time there were reasonable grounds for believing the transaction would benefit the company.

Transactions at an undervalue may, in theory, affect a bank in the following circumstances:

(a) G guarantees D's debt. G becomes insolvent. G made a transaction at an undervalue when he gave the guarantee to the bank. However, the Act permits the consideration to move to another, in this example from the bank to D.

(b) A bank has made an unsecured loan to D. The bank later takes a charge from D who then becomes insolvent. Any consideration given by the bank in return for the charge is past consideration, however, which is invalid in law. This point was argued unsuccessfully by the liquidator in

Re M.C. Bacon Ltd (1990). It was held that the consideration for the charge was the forbearance the bank showed in not calling in the overdraft at that time. Furthermore, the creation of the charge did not deplete the company's assets, but merely appropriated them to a particular creditor.

10.5 TRANSACTIONS DEFRAUDING CREDITORS

Sections 423-425 empower the court to make an order reversing a transaction which amounts to a fraudulent undervalue. This will be more difficult to prove than a transaction at an undervalue as it requires that the debtor made the transaction for the purpose of:

(a) putting assets out of reach of someone who has or will have a claim against him; or
(b) otherwise prejudicing such a person.

The provision is broader than the transaction at an undervalue, however, in that no time limits are set. Indeed, an order can be made even if no insolvency ever occurs.

This provision is generally helpful to a secured creditor, as the forerunner to it (s. 172 of the Law of Property Act 1925) established the right of a mortgagee of land to void a lease granted by a mortgagor in contravention of the terms of the mortgage deed (*Lloyds Bank Ltd* v *Marcan* (1973)).

10.6 EXTORTIONATE CREDIT TRANSACTIONS

Sections 244 and 343 give the court wide powers to reopen a transaction whereby the debtor obtained credit, if this was within three years before the commencement of the winding up or bankruptcy and the transaction was extortionate. The conditions are that either:

(a) it requires grossly exorbitant payments to be made; or
(b) it grossly contravenes ordinary principles of fair dealing.

The court has the power to make a variety of orders, including a forfeiture of security held by a lender.

Under a similar provision contained in the Consumer Credit Act 1974, an interest rate of 48% was held not to be extortionate (*Ketley* v *Scott* (1981)).

11 Taking Security from Individuals

11.1 INTRODUCTION

Whenever a bank takes a charge from a customer to secure a loan to that customer, the law now places certain duties on the bank, such as not to mislead the customer as to the effect of the charge. These duties will be considerably more onerous when the bank is taking a charge or a guarantee to secure a loan which is being made to another person.

The duties to be discussed are:

(a) Not to exert (or be involved in the exerting by another of) undue influence on the giver of the security.
(b) Not to misrepresent the effect of giving the security or any of the circumstances surrounding the giving of it.
(c) To advise the giver of the effect of giving the security (or to see that he obtains advice from elsewhere).

The duty, such as it exists, to advise a potential guarantor of matters concerning the principal debtor's account is discussed in chapter 12.

11.2 UNDUE INFLUENCE

It is a general principle of law that where one party to an agreement has been subject to the strong influence of the other party, so that he does not form an independent judgment as to whether to enter into the agreement, then the transaction becomes voidable for undue influence, i.e. the influenced party may choose to void it if he wishes. This defence is to be distinguished from that of duress, whereby physical force or the threat of it is used to obtain the other party's agreement. The legal effect of duress is also to make the transaction voidable.

The defence of undue influence is most obviously raised when one party has given something valuable to the other, either outright or by sale at an undervalue. This does not directly concern banks, who are rarely the recipients of such bounty. The defence is most commonly raised against banks in two scenarios:

225

(1) G provides a guarantee to secure the bank's loan to a relative, often a son of G. G's son squanders the money, the bank claims from G, and it is then argued that G's son had unduly influenced an elderly G.

(2) D approaches the bank for loan finance. The bank requires security which is available in the form of D's house. The house is jointly owned by D and Mrs D, or Mrs D has a right of occupation or overriding interest, and thus the bank requires Mrs D to execute the mortgage deed or a deed of postponement. D squanders the money, the bank seeks a possession order over the matrimonial home, whereupon Mrs D alleges that she was induced to sign by D's influence.

It is now clear that for a defendant to raise undue influence against a bank, two separate factors must both be present:

(a) The transaction in question must have been manifestly disadvantageous to him.
(b) Undue influence must either:
  (i) have been applied by the bank itself; or
  (ii) have been applied by someone acting as agent of the bank.

Illustrations

National Westminster Bank plc v *Morgan* (1985) HL. Mr and Mrs M owned a house which was charged to a building society. The mortgage payments fell into arrears and the society obtained a possession order. The bank was asked by Mr M to provide short-term bridging finance to pay off the society, pending money being raised from other sources. The bank had also made business loans to Mr M. The bank manager visited the Ms' house and Mrs M agreed to sign the charge form so long as the house was not used as security for the business loans. To this the manager agreed, although the charge form included the standard all-monies clause (see chapter 13). The bridging loan was defaulted upon and the bank sought a possession order, which was resisted by Mrs M on the grounds of undue influence. Her defence failed, as giving the charge to the bank was not disadvantageous to her. She was about to lose her house in any case when she signed the mortgage deed and the bank did not seek to rely on the all-monies clause. It also seems that the bank did not exert undue influence on Mrs M and neither did anyone acting as its agent.

Lloyds Bank v *Bundy* (1974) CA. Mr B provided a series of guarantees, backed by charges on his sole property, to secure the bank's business loans to his son. It was a feature of the case that the bank allowed the loan to increase beyond the agreed limit (and the limit on the guarantee) and then approached Mr B to increase his limit. Mr B was elderly, did not understand business matters well and placed a degree of trust in his bank. When the son defaulted, the bank sought a possession order against Mr B which the court refused on the basis that, due to the trust placed in the bank by Mr B, the bank had failed to recognise a conflict of interest. It should have declined to accept the guarantee until Mr B had obtained independent advice.

Avon Finance Co. Ltd v *Bridger* (1985) CA. Mr and Mrs B bought a retirement home, paid for with their savings, a building society mortgage loan and funds provided by their son. Unknown to Mr and Mrs B, their son defrayed the cost of his contribution by raising a loan from the plaintiff lender, which was secured by a second mortgage on Mr and Mrs B's new home. The son took his parents to the lender's solicitor's office and persuaded them to sign the charge forms by exerting influence over them (he also misled them as to the nature of the documents they were signing). The son defaulted on the loan and the lender sought a possession order of Mr and Mrs B's home. This was refused as the lender had used the son as its agent, and he had unduly influenced his parents in obtaining their signatures for the lender.

Coldunell Ltd v *Gallon* (1986) CA. Mr and Mrs G occupied a retirement bungalow which was registered in Mr G's name. Their son wished to raise short-term business finance, which the plaintiff lender was prepared to supply with the security of a charge on Mr and Mrs G's home. It was arranged that Mr G would grant a charge over his home and that Mrs G would sign a consent form. The lender's solicitors prepared the documents and intended to post them to Mr and Mrs G, along with letters advising them to obtain independent advice. Somehow the son got hold of the envelopes, withheld the letters and persuaded his parents to sign the forms. He soon defaulted on the loan and the lender sought a possession order against Mr and Mrs G. This was granted since, although the son undoubtedly exerted undue influence, he was not acting as the lender's agent. There was no evidence that the solicitors had handed over the envelopes to the son (he might have intercepted them at the parents' home, although he did not live there) and it was suggested that even had the solicitors done so, they would not have been using him as an agent but as a messenger.

Bank of Credit and Commerce International SA v *Aboody* (1989) CA. Mr A set up a company and persuaded Mrs A to be an officer of it. She took no part in business affairs, however, and signed any document put before her by Mr A. The matrimonial home was in Mrs A's sole name. Mr A arranged a bank loan for the company which was to be secured by a charge on Mrs A's house, and she obediently signed the necessary forms. The company defaulted on the loans and a possession order was sought against Mrs A. The court granted this as it found that, although undue influence had been present, Mrs A had enjoyed the benefits of the continued existence of the company for some time after the charge was given. There was thus no manifest disadvantage proved.

It must be noted that in certain relationships (none of which applied in the cases above) there is an automatic presumption of undue influence. These include solicitor/client, physician/patient, trustee/beneficiary, spiritual adviser/disciple and parent/offspring. In each relationship, it is the former who is presumed to influence the latter. In the last example, the offspring would have to be 18 years in order to have the legal title to property and in order to give a valid guarantee.

In the above relationships the presumption is rebuttable; the onus is on the bank to prove that there has not been any undue influence. In other cases the other party must prove the undue influence. It is widely believed that if he obtains independent expert advice before signing the relevant document, and signs in the presence of the giver of the advice, a defence of undue influence will not later be available to him. This may or may not be correct, as it seems possible that the influence of the stronger party might sometimes pervade the session with the advice-giver (imagine for instance a youthful follower of a powerful religious sect).

Finally, it is pertinent to recall that in the *Morgan* case, Lord Scarman issued a warning to the effect that the law leaves the dividing line, between mere folly on the one hand and unconscionable transactions on the other hand, deliberately uncertain. 'There is no precisely defined law setting limits to the equitable jurisdiction of a court to relieve against undue influence.'

11.3 MISREPRESENTATION

In this context, misrepresentation may take either of two forms.

(1) Some misrepresentation is made to the provider of the security which induces him to sign, something he would not otherwise have done.

The effect is akin to undue influence in that the victim may void the transaction. Either the bank must make the misrepresentation, or someone acting as its agent.

Illustrations

Kings North Trust Ltd v *Bell* (1986) CA. Mr B wished to buy a business property and approached the lender for bridging finance, pending the sale of another property. Part of the security for the loan was a charge on Mr B's house in which Mrs B had an overriding interest. The lender, in view of the *Boland* decision (see chapter 13), required Mrs B's signature on the mortgage deed, as well as that of Mr B. The lender's solicitors sent the documents to solicitors acting for Mr and Mrs B's company, who took them to Mr B to have signed by him; they were left with Mr B so that he could get them signed by Mrs B. Mrs B was accustomed to signing any document relating to their company that Mr B put before her. On this occasion, Mr B misled his wife by neglecting to mention the purpose of the loan. Rather harshly, the court considered this amounted to fraudulent misrepresentation by Mr B, which affected the lender since Mr B had acted as their sub-agent. Mr B defaulted on the loan and the court refused the lender's application for a possession order of the matrimonial home.

Lloyds Bank plc v *Waterhouse* (1990) CA. W's son approached the bank for funds to enable him to buy a farm. The bank took a charge on the farm but also required a guarantee from W. This guarantee was in standard form and therefore was described to be security for any borrowing the son made from the bank (known as the 'all-monies' clause). The son did borrow large amounts beyond what was necessary to purchase the farm. When the bank called on W to pay, he revealed that he was illiterate and thus had no idea of the written terms of the form. Furthermore, W had asked the bank about the terms of the guarantee and had been told that the purpose of the guarantee was to provide security for the loan, which was made to enable the son to buy the farm. It was held that W would not have signed the guarantee form had he known its terms made him liable for all borrowings his son might make from the bank. Accordingly the bank was unable to rely on the guarantee.

(2) Some negligent misstatement is made by a representative of the bank, the effect of which falls short of influencing the person to sign the

document but which does lead him to misunderstand the effect of it. The security will not be voidable but the bank will be liable in negligence.

Illustration

Cornish v *Midland Bank plc* (1985) CA. Mr and Mrs H purchased a farm and approached the bank for finance to renovate it. The bank agreed to do so, subject to a limit of £2,000 and to it taking a second mortgage. Mrs H was left with the impression that the bank had agreed not to lend more than the limit, whilst in reality the charge form included the standard 'all-monies' clause. Furthermore, she was unaware that she had executed any form of mortgage. Soon after, Mr and Mrs H separated (to the bank's knowledge), and Mr H alone operated the account until it was overdrawn well beyond the limit. The court held that the mortgage was valid but that the bank had been negligent in misleading Mrs H as to the limit, and it was therefore liable to compensate her for her loss resulting from this. It was also suggested that the bank owed her a duty not to allow Mr H to continue to borrow on the account and to notify her if he did. Furthermore, as she was also a personal customer, the bank owed her a duty to advise her as to the nature and effect of the document she was about to sign.

11.4 ADVICE

It has been noted that there were dicta in the *Cornish* case to the effect that a bank does have a duty to advise a provider of security, if that person is a personal customer of the bank. It is clear, however, that no such duty is owed to someone who is not a customer (*O'Hara* v *Allied Irish Banks Ltd* (1985)).

The duty to advise a customer was affirmed in *Midland Bank plc* v *Perry* (1987) CA. The effect of failing in that duty is the same as in *Cornish*; the security remains valid but the bank is liable in negligence to the customer who it should have advised.

11.5 *NON EST FACTUM*

In order to lose the benefit of a security or to be liable in negligence due to undue influence, misrepresentation or failure to advise, the bank must be culpable in some way. If, for example, there was undue influence but the person exerting it was not acting as an agent of the bank, the security is valid. The defence of *non est factum* is different in that a totally innocent third party can be prejudiced by it.

In effect the signatory of the document is saying that this was not his action. To be successful, this will require three elements:

(a) The signatory was unable to read the document, e.g. through blindness or illiteracy. In *Saunders* v *Anglia Building Society* (1971) HL, the disability was due to the signatory's glasses being broken.

(b) The document which was signed was fundamentally different from that which the signatory thought he was signing. This will perhaps result from a fraudulent misrepresentation by the person who stands to gain from the security being granted, such as a principal debtor who is deceiving a relative into signing what is really a guarantee form.

(c) The signatory was not negligent in signing the document. Thus in the ordinary case he should read it. In more exceptional circumstances, he should wait until he has his glasses available and then read it, or (if he is blind or illiterate) he should seek out some trustworthy person to read it to him before he signs it (*Saunders* v *Anglia Building Society* (1971) HL).

It follows that only in the most extreme circumstances will a signatory be able to dispute liability on a document on the basis of *non est factum*, but that where he is able to do so as a result of a third party's fraud, a bank cannot defend itself by pointing out that it acted properly.

12　Guarantees

12.1　INTRODUCTION

The word guarantee is used somewhat loosely in English legal terminology. It is a familiar term in the consumer durables market where it actually refers to a warranty made by the manufacturer of the goods, in favour of the ultimate purchaser. In law, this is not a true guarantee at all.

In the banking context, guarantees may be made by a bank in favour of a third party to guarantee payment by the bank's corporate customer of some liability to that third party. A performance bond is an example of such a bank guarantee. We are not concerned with these in this work.

Banks also take guarantees to secure loans they make to customers. The guarantor may typically be a relation of a personal borrower or a director of a company borrower. Such guarantees are usually executed on standard forms, which the bank prepares and which invariably include an indemnity clause. They then become indemnity contracts as well as guarantee contracts. This is reflected in the standard form contracts used by banks where the agreement is governed by the 'truth in lending' provisions of the Consumer Credit Act 1974; these documents are headed 'Guarantee and Indemnity'.

12.2　GUARANTEES AND INDEMNITIES

The distinction between a guarantee and an indemnity is significant for the following reasons:

(1) A guarantor is agreeing to pay if the principal debtor does not, whereas an indemnifier agrees to pay in any case. This is sometimes described as secondary liability of the guarantor and primary liability of the indemnifier. A bank creditor can demand payment from the indemnifier directly but must ask the principal debtor to repay before turning to the guarantor. A bank would have no objection to doing so, but what is more significant is that the bank cannot demand that the guarantor pay if the principal debtor is not liable in law to pay.

233

Illustration

Coutts & Co. v *Browne-Lecky* (1947). A bank had lent money to a person under 18, taking a guarantee as security. The loan was irrecoverable due to the minor's lack of capacity, and the guarantee was therefore also not enforceable without a clause specifically making the guarantor liable in these circumstances.

Section 2 of the Minors Contracts Act 1987 now provides that a guarantor will be liable even if the loan is irrecoverable from a minor. However, a loan made to an organisation acting *ultra vires* its powers can render a guarantee similarly unenforceable.

The above examples must be distinguished from those cases where the guarantor lacks capacity to enter into the guarantee contract. A guarantee from a minor is void for this reason under the Minors Contracts Act 1987, and a guarantee given by an organisation will be void when it acts beyond its powers.

(2) Section 4 of the Statute of Frauds 1677 requires that, to be enforceable, a guarantee (but not an indemnity) be in writing and signed by the guarantor. Banks are naturally keen to comply with these requirements for evidential purposes in any case. A guarantee (and indemnity), provided in connection with a credit agreement regulated by the Consumer Credit Act 1974, must be in properly executed written form, otherwise it will be unenforceable without a court order. The Act specifies in some detail the precise nature of the form to be used.

12.3 CONSIDERATION

Any contract not under seal requires consideration in order to be valid. A guarantor often makes his promise to pay and receives nothing in return. This does not matter, as the law only requires that consideration moves from the promisee. Thus the guarantor makes his promise to the bank which then makes its loan to its customer, the principal debtor. There is a potential problem where the money was lent before the guarantee was taken, as this could mean that the loan amounts to 'past consideration' and is therefore invalid. In this case, the consideration may consist of continuing the account, or even refraining from action to recover the debt; the requirement for consideration may be satisfied by a forbearance for a reasonable time (*Fullerton* v *Provincial Bank of Ireland* (1903) HL). It is the practice of banks to state these alternatives on the guarantee form. The legal requirement to state the consideration was abolished in 1854, and it is suggested that the statement achieves nothing if in fact the bank has not provided any consideration. If lack of consideration is ever a problem, the guarantee contract could simply be executed under seal. A $12\frac{1}{2}$% stamp duty on such deeds was abolished in 1971.

12.4 DUTY TO A GUARANTOR BEFORE THE GUARANTEE IS SIGNED

It is well established that a guarantee contract is not *uberrimae fidei*, and therefore there is no duty on the bank to warn a potential guarantor of circumstances about the principal debtor's account that might make the former think better of signing the form.

Illustration

Cooper v *National Provincial Bank Ltd* (1946). The principal debtor's account could be operated by her spouse, who was an undischarged bankrupt. The guarantor knew nothing of this and sought to have the guarantee contract set aside. The court declined to do so.

However, in *Hamilton* v *Watson* (1845) HL, it was stated that the bank should disclose 'anything that might not naturally be expected to take place between the ... debtor and creditor, to the effect that his [the surety's] position shall be different from that which the surety might naturally expect.' In *Cooper*, the court considered that the facts were within the category of what might be naturally expected. It appears, therefore, that the bank's duty to disclose is limited to extreme circumstances.

The above issue is to be distinguished from the bank's possible duty to see that the guarantor obtains independent advice (the undue influence defence), its duty not to misrepresent the effect of the guarantee document and its possible duty to explain the meaning of the document—all of which are discussed in chapter 11, since the principles can be applied to joint mortgages as well as to guarantees.

12.5 DEMAND, DETERMINATION AND THE LIMITATION ACT

Once a guarantee is signed, a contingent liability arises for the guarantor. Subject to any financial limit stated on the form, the guarantor will usually not know how much he will eventually be liable for, or when he will have to pay. It is possible that he will never have to pay anything.

The answer to these matters lies in the determination of the guarantee. When the form is signed, unless a temporal limit is stated, a liability is established which might crystallise any time in the future. This occurs when the guarantee is determined, which will commonly be either when the bank makes demand of the guarantor (assuming the form provides for this) or when the guarantor gives notice to determine. He is then liable for whatever the principal debtor owes the bank at that time, which may of course be nothing.

It follows that a contingent guarantee liability can continue for decades before determination. This does not fall foul of the Limitation Act 1980, since it has been held that the statutory time limit for enforcement of contracts (six years) does not begin to run until demand has been made (*Bradford Old Bank Ltd* v *Sutcliffe* (1918) CA).

12.6 JOINT GUARANTEES

Bank guarantee forms invariably provide for two or more guarantors of the same debt to be jointly and severally liable; the reasons for extending the liability of guarantors in this way are partly historical, but there is a remaining advantage in that on the death of one guarantor, his estate will assume liability instead of liability terminating on his death.

There are a number of cases which illustrate the principle that the liability of joint (or joint and several) guarantors is mutually dependent:

James Graham & Co. (Timber) Ltd v *Southgate Sands* (1985) CA. Where joint guarantors appear to have all signed but one signature later proves to be forged, all escape liability.

National Provincial Bank Ltd v *Brackenbury* (1906). It was intended that four persons would be joint guarantors; one declined to sign, and the other three (who had signed) were not liable.

Ellesmere Brewery Company v *Cooper* (1896). It was intended that four guarantors would each be liable up to specified limits. One altered his limit to a lower figure after the others had signed, with the result that none of them were liable at all.

Smith v *Wood* (1929). The release of one guarantor will discharge the others. This is not so, however, if the form includes a clause permitting release of a guarantor.

The logic underlying the above decisions, which might appear rather harsh for the bank creditor, is based on a co-guarantor's right of contribution (*Scholefield Goodman & Sons Ltd* v *Zyngier* (1986) PC). This means that if the co-guarantors each guarantee the same debt, any one can be obliged to pay the creditor (subject to his limit, if any), but if he has then paid more than his share, he has a right to be indemnified by the others. The appropriate shares will be equal ones, unless the limits vary, in which case the shares are proportionate to the limits (*Ellesmere Brewery Company* v *Cooper* (1896)).

12.7 STANDARD BANK GUARANTEE TERMS

The common law seeks to protect a guarantor, who often gains nothing from providing his promise to pay another's debt, by conferring on him a number of rights. Under the freedom of contract principle, however, the law recognises his right to give up those rights if he so chooses. Banks have long taken advantage of this principle by drafting standard form contracts which have just this effect, so far as is possible. Common law also provides that any clause in a contract which restricts the guarantor's rights is to be construed in his favour (*First National Finance Corporation* v *Goodman* (1983) CA). There is also a possibility that certain clauses may be rendered invalid by statute, namely s. 3(2) of the Unfair Contract Terms Act 1977.

The following standard clauses will not necessarily be found in every agreement, and the list is not exhaustive. Sometimes two or more of the following are combined in a single clause. References are made below to the Principal Debtor ('PD') and to the Guarantor ('G'):

Consideration

This is discussed in **12.3** above.

Demand

The guarantor's liability to pay commences with demand being made by the bank. This is discussed in **12.5** above. The demand is deemed to have been made the day after it is posted to the guarantor.

'All monies'

A guarantee of a specific debt would be discharged by repayment of that debt, and any further borrowing would not be secured; it is often important for a bank to know that all overdrafts, loans, guarantee liabilities, interest and charges owing by the principal debtor, are covered by the security.

Continuing security

Clayton's case would have the effect of discharging a current account debt in an active account, even if it never moved into credit. It is therefore made clear that the guarantee is continuing in nature and secures present and future loans.

Notice to determine

The continuing security clause will go on to say that if the guarantor wishes to determine the guarantee, he must give three months notice to the bank. This negates the common law position whereby a guarantor is entitled to instant determination (*Beckett* v *Addyman* (1882) CA). Again, at common law, notice of death of the guarantor will determine the guarantee instantly (*Bradbury* v *Morgan* (1862)). However, the bank can include a provision to the effect that notice of death will not determine it, and the personal representatives of the guarantor will have to give three months notice to do so. No attempt is made by banks to require a three month notice period in the event of the guarantor's mental capacity or bankruptcy. It seems unlikely that either would be effective. On the question of whether a bank is entitled to increase its loan to the principal debtor, during the three months period after notice to determine is given, and to hold the guarantor (or his personal representatives) liable for the full amount, the decided cases are not conclusive (*Coulthart* v *Clementson* (1879) and *Lloyd's* v *Harper* (1880) CA). It is generally agreed, however, that, in the unlikely event of a bank doing so, this would be within its legal rights.

The whole debt

The demand clause will specify that the guarantor will be liable for all monies owed to the bank by the principal debtor, and then go on to say the amount recoverable shall not exceed a given limit (if it is a limited guarantee). The purpose of this approach is to negate two common law rights of the guarantor. First, he would otherwise be entitled to take a proportionate part of any direct security that the bank is holding.

Illustration

Assume the bank had lent £2,000 and had taken a direct mortgage from PD worth £1,000 and a guarantee from G, limited to £1,000. Without the benefit of this clause, when G paid £1,000 to the bank, he would be entitled to £500 worth of the direct mortgage, since he had paid half PD's debt. The bank would then recover a total of £1,500 from its securities. With the benefit of the clause, the bank can refuse to give up any part of the direct mortgage unless it receives the full £2,000 from G. Thus the bank will recover £2,000 from its securities.

The second benefit is as follows. *Re Sass* (1896). G had guaranteed PD's account up to a limit of £300. PD became bankrupt when his account was overdrawn £755. The bank demanded £300 from G. This was paid and placed by the bank in a separate account, whereupon the bank proved in PD's bankruptcy for the full £755. The rule against double-proof prevents the bank from claiming this and G claiming his £300 from PD's trustee (*Ex parte European Bank* (1871)). It was held that the effect of the clause was to permit the bank to claim the full £755 and to prevent G from claiming at all, unless he chose to exceed his limit and to pay the full £755. This is beneficial for the bank if a dividend is paid by PD's trustee, so that (for example), if the bank received a dividend of 60p in the pound on its claim of £755, it obtains £453 from that source, which together with the £300 from G, would see it nearly repaid.

Variation, release, compounding and granting time

If the bank materially varies its agreement with PD, such as increasing a fixed rate of interest, this will discharge G's liability at common law (*Burnes v Trade Credits Ltd* (1981)). If the bank releases other securities it is holding to secure PD's debt (the effect of which may be to prejudice G's position if he loses his right of contribution), then G's liability is reduced by the amount of the lost contribution (*Wulff v Jay* (1872)). If the bank compounds the debt, i.e. accepts less than full payment, G's liability is discharged at common law (*Perry v National Provincial Bank of England* (1910)). Similarly, at common law, G is discharged when the bank grants time to PD (*Polak v Everett* (1876)). All of the above can be dealt with, however, by a suitably drafted clause.

Continuation of the principal debtor's account

There is a danger that continuation of the account after determination of the guarantee would lead to a technical repayment by PD under the rule in *Clayton*'s case, and thus a discharge of G's liability. The clause declares that subsequent credits into the account will not reduce the liability of G, even if the account is not ruled off. Such a clause was tested, and found effective, in *Westminster Bank Ltd v Cond* (1940)).

Restriction on guarantor taking security from principal debtor

If G were free to do so, the bank's claim against PD would be subordinated. However, if G contravenes the clause and does take a charge from PD, it seems the charge is valid. The clause will therefore go on to say that G's liability to the bank in these circumstances will be increased by the amount of the value of the charge. This is helpful if the guarantee is limited.

Independent security

In case a second guarantee from the same guarantor was construed to be a replacement of the earlier, this clause clarifies the position. Equally, any other security for the same debt will not limit the guarantee.

Changes and amalgamations of parties

If the bank changes its name or amalgamates with another, G may be discharged at common law (*First National Finance Corp v Goodman* (1983) CA). Where there is a change in the constitution of a partnership, there is a statutory provision (s. 18 of the Partnership Act 1890) which revokes (as to future debts) guarantees given by partnerships and also guarantees given to secure the debts of partnerships, unless the contrary is expressed. Naturally, the clause does so. The clause cannot, however, make a future partner liable, and therefore when a partnership guarantor admits a new partner, a fresh guarantee should be taken.

Conclusive evidence

For procedural convenience, in the event of litigation against G, it is provided that the extent of G's liability can be proved by a bank statement certified as correct by a bank employee of a certain seniority (usually Regional Manager). This would not otherwise be admissible evidence in court but it has been held that the clause is effective, due to the special reputation bankers enjoy for honesty (*Bache & Co. (London) Ltd* v *Banque Vernes et Commerciale de Paris SA* (1973) CA). Also, any admission of liability by, or on behalf of, PD will state to be binding on G. This is helpful if PD is insolvent and his trustee, or (if PD is a company) his administrative receiver or liquidator, accepts the bank's proof of PD's debt.

Avoided payments by PD will be ineffective

The preference and '12 month rule' provisions of the Insolvency Act 1986 are explained elsewhere. The concern is that PD will settle his debt with the bank, and the guarantee is determined with G's liability appearing to be nil. Soon after, PD is made bankrupt (or goes into liquidation), and his trustee (or liquidator) reclaims the payment. The clause proclaims that G's liability will remain in these circumstances and that the bank is entitled to retain the security for a period of 25 months (24 months being the maximum relation back period for preferences). It seems that the bank could in any case claim against G but the clause removes any possible doubt. Were the bank to permit the guarantee document to be destroyed when PD repays, however, it is doubtful whether the clause would assist. As a buttress to the above, it is provided that the guarantee document permanently remains the property of the bank.

12.8 THE GUARANTOR'S RIGHTS

Most of these are carefully removed by the clauses explained above. Those that remain are:

Right to know the extent of his liability

The authority for this is obscure but it is widely accepted that G can at any time and, presumably with any reasonable frequency, insist on knowing the current debt owed by PD to the bank. This seems to be an exception to the bank's duty of secrecy to its customer, PD; presumably as under compulsion of law or implied consent from PD. The bank should not, however, give more information than G needs. Thus if PD's debt is greater than the limit on G's liability, G should simply be told that his liability is fully relied upon, and if PD's account is in credit, G should be told he has no liability at present. Where the loan agreement is regulated by the Consumer Credit Act 1974, G also has a statutory right to a statement of PD's account (as well as to copies of the security document and the loan agreement) on written request with a fee of 50 pence. The bank may refuse to comply if PD at that time owes nothing, or if a similar request was complied with in the previous month. Otherwise it must respond within 12 days plus one month, failing which it commits an offence.

Right to be indemnified by PD

Assuming PD asked G to provide the guarantee and that G has paid the bank, G can call upon PD to reimburse him (but not prove in PD's insolvency unless he pays the whole debt, see above). Furthermore, if G wishes to take the initiative, he may determine the guarantee and he need not wait for demand to be made from him by the bank; he may take legal action to force PD to pay the debt (*Thomas* v *Nottingham Incorporated Football Club Ltd* (1972)).

Rights of subrogation and contribution

Where G pays off the whole debt (not simply his guarantee limit—see 'The whole debt' clause in **12.7** above), he is entitled by subrogation to the bank's rights. Therefore, he can take any security which the bank is holding from PD, and also a rateable share of any security which the bank is holding from other guarantors of PD's debt. In addition, G has a right of rateable contribution from other guarantors.

Right to set-off

G can only be asked to pay what PD owes, and if PD has a good defence to the bank's claim, G may also raise this as a defence (*Bechervaise* v *Lewis* (1872)). However, in *The Fedora* (1986) CA, it was held that a 'set-off' clause (which denies this right to G) is effective, at least where the defence is not clear cut. Such clauses may become a feature of guarantee forms.

12.9 ESTOPPEL BY CONVENTION

Where the parties to a guarantee both believe that certain debts are covered by the guarantee and they act accordingly, but in fact those debts are not so covered, an estoppel by convention may arise to prevent one party from relying on the express terms of the guarantee.

Illustration

Amalgamated Investment and Property Co. Ltd v *Texas Commerce International Bank* (1981) CA. It was agreed that G would guarantee a loan to A and the necessary form was signed. Later on, all parties agreed that the loan should be made to B, who would onlend to A. All parties assumed the guarantee would cover the new arrangement, but it did not. As all parties had made this assumption, they were all estopped from disputing it.

12.10 LETTERS OF COMFORT

In the corporate and international sectors of banking, a letter of comfort may be accepted by the lending bank in place of a full-blown guarantee. Such a letter may be provided by a parent company to secure a loan to a subsidiary, or by a central government in respect of a loan to a government agency. In the former case, the letter will normally contain a statement to the effect that the parent agrees to maintain its holding in the borrower, and that it is the parent's policy that the subsidiary's business will remain in a position to meet its liabilities to the bank.

Such a letter of comfort was examined by the courts in *Kleinwort Benson Ltd* v *Malaysian Mining Corp Berhad* (1989) CA. It was held that whilst there was a promise by the parent to maintain its holding in the subsidiary, nothing was said which gave rise to any promise that the latter would meet its debts.

It is therefore now established that the typical letter of comfort is not actionable. The relevant legal principle is that parties to a binding contract must intend to create legal relations. However, a letter of comfort is usually given with the express intention, on the part of the giver, that he should *not* be sued on it.

13 Land as Security

13.1 INTRODUCTION

Classification of land

Land is defined in English law as 'real property', as distinct from all other forms of asset which are 'personal property' or 'personalty'. An entirely different set of legal rules applies to real property.

In commercial terms one is usually concerned with the building on the land, such as the house or factory, but the law analyses this as a parcel of land which happens to have a building on it.

13.2 LEGAL ESTATES AND INTERESTS IN LAND

Under s. 1 of the Law of Property Act 1925 the forms of ownership of land are defined as 'estates' in land. There are two:

(a) Freehold. This is more technically referred to as the 'fee simple absolute in possession'.
(b) Leasehold. Or 'a term of years absolute'.

Freehold ownership of land is as close as one can get to absolute title. It will last indefinitely.

Leasehold ownership must expire at some date. A lease may be created out of a freehold, and grants a right of possession for any period of time—it is common to find periodic tenancies which are as short as one week (although this will be repeatedly renewed) or as long as 999 years. There is invariably a rent attached to a lease which the lessee must pay to his lessor or landlord. In commercial properties it is common to find a series of leases on one building, so that the freeholder leases to a head lessee who in turn leases to a sub-lessee and so on. In this case each sub-lease must not expire after the lease above it. When a lease (or head lease in the case of multiple leases) expires, the right of possession will revert to the freeholder. Thus freeholds which are subject to tenancies are referred to as 'reversions'. When a lease is granted at a periodic rental which is below market rents, a premium is charged. This is the price which is paid when a flat is 'bought' on a long leasehold subject to a ground rent. The purchaser is buying the right to possession of a flat at a low rental which is fixed for a long period of time.

Freehold or leasehold ownership of land may be subject to a range of legal and equitable interests. These include:

(a) Legal and equitable mortgages.
(b) Easements, e.g. the right of a landowner to go on to a neighbour's land (a right of way).
(c) Restrictive covenants, e.g. the right of a landowner to prevent his neighbour from building on some part of his land.

Leases may also incorporate positive covenants which, for instance, will oblige a lessor and lessee to maintain the structure of a building. Positive covenants on freeholds are not effective against subsequent purchasers, and this is the reason why flats are usually sold on long leases rather than freehold. It is commonly believed that the reason for this is that flats are often on an upper floor of a building. In fact there is no obstacle to what is known as a 'flying freehold'.

13.3 REGISTERED AND UNREGISTERED LAND

Land may also be classified as:

(a) Registered.
(b) Unregistered.

Most of England and Wales is now divided into areas of 'compulsory registration'. This means that all freeholds and leases with more than 40 years unexpired must be placed on their District Land Register on the next occasion they are transferred, if they are not already registered. When a property is registered, it is identified by a title number and there are three parts to the Register.

(1) The Property Register. With freehold property this usually consists simply of the street address and a reference to an attached plan of the locality, with a red line drawn around the property in question.

(2) The Proprietorship Register. This states the name or names (the

maximum is four) of the persons holding legal title to the property. Their title will normally be described as 'Title Absolute', known as state-guaranteed title. This means that if the person named is not the owner, the state will compensate any innocent purchaser. Title may also be described as 'Qualified', 'Possessory' or 'Good Leasehold', each of which does not carry the state guarantee.

(3) The Charges Register. This will incorporate such matters as legal mortgages and restrictive covenants.

Matters known as 'Minor interests' may be entered on the Proprietorship and Charges Registers. These are divided into:

(a) Notices.
(b) Cautions.
(c) Inhibitions.
(d) Restrictions.

These can deal with such matters as bankruptcy of the person with legal title, the right of a spouse to occupy residential property and equitable mortgages.

The Registers never leave the District Land Registries. The 'deeds' of registered land consist of a document known as the 'Land Certificate', which is a photocopy of the register stitched inside a rather grand looking cover. If the land is subject to a legal mortgage the 'deeds' will be a 'Charge Certificate', similarly a photocopy of the register but also with the original mortgage deed. The mortgagee holds this document. Where two or more mortgages are registered on the same title, each mortgagee will be given his own Charge Certificate, incorporating the original of his mortgage and showing, in the copy Charges Register, details of his mortgage and all previously registered mortgages.

Conveyancing of registered land is theoretically simple. The purchaser checks the Register of the property to see that the vendor is the registered owner and that no charges or minor interests affect the title, he pays his money to the vendor and then asks the District Land Registry to amend the Register so that he becomes the registered owner. In practice the Register is searched by reference to the copy in the Land or Charge Certificate, or Office Copies can be obtained from the Registry.

In any case a date is stamped on the copy and a Priority Search is then made, which is firstly a request of the Registry whether any entry has been made on the Register since the date the copy was made, and secondly the Registry grants a Priority period of 30 days, during which time it will not make any entry on the Register without the permission of the applicant, who must then complete his purchase and lodge the necessary documents with the Registry before this Priority Period expires. If the proper procedure is followed, the system protects the purchaser or mortgagee from everything except for overriding interests (see below).

Conveyancing of unregistered land is based upon the concept of the good root of title. A vendor must produce the conveyance or other document evidencing his acquisition of the legal title to the land. If this was less than 15 years previous, he must also produce earlier conveyances until he has established an unbroken chain of title going back in time at least 15 years. The deeds of unregistered land therefore consist of a collection of previous conveyances; prior mortgages and the discharges of them also form part of the chain. Matters such as bankruptcy of the vendor (dealt with as minor interests in the case of registered land) are this time entered on a special register that is kept for unregistered land—the Land Charges Registry, which must therefore be searched by an intending purchaser or mortgagee. The land is not registered, however, and a search is made against the name of the vendor.

Searches of other registers

Local land charges

A purchaser or mortgagee will search this register in order to discover matters which would adversely affect the value of the land, such as a compulsory purchase order. Standard form enquiries may also be made of the local authority, which would reveal matters such as plans to construct new roads in the local vicinity.

Companies register

Where the vendor or mortgagor is a corporate entity, the register of the company will reveal fixed charges over its land and floating charges over the whole of the company's undertaking.

13.4 TYPES OF OWNERSHIP OF LAND

The freehold or leasehold estate may be divided into:

(a) The legal title.
(b) The equitable or beneficial interest.

Where the two categories do not exactly coincide, a form of trust will exist whereby the person with the legal title holds it on trust for one or more persons (possibly including himself). For example, A may own the legal title and B and C may own the equitable title. Where land is conveyed to more than four persons, the first four named hold the legal title on trust for all of them as equitable owners. (See also the cases below in **13.5** to **13.8**.)

The person with legal title is then called a trustee. The beneficial interest belongs to the person entitled to the proceeds if the property is sold, for example because he paid some or all of the purchase price.

Legal title may be shared by a maximum of four persons who must all be adults. If five or more jointly own land, this will have to be achieved through a trust. There is no limit to the number that may have beneficial interests. Neither is there any age limit.

Where the legal title is shared this will take one of two forms:

(a) A joint tenancy.
(b) A tenancy in common.

The key to the difference lies in the 'right of survivorship'. In a joint tenancy of A and B where A dies, B automatically becomes sole owner of the legal title. If they were tenants in common, A's share would pass according to the terms of his Will or to the rules of intestacy.

Any beneficial interest in land can only exist behind a 'trust for sale', which means that a purchaser or mortgagee can safely pay his money to two or more owners of the legal title, and persons with a beneficial interest must claim from those vendors of the legal title (if they can). The purchaser will obtain a good title. This is a principle known as 'overreaching' the claims of the beneficial owners.

Where a purchaser takes his title from a sole legal owner, however, the position is more complex. He will still obtain a good title but only if he has no notice (actual or constructive) of the beneficial interest. Constructive notice consists of matters which the purchaser should be aware of, whether or not he is. An example are matters entered on the Registers which the purchaser is deemed to know, whether or not he in fact did search the Register.

These matters relating to beneficial interests are of vital interest to a bank accepting a mortgage of land, since the position of mortgagees is comparable to that of purchasers. The precise situation differs, at least in terminology, between registered and unregistered land.

13.5 INTERESTS IN REGISTERED LAND

As observed earlier, a purchaser of registered land need only ensure that the entries on the Register are satisfactory and follow the correct procedures; for instance, a wife could register a Notice, protecting her rights of occupation, under the Matrimonial Homes Act 1983. Matters became more complicated in 1980. Under s. 70 of the Land Registration Act 1925, a purchaser takes the land subject to any overriding interests which persons other than the legal owner enjoy. These overriding interests are the only matter relating to the land which need not and cannot be entered on the Register. The most obvious example in residential property is some form of tenancy protected under rent legislation. Such a tenancy of a property offered for sale or mortgage could reduce its value by as much as 50%. In practice, this has not caused many problems, either because vendors have not attempted this type of fraud or perhaps the true position would always be too evident to the purchaser, irrespective of the lack of notice from the register of the property.

Another category of overriding interest is that held by a person who has a beneficial interest in the property and who is in actual occupation of it.

Illustration

This suddenly became a serious problem for mortgagees with the decision in *Williams and Glyn's Bank* v *Boland* (1981) HL. The legal title was in the sole name of Mr Boland but Mrs Boland had contributed to the purchase price. Therefore Mr Boland held the legal title on trust for the benefit of himself and Mrs Boland, and of course her interest did not appear on the Register. The bank took its legal mortgage from Mr Boland, who later defaulted and the bank sought to exercise its power of sale. First it needed possession of the house and, as nobody can be evicted in these circumstances without a court order, the bank went to court for a possession order. Mrs Boland resisted this on the grounds that she had an overriding interest, based on her equitable interest and actual occupation coexisting at the time the bank took its mortgage from

Mr Boland. The House of Lords agreed, and the bank found itself not only without possession but also without a valid legal mortgage, since a legal mortgage must be on the whole property and Mr Boland did not own the whole property. It then had an equitable mortgage on Mr Boland's share. Presumably it waited until the Bolands voluntarily decided to move and then took its loan and accrued interest out of Mr Boland's share of the proceeds of sale. Mortgages of land sometimes enjoy the considerable advantage of price inflation which can be invaluable in these circumstances.

The overreaching principle is contained in s. 27(1) of the Law of Property Act 1925 and s. 17 of the Trustee Act 1925.

Illustration

City of London Building Society v *Flegg* (1988) HL. Mr and Mrs Maxwell-Brown purchased a house with funds supplied by her parents (Mr and Mrs Flegg) and by a mortgage lender. All four lived in the house. Later, the mortgage loan was refinanced by the plaintiffs, who took a legal mortgage from the Maxwell-Browns and in ignorance of the beneficial interest of the Fleggs. The Maxwell-Browns held the legal title on trust for themselves and for the Fleggs. Following default on this loan, the Building Society sought a possession order which the House of Lords held they were entitled to obtain, since the overriding interest of the Fleggs was overreached by the mortgaging of the property by *two* trustee legal owners.

13.6 INTERESTS IN UNREGISTERED LAND

A purchaser of unregistered land must ensure that the vendor can show a good root of legal title, and he must search the Land Charges Register against the name of the vendor. For instance, a wife may (as with registered land) protect her right of occupation by registering a Class F Charge in respect of the matrimonial home against her husband's name at the Land Charges Registry (Matrimonial Homes Act 1983).

If others have a beneficial interest in the property, the position will once again depend on whether there are two legal owners transferring the property. If there are two or more, the overreaching principles apply in exactly the same way as for registered land. If there is a sole legal owner, the position depends on whether the purchaser has notice (actual or constructive) of the beneficial interest. Actual notice is simple; if the purchaser knows of the interest at the time he makes the transaction, he does not get good title. The purchaser is deemed to have constructive notice of the interest when the legal owner does not occupy the land and the purchaser fails to make enquiry of whoever does occupy it. Where the legal owner does occupy the land, the case of *Caunce* v *Caunce* (1969) suggests that the purchaser will have no constructive notice of an interest of any other occupant (in this case a wife), unless the situation should raise some suspicion in his mind. In view of the judicial trend over the last decade or so to bolster the protection for spouses who are not legal owners, there must be some doubt as to whether this decision would be followed today.

13.7 THE MEANING OF OCCUPATION

For someone to have an overriding interest in registered land, occupation of the land is essential. In unregistered land, occupation is a considerable factor in deciding whether a purchaser has constructive notice of a beneficial interest. It is worth considering exactly what constitutes occupation. In *Kingsnorth Finance Co. Ltd* v *Tizard* (1986), an ex-wife, who had left the matrimonial home but who visited every afternoon and stayed one night in every fortnight, was held to be in occupation.

In *Abbey National Building Society* v *Cann* (1990) HL, the person claiming an overriding interest had never lived in the house and was in Holland at the time the mortgagee took its charge. Some personal belongings were moved in to the newly acquired house some 35 minutes before the mortgage was completed. This was considered to be insufficient for actual occupation.

13.8 THE POSITION OF A PURCHASER OR MORTGAGEE

Where a bank is offered a mortgage of land there is a danger that some person or persons other than the legal owner may have an overriding interest, or the bank will later be deemed to have had constructive notice of a beneficial interest. If so, the bank will be left with an equitable mortgage of the legal owner's beneficial share of the property (if any).

Registered land

Since occupation is a prerequisite of an overriding interest, the obvious approach is to discover who is in occupation and ask each if he has a beneficial interest (the Land Registration Act lays down that if enquiry is made of a person with an overriding interest and he fails to disclose it then the mortgagee gets good title). Asking the legal owner whether others have an overriding interest does not provide any protection against claims from those others. The danger is that the bank will not discover some person who occupies, especially where the broadest interpretation of that word is used, and visiting the property would not reveal that person's existence. So far the main concern has centred on spouses (usually wives), but any person who satisfies the criteria will have an overriding interest. Where the property is occupied by non-legal owners the usual practice is to have them sign a deed of postponement. There is no minimum age limit for a person to hold an overriding interest, and the idea of a young child being required to postpone his interest is a nightmare for mortgagees, who in practice only concern themselves with adults in occupation. The problem should now be limited to situations where the bank provides mortgage finance some time after the property was purchased, e.g. through refinancing. For many years, mortgagees had been concerned that an overriding interest could arise in favour of a person who moved into a house, newly acquired with funds from that mortgagee. Such concerns have been laid to rest by the following case.

Abbey National Building Society v *Cann* (1990) HL. C purchased a house in his sole name, partly with mortgage money from the AN and partly with the proceeds of sale of another house. He told AN he intended to live there alone. In fact he intended to live there with his mother, and she acquired a beneficial interest in the new house since first, she had a beneficial share in the previous house and second, had agreed to vacate the previous house on condition that she was allowed to live in the new one. The mother's claim to have an overriding interest in priority to AN's mortgage failed for three reasons. First, her beneficial interest did not come into existence until the moment of completion of the mortgage, which was held to be contemporaneous with the completion of the purchase. Since AN had advanced their mortgage monies to the son's solicitor a few days prior to completion, it had acquired an equitable charge before, and therefore in priority to, the mother's beneficial interest. Second, she was not considered to be in actual occupation at the time the mortgage was completed. An argument that the relevant time to consider occupation was the time of registering the mortgage (always some time after purchase), was dismissed. Third, she knew that her son had insufficient funds to purchase the house without a mortgage loan, and she was therefore taken to have impliedly authorised him to mortgage the house to AN, even though she knew nothing of that mortgage.

There is clearly an express authorisation when there is actual knowledge of the mortgage (*Bristol and West Building Society* v *Henning* (1985)).

Unregistered land

Occupation is again important and whilst the bank may acquire good title where a person with a beneficial interest occupies the property, the vagaries of the suspicious circumstances test are such that it is clearly good policy to apply the same procedure as that followed in the case of registered land.

The foolproof approach for both types of land would be to take the mortgage from two legal owners, and therefore to enjoy the protection of the overreaching principle. Where the land is owned by a sole legal owner, the bank could require him to convey to a fellow trustee as joint tenants. Even this approach may not suffice if the bank knew of the beneficial interest, as the overreaching principle requires good faith. Similarly, it would not assist where the mortgage monies did not accrue to both trustee legal owners but only to one of them.

13.9 THE MATRIMONIAL HOMES ACT 1983

Parliament has recognised the social problem of one spouse (usually the husband), who owned the matrimonial home as sole legal owner, secretly selling to an innocent third party and disappearing with the proceeds. In this situation, the non-owning spouse now has a right to occupy the matrimonial home (whether or not he or she does in fact occupy it), but this right must be registered to have any effect on a purchaser or mortgagee (see **13.6** above). Only spouses have this right, which does not extend to non-married partners.

13.10 TYPES OF MORTGAGE OVER LAND

(a) Legal
(b) Equitable.

Legal mortgage

The Law of Property Act 1925 permits two alternative methods of creating a legal mortgage over land. First, it may be by demise, which means by granting a long lease to the mortgagee. Second, it may be a charge by deed expressed to be by way of legal mortgage. The latter is universal but the legal consequences are similar whichever is used. The latter may be preferable in the case of mortgages of leasehold interests.

The legal mortgage must be by deed and the mortgagor's signature must be witnessed. Section 1 of the Law of Property (Miscellaneous Provisions) Act 1989 provides that a document is a deed if it is clearly intended to be a deed. Seals are no longer necessary. See chapter 16 for the means by which companies execute documents.

Equitable mortgage

Common law requires a minimum only of an intention by the owner to grant a security right in return for value given, such as a loan. In the case of land, s. 2 of the Law of Property (Miscellaneous Provisions) Act 1989 requires any contract for the future disposition of an interest in land to be in writing, signed by both parties, and to incorporate all the terms expressly agreed by the parties. An equitable mortgage over a legal interest in land will constitute an agreement to give a legal mortgage and will be within s. 2. Also, note the mortgagee must sign the mortgage, as well as the mortgagor. In practice, banks now require the title deeds to be deposited, a memorandum of deposit to be signed by the mortgagor and by the bank, and inclusion of all agreed terms in the memorandum. Note that the section does not apply to a legal mortgage, since this constitutes an actual disposition of an interest in land, not a contract to do so. Note also that s. 40 of the Law of Property Act 1925 is now repealed.

In the case of registered land, the equitable mortgage cannot be registered as such. Notice of Deposit of the Land Certificate can be registered (or Notice of Intended Deposit if the Land Certificate is not yet available). This is good protection against a subsequent legal mortgage.

With unregistered land, the mortgage only has to be registered as a Land Charge if the title deeds are not held.

If the mortgage (legal or equitable) is to secure a granting of credit which is regulated by the Consumer Credit Act 1974, a special procedure must be followed which includes a 'cooling-off' period, failing which the charge will be void (see chapter 3).

Registration and priority—registered land

A priority search of a title at HM Land Registry will give the searcher 30 working days during which nobody else can register an entry against that title.

Where two or more mortgages have been granted over the same piece of registered land, their priority ranks in order of registration on the Charges Register for the title to that land.

However, a subsequent mortgagee can only be fully registered with the consent of every prior mortgagee, since the Land Registry will not register the subsequent charge unless the existing Charge Certificates are all returned to the Land Registry for updating. This will give a prior, registered mortgagee the option to refuse to allow registration of the later charge or to agree the terms of a suitable priority document. This latter option will be important if the prior mortgagee wishes to continue lending on the security of his mortgage without the rule in *Clayton's* case running against him.

If a second mortgagee of registered land does not wish to, or cannot, obtain the consent of a prior mortgagee for registration of the later charge, the second mortgagee can protect his security by registering a Caution. This will give limited protection but will at least give everyone notice of his interest as mortgagee. His mortgage, being equitable (even if it is created by deed or expressed to be a legal mortgage), will rank after all legal, registered mortgages and should rank against other equitable mortgages in order of registration, whether they have been registered by a Caution or Notice.

Registration and priority—unregistered land

A search against a person's name at the Land Charges Registry will again give a 30 working-day period during which nobody except the searcher can register an entry against the name of the person searched against.

The first mortgagee in time, whether his mortgage is legal or equitable, is entitled to hold the title deeds to the property and, if he does so, he need not register his mortgage at the Land Charges Registry—in fact, he will not be able to register.

A second mortgagee is deemed to have constructive notice of the first charge by virtue of the mortgagor not being able to produce the title deeds.

A mortgage over unregistered land, unless protected by deposit of deeds, will be void against subsequent mortgages if it is not registered at the Land Charges Registry (s. 4(5) Land Charges Act 1972).

Subject to this, a legal charge can be registered as a Class C(i) puisne mortgage, and an equitable charge as a Class C(iii) general equitable charge.

By virtue of s. 97 Law of Property Act 1925, mortgages over unregistered land rank in order of date of registration at the Land Charges Registry, regardless of whether they are legal or equitable mortgages, save only that the first mortgagee in time who holds the title deeds will rank ahead of all subsequently created mortgages.

If the first mortgagee does not take the title deeds, he must register his security as a puisne charge in order that he will be protected by registration constituting notice to subsequent mortgagees (s. 198 Law of Property Act 1925). A subsequent mortgagee taking possession of the title deeds should give notice to the first mortgagee but he cannot register his subsequent charge at the Land Charges Registry. If the first mortgagee holds the title deeds but subsequently releases them and they are deposited with another mortgagee who is ignorant of the first mortgage (and innocent of any fraud on the first mortgagee), the first mortgagee may lose his priority (*Agra Bank Ltd* v *Barry* (1874) HL).

Any unregistered charges will rank after all registered charges, but will be void against a purchaser for value. However, they will be valid against the mortgagor who will therefore have to account for the sale proceeds to unregistered mortgagees.

13.11 STANDARD BANK MORTGAGE TERMS

These include:

(a) Exclusions of ss. 93 and 103 of the Law of Property Act 1925, permitting the bank to consolidate two or more mortgages it holds from the same customer and removing the waiting periods following default.

(b) Exclusion of the mortgagor's power to grant leases or sub-leases. Any such lease will therefore be invalid. This provision is not totally effective in the case of agricultural property.

(c) A promise by the mortgagor to keep the property in good repair and insured. Banks very sensibly take other steps to verify that the property is insured, e.g. by demanding receipts.

(d) A continuing security clause to cover further advances and to protect against the effects of *Clayton*'s case. Even so, if notice of second mortgage is received the bank will not enjoy first priority for further lending. Furthermore, in *Deeley* v *Lloyds Bank*, a current account secured by a first mortgage was not ruled off when notice of second mortgage was received, and the bank lost priority due to the effect of *Clayton*'s case, even though there was no real new lending.

(e) A power to grant leases at a premium. This will be a more useful remedy than a simple sale in the case of a mortgage of a developer's newly constructed freehold block of flats.

The memorandum of deposit

This will incorporate:

(a) A continuing security clause.

(b) A promise by the mortgagor to grant a legal mortgage to the bank if requested to do so. If the mortgagor agrees to such a request the bank will acquire a power of sale. If he will not agree, the bank may seek an order for specific performance from the court, which should be granted as this relates to a contract for the conveyance of an interest in land. (Note that, because of this, the memorandum of deposit must be signed by both the mortgagor and the mortgagee (s. 2 Law of Property (Miscellaneous Provisions) Act 1989).)

(c) The bank may be granted an irrevocable power of attorney by the mortgagor. In this event, as the bank holds the title deeds, it will enjoy automatic power of sale (*Re White Rose Cottage* (1965)).

13.12 REALISING THE MORTGAGE

A legal mortgagee has the following options:

(a) To exercise his power of sale.
(b) To appoint a Receiver.
(c) To foreclose.

(d) To enter into possession of the property.
(e) To sue on the mortgagor's covenant to repay the debt.

13.13 THE MORTGAGEE'S POWER OF SALE

A sale frequently permits a bank to obtain a large sum which can repay the customer's debt, and it is therefore the most popular remedy.

Once the mortgagor is in default, a mortgage by deed carries a statutory power of sale under s. 101 of the Law of Property Act 1925. This will include all legal mortgages, as well as equitable mortgages executed under seal or in accordance with s. 1 of the Law of Property (Miscellaneous Provisions) Act 1989. The property may be sold whole or in parts. For commercial reasons, the bank will invariably wish to offer the property for sale without the customer in occupation and, unless the latter has abandoned the property, a court order should be obtained in case an offence under the Protection from Eviction Act 1977 is committed by the bank. An order is always necessary in the case of residential property, unless it has been abandoned. The court has power to suspend the order for possession if it appears likely that the mortgagor can pay off the arrears within a reasonable period. In the case of an instalment mortgage, this means that the mortgagor must pay the normal instalments and a fixed proportion of the arrears each month until the arrears are repaid. If he misses a payment, the order will automatically become effective without the need for a further application to court. Where the mortgage is to secure an overdraft with no repayment by instalment, the court may only suspend its order if it is likely that the mortgagor can repay the whole debt. Where the order is not suspended, it will usually grant possession 28 days hence.

A spouse who has registered a right to occupy under the Matrimonial Homes Act will not be able to resist possession unless the registration was in place before the bank took its charge.

A residential tenant of the mortgagor cannot resist possession against the mortgagee even if he is entitled to Rent Act protection from eviction as against the mortgagor.

Mortgagee's duty to obtain a proper price

In strictly commercial terms, the mortgagee will not have an interest in obtaining a price for the property that is any higher than the debt owed to him. The law is therefore careful to protect the interest of the mortgagor, and imposes a duty on the mortgagee to act in good faith and to take reasonable care to sell at a proper price (*Cuckmere Brick Co. Ltd v Mutual Finance Ltd* (1971)). He is not, however, obliged to delay a sale in the expectation of a rising market. He may not sell the property to himself. Since *Standard Chartered Bank* v *Walker* (1983) CA, it cannot be regarded as safe to offer the property at auction and to have no regard to the location and advertising of the auction, or to the price obtained. The preferred practice is now to instruct professional agents to value the property and to sell at or near the valuation price, which is normally set on the low side. If the courts do regard the price to be improper, the mortgagee is still liable but he has a right to pursue a claim by way of indemnity against the valuer.

In *Swingcastle Ltd* v *Gibson* (1990) CA, S agreed to lend £10,000 to C, taking a legal charge over C's house which had been valued by a chartered surveyor (G) at £18,000. The agreed rate of interest was 36%, increasing on default to 45%. The house was later forcibly sold for £12,000, which left a shortfall after arrears of over £7,000. S would not have lent if it had known the house was worth so little and it sued G for his negligent valuation. S succeeded in claiming the full amount of the shortfall from G, including the default interest rate.

In *Parker-Tweedale* v *Dunbar Bank plc* (1989) CA, the matrimonial home of Mr and Mrs P was in Mrs P's sole name but Mr P had a beneficial interest. On default, D Bank, with Mrs P's consent, exercised their power of sale. Mr P objected that the sale price was too low. It was held that, as mere beneficiary under the trust for sale of the house, he had no grounds to object to the sale price, but would only have a claim against Mrs P for breach of trust.

Equity protects a guarantor as well as the mortgagor, however. This was established in *Standard Chartered Bank* v *Walker* (1983) CA and more recently in *China and South Sea Bank Ltd* v *Tan* (1990) PC. F Ltd borrowed from C bank, offering shares in another company as security, and a guarantee was taken from T. The shares were at one time adequate security but they eventually became worthless, and a claim was made against T for the HK$33 million then owing. T argued that the C bank owed him a duty to exercise care in timing its sale of the shares. This was rejected. A creditor may choose the timing of its sale, but when he does sell he must take care to obtain the best price. There are other duties, however, such as a duty to perfect the direct security (e.g. by registering it properly), and not to surrender it. These duties, and the extent to which they may be lessened by agreement between the parties, are discussed in chapter 12.

Applying the proceeds of sale

Assuming the mortgagee has a first charge, the order is:

(a) Proper expenses of the sale.
(b) His claim including costs.
(c) A second mortgagee (if one exists), or otherwise to the mortgagor, unless he is bankrupt, in which case to the trustee in bankruptcy.

If there are insufficient funds to repay junior mortgagees, their mortgages are discharged by the sale in any case.

In the unlikely event of a sale by a junior mortgagee, the senior mortgagee must be repaid first. If there is insufficient to repay that senior mortgagee, the purchaser acquires the property encumbered by that mortgage.

13.14 OTHER REMEDIES OF THE MORTGAGEE

Appoint a receiver

Under the terms of a standard mortgage, a receiver may be appointed when the debt has become due, which will be when demand is made. The appointment must be in writing and is effective from the moment the receiver accepts his appointment. The receiver is the agent of the mortgagor (Law of Property Act 1925 s. 109(2)) and the mortgagee is therefore not responsible for his acts or omissions. However, in *Standard Chartered Bank* v *Walker* the bank was liable for the receiver's negligence, as it had been directing him. It is common practice in any event for the receiver, when he is appointed, to seek an indemnity for any liability in negligence from the mortgagee.

The receiver is most commonly appointed when the mortgaged property is income-producing, such as the freehold of a block of flats which is let at market rents. The proceeds must then be applied according to s. 109(8) of the Law of Property Act:

(a) Payment of certain expenses of the property.

(b) Paying prior mortgagees (if any).
(c) Paying his commission, insurance premiums and proper repairs.
(d) Paying interest to the mortgagee.
(e) Paying principal to the mortgagee.

Foreclosure

In its true legal meaning this term refers to a process of applying for a court order of foreclosure, the effect of which is to render the mortgagee the owner of the mortgaged property, and to discharge the debt irrespective of the value of the property and the size of the debt. This remedy is not nowadays sought or obtained, and the term has become used to describe the process of obtaining possession and exercising power of sale.

Entering into possession

As discussed in **13.13** above, this process frequently precedes the exercising of the mortgagee's power of sale. In fact, most mortgagors would be surprised to learn that any legal mortgagee has the right to go into possession of the mortgaged property even if there is no default. The original legal concept of a mortgage being a transfer of the mortgaged property to the mortgagee means that it is the mortgagee, not the mortgagor, who is primarily entitled to possession. The mortgage will provide for the mortgagor to be entitled to possession while he complies with the terms of the mortgage. Taking possession by the mortgagee is, therefore, no more than the assertion of his common law right. In practice, possession may take place where the mortgagee wishes to let the property, and the acceptance by the mortgagee of rent will constitute taking possession. The mortgagee will be liable to the mortgagor for any damage, or for devaluing the property (e.g. by letting to a Rent Act tenant), or for rent received, or for rent which should have been received. He is allowed, however, to keep the property empty pending a sale without being liable for rent (*Shepard* v *Jones* (1882)).

A mortgagee in possession of empty property will be liable to third parties who go onto the property, or who own land adjacent to it, and who have a claim under the Occupiers Liability Act 1957 or in private nuisance. For these reasons, the mortgagee will appoint a receiver to act on his behalf, but as the agent of the mortgagor, thus avoiding being deemed at law to have taken possession himself.

A mortgage will usually provide that the mortgagor cannot grant leases. The mortgagee will thus be entitled to possession as against a tenant whose lease was not agreed by the mortgagee, unless the lease was granted before the mortgage was executed.

Suing on the covenant to repay

The mortgagee will, of course, be entitled to sue the borrower for repayment under the loan agreement which is secured by the mortgage. However, if the mortgage contains a covenant to repay, the mortgagee will have the additional right to sue the mortgagor for repayment under the terms of the mortgage. Where the mortgage secures lending to someone other than the mortgagor, the covenant to repay will, in effect, be a guarantee and will give the mortgagor the right to sue two parties (the borrower and the mortgagor) for repayment.

If the mortgage is a deed, the mortgagee will be entitled to sue on the covenant to repay for up to 12 years after demand has been made under the mortgage, and this period may start running some time after demand has been made under the loan agreement. An action for repayment under the loan agreement must usually be commenced within six years of demand, since the loan agreement will usually be under hand, not under seal.

Remedies of an equitable mortgagee

Sale

As explained above, this will only be available to an equitable mortgagee under seal. Otherwise an application must be made for a court order (s. 91 of the Law of Property Act 1925).

Possession

An equitable mortgagee has no inherent right to possession of the mortgaged property but may apply to the court for possession. In practical terms, this is much the same position as that of the legal mortgagee (discussed above).

Receiver

The equitable mortgagee has no right to appoint a receiver unless the mortgage is under seal and specifically grants this right.

Foreclosure

This right is in theory available to any equitable mortgagee who has the right to demand a legal mortgage but, as explained above, this remedy is, to all practical purposes, defunct.

Suing on the covenant to repay

The position is the same as for a legal mortgage.

Where the mortgage (legal or equitable) secures the grant of credit which is regulated by the Consumer Credit Act, a court order must be obtained before any enforcement takes place (s. 126 Consumer Credit Act 1974).

13.15 MORTGAGES OF LEASEHOLD PROPERTY

It will frequently be commercially attractive to lend against the value of leasehold property, as this may have a very high resale value. Clearly the value is likely to diminish over time as the lease shortens but this will not be a concern with long leases, and can in any case be taken into account when deciding the extent of the loan. There are several other matters, however, which are peculiar to mortgages of leaseholds:

(1) There is a possibility that the lessor may forfeit the lease, with the result that the lease vanishes and renders worthless any charge on it. Forfeiture may result from failure to pay rent or from persistent breaches of covenants in the lease. The law requires the lessor to follow a lengthy procedure in order to obtain forfeiture, and the court has power to grant relief against forfeiture, which it will give on any reasonable application by the lessee, but the mortgagee of the lease will not necessarily hear of the forfeiture proceedings until it is too late. The lessee would not normally sit idly by while a valuable lease is forfeited but he may not act if it is overmortgaged and he has no equity in it. If the mortgagee applies for relief from forfeiture, the court will commonly require him to rectify or pay the mortgagor's breach and to guarantee against future breaches, or take over the lease in the mortgagee's name as tenant. Some leases contain a clause which provides for automatic forfeiture in the event of the lessee's bankruptcy. Such a lease is obviously not suitable security for a mortgagee. In such a case the lessor would have to be approached to execute a Deed of Variation to the lease, in order to remove the clause.

(2) The lease may contain some restriction (absolute or conditional on the lessor's consent) on mortgaging or assigning the lease. If there is a restriction on mortgaging, a bank can decline to accept the lease as security, unless the lease is varied or the lessor's consent obtained. In the case of a restriction on assigning, a mortgage will be effective if the charge by way of legal mortgage is used, as opposed to the charge by demise. A problem may later arise if the mortgagee wishes to exercise his power of sale, which will require an assignment of the lease to a purchaser. Where the restriction is conditional, the lessor's consent may not be unreasonably refused (s. 89(1) of the Law of Property Act 1925). Where the restriction is absolute, the mortgagee would be well advised to have the lease varied before accepting it as security.

(3) The lease will commonly contain repair covenants, to deal with repair and maintenance of the building and contributions to the costs of these by the lessees. The lease may also contain easements to permit passage of services such as water, gas, drainage etc. through parts of the building demised to other lessees. These provisions are notoriously complex to draft, and care must be taken in each case to tailor them to the precise design of the building in question. It is false economy to avoid the expense of having a lawyer scrutinise the covenants and easements in the lease. Even when this precaution is taken, it is distressingly common to find that a matter has been overlooked and a purchaser refuses to buy the lease as it stands, and the lease is therefore heavily devalued unless it can be varied. If an independent lawyer was employed to examine the lease, an action should lie against him in these circumstances. In residential conveyancing, it is an odd fact of life that the lawyer's fees are based on the price of the property being purchased. The more expensive (usually freehold) houses present no special problems in most cases but the cheaper (leasehold) flats can be a nightmare. Thus the size of the lawyer's fees may be in inverse proportion to the amount of work involved.

13.16 DISCHARGE OF A MORTGAGE

This is usually by redemption, i.e. the mortgagor repays the full debt. Any provision in the mortgage which prevents redemption will be void, unless the mortgagor is a company granting a debenture. The mortgagee may refuse to release its charge if the loan has been repaid but contingent liabilities are outstanding which may give rise to a debt at a later date, e.g. liability under a guarantee (*Re Rudd &Son Ltd* (1986)).

Registered land

Discharge of a legal mortgage is by Form 53, signed by the mortgagee and sent to the District Land Registry with the Charge Certificate. The Registry delete the entry on the Charges Register and return the Land Certificate to the mortgagor, unless there are other mortgages outstanding.

Discharge of an equitable mortgage will involve notice to the Land Registry by the mortgagee that the Notice of Deposit on the Charges Register should be deleted. The mortgagee will return the Land Certificate to the mortgagor and cancel any Memorandum of Deposit or Deed (if under seal).

Unregistered land

Discharge of a legal mortgage is by signed receipt, usually on the back of the mortgage deed itself. This receipt now forms part of the title deeds and must be preserved with them. The title deeds are returned to the mortgagor unless notice of second mortgage has been received. There is no duty to search for second mortgages (Law of Property Amendment Act 1926 s. 7 and Schedule) but it is good practice to do so in case an earlier notice has been misfiled. Any registered land charge should be vacated by notice to the Land Charges Registry.

Discharge of an equitable mortgage involves return of the title deeds (subject to notice of second mortgage), and cancellation of the memorandum of deposit and any deed. Any land charge should be vacated.

In practice, a mortgage is frequently redeemed when the mortgagor sells his property and the purchase price is used to redeem. A problem arises if the purchaser or his mortgagee will not hand over the purchase price until he receives the Form 53, and the mortgagee of the vendor refuses to hand over the Form 53 until he receives his redemption monies (and, in any case, will not have the Form 53 available for a week or so as it has to be prepared at Head Office). The solution is for the vendor's mortgagee to hand over the Charge Certificate and signed Transfer on completion, and for his solicitor to give a signed undertaking to send the Form 53 as soon as it is available.

13.17 RISKS FOR A LENDER

To summarise:

(a) Some defect in the mortgagor's title, which may not be clear from search of the Land Register or Land Charges Register and Local Land Charges Register. This may be an overriding interest accruing to another in the case of registered land, or a beneficial interest in the case of unregistered land.

(b) A forged signature on the mortgage deed. The charge will then be void. If there are two co-owners and the signature of one is forged, the mortgagee has an equitable mortgage over the share of the property beneficially owned by the genuine signatory (*First National Securities Ltd v Hegerty* (1984)).

(c) The various pitfalls which present themselves in the case of mortgages of leaseholds (discussed above).

(d) A claim of undue influence or *non est factum* by one of the mortgagors (see chapter 11).

14 Shares as Security

14.1 INTRODUCTION

Types of stocks and shares

We are concerned here primarily with two types:

(a) Registered shares in companies registered under the Companies Acts, whether listed on the Stock Exchange or not.
(b) British Government Stocks, known as 'gilts'.

Securities may also be offered in the form of debenture stock issued by companies, bearer shares, shares issued by foreign companies, certificates of deposit issued by banks, commercial paper and Euronotes and Eurobonds issued by companies, savings certificates and bonds issued by the UK or foreign governments—to name only some of the possibilities. To a large extent the principles that follow will apply irrespective of the type of security, bearing in mind that title to a bearer instrument will be transferred by mere delivery.

Basis of lending

Any quoted security may be easily valued. However, this value is likely to be far more volatile than in the case of life policies and land. Valuation of unquoted shares is basically an exercise in balance sheet interpretation, with strong reference to the value of overall control of a company.

14.2 TYPES OF MORTGAGE

The mortgage may be:

(a) A Legal mortgage.
(b) An Equitable mortgage.

Legal mortgage

This is effected by transferring title to the security from customer to the bank, in much the same way as if the bank had purchased it. The bank mortgagee thus becomes the registered holder of shares which are mortgaged to it. Assuming the mortgage is of company shares, the bank will take from the customer:

(a) The Share Certificate.
(b) A signed and completed share transfer form.

The transfer will have to be stamped but Stamp Duty is applied at a flat rate of 50 pence when the transfer is by way of mortgage. The two documents are sent to the Registrar of the Company concerned, who will issue and send to the mortgagee a Share Certificate in his name. For the sake of convenience, most banks maintain nominee companies for the purpose of holding shares that have been transferred by way of legal mortgage.

The above documents are sufficient to create a valid legal mortgage and there is no requirement for any further mortgage form, nor for any documents to be under seal. However, it is invariably bank practice to take a memorandum of deposit from the customer incorporating various protective clauses.

Equitable mortgage

In law this requires a minimum only of an intention for the bank to assume an equitable interest in the shares, in return for some valuable consideration provided to the customer. Unless clearly deposited by way of safe custody, the deposit of a Share Certificate will create an equitable mortgage over the shares (*Harrold* v *Plenty* (1901)). In practice, the bank will require deposit of the Share Certificate and a signed memorandum of deposit in order to clarify the terms of the mortgage (see **14.3**). A transfer form signed by the customer but otherwise left blank is often taken.

14.3 THE MEMORANDUM OF DEPOSIT

This will incorporate:

(a) A continuing security clause to cover further advances and to exclude *Clayton's* case.
(b) A clause excluding the waiting periods after default, which would otherwise apply under s. 103 of the Law of Property Act 1925.

SHARES AS SECURITY

(c) A statement that dividends from the shares will form part of the security.

(d) A statement that the bank holds the shares as security. Otherwise, it might be argued in the case of an equitable mortgage that the customer had merely deposited the shares under safe deposit arrangements, or in the case of a legal mortgage that the bank had purchased the shares.

(e) In an equitable mortgage, the customer agrees to execute any transfer which the bank requests him to complete.

14.4 REALISING THE MORTGAGE

Legal mortgages

Once the customer is in default, the bank has a power of sale of the shares, which it can easily exercise since the shares are registered in its name.

Equitable mortgages

A court order would be required for the bank to sell the shares. However, the bank normally holds a blank, signed transfer form which it may complete and thereby effect a sale. Alternatively, a sale will be possible if the equitable mortgage is under seal, i.e. the bank holds irrevocable power of attorney granted by the customer.

14.5 RISKS FOR THE LENDER

Legal mortgages

Shares in a private limited company may be difficult to transfer or to sell at a satisfactory price. The company's Articles of Association may prohibit registration of a transfer of shares save in the directors' absolute discretion. Alternatively, the Articles may require a selling shareholder to offer his shares to existing members of the company.

There is no system of registering equitable or beneficial interests in shares, and therefore any such interest will only bind a legal mortgagee if he has notice of it. Such notice must be actual or constructive, in the sense that it is clear from the situation that a beneficial interest may exist. In other words, when a customer presents a genuine share certificate in his name, this proves that he holds the legal title to the shares. It is quite possible that he holds the legal title as trustee, so that some other person has a beneficial interest. However, it is only if the bank knows or ought to surmise from the situation that this is a nominee holding (and knows this at the time it takes its legal mortgage), that its title is defective. Note that the legal mortgage is not complete until the bank is registered as owner of the shares, and this may be some time after the customer signs over the documents.

There is, however, a risk from a forged transfer document, and it will not assist if the shares have since been registered in the bank's name or even if the shares have been sold.

Illustration

Sheffield Corporation v *Barclay* (1905) HL. A genuine but stolen share certificate was presented to the bank with a forged transfer document. The bank sent these in for registration and obtained a share certificate in its own name. Later the shares were sold by the bank to an innocent purchaser. When the original owner realised his loss, he sued the company. Naturally, the company had two innocent persons claiming ownership of the same block of shares, and had to recognise both. The bank was held responsible to the company for having misrepresented the situation by submitting a forged transfer.

Where the share certificate is forged, the company will presumably decline to complete the transfer.

Where the shares are partly paid, the bank holding a legal mortgage will be liable for further calls from the company. However, demand may be made of the customer at this time and the shares sold if a default occurs. It could only involve the bank in a loss if the company were in insolvent liquidation.

As legal owner of the shares, the bank will receive dividends, bonus and rights issues, and must account to the customer for these unless the memorandum of deposit provides otherwise.

A variety of consequences may flow from the legal mortgage for the company whose shares are mortgaged to the bank. If the bank's holding in the company exceeds 50%, the company may be considered a subsidiary of the bank for certain purposes, and thus the company will cease to be a member of its original group. Thus a company's Value Added Tax grouping may be jeopardised and there may also be complications in connection with group accounting. Of interest to the bank is the consideration that much smaller holdings may come within the disclosure of interests rules. A solution to these problems can be found if the bank mortgagee disclaims all voting rights in the company whose shares are mortgaged to it until the bank makes demand.

Equitable mortgages

Unlike a legal mortgagee, the equitable mortgagee takes subject to prior equitable interests of which he is unaware.

Illustration

Coleman v *London County and Westminster Bank* (1916). The bank took an equitable mortgage of shares fraudulently offered by a nominee holder. Later, the beneficial owner declared his interest, whereupon the bank completed the blank signed transfers it was holding and had the shares registered in its name. The bank's claim to the shares failed, since as equitable mortgagee its title was inferior to that of the person with the prior beneficial interest and as legal mortgagee, it could not obtain good title when it was aware of a beneficial interest at the time it completed its legal mortgage.

There is a risk that a fraudulent customer may deposit the share certificate with an equitable mortgagee, and then claim to the company that the certificate is lost, obtain a new certificate and sell the shares. The bank's title will be inferior to that of an innocent purchaser. There is a procedure whereby the equitable mortgagee may utilise the Rules of the Supreme Court Order 50 to serve a 'Stop Notice' on the company, which will then be obliged to give the mortgagee 14 days notice before registering any transfer of ownership. In this time the bank can seek an injunction from the court to stop its customer from selling the shares. This procedure is not appropriate as a matter of routine, however, and if there is any concern about fraud on the part of the customer, it would be far simpler to take a legal mortgage from the start.

As the bank does not hold legal title to the shares, any dividend or rights or bonus issue will go to the customer. Rights and bonus issues, of course, may dilute the equity, making the block of shares held under the bank's charge less valuable.

Some banks take the view that the risks attached to equitable mortgages of shares are so great that it is their policy always to take a full legal charge.

15 Life Assurance Policies as Security

15.1 INTRODUCTION

Life assurance policies may take one of three different forms:

(a) Whole life policy. This matures on death of the life assured.

(b) Endowment policy. This matures on expiration of a fixed term or on earlier death of the life assured. Endowment policies may be either low-cost or full-cost. The former is commonly used in conjunction with a house-purchase mortgage loan. During the term of the mortgage loan, interest only is paid to the lender, and at the end of the term the endowment policy matures in order to repay the principal.

(c) Term policy. This provides cover against death of the life assured during a fixed term. If the life assured survives this term, no monies are paid.

In the first two types of policy there will inevitably be a claim at some stage. In the third there will not necessarily be a claim, and consequently this type of policy has no surrender value.

Basis of lending

When a lender is using a life policy as security for a loan, it is a simple matter to discover the present surrender value of the policy, i.e. what it can be cashed in for. Assuming premiums are paid, the surrender value should increase as time passes. A policy with no surrender value, such as a term policy or a newly enacted policy, may still be assigned in order to protect the lender against death of the borrower.

Parties involved in a life policy contract

(a) The Insurer, i.e. the Life Company.

(b) The Policyholder. Usually he takes out cover on his own life for his own benefit (or for the benefit of his beneficiaries on his death).

(c) The Life Assured. It may be that the policyholder takes out cover on the life of another.

(d) The Beneficiary. It may be that the policyholder has declared that some other person will receive payment when the policy matures. This is a policy written in trust, and includes settlement policies made under the provisions of the Married Women's Property Act 1882.

15.2 TYPES OF MORTGAGE ON LIFE POLICIES

Mortgages of life policies are truly assignments of the debt owed by the Insurer. There are two types:

(a) Legal Assignment.
(b) Equitable Assignment.

In both types, the policyholder (or such other beneficiary as may exist) assigns to the lender the benefit he is entitled to receive at some future date from the Insurer. The Assignee can only receive as good an interest as the Assignor holds; life policies are not negotiable instruments.

Legal assignment

This is usually effected under the Policies of Assurance Act 1867. The procedure under the Act requires:

(a) A written assignment. It need not be under seal.

(b) The assignor's signature must be witnessed.

(c) Written notice of the assignment must be given to the Insurer. If a written request is made to the Insurer, the Act requires him to issue a written acknowledgement of notice. For this service the Insurer is entitled to charge a sum not exceeding five shillings (now 25 pence), which inflation has devalued somewhat since 1867!

Once the legal assignment has been perfected, the assignee acquires the right to receive payment (subject to prior assignments) and can give a good discharge to the Insurer.

A legal assignment may also be effected under the general provision relating to assignments in s. 136 of the Law of Property Act 1925, which requires:

(a) An assignment of the whole debt.
(b) An assignment in writing (not necessarily under seal).
(c) Written notice is given to the debtor (the Insurer). There is no provision for acknowledgement of notice.

Equitable assignments

The law only requires that the parties intend that the equitable rights of the policyholder pass to the assignee, supported by valuable consideration. As with Share Certificates, the deposit of a life policy otherwise than for safe custody will create an equitable mortgage (*Spencer* v *Clarke* (1878)). It is bank practice, however, to bolster its position by having a memorandum of deposit signed by the customer assignor and by giving notice of assignment to the Insurer, for the reasons explained below. Power of sale without reference to the court can be achieved by taking the equitable assignment under seal.

15.3 PRIORITIES BETWEEN DIFFERENT ASSIGNEES

This is determined by the rule in *Dearle* v *Hall* (1828), which provides that the first to give notice to the Insurer has first priority, irrespective of whether the assignments are legal or equitable.

Constructive notice of prior assignment

Illustration

Spencer v *Clarke* (1878) establishes that non-production by the policyholder of the original policy may be constructive notice to the assignee of prior assignment, even if the first assignee did not give notice to the Insurer.

It follows from the above that an assignee who takes the original policy and is the first to give notice of assignment to the Insurer, will enjoy first priority whether his assignment is legal or equitable.

15.4 STANDARD TERMS

(a) A continuing security clause to counteract the effect of the rule in *Clayton*'s case.

(b) A promise by the assignor to pay the premiums and his agreement to the bank paying them for him, and the bank debiting his account accordingly.

(c) In a legal assignment, the bank has the right to sell and surrender the policy, and the statutory waiting periods in s. 103 of the Law of Property Act 1925 are excluded.

(d) Section 93 of the Law of Property Act 1925, which would prevent the assignee from consolidating, is also excluded.

(e) In an equitable assignment, the bank can require the assignor to provide a legal assignment on demand by the bank.

15.5 REMEDIES OF THE ASSIGNEE

(a) The legal assignee may surrender the policy to the Insurer and is entitled to receive the full surrender value. Alternatively, he may sell the policy to a third party. After deducting his loan, interest and expenses he will pass on the balance to the policyholder. A higher figure may be obtained by sale of the policy to an investor, and it may be that the assignee is under a duty to do so in order to obtain the best possible price, as laid down in *Standard Chartered Bank* v *Walker* (1982) CA. If the policy has matured, the assignee is entitled to the full capital value from the Insurer, subject to the same duty to pass on the balance.

(b) An equitable assignee's rights depend on whether his assignment is under hand or under seal. If under hand, a sale can only occur with a court order. If under seal, the accompanying irrevocable power of attorney in favour of the assignee will permit a sale by him.

15.6 POTENTIAL RISKS FOR THE LENDER

Beneficiaries

As mentioned earlier, the assignment must always be taken from the person entitled to receive payment on maturity of the policy, and this may be someone other than the policyholder or his personal representatives. If so, the lender must ensure:

(a) None of the beneficiaries are under 18 when making the assignment, as it would then be ineffective.
(b) The beneficiary must be named. If a policy in favour of 'the wife of X' is assigned, this would not bind a later (different) wife.
(c) The lender must be conscious of the possibility of the beneficiary raising undue influence when the security is realised, particularly when all the benefit of the loan accrues to another.

Insurable interest

It is possible for a policyholder to insure the life of another but, under the Life Assurance Act 1774, which was passed to prevent '... a mischievous kind of gaming', this is restricted to certain relationships. Apart from one's own life, one can insure the life of one's spouse. The life of a parent, that of an employee and that of a debtor (among others) may be insured but only to a limited extent.

Where insurable interest is lacking, the Act declares the life insurance contract null and void. Therefore the Insurer may refuse to pay on maturity of the policy and may refuse to return premiums. However, in *Hughes* v *Liverpool Victoria Friendly Society* (1916), an agent of the Insurer had told the policyholder that the policies were valid; the court considered this to be fraud and the premiums had to be returned.

Insurers on occasions do issue policies where it is doubtful whether any insurable interest exists.

Where the policy has been assigned, there is no requirement that the assignee has an insurable interest. Also where an insurable interest has ceased to exist, e.g. due to divorce, this will not affect the policy.

Non-disclosure and misrepresentation

Insurers are protected by the *uberrima fides* rule, which requires the proposer to disclose all facts which would be material to the Insurer when deciding whether to issue cover, or how much premium to charge for doing so. Therefore, the proposer is under a duty to disclose material facts, even if he is not asked a relevant question, and he must honestly answer all questions he is asked.

Where the policyholder has failed in this duty, the Insurer is entitled to void the policy and therefore to refuse to pay on a claim. Premiums are returnable unless the policyholder acted fraudulently.

Suicide

The policyholder and life assured may seek to bring about maturity of the policy by committing suicide. Most Insurers include a clause excluding liability to pay if death is caused in this manner during the first year of the policy. Such a clause will be effective, but it was held in *Beresford* v *Royal Insurance Co. Ltd* (1938) HL that it raises an implication that the Insurer agrees to pay where suicide occurs after the initial period. The clause usually goes on to say that if death is caused by suicide during the first year, the Insurer will pay any assignee of the policy.

Illustration

In the *Beresford* case, a 'sane' suicide occurred after the initial period. It was held that normally the Insurer would not be obliged to pay, as the policyholder should not be able to deliberately cause the insured event to occur and cause the insurance monies to be paid, in the same way as an Insurer could not be forced to pay on a buildings policy if the policyholder burned his own house. However, the effect of the clause was held to be that the Insurer had impliedly agreed to pay in these circumstances. The Insurer won the *Beresford* case as suicide was at that time illegal and the court refused to enforce the contract on public policy grounds. The Suicide Act 1961 'legalised' suicide, and on the same facts the Insurer would now be obliged to pay.

Where no suicide clause is included in the policy, the basic rule applies, and any 'sane' suicide will not produce a valid claim. An 'insane' suicide, however, will do so. This is because it is not a deliberate act.

Where the Insurer is entitled to refuse to pay, he is not obliged to return premiums as he has been on risk until the suicide, when death might have been caused by other means.

Murder and unlawful killing

Where the life assured is murdered either by the policyholder, the beneficiary or by anyone entitled indirectly to the insurance monies through the deceased's will or under the rules of intestacy, the Insurer is not obliged to pay. It seems likely that the same applies to a manslaughter killing. The Insurer would not be obliged to return premiums.

Non-payment of premiums

In practice a bank will wish to monitor payment of premiums by establishing a direct debit from the policyholder's account. An Insurer to whom notice of assignment has been given may warn a bank when a policy is about to lapse due to non-payment of premiums. Where the bank is aware that the policy is about to lapse, its mortgage will normally give it the right to pay the premiums itself, to convert the policy into a paid-up state or to surrender the policy.

Where the bank has not taken any action, the position will depend on the terms in the policy. Frequently the Insurer will use the surrender value of the policy to pay premiums, and after a given time convert it into a paid-up state. In the absence of such provisions, however, there has to be a risk that the policy will lapse with no return of premiums.

16 Taking Security from Companies

16.1 INTRODUCTION

If a secured loan is made to a registered company, the legal position is often similar to that pertaining when the security is taken from an individual. If the asset charged is land, the same considerations of registration apply. If it concerns a life or other insurance policy, the same doctrine of notice applies.

As a general rule, it is fair to say that when a fixed charge is granted by a company, all the law which applies in the 'individual' case applies but there may be extra considerations due to a company being involved. One must also be aware that companies are able to create a special type of charge known as a floating charge. When a bank lends to a corporate customer, any security it takes is likely to be in the form of a 'debenture'. This has no connection with loan stock debentures which may be traded on the Stock Exchange, it is simply a practice term used to describe the typical form of charge taken by a bank from a company customer. This debenture will incorporate a fixed charge over the book debts and the fixed assets of any value which the company owns, and a floating charge on the company's assets in general.

The law relating to companies is contained chiefly in a consolidating enactment, namely the Companies Act 1985. This has been amended and supplemented, however, by the Companies Act 1989. Matters relating to liquidation and receivership are contained in the Insolvency Act 1986.

16.2 CORPORATE CAPACITY

The long-established *ultra vires* rule was abolished by the Companies Act 1989. A new s. 35 is inserted into the Companies Act 1985, which declares that the validity of an act done by a company shall not be called into question on the ground of lack of capacity by reason of anything in the company's memorandum. A company therefore will continue to have a memorandum setting out the objects of the company but a third party will not be affected by it whether or not he knows of the contents of the company's 'objects clause'.

A new s. 35A provides that in favour of a person dealing with a company in good faith, the power of the board of directors to bind the company shall be deemed to be free of any limitation under the company's constitution. It is expressly provided that a person shall not be regarded as acting in bad faith, by reason only of his knowing that an act is beyond the powers of the directors.

In s. 35B it is stated that a party entering into a transaction with a company is not bound to enquire as to whether the transaction is within the company's memorandum or whether it is within the powers of the directors acting on behalf of the company.

Under these rules, a bank lending to a company need not be concerned to look at the company's memorandum and articles of association to determine whether the company or its agents are acting properly. Nor will it be put on notice of lack of capacity by having seen these documents.

The *ultra vires* rule still applies in some situations, however. For example, where the directors exceed their powers and the other party to the transaction includes a director of the company (s. 322A). A bank may have to be careful if, for instance, it lends to a company under a loan agreement containing a directors' guarantee.

16.3 EXECUTION OF DOCUMENTS BY A COMPANY

These rules affect the form of documents whereby a company grants security to a bank.

Section 36A declares that a company need no longer have its own company seal. Whether it has one or not, a document signed by two directors, or by one director and the company secretary, has the same effect as if it had the company's seal on it.

If it is clear from the document's face that it is intended to be a deed, then it takes effect as a deed. The company's seal is not necessary.

Similar rules apply to Scottish companies.

16.4 THE FLOATING CHARGE

When a fixed charge is taken over the assets of an individual or of a company, the chargee has the comfort of knowing that he enjoys first priority over the asset (assuming it is a first charge and is perfected) and that the chargor is not able to validly dispose of the asset without his permission. Thus a first fixed charge over an asset which is unlikely to decline in value (such as some types of land and insurance policies), is a good security. Fixed charges over assets which will decline in value (such as some types of plant and machinery which will have to be replaced after a few years), are good security only in the early years. The replacement asset will not automatically be covered by the charge, although the customer can be asked to provide a new charge.

It is possible to take fixed charges over current assets (such as stock in trade) but it is likely to be highly inconvenient, for both bank and customer, for permission to have to be sought each time the asset is disposed of and for a fresh charge to be granted to cover the replacement items. Fortunately this is not a problem with one form of current asset, namely book debts. The law does permit a fixed charge to be taken which covers future book debts (see chapter 18).

The floating charge therefore has two great advantages over the fixed charge:

(a) It can conveniently cover the stock in trade of a business customer; and

(b) It can automatically cover all assets which are acquired in the future.

An effective floating charge cannot be created by a non-corporate entity, as non-possessory charges created by individuals must be registered under the Bills of Sale Act, with details entered of all the specific items covered by the charge. An exception to this rule is a form of agricultural floating charge which may be created under the Agricultural Credits Act 1928 (see chapter 19).

The floating charge may in theory be expressed to be over certain classes of asset but in practice it is invariably expressed to be over all of the assets of the company chargor. In this case it is an equitable charge which 'hovers' until some event crystallises the charge, at which time it becomes a fixed equitable charge on the assets which the company happens to own at that time (*Re Yorkshire Woolcombers Association Ltd* (1903) CA). The crystallising events would typically be either the company going into liquidation or the chargeholder appointing administrative receivers, following a default by the company.

16.5 STANDARD DEBENTURE TERMS

(1) The company agrees to pay on written demand all monies owing, and demand may be made at the company's registered office.

(2) The company grants fixed charges over the assets listed in a schedule and a floating charge over all the assets present and future.

(3) A promise by the company not to grant any charge which would rank equally with or ahead of the bank's floating charge, and a promise not to dispose of assets except in the ordinary course of business.

(4) The company, on the bank's written demand, will grant a legal mortgage to the bank of any land it acquires in the future.

(5) A 'continuing security' clause (see **13.11** above).

(6) Power for the bank to appoint receivers (or administrative receivers) and managers at any time after the bank has made demand, or if the company so requests, or a petition has been presented to the court under s. 9 of the Insolvency Act 1986 for the making of an administration order in respect of the company (see below for details of administration orders). The receiver is to be the agent of the company and is granted specific powers, including sale of company property and to carry on its business. Irrevocable power is granted to the bank and to the receiver to execute deeds on the company's behalf. The bank may determine the remuneration of the receiver.

(7) Exclusion of ss. 93 and 103 of the Law of Property Act 1925 (see **13.11**).

(8) A promise by the company not to assign its book debts to third parties and to pay those debts into its account with the bank when they are received (see chapter 18 for an explanation of the considerable importance of this clause).

(9) To provide copies of the annual accounts of the company.

(10) To keep its assets in good repair and insured.

16.6 FIXED AND FLOATING CHARGES COMPARED

(a) The company is free to buy and sell those assets which are covered only by the floating charge. The danger for the bank is that the company will run down the level of its assets, so that when the charge crystallises, it fixes onto very few assets. This may constitute a breach of clause (3) above (see **16.5**) but if the company is insolvent, this will not assist.

(b) Nothing can subordinate a first fixed perfected charge. However, the floating charge is subordinated to a subsequent fixed charge (*Wheatley* v *Silkstone and Haigh Moor Coal Co.* (1885)). If a company does grant a fixed charge to a different creditor after giving a bank the standard debenture, it will contravene clause (3) above but this in itself would not invalidate the charge unless the chargee had notice of the clause. Such notice may be constructive in the form of registration of particulars of the clause (s. 199(1) of the Law of Property Act 1925 and see the new rules on registration of charges in **16.11** below). A floating charge may also, in effect, be subordinated by a judgment creditor who successfully sues the company and enforces the judgment (e.g. by bailiffs seizing stock) before the charge crystallises (*Re Opera Ltd* (1891)).

(c) Holders of a first fixed charge will have first priority to the proceeds of sale of the asset they have a charge over, after sale expenses have been met. The floating charge holder will be subordinated to preferential creditors, as defined in s. 386 and Sch. 6 of the Insolvency Act 1986.

(d) Any charge which is granted to secure a previously unsecured debt is potentially vulnerable as a preference under s. 239 of the Insolvency Act 1986, if the company commences winding-up within the next six months (24 months if the parties are 'connected persons') and the company was influenced by a desire to prefer the bank over other creditors. Floating charges are additionally vulnerable under s. 245, which provides that such charges which are granted to secure a prior debt will be invalid if the company commences winding-up within the following 12 months (24 months if the parties are connected), unless it can be proved that the company was solvent immediately after the giving of the charge. A desire to prefer does not this time have to be proved. The charge will be valid to the extent that money is provided at the time the charge is given, or after it is given and interest at a fixed rate may be added (it is currently fixed at 5%). An already complex provision may be further compounded by the effect of the rule in *Clayton*'s case.

Illustration

Re Yeovil Glove Co. Ltd (1965) CA. Y Ltd had an overdraft of £67,500 with the bank which then required a floating charge from the company. The overdraft balance remained at a similar figure but it was an active account and around £110,000 was paid in and out. Within 12 months of the charge being taken, winding-up of the company commenced. The liquidator claimed the charge was void but the court held that the effect of *Clayton*'s case was to bring forward the effective date of the debt so that it post-dated the creation of the charge, which was therefore fully valid.

However, if there is no genuine activity on the account and the court considers the later debits on the account do not represent fresh payments, the *Clayton*'s case rule will not be applied (*Re Destone Fabrics Ltd* (1941)).

(e) The stock covered by the floating charge may not belong to the company at all, due to a 'retention of title' clause in the contract of sale which operates for the benefit of the supplier of the stock. If, as a result, the stock never became the property of the company in the first place, no chargeholder or other creditor can receive the proceeds of its sale. This naturally is more likely to prejudice a floating charge than a fixed charge (see **16.9** below for a fuller discussion of retention of title clauses).

(f) The holder of a floating charge is able to prevent the making of an administration order by the court under s. 9 of the Insolvency Act 1986 (see **16.10** below for details of administration orders). A fixed charge holder does not have this ability. In practice this is a powerful reason for a bank to take a floating charge on every occasion it takes company security.

16.7 CRYSTALLISATION OF A FLOATING CHARGE

This is the process by which the charge becomes a fixed one over the assets which the company owns at the relevant time. This will occur when the bank appoints a receiver pursuant to its powers in the debenture (*Governments Stocks and Other Securities Investment Co. Ltd v Manila Railway Co. Ltd* (1897) HL), or if the company commences winding-up, whether or not the company is in default (*Hodson v Tea Company* (1880)), or if the company completely ceases to carry on business (*Re Woodroffes (Musical Instruments) Ltd* (1986)). The appointment of an administrator may also crystallise a floating charge, although this is not yet certain, and most floating charges will make express provision for administration to crystallise the security. Such a provision may be one of several in a floating charge which specify particular events which will cause the security to crystallise. For instance, the floating charge may provide that the mortgagee can crystallise the security at any time simply by giving notice to the company (*Re Brightlife Ltd* (1987)). However, the attraction of these procedures has been greatly reduced by certain provisions of the Insolvency Act 1986 because only sale proceeds recovered from a voluntary sale by the company before winding up or receivership can now be treated as fixed charge recoveries, free from preferential creditors' claims. In addition, s. 410 of the Companies Act 1985 (as amended) now provides that regulations may be introduced which require registration of crystallisation within a certain time period.

16.8 ADMINISTRATIVE RECEIVERS

'Administrative receiver' is the term used in the Insolvency Act 1986 for a receiver appointed under a floating charge, to distinguish him from receivers appointed by the court and receivers of rent appointed under the Law of Property Act 1925. However, administrative receivers are referred to in this book simply as receivers.

The following discussion of the law relating to receivers is from a banker's point of view, in that much law which would not always concern the appointing bank (but which would concern a receiver) is excluded. Also it is assumed that a standard form debenture has been executed.

Appointment of receiver

Where the bank has become concerned about a company account, in practice the bank may suggest that the directors invite the bank to appoint a receiver. An appointment at the directors' invitation will avoid the receiver being a trespasser on the company's property, even if his appointment is invalid. If they decline, the bank may appoint in any case, and assuming the appointment is legally valid and bona fide, the appointment cannot be challenged (*Shamji* v *Johnson Matthey Bankers Ltd* (1986)).

A fixed chargeholder will appoint a receiver, as explained in chapter 13. A floating chargeholder will appoint administrative receivers. A bank normally appoints the latter, and the following references to 'receivers' refers to these. The appointment must be in writing, s. 109(1) of the Law of Property Act 1925 and the standard debenture so provides, but it need not be under seal (*Windsor Refrigerator Co. Ltd* v *Branch Nominees Ltd* (1961)). The appointed receiver must be an insolvency practitioner, authorised to act as such.

Companies are not permitted to act as receivers. It is common practice for two receivers to be appointed jointly, to minimise possible succession problems if one retires or dies.

Receivers will not be displaced by a subsequent liquidation of the company, and they may be appointed even after the winding-up has commenced (*Re Stubbs (Joshua) Ltd, Barney* v *Stubbs (Joshua) Ltd* (1891)). Under the Insolvency Act 1986, after being appointed, the receivers must publish the appointment, notify the company, notify creditors and notice of it must appear on company stationery. The bank must notify the Registrar of Companies within seven days and the appointment will appear on the company's charges register.

If time is of the essence, e.g. because a judgment creditor is about to have the company's assets seized, the bank can move very quickly to appoint a receiver.

Illustration

R.A. Cripps & Son Ltd v *Wickenden* (1973). Demand was effectively made to the company at 10.45 a.m. No monies having been forthcoming, the receiver was appointed at 12.30 p.m. on the same day. This was held to have allowed sufficient time for the company to comply with the demand, since the law only recognised the need to physically move the money to the bank, and not the need to negotiate the raising of the necessary funds from another source.

Receivers are expressed to be agents of the company in the debenture. This is a strange form of agency since the receiver, for obvious reasons, does not take instructions from the company and he is personally liable on contracts he makes for the company, unless the contrary is stated in each contract. As he is agent of the company, however, the bank that appointed him cannot be held liable for his negligence. In practice, the receiver will demand an indemnity from the bank before accepting. Furthermore, the bank's actions may negate the written terms of the debenture.

Illustration

Standard Chartered Bank Ltd v *Walker* (1982) CA. The bank had taken a standard debenture from JW Ltd and also had personal guarantees from Mr and Mrs W. A receiver was appointed (as agent of the company) and, responding to pressure from the bank, put the company's plant and machinery in an unsuitable auction sale. The bank also called on Mr and Mrs W to pay but the defence was that if a proper price had been obtained for the assets, there would have been a lower claim under the guarantee. The bank was unable to deny liability for the receiver's negligence, as it had chosen to instruct the receiver to make an early sale of the assets and thus make him its agent, regardless of the terms of the debenture.

The amount of the receiver's remuneration may be determined by the bank if the debenture so specifies.

Obligations of the receiver

After the appointment, the Companies Act 1985 and the Insolvency Act 1986 require the directors of the company to prepare a statement of affairs for the receiver who must, in turn, send a copy of it to the Registrar of Companies. Thereafter he must prepare annual (and final) accounts of his receipts and payments for the Registrar, and keep sufficient records for the company's accounts to be prepared.

The receiver must pay off the preferential creditors before the floating chargeholder, although inasmuch as the bank has fixed charges, the proceeds of sale of these assets will go to the bank before the preferential creditors.

It has been seen in chapter 2 that a bank may become a preferential creditor by having advanced money for the payment of the company employees' wages. Where the bank's claim against a company in liquidation is partly preferential and partly non-preferential and it holds some fixed and floating charges, it is entitled to set the proceeds of sale from the assets subject to the fixed charge against the non-preferential element, permitting the bank to claim as a preferential creditor for the balance still owing after realisation of the fixed charges (*Re William Hall (Contractors) Ltd* (1967)).

Powers of the receiver

The debenture will grant considerable power to sell assets and manage the company's business. Schedule 1 to the Insolvency Act 1986 grants wide powers in any case.

The receiver may petition the court for a winding-up order if this may lead to preservation of the assets of the company (*Re Emmadart Ltd* (1979)). In any case where the court orders a winding-up, a receiver who was appointed before the liquidator may continue to sell assets (*Sowman v David Samuel Trust Ltd* (1978)). One appointed after the liquidator may not (*Re Henry Pound, Son & Hutchins Ltd* (1889)). In a voluntary winding-up, the receiver may sell assets after the liquidator is appointed, even if the receiver was appointed later.

16.9 RETENTION OF TITLE OR 'ROMALPA' CLAUSES

As mentioned above, the value of a floating charge may be diminished by the effect of these clauses. It is always vexing, however, for a supplier of goods to see goods he has just delivered to a company purchaser and which have not yet been paid for, being sold off to pay the company's preferential creditors and floating charge holder while, as an unsecured creditor, he receives nothing. It is unsurprising, therefore, that he will do his best to improve his position, which can in fact be achieved by the simple expedient of inserting a clause into his standard form conditions of sale. Such an approach may or may not assist, however, depending on the exact clause used and the exact circumstances of the case. The law relating to these clauses is regrettably complex.

Under the Sale of Goods Act 1979, the parties to a sale of goods contract are free to express the time when the title to the goods being sold will pass. The seller of the goods will therefore prefer to express that title will pass at the time when the goods are fully paid for.

Illustration

Aluminium Industrie Vaasen BV v *Romalpa Aluminium Ltd* (1976) CA. A supplied foil to R on terms that legal and beneficial ownership was to remain with A until the foil was fully paid for. Meanwhile R agreed to keep the foil separate from other goods in its possession and, at A's request, to assign to A the proceeds of any sale of the foil to a sub-purchaser. R had borrowed from a bank against the security of a floating charge. At the time the bank appointed a receiver, there was a large amount of foil in R's possession which had been supplied by A, which was unpaid for, and which had been kept separate. Also there was a sum of money which R had obtained from sub-purchasers of foil, for which A was unpaid. A successfully claimed both the foil and the proceeds of sale in priority to the bank's floating charge. It was held that the contract made R a bailee of the foil until it was paid for, and therefore the foil in R's possession was still the property of A, and that the foil which had been sold on to sub-purchasers had been sold by R as A's agent, and A was therefore able to trace the proceeds of sale from A's bank account.

A series of subsequent cases has failed to extend significantly the parameters of the *Romalpa* decision. In particular, it seems it is not possible to reclaim goods if they have simply been mixed with other (similar) goods from other suppliers, such as oil or other liquid goods stored in a vat so that it is impossible to identify precisely the supplier's goods. If the goods have been mixed with other products in a manufacturing process, any right to trace the goods into the finished product seems to be fraught with problems, and to trace the proceeds of sale of the finished product is impossible. Any other form of clause (such as one which permits the purchaser to acquire the legal title to the goods and the right to use them in a manufacturing process but yet reserving an equitable right over them) can only be effective as a charge over the goods which requires registration under s. 395 of the Companies Act 1985, and if it is not so registered within 21 days of the contract being made, it is void against a liquidator of the purchasing company. It is clearly not practical for suppliers to register a charge on each occasion they supply goods to a company but it has been argued that where a supplier and a company purchaser have made a specific agreement to insert a retention of title clause into all their contracts, one registration of this agreement will suffice.

16.10 ADMINISTRATION ORDERS

It has been seen above that a floating chargeholder's rights are largely unaffected by the commencement of a company's winding-up and the appointment of a liquidator. This is not true, however, of an administration order and the appointment of an administrator.

Section 8 of the Insolvency Act 1986 provides that the court may make an administration order where:

(a) the company is, or is likely to become, unable to pay its debts; and
(b) the making of an order is likely to achieve either:

 (i) a more advantageous realisation of the company's assets than would a liquidation; or
 (ii) the survival of at least part of the company's business.

If the order is made and an administrator appointed, then from that moment no chargeholder may realise his security. Fixed chargeholders may not sell assets and floating chargeholders may not appoint receivers. Assets subject to a fixed charge may be sold by agreement between the administrator and the chargeholder or, failing this, by court order. The chargeholder must receive the proceeds of sale of the asset in the usual way when it is sold, although meanwhile interest may have built up or the asset may have depreciated in value.

The floating chargeholder, however, will lose priority to the expenses of the administration and to the trade debts incurred during the administration. Furthermore, the administrator has complete control over the timing of sales of assets subject to the floating charge. The administrator cannot, however, profit from the company's assets in disregard of third-party interests in them, and third parties may apply for a court order to protect their position.

It is provided in s. 9 that once a petition is made to the court for the making of an administration order, the court must give notice of this petition to any floating chargeholder (assuming he has a charge over substantially the whole of the company's assets, which a standard bank debenture will grant). It is further provided that the court is unable to make the order if administrative receivers are in place.

The effect of the above is that a floating chargeholder is always able to prevent the making of an administration order if he so wishes (by appointing administrative receivers before the court makes the administration order), but that a fixed chargeholder does not have this power. Accordingly, it is now bank practice to take fixed and floating charges in all cases.

The concept of the administration order has yet to become popular. In 1989 there were 129 orders, down from 198 the previous year.

16.11 PRIORITY OF CHARGES AND REGISTRATION

These rules are substantially affected by the Companies Act 1989. The new law is described here and is expected to come into force in June 1991.

Charges requiring registration

Section 395 of the Companies Act 1985 requires that certain types of charge created by companies must be registered with the Registrar of Companies at Companies House. Section 396 (as amended) lists the charges which must be registered and these now are as follows:

(a) a floating charge;
(b) a charge on land, or any interest in land;
(c) a charge on goodwill, intellectual property, book debts or uncalled share capital;
(d) a non-possessory charge on goods;
(e) a charge for securing an issue of debenture stock.

Clearly the standard bank debenture does require registration as it incorporates a floating charge.

Registration consists of supplying the prescribed particulars of the charge in the prescribed form to the Registrar of Companies (regulations will be made to specify what is prescribed).

It is advantageous to include specific details of the term in the debenture which prohibits the company from granting subsequent charges to other lenders which would rank *pari passu* with, or ahead of, the debenture (as explained in **16.6** above). Section 416 now states that a person taking a charge is deemed to have notice of any matter requiring registration and disclosed on the register at the time he takes his charge. It is specifically stated in s. 415 that the prescribed particulars may include whether the company has undertaken not to create other charges ranking in priority or *pari passu* with the charge being registered, and the regulations will almost certainly adopt this.

It is the company's duty to register a charge it creates and it commits an offence if the charge is not registered. However, any person interested in the charge may register it and banks prefer to do so for obvious reasons. The Registrar must send both a copy of the registered particulars and a note of the date of their delivery to the company and to the chargee (s. 398).

On request by the chargee, the Registrar must provide a certificate stating the date on which the particulars of the charge were registered. This certificate is conclusive evidence that the particulars of the charge were delivered no later than the date stated (s. 397). It will still be open to a liquidator to dispute the validity of the charge, however. For instance, it could be argued that incomplete particulars were delivered or even that complete particulars were delivered but that the Registrar omitted to register some of them. As a consequence of this (and of s. 416 above), a bank will be well advised to examine closely its copy of the registered particulars of its charge. Alternatively, it could be argued that the charge was registered late (perhaps because the charge was held undated for some time before a date was entered on it). For those familiar with the old law, if the same facts arose today as occurred in the cases of *Re C.L. Nye Ltd* (1970) CA and *National Provincial and Union Bank of England* v *Charnley* (1924) CA, opposite conclusions would now have to be reached.

Consequence of failing to register

The requirement is to register the charge within 21 days of the creation of the charge, failing which it becomes void against:

(a) any liquidator or administrator of the company;

(b) any person who for value acquires an interest in the property subject to the charge (such as a purchaser of the property or a second mortgagee of it) (s. 399).

By s. 414 a charge is deemed to be created when:

(a) an unconditional instrument is executed; or
(b) the conditions of a conditional instrument are fulfilled; or
(c) where there is no instrument creating the charge (which would be unusual in the banking context), when an agreement is entered into by the company conferring a security interest.

This means that a bank which holds an executed but undated

company charge risks losing its security by waiting before dating and registering it. The creditor whose charge is unregistered becomes an unsecured creditor in a liquidation. Note, however, that the charge is valid when created but becomes void on the 22nd day after its creation, if it is not registered by then. Even then, the charge will still be valid against the company itself, and can be enforced so long as the company is not in liquidation.

Late registration

A charge may now be registered late, however, and where the charge is registered after 21 days have passed, the charge will still be valid, although the rights of creditors who have registered charges in the meantime are protected. In addition, a late registered charge will be void against a liquidator or administrator of the company if the company was unable to pay its debts at the time the charge was registered and insolvency proceedings begin within six months of the charge being registered (12 months in the case of a floating charge) (s. 400).

Errors and omissions

Section 402 now provides that where the registered particulars of a charge are not complete and accurate, the charge is void to the extent that rights are not disclosed due to the inaccuracy or incompleteness of the particulars.

The court may make an order validating such a charge if it is satisfied that no unsecured creditor has been materially misled or that no person became an unsecured creditor while the registered particulars were inaccurate or incomplete (s. 402).

Further particulars of a charge, supplementing or varying the registered particulars may be made at any time in the prescribed form (s. 401).

Release of charges

Upon release of the charge, a memorandum should be delivered to the Registrar. The memorandum should be in prescribed form and signed by, or on behalf of, the company and the chargee (s. 403).

17 Charges Over Bank Balances

17.1 INTRODUCTION

In practice it is quite common for a bank to wish to use a customer's credit balance as a form of security for some liability which the customer owes or might in the future owe to the bank.

The concept of set-off has been discussed in 1.14 above. This will permit, for example, a bank which has lent money on current account to set this off against a credit balance held on deposit, and thus provides an ideal form of security for the bank since no formal procedures are involved such as application to the court; the bank can simply take the money. Nor is any advance documentation necessary. In the event of insolvency of the customer, the statutory set-off rules in the Insolvency Act 1986 apply, with the same effect.

A simple reliance on common law and statutory set-off will not always be sufficient, however. For instance, the customer may withdraw the funds in the credit balance, or he may assign the credit balance to some third party, or the bank may wish to look to the deposit as security for the debt of a third party, or may wish it to secure a contingent liability (such as a guarantor's liability, which will only ever become operative if the principal debtor defaults). In these events the right of set-off may not be available to the bank.

There is a clear commercial need, therefore, for a simple and effective form of charging a bank deposit to the bank where it is deposited, in the same way that other property of the customer, such as shares, can be charged. Much the same need arises in the insurance industry, where companies lend money to their policyholders against the security of the life policy issued by themselves.

Unfortunately, the law fails to meet these needs and something which ought in theory to be quite simple becomes labyrinthine in practice.

The following discussion assumes that a bank wishes (in effect) to take a charge over a credit balance, so that it may prevent the customer from withdrawing it and so that it will be a good security in the event of the customer's insolvency. There are three recognised means of attempting

299

to do so, and in true belt and braces fashion, banks commonly adopt all three in combination.

The key to understanding what follows is to remember that when a customer has 'money in a bank account', the law analyses this as the bank owning the money but owing a debt to the customer, who therefore owns the right to receive that debt from the bank (called a chose in action).

17.2 CONTRACTUALLY EXTENDING THE RIGHT OF SET-OFF

As explained earlier, the right of set-off prior to insolvency is based on common law and, subsequent to insolvency, on statute. Common law will not permit a contingent liability, an unmatured liability nor a third party liability to be set off against a cash balance. Furthermore, the bank may at any time receive notice that the benefit of the credit balance has been assigned to some third party or attached under a Garnishee order of the court, and this will prevent a set-off of contingent or subsequent liabilities when they mature or crystallize. Common law is also prepared to perceive an implied agreement between bank and customer not to set-off (see *Buckingham* v *London & Midland Bank Ltd* (1895)).

A properly drafted deposit agreement or letter of set-off will deal with all of the above concerns, with the possible exceptions of the assignment and the Garnishee (on one view of the law). The agreement should precisely specify which deposits and which liabilities are to be the basis of the set-off. The bank will be granted irrevocable authority to debit the credit balance with the debts, and the customer will be restrained from drawing from the account.

In the event of the customer's insolvency, statutory set-off under s. 323 of the Insolvency Act 1986 will apply (for insolvent companies, the Insolvency Rules 1986, rule 4.90 has the same effect). This provides for the setting off of mutual credits and debts. Any unmatured debts are accelerated, and it seems from *Re Charge Card Services Ltd* (1987), a case based on s. 31 of the now repealed Bankruptcy Act 1914, that contingent liabilities may also be set off. This is probably just as well, since *British Eagle International Airlines Ltd* v *Compagnie Nationale Air France* (1975) HL, interprets what is now s. 107 of the Insolvency Act 1986 to mean that any contractual provision which seeks to improve the position of an unsecured creditor in the event of insolvency is void. The thrust of s. 107 is that all unsecured creditors should be treated on a *pari passu* basis.

Notwithstanding the above assumption that a letter of set-off does not create a charge (and this conclusion was reached in *Re Charge Card Services Ltd*), it is conceivable that another (higher) court might analyse it as such. If this occurred with a corporate customer then there might be a requirement to register the 'charge' under the terms of ss. 395 and 396 of the Companies Act 1985, and failure to do so within 21 days of its creation would render it void as against a liquidator and other creditors. As it would be far too late to register when the case came to court, it may seem a sensible precaution to register all set-off agreements as charges within 21 days of their being made. However, in *Re Charge Card Services Ltd*, it was also held to be impossible for someone to take charge over a debt owing by him to the creditor/mortgagor. This is because a charge on a debt takes effect as an assignment and an assignment to the creditor extinguishes the debt.

The set-off agreement, if it is a charge, is one that requires registration if the credit balance constitutes a 'segregated fund' (*Swiss Bank Corporation* v *Lloyds Bank Ltd* (1982) HL), which seems to apply if the money is held in a separate account.

17.3 TAKING A CHARGE OVER THE CREDIT BALANCE

As explained above, the current state of the law holds that this is an impossibility. It was stated in *Halesowen Presswork and Assemblies Ltd* v *Westminster Bank* (1972) HL that a bank could not take a lien over a deposit with it, and this was applied in the first instance decision of *Re Charge Card Services Ltd* (1987) to conclude that a debtor (such as a bank) could not take a charge over a debt owed to itself. In *Re Hart, ex parte Caldicott* (1884) CA, however, it was held to be possible.

If a charge is taken over the credit balance, it may require registration as a charge over a book debt under s. 395 of the Companies Act 1985, if the chargor is a company. Once again, there is some doubt as to whether the law does require registration, this time because it is not clear whether the credit balance constitutes a 'book debt' but caution demands that the charge is registered within 21 days. It is current practice of the Companies Registration Office to accept applications for registration of charges of credit balances. Where the charge is granted by a non-corporate customer, it appears that registration as a bill of sale is not required.

17.4 THE FLAWED ASSET

In the event that a set-off is not available and it is confirmed that a charge taken is not effective, a backstop is provided by an agreement between bank and customer, which is part of the contract of deposit, and which restricts the ability of the customer to withdraw his funds until his liability to the bank has been discharged or can no longer arise (if it is contingent), such as a guarantee being determined with no debt due from the principal debtor and thus no liability on the part of the guarantor.

There must be some concern that the flawed asset agreement would not survive an insolvency of the customer, due to the *pari passu* principle enacted in s. 107 of the Insolvency Act 1986, discussed above. Equally, if it secures a contingent or subsequent liability, it may be subordinated to an assignment or a Garnishee order in the same way as a contractual set-off may be.

18 Charges Over Book Debts

18.1 INTRODUCTION

As explained in chapter 16, charges over a company's assets may be either fixed or floating, and fixed charges enjoy a considerable advantage over floating charges in that they rank higher in a company's liquidation. Floating charges, on the other hand, have the advantage of easily being attached to future property, i.e. property which the company will acquire after the charge is taken.

The item 'Current debtors' is frequently an important asset on a trading company's balance sheet. If a charge is taken over the company's assets and one year later the company goes into liquidation, the 'current debtors' asset is likely to be made up of entirely different debts owed to the company after this one year. Clearly a floating charge will encompass the new debts but it is also possible for a bank to take a fixed charge over these future debts, although this can only be an equitable fixed charge (*Tailby* v *Official Receiver* (1888) HL).

18.2 PROCEDURE FOR TAKING THE CHARGE

A charge over a company's book debts is one of the categories of charges which must be registered within 21 days (s. 396 of the Companies Act 1985).

A number of complications arise, however, with equitable fixed charges over future book debts, such as the requirement that the charge takes the correct form and that certain details of it be registered.

Illustrations

Siebe Gorman & Co. Ltd v *Barclays Bank Ltd* (1979). The bank took a debenture from a company, which included a fixed charge over future book debts. Under the terms of the debenture, the company was legally obliged to pay the proceeds of the debts, when received, into its account with the bank, and was prohibited from assigning the debts to other parties. The bank registered the debenture but the above terms were not noted on the register. The company subsequently did assign the debts to the plaintiff in payment of a debt that it owed to the plaintiff, and the bank was given notice of this assignment. The bank continued to operate the company's current account. The court held that a valid fixed charge had been created over the debts as they came into existence. It further held that the registration of the debenture did not give notice to the plaintiff of the specific terms relating to the charge over the debts. At the moment the bank received notice of assignment of the debts, it enjoyed priority but that (due to the lack of notice of the terms of the debenture) further advances would rank after the plaintiff's claim. Since the bank's loan to the company was on current account and the account was not broken, *Clayton*'s case operated to discharge the earlier debt which enjoyed priority, to be replaced by a later debt which did not.

Re Brightlife Ltd (1987). A non-bank creditor took a fixed charge over a company's future book debts but the company was legally entitled to pay the cheques it received from its debtors into its bank account and to withdraw the proceeds. The charge was held to be merely a floating charge because the chargee could not show that it was capable of exercising effective control over the company's debts.

Conclusions

It follows from the above that:

(a) It is not enough to simply describe the charge on future book debts as fixed; the terms of the charge must legally oblige the company to pay the debts into its account with the bank, and to (effectively or specifically) entitle the bank to refuse withdrawals against these credits. It is therefore problematic for a non-bank to take an effective fixed charge over future book debts.

(b) The terms of the charge must also prohibit assignments of the book debts, and details of this and of the obligations in (a) above must be entered on the company's register when the charge itself is registered, which must be within 21 days of its creation.

(c) Alternatively to (b) above, no further advances should be made to the company and current accounts should be ruled off, when notice of assignment is received.

(d) It should be noted that if the company does not comply with its obligation to pay the proceeds of the debts into its bank account, the bank may have no recourse other than to the company itself. This is because the debtors paying the debts can get a good discharge by paying the company and therefore cannot be held liable to the bank which has a charge on the debts. This may be different if the debtors have notice of the charge but they presumably cannot be deemed to know of the charge simply because it is registered.

19 Agricultural Charges

19.1 INTRODUCTION

It is always possible for agricultural land to be mortgaged in the same manner as any land, and a land mortgage will normally include fixtures attached to the land. However, some farmers are tenants and thus do not own an interest in the land which is mortgageable, and in any case the assets of a farm will consist of considerably more than the land it occupies.

Corporate farmers may grant a floating charge. A non-corporate farmer will be able to grant a non-possessory chattel mortgage by executing a bill of sale but this procedure has a number of drawbacks, and thus special forms of agricultural charge were established by the Agricultural Credits Act 1928.

The Act defines a farmer as an individual owner or tenant of an agricultural holding. The Act permits a farmer to charge any of his 'farming stock and other agricultural assets'. These are widely defined to include crops and horticultural produce (growing or harvested), livestock (including bees) and the produce and progeny thereof, seeds, manures, agricultural plant and machinery and rights to compensation. Charges may be fixed or floating.

19.2 FIXED CHARGES

This will specify the charged assets, but it will include the progeny of charged livestock born after the date of the charge and also any plant which is acquired to replace that charged. The standard form of charge will permit the bank to appoint a receiver of the property, or to sell it, if the chargor fails to pay on the bank's demand. Power of sale will also arise on other events such as a judgment creditor enforcing against any of the property, the chargor's death, bankruptcy or arrangement with creditors.

Unlike a normal fixed charge, the chargor is free to sell the assets but is obliged to pay the proceeds of sale to the bank. If he fails to do so with intention to defraud the bank, he commits a criminal offence.

The standard form charge will give the bank power to inspect the charged property. It will also oblige the chargor to keep the property in good repair and insured. Any money received from an insurance claim in respect of the property must be paid to the bank.

19.3 FLOATING CHARGES

Somewhat similar in its nature to the company floating charge, this covers 'the farming stock and other agricultural assets from time to time belonging to the farmer'. Unlike the company floating charge, he must pay over to the bank the proceeds of sale of any of the property covered by the charge, except for money he spends on farming stock, which will be subject to the charge.

The charge fixes automatically on the chargor's death or bankruptcy, or on dissolution of a partnership where the charged property is partnership property. The bank may give written notice to fix the charge, and the standard form will permit this on failure to repay on demand.

19.4 REGISTRATION AND PRIORITY

The charge must be registered within seven clear working days of its creation, failing which it becomes void (except against the chargor). There is a procedure for applying for a court extension of this period, however, if the omission to register was accidental or inadvertent. It is registered at the Agricultural Credits Department of the Land Registry under the name of the chargor. Registration constitutes notice to the world at large but when a charge expressly secures a current account or further lending (as bank charges do), the chargee is not deemed to have notice of a later charge if it is registered after he last searched.

It is possible, and clearly desirable, to search the Register before taking the charge. The bank will be deemed to have notice of charges already on the register. Very low fees are payable for searching and registering.

Priority between charges is determined by the order in which they are registered. Once a floating charge is registered, a subsequent fixed charge will be void as respects property covered by the earlier floating charge. Agricultural charges of crops attached to the land take priority over mortgages of that land, in respect of the crops, even if the land mortgage was created first.

AGRICULTURAL CHARGES

Claims for rent and taxes normally take priority to fixed and floating agricultural charges.

There is a preference rule for all agricultural charges which is analogous to the 12-month rule for company floating charges under s. 245, Insolvency Act 1986. If a bankruptcy order is made against a chargor, and the charge was created within three months prior to the petition being presented, then unless it can be proved that the chargor was solvent when he created the charge, the amount secured by the charge will be reduced by the sum owed to the bank prior to the creation of the charge.

Illustration

F owes the bank £10,000, unsecured. On 1 March, an agricultural charge is taken. On 1 May, when the bank is owed £15,000, a petition is presented against F and the court makes the bankruptcy order on 1 July. The charge is vulnerable because the petition was presented within three months of the creation of the charge (although the bankruptcy order was not), and the amount covered by it must therefore be reduced by the sum owed to the bank immediately before the creation of the charge. Thus the charge is good security for £5,000. Note that the provision is worded differently from s. 245 and the bank cannot obtain the benefit of the operation of *Clayton*'s case when the loan is made on current account.

Appendix 1 Relevant Statutory Provisions

Bills of Exchange Act 1882
Sections 2, 3, 20-27, 29, 30, 45, 59, 60, 75-81 and 90.

Cheques Act 1957
Sections 1, 2 and 4.

Law of Property (Miscellaneous Provisions) Act 1989
Sections 1 and 2.

Companies Act 1989
Sections 108, 130 and 142

Insolvency Act 1986
Sections 44, 84, 122, 123, 175, 213, 214, 238-241, 245, 247, 249, 251 ('shadow director' definition only), 267, 268, 284, 323, 328, 386, 387 and Schedule 6 (paras. 1-15 only).

Consumer Credit Act 1974
Sections 8-14, 16, 48-51, 60, 61, 65, 75, 83, 84, 126 and 127.

BILLS OF EXCHANGE ACT 1882

2 *Interpretation of terms* In this Act, unless the context otherwise requires,
'Acceptance' means an acceptance completed by delivery or notification.
'Action' includes counter claim and set off.
'Banker' includes a body of persons whether incorporated or not who carry on the business of banking.
'Bankrupt' includes any person whose estate is vested in a trustee or assignee under the law for the time being in force relating to bankruptcy.
'Bearer' means the person in possession of a bill or note which is payable to bearer.
'Bill' means bill of exchange, and 'note' means promissory note.
'Delivery' means transfer of possession, actual or constructive, from one person to another.
'Holder' means the payee or indorsee of a bill or note who is in possession of it, or the bearer thereof.
'Indorsement' means an indorsement completed by delivery.

'Issue' means the first delivery of a bill or note, complete in form to a person who takes it as a holder.
'Person' includes a body of persons whether incorporated or not.
'Value' means valuable consideration.
'Written' includes printed, and 'writing' includes print.

3 *Bill of exchange defined* (1) A bill of exchange is an unconditional order in writing, addressed by one person to another, signed by the person giving it, requiring the person to whom it is addressed to pay on demand or at a fixed or determinable future time a sum certain in money to or to the order of a specified person, or to bearer.
(2) An instrument which does not comply with these conditions, or which orders any act to be done in addition to the payment of money, is not a bill of exchange.
(3) An order to pay out of a particular fund is not unconditional within the meaning of this section; but an unqualified order to pay, coupled with (a) an indication of a particular fund out of which the drawee is to re-imburse himself or a particular account to be debited with the amount, or (b) a statement of the transaction which gives rise to the bill, is unconditional.
(4) A bill is not invalid by reason—
(a) That it is not dated;
(b) That it does not specify the value given, or that any value has been given therefor;
(c) That it does not specify the place where it is drawn or the place where it is payable.

20 *Inchoate instruments* (1) Where a simple signature on a blank ... paper is delivered by the signer in order that it may be converted into a bill, it operates as a prima facie authority to fill it up as a complete bill for any amount ... using the signature for that of the drawer, or the acceptor, or an indorser; and, in like manner, when a bill is wanting in any material particular, the person in possession of it has a prima facie authority to fill up the omission in any way he thinks fit.
(2) In order that any such instrument when completed may be enforceable against any person who became a party thereto prior to its completion, it must be filled up within a reasonable time, and strictly in accordance with the authority given. Reasonable time for this purpose is a question of fact.
Provided that if any such instrument after completion is negotiated to a holder in due course it shall be valid and effectual for all purposes in his hands, and he may enforce it as if it had been filled up within a reasonable time and strictly in accordance with the authority given.

21 *Delivery* (1) Every contract on a bill, whether it be the drawer's, the acceptor's, or an indorser's, is incomplete and revocable, until delivery of the instrument in order to give effect thereto.
Provided that where an acceptance is written on a bill, and the drawee gives notice to or according to the directions of the person entitled to the bill that he has accepted it, the acceptance then becomes complete and irrevocable.

(2) As between immediate parties, and as regards a remote party other than a holder in due course, the delivery—
(a) in order to be effectual must be made either by or under the authority of the party drawing, accepting, or indorsing, as the case may be:
(b) may be shown to have been conditional or for a special purpose only, and not for the purpose of transferring the property in the bill.
But if the bill be in the hands of a holder in due course a valid delivery of the bill by all parties prior to him so as to make them liable to him is conclusively presumed.
(3) Where a bill is no longer in the possession of a party who has signed it as drawer, acceptor, or indorser, a valid and unconditional delivery by him is presumed until the contrary is proved.

22 *Capacity of parties* (1) Capacity to incur liability as a party to a bill is co-extensive with capacity to contract.
Provided that nothing in this section shall enable a corporation to make itself liable as drawer, acceptor, or indorser of a bill unless it is competent to it so to do under the law for the time being in force relating to corporations.
(2) Where a bill is drawn or indorsed by an infant, minor, or corporation having no capacity or power to incur liability on a bill, the drawing or indorsement entitles the holder to receive payment of the bill, and to enforce it against any other party thereto.

23 *Signature essential to liability* No person is liable as drawer, indorser, or acceptor of a bill who has not signed it as such: Provided that
(1) Where a person signs a bill in a trade or assumed name, he is liable thereon as if he had signed it in his own name:
(2) The signature of the name of a firm is equivalent to the signature by the person so signing of the names of all persons liable as partners in that firm.

24 *Forged or unauthorised signature* Subject to the provisions of this Act, where a signature on a bill is forged or placed thereon without the authority of the person whose signature it purports to be, the forged or unauthorised signature is wholly inoperative, and no right to retain the bill or to give a discharge therefor or to enforce payment thereof against any party thereto can be acquired through or under that signature, unless the party against whom it is sought to retain or enforce payment of the bill is precluded from setting up the forgery or want of authority.
Provided that nothing in this section shall affect the ratification of an unauthorised signature not amounting to a forgery.

25 *Procuration signatures* A signature by procuration operates as notice that the agent has but a limited authority to sign, and the principal is only bound by such signature if the agent in so signing was acting within the actual limits of his authority.

26 *Person signing as agent or in representative capacity* (1) Where a person

signs a bill as drawer, indorser, or acceptor, and adds words to his signature, indicating that he signs for or on behalf of a principal, or in a representative character, he is not personally liable thereon; but the mere addition to his signature of words describing him as an agent, or as filling a representative character, does not exempt him from personal liability.
(2) In determining whether a signature on a bill is that of the principal or that of the agent by whose hand it is written, the construction most favourable to the validity of the instrument shall be adopted.

27 *Value and holder for value* (1) Valuable consideration for a bill may be constituted by,—
(a) Any consideration sufficient to support a simple contract;
(b) Any antecedent debt or liability. Such a debt or liability is deemed valuable consideration whether the bill is payable on demand or at a future time.
(2) Where value has at any time been given for a bill the holder is deemed to be a holder for value as regards the acceptor and all parties to the bill who became parties prior to such time.
(3) Where the holder of a bill has a lien on it, arising either from contract or by implication of law, he is deemed to be a holder for value to the extent of the sum for which he has a lien.

29 *Holder in due course* (1) A holder in due course is a holder who has taken a bill, complete and regular on the face of it, under the following conditions; namely,
(a) That he became the holder of it before it was overdue, and without notice that it had been previously dishonoured, if such was the fact:
(b) That he took the bill in good faith and for value, and that at the time the bill was negotiated to him he had no notice of any defect in the title of the person who negotiated it.
(2) In particular the title of a person who negotiates a bill is defective within the meaning of this Act when he obtained the bill, or the acceptance thereof, by fraud, duress, or force and fear, or other unlawful means, or for an illegal consideration, or when he negotiates it in breach of faith, or under such circumstances as amount to a fraud.
(3) A holder (whether for value or not), who derives his title to a bill through a holder in due course, and who is not himself a party to any fraud or illegality affecting it, has all the rights of that holder in due course as regards the acceptor and all parties to the bill prior to that holder.

30 *Presumption of value and good faith* (1) Every party whose signature appears on a bill is prima facie deemed to have become a party thereto for value.
(2) Every holder of a bill is prima facie deemed to be a holder in due course; but if in an action on a bill it is admitted or proved that the acceptance, issue, or subsequent negotiation of the bill is affected with fraud, duress, or force and fear, or illegality, the burden of proof is shifted, unless and until the holder proves that, subsequent to the alleged fraud or illegality, value has in good faith been given for the bill.

APPENDIX 1

45 *Rules as to presentment for payment* Subject to the provisions of this Act a bill must be duly presented for payment. If it be not so presented the drawer and indorsers shall be discharged.
A bill is duly presented for payment which is presented in accordance with the following rules:—
(1) Where the bill is not payable on demand, presentment must be made on the day it falls due.
(2) Where the bill is payable on demand, then, subject to the provisions of this Act, presentment must be made within a reasonable time after its issue in order to render the drawer liable, and within a reasonable time after its indorsement, in order to render the indorser liable.
In determining what is a reasonable time, regard shall be had to the nature of the bill, the usage of trade with regard to similar bills, and the facts of the particular case.
(3) Presentment must be made by the holder or by some person authorised to receive payment on his behalf at a reasonable hour on a business day, at the proper place as herein-after defined, either to the person designated by the bill as payer, or to some person authorised to pay or refuse payment on his behalf if with the exercise of reasonable diligence such person can there be found.
(4) A bill is presented at the proper place:—
(a) Where a place of payment is specified in the bill and the bill is there presented.
(b) Where no place of payment is specified, but the address of the drawee or acceptor is given in the bill, and the bill is there presented.
(c) Where no place of payment is specified and no address given, and the bill is presented at the drawee's or acceptor's place of business if known, and if not, at his ordinary residence if known.
(d) In any other case if presented to the drawee or acceptor wherever he can be found, or if presented at his last known place of business or residence.
(5) Where a bill is presented at the proper place, and after the exercise of reasonable diligence no person authorised to pay or refuse payment can be found there, no further presentment to the drawee or acceptor is required.
(6) Where a bill is drawn upon, or accepted by two or more persons who are not partners, and no place of payment is specified, presentment must be made to them all.
(7) Where the drawee or acceptor of a bill is dead, and no place of payment is specified, presentment must be made to a personal representative, if such there be, and with the exercise of reasonable diligence he can be found.
(8) Where authorised by agreement or usage a presentment through the post office is sufficient.

59 *Payment in due course* (1) A bill is discharged by payment in due course by or on behalf of the drawee or acceptor.
'Payment in due course' means payment made at or after the maturity of the bill to the holder thereof in good faith and without notice that his title to the bill is defective.

(2) Subject to the provisions herein-after contained, when a bill is paid by the drawer or an indorser it is not discharged; but
(a) Where a bill payable to, or to the order of, a third party is paid by the drawer, the drawer may enforce payment thereof against the acceptor, but may not re-issue the bill.
(b) Where a bill is paid by an indorser, or where a bill payable to drawer's order is paid by the drawer, the party paying it is remitted to his former rights as regards the acceptor or antecedent parties, and he may, if he thinks fit, strike out his own and subsequent indorsements, and again negotiate the bill.
(3) Where an accommodation bill is paid in due course by the party accommodated the bill is discharged.

60 *Banker paying demand draft whereon indorsement is forged* When a bill payable to order on demand is drawn on a banker, and the banker on whom it is drawn pays the bill in good faith and in the ordinary course of business, it is not incumbent on the banker to show that the indorsement of the payee or any subsequent indorsement was made by or under the authority of the person whose indorsement it purports to be, and the banker is deemed to have paid the bill in due course, although such indorsement has been forged or made without authority.

75 *Revocation of banker's authority* The duty and authority of a banker to pay a cheque drawn on him by his customer are determined by—
(1) Countermand of payment:
(2) Notice of the customer's death.

76 *General and special crossings defined* (1) Where a cheque bears across its face an addition of—
(a) The words 'and company' or any abbreviation thereof between two parallel transverse lines, either with or without the words 'not negotiable';
or
(b) Two parallel transverse lines simply, either with or without the words 'not negotiable';
that addition constitutes a crossing, and the cheque is crossed generally.
(2) Where a cheque bears across its face an addition of the name of a banker, either with or without the words 'not negotiable', that addition constitutes a crossing, and the cheque is crossed specially and to that banker.

77 *Crossing by drawer or after issue* (1) A cheque may be crossed generally or specially by the drawer.
(2) Where a cheque is uncrossed, the holder may cross it generally or specially.
(3) Where a cheque is crossed generally the holder may cross it specially.
(4) Where a cheque is crossed generally or specially, the holder may add the words 'not negotiable'.
(5) Where a cheque is crossed specially, the banker to whom it is crossed may again cross it specially to another banker for collection.

(6) Where an uncrossed cheque, or a cheque crossed generally, is sent to a banker for collection, he may cross it specially to himself.

78 *Crossing a material part of cheque* A crossing authorised by this Act is a material part of the cheque; it shall not be lawful for any person to obliterate or, except as authorised by this Act, to add to or alter the crossing.

79 *Duties of banker as to crossed cheques* (1) Where a cheque is crossed specially to more than one banker except when crossed to an agent for collection being a banker, the banker on whom it is drawn shall refuse payment thereof.
(2) Where the banker on whom a cheque is drawn which is so crossed nevertheless pays the same, or pays a cheque crossed generally otherwise than to a banker, or if crossed specially otherwise than to the banker to whom it is crossed, or his agent for collection being a banker, he is liable to the true owner of the cheque for any loss he may sustain owing to the cheque having been so paid.
Provided that where a cheque is presented for payment which does not at the time of presentment appear to be crossed, or to have had a crossing which has been obliterated, or to have been added to or altered otherwise than as authorised by this Act, the banker paying the cheque in good faith and without negligence shall not be responsible or incur any liability, nor shall the payment be questioned by reason of the cheque having been crossed, or of the crossing having been obliterated or having been added to or altered otherwise than as authorised by this Act, and of payment having been made otherwise than to a banker or to the banker to whom the cheque is or was crossed, or to his agent for collection being a banker, as the case may be.

80 *Protection to banker and drawer where cheque is crossed* Where the banker, on whom a crossed cheque is drawn, in good faith and without negligence pays it, if crossed generally, to a banker, and if crossed specially, to the banker to whom it is crossed, or his agent for collection being a banker, the banker paying the cheque, and, if the cheque has come into the hands of the payee, the drawer, shall respectively be entitled to the same rights and be placed in the same position as if payment of the cheque had been made to the true owner thereof.

81 *Effect of crossing on holder* Where a person takes a crossed cheque which bears on it the words 'not negotiable', he shall not have and shall not be capable of giving a better title to the cheque than that which the person from whom he took it had.

90 *Good faith* A thing is deemed to be done in good faith, within the meaning of this Act, where it is in fact done honestly, whether it is done negligently or not.

CHEQUES ACT 1957

1 *Protection of bankers paying unindorsed or irregularly indorsed cheques, etc.*
(1) Where a banker in good faith and in the ordinary course of business pays a cheque drawn on him which is not indorsed or is irregularly indorsed, he does not, in doing so, incur any liability by reason only of the absence of, or irregularity in, indorsement, and he is deemed to have paid it in due course.
(2) Where a banker in good faith and in the ordinary course of business pays any such instrument as the following, namely,—
(a) a document issued by a customer of his which, though not a bill of exchange, is intended to enable a person to obtain payment from him of the sum mentioned in the document;
(b) a draft payable on demand drawn by him upon himself, whether payable at the head office or some other office of his bank;
he does not, in doing so, incur any liability by reason only of the absence of, or irregularity in, indorsement, and the payment discharges the instrument.

2 *Rights of bankers collecting cheques not indorsed by holders* A banker who gives value for, or has a lien on, a cheque payable to order which the holder delivers to him for collection without indorsing it, has such (if any) rights as he would have had if, upon delivery, the holder had indorsed it in blank.

4 *Protection of bankers collecting payment of cheques, etc.* (1) Where a banker, in good faith and without negligence,—
(a) receives payment for a customer of an instrument to which this section applies; or
(b) having credited a customer's account with the amount of such an instrument, receives payment thereof for himself;
and the customer has no title, or a defective title, to the instrument, the banker does not incur any liability to the true owner of the instrument by reason only of having received payment thereof.
(2) This section applies to the following instruments, namely,—
(a) cheques;
(b) any document issued by a customer of a banker which, though not a bill of exchange, is intended to enable a person to obtain payment from that banker of the sum mentioned in the document;
(c) any document issued by a public officer which is intended to enable a person to obtain payment from the Paymaster General or the Queen's and Lord Treasurer's Remembrancer of the sum mentioned in the document but is not a bill of exchange;
(d) any draft payable on demand drawn by a banker upon himself, whether payable at the head office or some other office of his bank.
(3) A banker is not to be treated for the purposes of this section as having been negligent by reason only of his failure to concern himself with absence of, or irregularity in, indorsement of an instrument.

APPENDIX 1

LAW OF PROPERTY (MISCELLANEOUS PROVISIONS) ACT 1989

1 *Deeds and their execution*
(1) Any rule of law which—
(a) restricts the substances on which a deed may be written;
(b) requires a seal for the valid execution of an instrument as a deed by an individual; or
(c) requires authority by one person to another to deliver an instrument as a deed on his behalf to be given by deed,
is abolished.
(2) An instrument shall not be a deed unless—
(a) it makes it clear on its face that it is intended to be a deed by the person making it or, as the case may be, by the parties to it (whether by describing itself as a deed or expressing itself to be executed or signed as a deed or otherwise); and
(b) it is validly executed as a deed by that person or, as the case may be, one or more of those parties.
(3) An instrument is validly executed as a deed by an individual if, and only if—
(a) it is signed—
  (i) by him in the presence of a witness who attests the signature; or
  (ii) at his direction and in his presence and the presence of two witnesses who each attest the signature; and
(b) it is delivered as a deed by him or a person authorised to do so on his behalf.
(4) In subsections (2) and (3) above 'sign', in relation to an instrument, includes making one's mark on the instrument and 'signature' is to be construed accordingly.
(5) Where a solicitor or licensed conveyancer, or an agent or employee of a solicitor or licensed conveyancer, in the course of or in connection with a transaction involving the disposition or creation of an interest in land, purports to deliver an instrument as a deed on behalf of a party to the instrument, it shall be conclusively presumed in favour of a purchaser that he is authorised so to deliver the instrument.
(6) In subsection (5) above—
'disposition' and 'purchaser' have the same meanings as in the Law of Property Act 1925; and
'interest in land' means any estate, interest or charge in or over land or in or over the proceeds of sale of land.
(7) Where an instrument under seal that constitutes a deed is required for the purposes of an Act passed before this section comes into force, this section shall have effect as to signing, sealing or delivery of an instrument by an individual in place of any provision of that Act as to signing, sealing or delivery.

2 *Contracts for sale etc. of land to be made by signed writing*
(1) A contract for the sale or other disposition of an interest in land can only be made in writing and only by incorporating all the terms which the parties have expressly agreed in one document or, where contracts are exchanged, in each.

(2) The terms may be incorporated in a document either by being set out in it or by reference to some other document.
(3) The document incorporating the terms or, where contracts are exchanged, one of the documents incorporating them (but not necessarily the same one) must be signed by or on behalf of each party to the contract.
(4) Where a contract for the sale or other disposition of an interest in land satisfies the conditions of this section by reason only of the rectification of one or more documents in pursuance of an order of a court, the contract shall come into being, or be deemed to have come into being, at such time as may be specified in the order.
(5) This section does not apply in relation to—
(a) a contract to grant such a lease as is mentioned in section 54(2) of the Law of Property Act 1926 (short leases);
(b) a contract made in the course of a public auction; or
(c) a contract regulated under the Financial Services Act 1986;
and nothing in this section affects the creation or operation of resulting, implied or constructive trusts.
(6) In this section—
'disposition' has the same meaning as in the Law of Property Act 1925;
'interest in land' means any estate, interest or charge in or over land or in or over the proceeds of sale of land.
(7) Nothing in this section shall apply in relation to contracts made before this section comes into force.
(8) Section 40 of the Law of Property Act 1925 (which is superseded by this section) shall cease to have effect.

COMPANIES ACT 1989

A company's capacity and the power of the directors to bind it.

108 (1) In Chapter III of Part I of the Companies Act 1985 (a company's capacity; formalities of carrying on business), for section 35 substitute—

A company's capacity not limited by its memorandum.

35 (1) The validity of an act done by a company shall not be called into question on the ground of lack of capacity by reason of anything in the company's memorandum.
(2) A member of a company may bring proceedings to restrain the doing of an act which but for subsection (1) would be beyond the company's capacity; but no such proceedings shall lie in respect of an act to be done in fulfilment of a legal obligation arising from a previous act of the company.
(3) It remains the duty of the directors to observe any limitations on their powers flowing from the company's memorandum; and action by the directors which but for subsection (1) would be beyond the company's capacity may only be ratified by the company by special resolution.
A resolution ratifying such action shall not affect any liability incurred by the directors or any other person; relief from any such liability must be agreed to separately by special resolution.
(4) The operation of this section is restricted by section 30B(1) of the Charities Act 1960 and section 112(3) of the Companies Act 1989 in relation to companies which are charities; and section 322A below (invalidity of certain transactions to which directors or their associates are parties) has effect notwithstanding this section.

Power of directors to bind the company.

35A (1) In favour of a person dealing with a company in good faith, the power of the board of directors to bind the company, or authorise others to do so, shall be deemed to be free of any limitation under the company's constitution.
(2) For this purpose—
(a) a person 'deals with' a company if he is a party to any transaction or other act to which the company is a party;
(b) a person shall not be regarded as acting in bad faith by reason only of his knowing that an act is beyond the powers of the directors under the company's constitution; and
(c) a person shall be presumed to have acted in good faith unless the contrary is proved.
(3) The references above to limitations on the directors' powers under the company's constitution include limitations deriving—
(a) from a resolution of the company in general meeting or a meeting of any class of shareholders, or

(b) from any agreement between the members of the company or of any class of shareholders.

(4) Subsection (1) does not affect any right of a member of the company to bring proceedings to restrain the doing of an act which is beyond the powers of the directors; but no such proceedings shall lie in respect of an act to be done in fulfilment of a legal obligation arising from a previous act of the company.

(5) Nor does that subsection affect any liability incurred by the directors, or any other person, by reason of the directors' exceeding their powers.

(6) The operation of this section is restricted by section 30B(1) of the Charities Act 1960 and section 112(3) of the Companies Act 1989 in relation to companies which are charities; and section 322A below (invalidity of certain transactions to which directors or their associates are parties) has effect notwithstanding this section.

No duty to enquire as to capacity of company or authority of directors.

35B A party to a transaction with a company is not bound to enquire as to whether it is permitted by the company's memorandum or as to any limitation on the powers of the board of directors to bind the company or authorise others to do so.

(2) In Schedule 21 to the Companies Act 1985 (effect of registration of companies not formed under that Act), in paragraph 6 (general application of provisions of Act), after sub-paragraph (5) insert—

'(6) Where by virtue of sub-paragraph (4) or (5) a company does not have power to alter a provision, it does not have power to ratify acts of the directors in contravention of the provision.'

(3) In Schedule 22 to the Companies Act 1985 (provisions applying to unregistered companies), in the entries relating to Part I, in the first column for 'section 35' substitute 'sections 35 to 35B'.

Company contracts and execution of documents by companies.

130 (1) In Chapter III of Part I of the Companies Act 1985 (a company's capacity; the formalities of carrying on business), for section 36 (form of company contracts) substitute—

'*Company contracts: England and Wales.*

36 Under the law of England and Wales a contract may be made—
(a) by a company, by writing under its common seal, or
(b) on behalf of a company, by any person acting under its authority, express or implied;
and any formalities required by law in the case of a contract made by an individual also apply, unless a contrary intention appears, to a contract made by or on behalf of a company.'

(2) After that section insert—

'*Execution of documents: England and Wales.*

36A (1) Under the law of England and Wales the following provisions have effect with respect to the execution of documents by a company.
(2) A document is executed by a company by the affixing of its common seal.
(3) A company need not have a common seal, however, and the following subsections apply whether it does or not.
(4) A document signed by a director and the secretary of a company, or by two directors of a company, and expressed (in whatever form of words) to be executed by the company has the same effect as if executed under the common seal of the company.
(5) A document executed by a company which makes it clear on its face that it is intended by the person or persons making it to be a deed has effect, upon delivery, as a deed; and it shall be presumed, unless a contrary intention is proved, to be delivered upon its being so executed.
(6) In favour of a purchaser a document shall be deemed to have been duly executed by a company if it purports to be signed by a director and the secretary of the company, or by two directors of the company, and, where it makes it clear on its face that it is intended by the person or persons making it to be a deed, to have been delivered upon its being executed.
A 'purchaser' means a purchaser in good faith for valuable consideration and includes a lessee, mortgagee or other person who for valuable consideration acquires an interest in property.'

(3) After the section inserted by subsection (2) insert—

'*Execution of documents: Scotland.*

36B (1) Under the law of Scotland the following provisions have effect with respect to the execution of documents by a company.
(2) A document—
(a) is signed by a company if it is signed on its behalf by a director, or by the secretary, of the company or by a person authorised to sign the document on its behalf, and
(b) is subscribed by a company if it is subscribed on its behalf by being signed in accordance with the provisions of paragraph (a) at the end of the last page.
(3) A document shall be presumed, unless the contrary is shown, to have been subscribed by a company in accordance with subsection (2) if—
(a) it bears to have been subscribed on behalf of the company by a director, or by the secretary, of the company or by a person bearing to have been authorised to subscribe the document on its behalf; and
(b) it bears—
    (i) to have been signed by a person as a witness of the subscription of the director, secretary or other person subscribing on behalf of the company; or
    (ii) (if the subscription is not so witnessed) to have been sealed with the common seal of the company.

(4) A presumption under subsection (3) as to subscription of a document does not include a presumption—
(a) that a person bearing to subscribe the document as a director or the secretary of the company was such director or secretary; or
(b) that a person subscribing the document on behalf of the company bearing to have been authorised to do so was authorised to do so.
(5) Notwithstanding subsection (3)(b)(ii), a company need not have a common seal.
(6) Any reference in any enactment (including an enactment contained in a subordinate instrument) to a probative document shall, in relation to a document executed by a company after the commencement of section 130 of the Companies Act 1989, be construed as a reference to a document which is presumed under subsection (3) above to be subscribed by the company.
(7) Subsections (1) to (4) above do not apply where an enactment (including an enactment contained in a subordinate instrument) provides otherwise.'

(4) After the section inserted by subsection (3) insert—

'*Pre-incorporation contracts, deeds and obligations.*

36C (1) A contract which purports to be made by or on behalf of a company at a time when the company has not been formed has effect, subject to any agreement to the contrary, as one made with the person purporting to act for the company or as agent for it, and he is personally liable on the contract accordingly.
(2) Subsection (1) applies—
(a) to the making of a deed under the law of England and Wales, and
(b) to the undertaking of an obligation under the law of Scotland,
as it applies to the making of a contract.'

Abolition of doctrine of deemed notice.

142 (1) In Part XXIV of the Companies Act 1985 (the registrar of companies, his functions and offices), after section 711 insert—

'*Exclusion of deemed notice.*

711A (1) A person shall not be taken to have notice of any matter merely because of its being disclosed in any document kept by the registrar of companies (and thus available for inspection) or made available by the company for inspection.
(2) This does not affect the question whether a person is affected by notice of any matter by reason of a failure to make such inquiries as ought reasonably to be made.
(3) In this section 'document' includes any material which contains information.
(4) Nothing in this section affects the operation of—
(a) section 416 of this Act (under which a person taking a charge over a

company's property is deemed to have notice of matters disclosed on the companies charges register), or

(b) section 198 of the Law of Property Act 1925 as it applies by virtue of section 3(7) of the Land Charges Act 1972 (under which the registration of certain land charges under Part XII, or Chapter III of Part XXIII, of this Act is deemed to constitute actual notice for all purposes connected with the land affected).'

INSOLVENCY ACT 1986

44 *Agency and liability for contracts* (1) The administrative receiver of a company—
(a) is deemed to be the company's agent, unless and until the company goes into liquidation;
(b) is personally liable on any contract entered into by him in the carrying out of his functions (except in so far as the contract otherwise provides) and on any contract of employment adopted by him in the carrying out of those functions; and
(c) is entitled in respect of that liability to an indemnity out of the assets of the company.

(2) For the purposes of subsection (1)(b) the administrative receiver is not to be taken to have adopted a contract of employment by reason of anything done or omitted to be done within 14 days after his appointment.

(3) This section does not limit any right to indemnity which the administrative receiver would have apart from it, nor limit his liability on contracts entered into or adopted without authority, nor confer any right to indemnity in respect of that liability.

84 *Circumstances in which company may be wound up voluntarily* (1) A company may be wound up voluntarily—
(a) when the period (if any) fixed for the duration of the company by the articles expires, or the event (if any) occurs, on the occurrence of which the articles provide that the company is to be dissolved, and the company in general meeting has passed a resolution requiring it to be wound up voluntarily;
(b) if the company resolves by special resolution that it be wound up voluntarily;
(c) if the company resolves by extraordinary resolution to the effect that it cannot by reason of its liabilities continue its business, and that it is advisable to wind up.

(2) In this Act the expression 'a resolution for voluntary winding up' means a resolution passed under any of the paragraphs of subsection (1).

(3) A resolution passed under paragraph (a) of subsection (1), as well as a special resolution under paragraph (b) and an extraordinary resolution under paragraph (c), is subject to section 380 of the Companies Act (copy of resolution to be forwarded to registrar of companies within 15 days).

122 *Circumstances in which company may be wound up by the court* (1) A company may be wound up by the court if—
(a) the company has by special resolution resolved that the company be wound up by the court,
(b) being a public company which was registered as such on its original incorporation, the company has not been issued with a certificate under section 117 of the Companies Act (public company share capital requirements) and more than a year has expired since it was so registered,
(c) it is an old public company, within the meaning of the Consequential Provisions Act,

APPENDIX 1

(d) the company does not commence its business within a year from its incorporation or suspends its business for a whole year,
(e) the number of members is reduced below 2,
(f) the company is unable to pay its debts,
(g) the court is of the opinion that it is just and equitable that the company should be wound up.

(2) In Scotland, a company which the Court of Session has jurisdiction to wind up may be wound up by the Court if there is subsisting a floating charge over property comprised in the company's property and undertaking, and the court is satisfied that the security of the creditor entitled to the benefit of the floating charge is in jeopardy.

For this purpose a creditor's security is deemed to be in jeopardy if the Court is satisfied that events have occurred or are about to occur which render it unreasonable in the creditor's interests that the company should retain power to dispose of the property which is subject to the floating charge.

123 *Definition of inability to pay debts* (1) A company is deemed unable to pay its debts—
(a) if a creditor (by assignment or otherwise) to whom the company is indebted in a sum exceeding £750 then due has served on the company, by leaving it at the company's registered office, a written demand (in the prescribed form) requiring the company to pay the sum so due and the company has for 3 weeks thereafter neglected to pay the sum or to secure or compound for it to the reasonable satisfaction of the creditor, or
(b) if, in England and Wales, execution or other process issued on a judgment, decree or order of any court in favour of a creditor of the company is returned unsatisfied in whole or in part, or
(c) if, in Scotland, the induciae of a charge for payment on an extract decree, or an extracted registered bond, or an extract registered protest, have expired without payment being made, or
(d) if, in Northern Ireland, a certificate of unenforceability has been granted in respect of a judgment against the company, or
(e) if it is proved to the satisfaction of the court that the company is unable to pay its debts as they fall due.

(2) A company is also deemed unable to pay its debts if it is proved to the satisfaction of the court that the value of the company's assets is less than the amount of its liabilities, taking into account its contingent and prospective liabilities.

(3) The money sum for the time being specified in subsection (1)(a) is subject to increase or reduction by order under section 416 in Part XV.

175 *Preferential debts (general provision)* (1) In a winding up the company's preferential debts (within the meaning given by section 386 in Part XII) shall be paid in priority to all other debts.
(2) Preferential debts—
(a) rank equally among themselves after the expenses of the winding up and shall be paid in full, unless the assets are insufficient to meet them, in which case they abate in equal proportions; and

(b) so far as the assets of the company available for payment of general creditors are insufficient to meet them, have priority over the claims of holders of debentures secured by, or holders of, any floating charge created by the company, and shall be paid accordingly out of any property comprised in or subject to that charge.

213 *Fraudulent trading* (1) If in the course of the winding up of a company it appears that any business of the company has been carried on with intent to defraud creditors of the company or creditors of any other person, or for any fraudulent purpose, the following has effect.
(2) The court, on the application of the liquidator may declare that any persons who were knowingly parties to the carrying on of the business in the manner above-mentioned are to be liable to make such contributions (if any) to the company's assets as the court thinks proper.

214 *Wrongful trading* (1) Subject to subsection (3) below, if in the course of the winding up of a company it appears that subsection (2) of this section applies in relation to a person who is or has been a director of the company, the court, on the application of the liquidator, may declare that that person is to be liable to make such contribution (if any) to the company's assets as the court thinks proper.
(2) This subsection applies in relation to a person if—
(a) the company has gone into insolvent liquidation,
(b) at some time before the commencement of the winding up of the company, that person knew or ought to have concluded that there was no reasonable prospect that the company would avoid going into insolvent liquidation, and
(c) that person was a director of the company at that time;
but the court shall not make a declaration under this section in any case where the time mentioned in paragraph (b) above was before 28th April 1986.
(3) The court shall not make a declaration under this section with respect to any person if it is satisfied that after the condition specified in subsection (2)(b) was first satisfied in relation to him that person took every step with a view to minimising the potential loss of the company's creditors as (assuming him to have known that there was no reasonable prospect that the company would avoid going into insolvent liquidation) he ought to have taken.
(4) For the purposes of subsections (2) and (3), the facts which a director of a company ought to know or ascertain, the conclusions which he ought to reach and the steps which he ought to take are those which would be known or ascertained, or reached or taken, by a reasonably diligent person having both—
(a) the general knowledge, skill and experience that may reasonably be expected of a person carrying out the same functions as are carried out by that director in relation to the company, and
(b) the general knowledge, skill and experience that that director has.
(5) The reference in subsection (4) to the functions carried out in relation to a company by a director of the company includes any functions which he does not carry out but which have been entrusted to him.
(6) For the purposes of this section a company goes into insolvent liquidation if

it goes into liquidation at a time when its assets are insufficient for the payment of its debts and other liabilities and the expenses of the winding up.
(7) In this section 'director' includes a shadow director.
(8) This section is without prejudice to section 213.

238 *Transactions at an undervalue (England and Wales)* (1) This section applies in the case of a company where—
(a) an administration order is made in relation to the company, or
(b) the company goes into liquidation;
and 'the office-holder' means the administrator or the liquidator, as the case may be.
(2) Where the company has at a relevant time (defined in section 240) entered into a transaction with any person at an undervalue, the office-holder may apply to the court for an order under this section.
(3) Subject as follows, the court shall, on such an application, make such order as it thinks fit for restoring the position to what it would have been if the company had not entered into that transaction.
(4) For the purposes of this section and section 241, a company enters into a transaction with a person at an undervalue if—
(a) the company makes a gift to that person or otherwise enters into a transaction with that person on terms that provide for the company to receive no consideration, or
(b) the company enters into a transaction with that person for a consideration the value of which, in money or money's worth is significantly less than the value, in money or money's worth, of the consideration provided by the company.
(5) The court shall not make an order under this section in respect of a transaction at an undervalue if it is satisfied—
(a) that the company which entered into the transaction did so in good faith and for the purpose of carrying on its business, and
(b) that at the time it did so there were reasonable grounds for believing that the transaction would benefit the company.

239 *Preferences (England and Wales)* (1) This section applies as does section 238.
(2) Where the company has at a relevant time (defined in the next section) given a preference to any person, the office-holder may apply to the court for an order under this section.
(3) Subject as follows, the court shall, on such an application, make such order as it thinks fit for restoring the position to what it would have been if the company had not given that preference.
(4) For the purposes of this section and section 241, a company gives a preference to a person if—
(a) that person is one of the company's creditors or a surety or guarantor for any of the company's debts or other liabilities, and
(b) the company does anything or suffers anything to be done which (in either case) has the effect of putting that person into a position which, in the event

of the company going into insolvent liquidation, will be better than the position he would have been in if that thing had not been done.

(5) The court shall not make an order under this section in respect of a preference given to any person unless the company which gave the preference was influenced in deciding to give it by a desire to produce in relation to that person the effect mentioned in subsection (4)(b).

(6) A company which has given a preference to a person connected with the company (otherwise than by reason only of being its employee) at the time the preference was given is presumed, unless the contrary is shown, to have been influenced in deciding to give it by such a desire as is mentioned in subsection (5).

(7) The fact that something has been done in pursuance of the order of a court does not, without more, prevent the doing or suffering of that thing from constituting the giving of a preference.

240 *'Relevant time' under ss. 238, 239* (1) Subject to the next subsection, the time at which a company enters into a transaction at an undervalue or gives a preference is a relevant time if the transaction is entered into, or the preference given—

(a) in the case of a transaction at an undervalue or of a preference which is given to a person who is connected with the company (otherwise than by reason only of being its employee), at a time in the period of 2 years ending with the onset of insolvency (which expression is defined below),

(b) in the case of a preference which is not such a transaction and is not so given, at a time in the period of 6 months ending with the onset of insolvency, and

(c) in either case, at a time between the presentation of a petition for the making of an administration order in relation to the company and the making of such an order on that petition.

(2) Where a company enters into a transaction at an undervalue or gives a preference at a time mentioned in subsection (1)(a) or (b), that time is not a relevant time for the purposes of section 238 or 239 unless the company—

(a) is at that time unable to pay its debts within the meaning of section 123 in Chapter VI of Part IV, or

(b) becomes unable to pay its debts within the meaning of that section in consequence of the transaction or preference;

but the requirements of this subsection are presumed to be satisfied, unless the contrary is shown, in relation to any transaction at an undervalue which is entered into by a company with a person who is connected with the company.

(3) For the purposes of subsection (1), the onset of insolvency is—

(a) in a case where section 238 or 239 applies by reason of the making of an administration order or of a company going into liquidation immediately upon the discharge of an administration order, the date of the presentation of the petition on which the administration order was made, and

(b) in a case where the section applies by reason of a company going into liquidation at any other time, the date of the commencement of the winding up.

241 *Orders under ss. 238, 239* (1) Without prejudice to the generality of

sections 238(3) and 239(3), an order under either of those sections with respect to a transaction or preference entered into or given by a company may (subject to the next subsection)—
(a) require any property transferred as part of the transaction, or in connection with the giving of the preference, to be vested in the company,
(b) require any property to be so vested if it represents in any person's hands the application either of the proceeds of sale of property so transferred or of money so transferred,
(c) release or discharge (in whole or in part) any security given by the company,
(d) require any person to pay, in respect of benefits received by him from the company, such sums to the office-holder as the court may direct,
(e) provide for any surety or guarantor whose obligations to any person were released or discharged (in whole or in part) under the transaction, or by the giving of the preference, to be under such new or revived obligations to that person as the court thinks appropriate,
(f) provide for security to be provided for the discharge of any obligation imposed by or arising under the order, for such an obligation to be charged on any property and for the security or charge to have the same priority as a security or charge released or discharged (in whole or in part) under the transaction or by the giving of the preference, and
(g) provide for the extent to which any person whose property is vested by the order in the company, or on whom obligations are imposed by the order, is to be able to prove in the winding up of the company for debts or other liabilities which arose from, or were released or discharged (in whole or in part) under or by, the transaction or the giving of the preference.
(2) An order under section 238 or 239 may affect the property of, or impose any obligation on, any person whether or not he is the person with whom the company in question entered into the transaction or (as the case may be) the person to whom the preference was given; but such an order—
(a) shall not prejudice any interest in property which was acquired from a person other than the company and was acquired in good faith, for value and without notice of the relevant circumstances, or prejudice any interest deriving from such an interest, and
(b) shall not require a person who received a benefit from the transaction or preference in good faith, for value and without notice of the relevant circumstances to pay a sum to the office-holder, except where that person was a party to the transaction or the payment is to be in respect of a preference given to that person at a time when he was a creditor of the company.
(3) For the purposes of this section the relevant circumstances, in relation to a transaction or preference, are—
(a) the circumstances by virtue of which an order under section 238 or (as the case may be) 239 could be made in respect of the transaction or preference if the company were to go into liquidation, or an administration order were made in relation to the company, within a particular period after the transaction is entered into or the preference given, and
(b) if that period has expired, the fact that the company has gone into liquidation or that such an order has been made.

(4) The provisions of sections 238 to 241 apply without prejudice to the availability of any other remedy, even in relation to a transaction or preference which the company had no power to enter into or give.

245 *Avoidance of certain floating charges* (1) This section applies as does section 238, but applies to Scotland as well as to England and Wales.
(2) Subject as follows, a floating charge on the company's undertaking or property created at a relevant time is invalid except to the extent of the aggregate of—
(a) the value of so much of the consideration for the creation of the charge as consists of money paid, or goods or services supplied, to the company at the same time as, or after, the creation of the charge,
(b) the value of so much of that consideration as consists of the discharge or reduction, at the same time as, or after, the creation of the charge, of any debt of the company, and
(c) the amount of such interest (if any) as is payable on the amount falling within paragraph (a) or (b) in pursuance of any agreement under which the money was so paid, the goods or services were so supplied or the debt was so discharged or reduced.
(3) Subject to the next subsection, the time at which a floating charge is created by a company is a relevant time for the purposes of this section if the charge is created—
(a) in the case of a charge which is created in favour of a person who is connected with the company, at a time in the period of 2 years ending with the onset of insolvency,
(b) in the case of a charge which is created in favour of any other person, at a time in the period of 12 months ending with the onset of insolvency, or
(c) in either case, at a time between the presentation of a petition for the making of an administration order in relation to the company and the making of such an order on that petition.
(4) Where a company creates a floating charge at a time mentioned in subsection (3)(b) and the person in favour of whom the charge is created is not connected with the company, that time is not a relevant time for the purposes of this section unless the company—
(a) is at that time unable to pay its debts within the meaning of section 123 in Chapter VI of Part IV, or
(b) becomes unable to pay its debts within the meaning of that section in consequence of the transaction under which the charge is created.
(5) For the purposes of subsection (3), the onset of insolvency is—
(a) in a case where this section applies by reason of the making of an administration order, the date of the presentation of the petition on which the order was made, and
(b) in a case where this section applies by reason of a company going into liquidation, the date of the commencement of the winding up.
(6) For the purposes of subsection (2)(a) the value of any goods or services supplied by way of consideration for a floating charge is the amount in money which at the time they were supplied could reasonably have been expected to be

obtained for supplying the goods or services in the ordinary course of business and on the same terms (apart from the consideration) as those on which they were supplied to the company.

247 *'Insolvency' and 'go into liquidation'* (1) In this Group of Parts, except in so far as the context otherwise requires, 'insolvency', in relation to a company, includes the approval of a voluntary arrangement under Part I, the making of an administration order or the appointment of an administrative receiver.
(2) For the purposes of any provision in this Group of Parts, a company goes into liquidation if it passes a resolution for voluntary winding up or an order for its winding up is made by the court at a time when it has not already gone into liquidation by passing such a resolution.

249 *'Connected' with a company* For the purposes of any provision in this Group of Parts, a person is connected with a company if—
(a) he is a director or shadow director of the company or an associate of such a director or shadow director, or
(b) he is an associate of the company;
and 'associate' has the meaning given by section 435 in Part XVIII of this Act.

251 *Expressions used generally* In this Group of Parts, except in so far as the context otherwise requires—
... 'shadow director', in relation to a company, means a person in accordance with whose directions or instructions the directors of the company are accustomed to act (but so that a person is not deemed a shadow director by reason only that the directors act on advice given by him in a professional capacity);

267 *Grounds of creditor's petition* (1) A creditor's petition must be in respect of one or more debts owed by the debtor, and the petitioning creditor or each of the petitioning creditors must be a person to whom the debt or (as the case may be) at least one of the debts is owed.
(2) Subject to the next three sections, a creditor's petition may be presented to the court in respect of a debt or debts only if, at the time the petition is presented—
(a) the amount of the debt, or the aggregate amount of the debts, is equal to or exceeds the bankruptcy level,
(b) the debt, or each of the debts, is for a liquidated sum payable to the petitioning creditor, or one or more of the petitioning creditors, either immediately or at some certain, future time, and is unsecured,
(c) the debt, or each of the debts, is a debt which the debtor appears either to be unable to pay or to have no reasonable prospect of being able to pay, and
(d) there is no outstanding application to set aside a statutory demand served (under section 268 below) in respect of the debt or any of the debts.
(3) A debt is not to be regarded for the purposes of subsection (2) as a debt for a liquidated sum by reason only that the amount of the debt is specified in a criminal bankruptcy order.

(4) 'The bankruptcy level' is £750; but the Secretary of State may by order in a statutory instrument substitute any amount specified in the order for that amount or (as the case may be) for the amount which by virtue of such an order is for the time being the amount of the bankruptcy level.
(5) An order shall not be made under subsection (4) unless a draft of it has been laid before, and approved by a resolution of, each House of Parliament.

268 *Definition of 'inability to pay', etc.; the statutory demand* (1) For the purposes of section 267(2)(c), the debtor appears to be unable to pay a debt if, but only if, the debt is payable immediately and either—
(a) the petitioning creditor to whom the debt is owed has served on the debtor a demand (known as 'the statutory demand') in the prescribed form requiring him to pay the debt or to secure or compound for it to the satisfaction of the creditor, at least 3 weeks have elapsed since the demand was served and the demand has been neither complied with nor set aside in accordance with the rules, or
(b) execution or other process issued in respect of the debt on a judgment or order of any court in favour of the petitioning creditor, or one or more of the petitioning creditors to whom the debt is owed, has been returned unsatisfied in whole or in part.
(2) For the purposes of section 267(2)(c) the debtor appears to have no reasonable prospect of being able to pay a debt if, but only if, the debt is not immediately payable and—
(a) the petitioning creditor to whom it is owed has served on the debtor a demand (also known as 'the statutory demand') in the prescribed form requiring him to establish to the satisfaction of the creditor that there is a reasonable prospect that the debtor will be able to pay the debt when it falls due,
(b) at least 3 weeks have elapsed since the demand was served, and
(c) the demand has been neither complied with nor set aside in accordance with the rules.

284 *Restrictions on dispositions of property* (1) Where a person is adjudged bankrupt, any disposition of property made by that person in the period to which this section applies is void except to the extent that it is or was made with the consent of the court, or is or was subsequently ratified by the court.
(2) Subsection (1) applies to a payment (whether in cash or otherwise) as it applies to a disposition of property and, accordingly, where any payment is void by virtue of that subsection, the person paid shall hold the sum paid for the bankrupt as part of his estate.
(3) This section applies to the period beginning with the day of the presentation of the petition for the bankruptcy order and ending with the vesting, under Chapter IV of this Part, of the bankrupt's estate in a trustee.
(4) The preceding provisions of this section do not give a remedy against any person—
(a) in respect of any property or payment which he received before the

commencement of the bankruptcy in good faith, for value and without notice that the petition had been presented, or
(b) in respect of any interest in property which derives from an interest in respect of which there is, by virtue of this subsection, no remedy.
(5) Where after the commencement of his bankruptcy the bankrupt has incurred a debt to a banker or other person by reason of the making of a payment which is void under this section, that debt is deemed for the purposes of any of this Group of Parts to have been incurred before the commencement of the bankruptcy unless—
(a) that banker or person had notice of the bankruptcy before the debt was incurred, or
(b) it is not reasonably practicable for the amount of the payment to be recovered from the person to whom it was made.
(6) A disposition of property is void under this section notwithstanding that the property is not or, as the case may be, would not be comprised in the bankrupt's estate; but nothing in this section affects any disposition made by a person of property held by him on trust for any other person.

323 *Mutual credit and set-off* (1) This section applies where before the commencement of the bankruptcy there have been mutual credits, mutual debts or other mutual dealings between the bankrupt and any creditor of the bankrupt proving or claiming to prove for a bankruptcy debt.
(2) An account shall be taken of what is due from each party to the other in respect of the mutual dealings and the sums due from one party shall be set off against the sums due from the other.
(3) Sums due from the bankrupt to another party shall not be included in the account taken under subsection (2) if that other party had notice at the time they became due that a bankruptcy petition relating to the bankrupt was pending.
(4) Only the balance (if any) of the account taken under subsection (2) is provable as a bankruptcy debt or, as the case may be, to be paid to the trustee as part of the bankrupt's estate.

328 *Priority of debts* (1) In the distribution of the bankrupt's estate, his preferential debts (within the meaning given by section 386 in Part XII) shall be paid in priority to other debts.
(2) Preferential debts rank equally between themselves after the expenses of the bankruptcy and shall be paid in full unless the bankrupt's estate is insufficient for meeting them, in which case they abate in equal proportions between themselves.
(3) Debts which are neither preferential debts nor debts to which the next section applies also rank equally between themselves and, after the preferential debts, shall be paid in full unless the bankrupt's estate is insufficient for meeting them, in which case they abate in equal proportions between themselves.
(4) Any surplus remaining after the payment of the debts that are preferential or rank equally under subsection (3) shall be applied in paying interest on those debts in respect of the periods during which they have been outstanding since the commencement of the bankruptcy; and interest on preferential debts ranks equally with interest on debts other than preferential debts.

(5) The rate of interest payable under subsection (4) in respect of any debt is whichever is the greater of the following—
(a) the rate specified in section 17 of the Judgments Act 1838 at the commencement of the bankruptcy, and
(b) the rate applicable to that debt apart from the bankruptcy.
(6) This section and the next are without prejudice to any provision of this Act or any other Act under which the payment of any debt or the making of any other payment is, in the event of bankruptcy, to have a particular priority or to be postponed.

386 *Categories of preferential debts* (1) A reference in this Act to the preferential debts of a company or an individual is to the debts listed in Schedule 6 to this Act (money owed to the Inland Revenue for income tax deducted at source; VAT, car tax, betting and gaming duties; social security and pension scheme contributions; remuneration etc. of employees); and references to preferential creditors are to be read accordingly.
(2) In that Schedule 'the debtor' means the company or the individual concerned.
(3) Schedule 6 is to be read with Schedule 3 to the Social Security Pensions Act 1975 (occupational pension scheme contributions).

387 *'The relevant date'* (1) This section explains references in Schedule 6 to the relevant date (being the date which determines the existence and amount of a preferential debt).
(2) For the purposes of section 4 in Part I (meeting to consider company voluntary arrangement), the relevant date in relation to a company which is not being wound up is—
(a) where an administration order is in force in relation to the company, the date of the making of that order, and
(b) where no such order has been made, the date of the approval of the voluntary arrangement.
(3) In relation to a company which is being wound up, the following applies—
(a) if the winding up is by the court, and the winding-up order was made immediately upon the discharge of an administration order, the relevant date is the date of the making of the administration order;
(b) if the case does not fall within paragraph (a) and the company—
   (i) is being wound up by the court, and
   (ii) had not commenced to be wound up voluntarily before the date of the making of the winding-up order,
   the relevant date is the date of the appointment (or first appointment) of a provisional liquidator or, if no such appointment has been made, the date of the winding-up order;
(c) if the case does not fall within either paragraph (a) or (b), the relevant date is the date of the passing of the resolution for the winding up of the company.
(4) In relation to a company in receivership (where section 40 or, as the case may be, section 59 applies), the relevant date is—

(a) in England and Wales, the date of the appointment of the receiver by debenture-holders, and
(b) in Scotland, the date of the appointment of the receiver under section 53(6) or (as the case may be) 54(5).

(5) For the purposes of section 258 in Part VIII (individual voluntary arrangements), the relevant date is, in relation to a debtor who is not an undischarged bankrupt, the date of the interim order made under section 252 with respect to his proposal.

(6) In relation to a bankrupt, the following applies—
(a) where at the time the bankruptcy order was made there was an interim receiver appointed under section 286, the relevant date is the date on which the interim receiver was first appointed after the presentation of the bankruptcy petition;
(b) otherwise, the relevant date is the date of the making of the bankruptcy order.

Schedule 6   The Categories of Preferential Debts

Category 1: Debts due to Inland Revenue
    1. Sums due at the relevant date from the debtor on account of deductions of income tax from emoluments paid during the period of 12 months next before that date.
The deductions here referred to are those which the debtor was liable to make under section 204 of the Income and Corporation Taxes Act 1970 (pay as you earn), less the amount of the repayments of income tax which the debtor was liable to make during that period.
    2. Sums due at the relevant date from the debtor in respect of such deductions as are required to be made by the debtor for that period under section 69 of the Finance (No. 2) Act 1975 (sub-contractors in the construction industry).

Category 2: Debts due to Customs and Excise
    3. Any value added tax which is referable to the period of 6 months next before the relevant date (which period is referred to below as 'the 6-month period').
For the purposes of this paragraph—
(a) where the whole of the prescribed accounting period to which any value added tax is attributable falls within the 6-month period, the whole amount of that tax is referable to that period; and
(b) in any other case the amount of any value added tax which is referable to the 6-month period is the proportion of the tax which is equal to such proportion (if any) of the accounting reference period in question as falls within the 6-month period;
and in sub-paragraph (a) 'prescribed' means prescribed by regulations under the Value Added Tax Act 1983.
    4. The amount of any car tax which is due at the relevant date from the debtor and which became due within a period of 12 months next before that date.

5. Any amount which is due—
(a) by way of general betting duty or bingo duty, or
(b) under section 12(1) of the Betting and Gaming Duties Act 1981 (general betting duty and pool betting duty recoverable from agent collecting stakes), or
(c) under section 14 of, or Schedule 2 to, that Act (gaming licence duty),
from the debtor at the relevant date and which became due within the period of 12 months next before that date.

Category 3: Social security contributions
6. All sums which on the relevant date are due from the debtor on account of Class 1 or Class 2 contributions under the Social Security Act 1975 or the Social Security (Northern Ireland) Act 1975 and which became due from the debtor in the 12 months next before the relevant date.
7. All sums which on the relevant date have been assessed on and are due from the debtor on account of Class 4 contributions under either of those Acts of 1975, being sums which—
(a) are due to the Commissioners of Inland Revenue (rather than to the Secretary of State or a Northern Ireland department), and
(b) are assessed on the debtor up to 5th April next before the relevant date,
but not exceeding, in the whole, any one year's assessment.

Category 4: Contributions to occupational pension schemes, etc.
8. Any sum which is owed by the debtor and is a sum to which Schedule 3 to the Social Pensions Act 1975 applies (contributions to occupational pension schemes and state scheme premiums).

Category 5: Remuneration, etc., of employees
9. So much of any amount which—
(a) is owed by the debtor to a person who is or has been an employee of the debtor, and
(b) is payable by way of remuneration in respect of the whole or any part of the period of 4 months next before the relevant date,
as does not exceed so much as may be prescribed by order made by the Secretary of State.
10. An amount owed by way of accrued holiday remuneration, in respect of any period of employment before the relevant date, to a person whose employment by the debtor has been terminated, whether before, on or after that date.
11. So much of any sum owed in respect of money advanced for the purpose as has been applied for the payment of a debt which, if it had not been paid, would have been a debt falling within paragraph 9 or 10.
12. So much of any amount which—
(a) is ordered (whether before or after the relevant date) to be paid by the debtor under the Reserve Forces (Safeguard of Employment) Act 1985, and
(b) is so ordered in respect of a default made by the debtor before that date in the discharge of his obligations under that Act,
as does not exceed such amount as may be prescribed by order made by the Secretary of State.

APPENDIX 1

Interpretation for Category 5

13. (1) For the purposes of paragraphs 9 to 12, a sum is payable by the debtor to a person by way of remuneration in respect of any period if—
(a) it is paid as wages or salary (whether payable for time or for piece work or earned wholly or partly by way of commissioning) in respect of services rendered to the debtor in that period, or
(b) it is an amount falling within the following sub-paragraph and is payable by the debtor in respect of that period.
(2) An amount falls within this sub-paragraph if it is—
(a) a guarantee payment under section 12(1) of the Employment Protection (Consolidation) Act 1978 (employee without work to do for a day or part of a day);
(b) remuneration on suspension on medical grounds under section 19 of that Act;
(c) any payment for time off under section 27(3) (trade union duties), 31(3) (looking for work, etc.) or 31A(4) (ante-natal care) of that Act; or
(d) remuneration under a protective award made by an industrial tribunal under section 101 of the Employment Protection Act 1975 (redundancy dismissal with compensation).

14. (1) This paragraph relates to a case in which a person's employment has been terminated by or in consequence of his employer going into liquidation or being adjudged bankrupt or (his employer being a company not in liquidation) by or in consequence of—
(a) a receiver being appointed as mentioned in section 40 of this Act (debenture-holders secured by floating charge), or
(b) the appointment of a receiver under section 53(6) or 54(5) of this Act (Scottish company with property subject to floating charge), or
(c) the taking of possession by debenture-holders (so secured), as mentioned in section 196 of the Companies Act.
(2) For the purposes of paragraphs 9 to 12, holiday remuneration is deemed to have accrued to that person in respect of any period of employment if, by virtue of his contract of employment or of any enactment that remuneration would have accrued in respect of that period if his employment had continued until he became entitled to be allowed the holiday.
(3) The reference in sub-paragraph (2) to any enactment includes an order or direction made under an enactment.

15. Without prejudice to paragraphs 13 and 14—
(a) any remuneration payable by the debtor to a person in respect of a period of holiday or of absence from work through sickness or other good cause is deemed to be wages or (as the case may be) salary in respect of services rendered to the debtor in that period, and
(b) references here and in those paragraphs to remuneration in respect of a period of holiday include any sums which, if they had been paid, would have been treated for the purposes of the enactments relating to social security as earnings in respect of that period.

CONSUMER CREDIT ACT 1974

8 *Consumer credit agreements* (1) A personal credit agreement is an agreement between an individual ('the debtor') and any other person ('the creditor') by which the creditor provides the debtor with credit of any amount.
(2) A consumer credit agreement is a personal credit agreement by which the creditor provides the debtor with credit not exceeding [£15,000].
(3) A consumer credit agreement is a regulated agreement within the meaning of this Act if it is not an agreement (an 'exempt agreement') specified in or under section 16.

9 *Meaning of credit* (1) In this Act 'credit' includes a cash loan, and any other form of financial accommodation.
(2) Where credit is provided otherwise than in sterling it shall be treated for the purposes of this Act as provided in sterling of an equivalent amount.
(3) Without prejudice to the generality of subsection (1), the person by whom goods are bailed or (in Scotland) hired to an individual under a hire-purchase agreement shall be taken to provide him with fixed-sum credit to finance the transaction of an amount equal to the total price of the goods less the aggregate of the deposit (if any) and the total charge for credit.
(4) For the purposes of this Act, an item entering into the total charge for credit shall not be treated as credit even though time is allowed for its payment.

10 *Running-account credit and fixed-sum credit* (1) For the purposes of this Act—
(a) running-account credit is a facility under a personal credit agreement whereby the debtor is enabled to receive from time to time (whether in his own person, or by another person) from the creditor or a third party cash, goods and services (or any of them) to an amount or value such that, taking into account payments made by or to the credit of the debtor, the credit limit (if any) is not at any time exceeded; and
(b) fixed-sum credit is any other facility under a personal credit agreement whereby the debtor is enabled to receive credit (whether in one amount or by instalments).
(2) In relation to running-account credit, 'credit limit' means, as respects any period, the maximum debit balance which, under the credit agreement, is allowed to stand on the account during that period, disregarding any term of the agreement allowing that maximum to be exceeded merely temporarily.
(3) For the purposes of section 8(2), running-account credit shall be taken not to exceed the amount specified in that subsection ('the specified amount') if—
(a) the credit limit does not exceed the specified amount; or
(b) whether or not there is a credit limit, and if there is, notwithstanding that it exceeds the specified amount,—
    (i) the debtor is not enabled to draw at any one time an amount which, so far as (having regard to section 9(4)) it represents credit, exceeds the specified amount, or
    (ii) the agreement provides that, if the debit balance rises above a given

amount (not exceeding the specified amount), the rate of the total charge for credit increases or any other condition favouring the creditor or his associate comes into operation, or
(iii) at the time the agreement is made it is probable, having regard to the terms of the agreement and any other relevant considerations, that the debit balance will not at any time rise above the specified amount.

11 *Restricted-use credit and unrestricted-use credit* (1) A restricted-use credit agreement is a regulated consumer credit agreement—
(a) to finance a transaction between the debtor and the creditor, whether forming part of that agreement or not, or
(b) to finance a transaction between the debtor and a person (the 'supplier') other than the creditor, or
(c) to refinance any existing indebtedness of the debtor's, whether to the creditor or another person,
and 'restricted-use credit' shall be construed accordingly.
(2) An unrestricted-use credit agreement is a regulated consumer credit agreement not falling within subsection (1), and 'unrestricted-use credit' shall be construed accordingly.
(3) An agreement does not fall within subsection (1) if the credit is in fact provided in such a way as to leave the debtor free to use it as he chooses, even though certain uses would contravene that or any other agreement.
(4) An agreement may fall within subsection (1)(b) although the identity of the supplier is unknown at the time the agreement is made.

12 *Debtor–creditor–supplier agreements* A debtor–creditor–supplier agreement is a regulated consumer credit agreement being—
(a) a restricted-use credit agreement which falls within section 11(1)(a), or
(b) a restricted-use credit agreement which falls within section 11(1)(b) and is made by the creditor under pre-existing arrangements, or in contemplation of future arrangements, between himself and the supplier, or
(c) an unrestricted-use credit agreement which is made by the creditor under pre-existing arrangements between himself and a person (the 'supplier') other than the debtor in the knowledge that the credit is to be used to finance a transaction between the debtor and the supplier.

13 *Debtor–creditor agreements* A debtor–creditor agreement is a regulated consumer credit agreement being—
(a) a restricted-use credit agreement which falls within section 11(1)(b) but is not made by the creditor under pre-existing arrangements, or in contemplation of future arrangements, between himself and the supplier, or
(b) a restricted-use credit agreement which falls within section 11(1)(c), or
(c) an unrestricted-use credit agreement which is not made by the creditor under pre-existing arrangements between himself and a person (the 'supplier') other than the debtor in the knowledge that the credit is to be used to finance a transaction between the debtor and the supplier.

14 *Credit-token agreements* (1) A credit-token is a card, check, voucher, coupon, stamp, form, booklet or other document or thing given to an individual by a person carrying on a consumer credit business, who undertakes—
(a) that on the production of it (whether or not some other action is also required) he will supply cash, goods and services (or any of them) on credit, or
(b) that where, on the production of it to a third party (whether or not any other action is also required), the third party supplies cash, goods and services (or any of them), he will pay the third party for them (whether or not deducting any discount or commission), in return for payment to him by the individual.
(2) A credit-token agreement is a regulated agreement for the provision of credit in connection with the use of a credit-token.
(3) Without prejudice to the generality of section 9(1), the person who gives to an individual an undertaking falling within subsection (1)(b) shall be taken to provide him with credit drawn on whenever a third party supplies him with cash, goods or services.
(4) For the purposes of subsection (1), use of an object to operate a machine provided by the person giving the object or a third party shall be treated as the production of the object to him.

16 *Exempt agreements* (1) This Act does not regulate a consumer credit agreement where the creditor is a local authority ..., or a body specified, or of a description specified, in an order made by the Secretary of State, being—
(a) an insurance company,
(b) a friendly society,
(c) an organisation of employers or organisation of workers,
(d) a charity,
(e) a land improvement company, or
(f) a body corporate named or specifically referred to in any public general Act,
 [(ff) a body corporate named or specifically referred to in an order made under—
  section 156(4), 444(1) or 447(2)(a) of the Housing Act 1985,
  section 2 of the Home Purchase Assistance and Housing Corporation Guarantee Act 1978 or section 31 of the Tenants' Rights, &c. (Scotland) Act 1980, or
  Article 154(1)(a) or 156AA of the Housing (Northern Ireland) Order 1981 or Article 10(6A) of the Housing (Northern Ireland) Order 1983;] [, or
(g) a building society] [, or
(h) an authorised institution or wholly-owned subsidiary (within the meaning of the Companies Act 1985) of such an institution.]
(2) Subsection (1) applies only where the agreement is—
(a) a debtor–creditor–supplier agreement financing—
 (i) the purchase of land, or
 (ii) the provision of dwellings on any land,
 and secured by a land mortgage on that land; or
(b) a debtor–creditor agreement secured by any land mortgage; or

(c) a debtor-creditor-supplier agreement financing a transaction which is a linked transaction in relation to—
  (i) an agreement falling within paragraph (a), or
  (ii) an agreement falling within paragraph (b) financing—
    (aa) the purchase of any land, or
    (bb) the provision of dwellings on any land,
and secured by a land mortgage on the land referred to in paragraph (a) or, as the case may be, the land referred to in sub-paragraph (ii).
(3) The Secretary of State shall not make, vary or revoke an order—
(a) under section (1)(a) without consulting the Minister of the Crown responsible for insurance companies,
(b) under subsection (1)(b) ... without consulting the Chief Registrar of Friendly Societies,
(c) under subsection (1)(d) without consulting the Charity Commissioners, or
(d) under subsection (1)(e) [, (f) or (ff)] without consulting any Minister of the Crown with responsibilities concerning the body in question[, or
(e) under subsection (1)(g) without consulting the Building Societies Commission and the Treasury.] [or
(f) under sub-section (1)(h) without consulting the Treasury and the Bank of England.]
(4) An order under subsection (1) relating to a body may be limited so as to apply only to agreements by that body of a description specified in the order.
(5) The Secretary of State may by order provide that this Act shall not regulate other consumer credit agreements where—
(a) the number of payments to be made by the debtor does not exceed the number specified for that purpose in the order, or
(b) the rate of the total charge for credit does not exceed the rate so specified, or
(c) an agreement has a connection with a country outside the United Kingdom.
(6) The Secretary of State may by order provide that this Act shall not regulate consumer hire agreements of a description specified in the order where—
(a) the owner is a body corporate authorised by or under any enactment to supply electricity, gas or water, and
(b) the subject of the agreement is a meter or metering equipment,
or where the owner is [*British Telecommunications*] [or where the owner is a public telecommunications operator specified in the order].
[(6A) This Act does not regulate a consumer credit agreement where the creditor is a housing authority and the agreement is secured by a land mortgage of a dwelling.
(6B) In subsection (6A) 'housing authority' means—
(a) as regards England and Wales, an authority or body within section 80(1) of the Housing Act 1985 (the landlord condition for secure tenancies), other than a housing association or a housing trust which is a charity;
(b) as regards Scotland, a development corporation established under an order made, or having effect as if made under the New Towns (Scotland) Act 1968, the Scottish Special Housing Association or the Housing Corporation;
(c) as regards Northern Ireland, the Northern Ireland Housing Executive.]
(7) Nothing in this section affects the application of sections 137–140 (extortionate credit bargains).

(8) In the application of this section to Scotland subsection (3)(c) shall not have effect.
(9) In the application of this section to Northern Ireland subsection (3) shall have effect as if any reference to a Minister of the Crown were a reference to a Northern Ireland department, any reference to the Chief Registrar of Friendly Societies were a reference to the Registrar of Friendly Societies for Northern Ireland, and any reference to the Charity Commissioners were a reference to the Department of Finance for Northern Ireland.

48 *Definition of canvassing off trade premises (regulated agreements)* (1) An individual (the 'canvasser') canvasses a regulated agreement off trade premises if he solicits the entry (as debtor or hirer) of another individual (the 'consumer') into the agreement by making oral representations to the consumer, or any other individual, during a visit by the canvasser to any place (not excluded by subsection (2)) where the consumer, or that other individual, as the case may be, is, being a visit—
(a) carried out for the purpose of making such oral representations to individuals who are at that place, but
(b) not carried out in response to a request made on a previous occasion.
(2) A place is excluded from subsection (1) if it is a place where a business is carried on (whether on a permanent or temporary basis) by—
(a) the creditor or owner, or
(b) a supplier, or
(c) the canvasser, or the person whose employee or agent the canvasser is, or
(d) the consumer.

49 *Prohibition of canvassing debtor–creditor agreements off trade premises*
(1) It is an offence to canvass debtor–creditor agreement off trade premises.
(2) It is also an offence to solicit the entry of an individual (as debtor) into a debtor–creditor agreement during a visit carried out in response to a request made on a previous occasion, where—
(a) the request was not in writing signed by or on behalf of the person making it, and
(b) if no request for the visit had been made, the soliciting would have constituted the canvassing of a debtor–creditor agreement off trade premises.
(3) Subsections (1) and (2) do not apply to any soliciting for an agreement enabling the debtor to overdraw on a current account of any description kept with the creditor, where—
(a) the Director has determined that current accounts of that description kept with the creditor are excluded from subsections (1) and (2), and
(b) the debtor already keeps an account with the creditor (whether a current account or not).
(4) A determination under subsection (3)(a)—
(a) may be made subject to such conditions as the Director thinks fit, and
(b) shall be made only where the Director is of opinion that it is not against the interests of debtors.

(5) If soliciting is done in breach of a condition imposed under subsection (4)(a), the determination under subsection (3)(a) does not apply to it.

50 *Circulars to minors* (1) A person commits an offence who, with a view to financial gain, sends to a minor any document inviting him to—
(a) borrow money, or
(b) obtain goods on credit or hire, or
(c) obtain services on credit, or
(d) apply for information or advice on borrowing money or otherwise obtaining credit, or hiring goods.
(2) In proceedings under subsection (1) in respect of the sending of a document to a minor, it is a defence for the person charged to prove that he did not know, and had no reasonable cause to suspect, that he was a minor.
(3) Where a document is received by a minor at any school or educational establishment for minors, a person sending it to him at that establishment knowing or suspecting it to be such an establishment shall be taken to have reasonable cause to suspect that he is a minor.

51 *Prohibition of unsolicited credit-tokens* (1) It is an offence to give a person a credit-token if he has not asked for it.
(2) To comply with subsection (1) a request must be contained in a document signed by the person making the request, unless the credit-token agreement is a small debtor–creditor–supplier agreement.
(3) Subsection (1) does not apply to the giving of a credit-token to a person—
(a) for use under a credit-token agreement already made, or
(b) in renewal or replacement of a credit-token previously accepted by him under a credit-token agreement which continues in force, whether or not varied.

60 *Form and content of agreements* (1) The Secretary of State shall make regulations as to the form and content of documents embodying regulated agreements, and the regulations shall contain such provisions as appear to him appropriate with a view to ensuring that the debtor or hirer is made aware of—
(a) the right and duties conferred or imposed on him by the agreement,
(b) the amount and rate of the total charge for credit (in the case of a consumer credit agreement),
(c) the protection and remedies available to him under this Act, and
(d) any other matters which, in the opinion of the Secretary of State, it is desirable for him to know about in connection with the agreement.
(2) Regulations under subsection (1) may in particular—
(a) require specified information to be included in the prescribed manner in documents, and other specified material to be excluded;
(b) contain requirements to ensure that specified information is clearly brought to the attention of the debtor or hirer, and that one part of a document is not given insufficient or excessive prominence compared with another.
(3) If, on an application made to the Director by a person carrying on a consumer credit business or a consumer hire business, it appears to the Director

impracticable for the applicant to comply with any requirement of regulations under subsection (1) in a particular case, he may, by notice to the applicant, direct that the requirement be waived or varied in relation to such agreements, and subject to such conditions (if any), as he may specify, and this Act and the regulations shall have effect accordingly.
(4) The Director shall give a notice under subsection (3) only if he is satisfied that to do so would not prejudice the interests of debtors or hirers.

61 *Signing of agreement* (1) A regulated agreement is not properly executed unless—
(a) a document in the prescribed form itself containing all the prescribed terms and conforming to regulations under section 60(1) is signed in the prescribed manner both by the debtor or hirer and by or on behalf of the creditor or owner, and
(b) the document embodies all the terms of the agreement, other than implied terms, and
(c) the document is, when presented or sent to the debtor or hirer for signature, in such a state that all its terms are readily legible.
(2) In addition, where the agreement is one to which section 58(1) applies, it is not properly executed unless—
(a) the requirements of section 58(1) were complied with, and
(b) the unexecuted agreement was sent, for his signature, to the debtor or hirer by post not less than seven days after a copy of it was given to him under section 58(1), and
(c) during the consideration period, the creditor or owner refrained from approaching the debtor or hirer (whether in person, by telephone or letter, or in any other way) except in response to a specific request made by the debtor or hirer after the beginning of the consideration period, and
(d) no notice of withdrawal by the debtor or hirer was received by the creditor or owner before the sending of the unexecuted agreement.
(3) In subsection (2)(c), 'the consideration period' means the period beginning with the giving of the copy under section 58(1) and ending—
(a) at the expiry of seven days after the day on which the unexecuted agreement is sent, for his signature, to the debtor or hirer, or
(b) on its return by the debtor or hirer after signature by him,
whichever first occurs.
(4) Where the debtor or hirer is a partnership or an unincorporated body of persons, subsection (1)(a) shall apply with the substitution for 'by the debtor or hirer' of 'by or on behalf of the debtor or hirer'.

65 *Consequences of improper execution* (1) An improperly executed regulated agreement is enforceable against the debtor or hirer on an order of the court only.
(2) A retaking of goods or land to which a regulated agreement relates is an enforcement of the agreement.

75 *Liability of creditor for breaches by supplier* (1) If the debtor under a debtor–creditor–supplier agreement falling within section 12(b) or (c) has, in relation to a transaction financed by the agreement, any claim against the supplier in respect of a misrepresentation or breach of contract, he shall have a like claim against the creditor, who, with the supplier, shall accordingly be jointly and severally liable to the debtor.

(2) Subject to any agreement between them, the creditor shall be entitled to be indemnified by the supplier for loss suffered by the creditor in satisfying his liability under subsection (1), including costs reasonably incurred by him in defending proceedings instituted by the debtor.

(3) Subsection (1) does not apply to a claim—

(a) under a non-commercial agreement, or

(b) so far as the claim relates to any single item to which the supplier has attached a cash price not exceeding [£100] or more than [£30,000].

(4) This section applies notwithstanding that the debtor, in entering into the transaction, exceeded the credit limit or otherwise contravened any term of the agreement.

(5) In an action brought against the creditor under subsection (1) he shall be entitled, in accordance with rules of court, to have the supplier made a party to the proceedings.

83 *Liability for misuse of credit facilities* (1) The debtor under a regulated consumer credit agreement shall not be liable to the creditor for any loss arising from use of the credit facility by another person not acting, or to be treated as acting, as the debtor's agent.

(2) This section does not apply to a non-commercial agreement or to any loss in so far as it arises from misuse of an instrument to which section 4 of the Cheques Act 1957 applies.

84 *Misuse of credit-tokens* (1) Section 83 does not prevent the debtor under a credit-token agreement from being made liable to the extent of [£50] (or the credit limit if lower) for loss to the creditor arising from use of the credit-token by other persons during a period beginning when the credit-token ceases to be in the possession of any authorised person and ending when the credit-token is once more in the possession of an authorised person.

(2) Section 83 does not prevent the debtor under a credit-token agreement from being made liable to any extent for loss to the creditor from use of the credit-token by a person who acquired possession of it with the debtor's consent.

(3) Subsections (1) and (2) shall not apply to any use of the credit-token after the creditor has been given oral or written notice that it is lost or stolen, or is for any other reason liable to misuse.

(4) Subsections (1) and (2) shall not apply unless there are contained in the credit-token agreement in the prescribed manner particulars of the name, address and telephone number of a person stated to be the person to whom notice is to be given under subsection (3).

(5) Notice under subsection (3) takes effect when received, but where it is given orally, and all the agreement so requires, it shall be treated as not taking effect if not confirmed in writing within seven days.

(6) Any sum paid by the debtor for the issue of the credit-token, to the extent (if any) that it had not been previously offset by use made of the credit-token, shall be treated as paid towards satisfaction of any liability under subsection (1) or (2).
(7) The debtor, the creditor, and any person authorised by the debtor to use the credit-token shall be authorised persons for the purposes of subsection (1).
(8) Where two or more credit-tokens are given under one credit-token agreement, the preceding provisions of this section apply to each credit-token separately.

126 *Enforcement of land mortgages* A land mortgage securing a regulated agreement is enforceable (so far as provided in relation to the agreement) on an order of the court only.

127 *Enforcement orders in cases of infringement* (1) In the case of an application for an enforcement order under—
(a) section 65(1) (improperly executed agreements), or
(b) section 105(7)(a) or (b) (improperly executed security instruments), or
(c) section 111(2) (failure to serve copy of notice on surety), or
(d) section 124(1) or (2) (taking of negotiable instrument in contravention of section 123),
the court shall dismiss the application if, but (subject to subsections (3) and (4)) only if, it considers it just to do so having regard to—
  (i) prejudice caused to any person by the contravention in question, and the degree of culpability for it; and
  (ii) the powers conferred on the court by subsection (2) and sections 135 and 136.
(2) If it appears to the court just to do so, it may in an enforcement order reduce or discharge any sum payable by the debtor or hirer, or any surety, so as to compensate him for prejudice suffered as a result of the contravention in question.
(3) The court shall not make an enforcement order under section 65(1) if section 61(1)(a) (signing of agreements) was not complied with unless a document (whether or not in the prescribed form and complying with regulations under section 60(1)) itself containing all the prescribed terms of the agreement was signed by the debtor or hirer (whether or not in the prescribed manner).
(4) The court shall not make an enforcement order under section 65(1) in the case of a cancellable agreement if—
(a) a provision of section 62 or 63 was not complied with, and the creditor or owner did not give a copy of the executed agreement, and of any other document referred to in it, to the debtor or hirer before the commencement of the proceedings in which the order is sought, or
(b) section 64(1) was not complied with.
(5) Where an enforcement order is made in a case to which subsection (3) applies, the order may direct that the regulated agreement is to have effect as if it did not include a term omitted from the document signed by the debtor or hirer.

Appendix 2 Proposed Legislation: Extract from 'Banking Services: Law and Practice' White Paper

LEGISLATION PROPOSED FOLLOWING THE JACK REPORT
(Annex 9 of the White Paper entitled
Banking Services: Law and Practice: CM 1026
Published March 1990)

Legislation will be introduced, when other pressures on the legislative timetable permit, for the following purposes:
(a) banning the unsolicited mailing of all payment cards (Committee recommendation 10(2)/paras. 4.4–5);
(b) restricting a customer's liability for loss in the case of payment cards (recommendation 10(10)/paras. 4.6);
(c) imposing on banks liability for the failure of electronic funds transfer equipment (recommendation 10(11)/paras. 4.7);
(d) clarifying the meaning of crossings on cheques and giving statutory recognition to the words 'account payee' (recommendations 7(2), 7(4)/paras. 5.6);
(e) permitting the truncation of cheques (recommendation 7(8)/paras. 5.11–13);
(f) clarifying the status of payable orders and bank giro credits (recommendations 7(11), (12), (13)/paras. 5.19–22);
(g) extending section 5(5) of the Forgery and Counterfeiting Act 1981 to apply to all payment cards (recommendation 11(5)/paras. 4.12–13);
(h) repealing sections 3 to 5 of Bankers' Books Evidence Act 1879 (which relate to the admissibility in evidence of copies of entries in bankers' books) (recommendation 13(6)/paras. 7.2, 7.5);
(i) amending the Bankers' Books Evidence Act 1879:—
  (i) to extend the definition of 'bankers' books' in section 9 to include cheques and credit slips (recommendation 13(8)/para. 7.8);
  (ii) to extend the definition of 'bank' and 'banker' in section 9 to include the Bank of England (recommendation 13(9)/para. 7.9); and
  (iii) to give a court discretion when making an order under section 7 to order payment of a fee to reimburse the bank for the cost of compliance (recommendation 13(10)/para. 7.11);
(j) restructuring the various statutory protections available to the paying bank under the Cheques Act 1957, the Bills of Exchange Act 1882 and the Stamp Act 1853 (recommendation 7(5)/para. 5.9);
(k) updating the Bills of Exchange Act 1882:—
  (i) to provide that the sum payable on a negotiable instrument may include a sum denominated in a unit of account established by an inter-govern-

mental institution or by agreement between two or more States (recommendation 8(5)/para. 6.4);
(ii) to remove the mandatory requirement for noting a protest of a dishonoured foreign bill, while retaining the procedure for use on a voluntary basis (recommendation 8(8)/paras. 6.6–7);
(iii) to permit transactions by way of screen based or book entry depository systems operated by an approved depository including transactions in 'dematerialised' instruments (recommendation 8(9)/paras. 6.9–10); and
(iv) to allow notice of dishonour to be given by electronic communication or by telecommunication (Technical Recommendation 36) (recommendation 8(10)/para. 6.11).

Index

Access cards   *68–9, 73*
Administration orders   *50, 220, 293–5*
Administrative receivers   *50, 289–92*
  as agents   *290–1*
  appointment   *289–91*
  obligations of   *291–2*
  power of bank to appoint   *286*
  powers of   *292*
Advertising, FSA and   *104–5*
Advertising of credit   *90–3*
  advertiser definition   *91*
  advertiser and regulated agreements   *90–1*
  categories of regulated advertisements   *91–3*
  form and contents   *91*
  full advertisements   *93*
  fundamental principle   *91*
  intermediate advertisements   *92–3*
  quotations   *92, 93–4*
  Regulations   *90*
  simple advertisements   *92*
  statutory warnings   *92, 93*
Advice
  'best advice' rule   *106*
  to provider of security   *230*
AFBD   *101*
Agency
  agent for payee bank   *169*
  agent for payer   *168*
  independent contractor   *168*

Agency—*continued*
  receivers as agents   *290–1*
Agricultural charges   *307–9*
  farmer defined   *307*
  fixed charges   *307–8*
  floating charges   *308*
  priority of charges   *308–9*
  progeny of charged livestock   *307*
  registration of charges   *308–9*
American Express cards   *68*
Annual Percentage Rate (APR)   *83, 84–5*
Appointed representatives   *103*
Appropriation of payments   *25–6, 53*
  Clayton's case   *26–8*
APR   *83, 84–5*
Arrangements   *220*
Assignment   *167*
'Associates'   *221*
Association of Futures Brokers and Dealers (AFBD)   *101*
Attorney, power of *see* Power of attorney
Automatic Teller Machines (ATMs)   *66–7, 189–202*
  balance enquiries   *201–2*
  bank's duties   *195–8*
  card issuers' ATMs   *190–2*
  confidentiality duty   *202*
  contributory negligence   *197*
  defamation claims   *197*
  limitation of liability   *198–9*

351

Automatic Teller Machines
(ATMs)—*continued*
  machine failure or error *195–9*
  'not in use' notice *196*
  records of transactions *195, 198*
  retention of card *196*
  services provided *201–2*
  third party's ATMs *192–4*
  see also Cash cards: Personal Identification Number (PIN)

BACS
  countermanding debit transfers *180*
  credit transfers *171–2*
  debit transfers *172, 180*
  direct remitter to *180*
Bailment
  bailment for reward *33*
  gratuitous bailment *33*
  liability of bank as bailee *33*
  voluntary bailment *33*
Bank
  definition of *4*
  see also individual types e.g. Collecting bank: Paying bank *etc.*
Bank balance charges *299–302*
  charge over credit balance *301*
  contract of deposit *302*
  contractually extending set-off *300–1*
  deposit agreement *300*
  flawed assets *302*
  registration of charge *301*
  segregated fund *301*
  set-off and *299–300*
Bank of England *102*
Bank notes *112*

Banker–customer relationship *3–35*
  access to information *see* Data Protection Act
  accounts held in different countries *6–7*
  after termination of contract *19*
  appropriation of payments *25–6, 53*
  banker's lien *see* Banker's lien
  charges *15*
  cheque collection *5, 141–6, 168*
  Clayton's case *26–8*
  combination of accounts *see* Combination of accounts
  conclusive evidence clause *9*
  customers *see* Customers
  debtor–creditor relationship *5–6*
  definition of bank *4*
  definition of customer *4–5*
  duty of care
    as agent *10–12*
    as trustee *see* Duty of care as trustee
  duty of confidentiality *see* Duty of confidentiality
  duty to collect cheques *168*
  express terms of contract *9–10*
  forged cheques *7–9*
  implied terms of contract *6–9*
  interest right *14–15*
  limitation to demand repayment *24–5*
  negligent advice to non-customer *5*
  opening account *see* Opening account

Banker–customer relationship—
    continued
  repayment on demand   *24*
  set-off *see* Set-off
  termination of contract   *34–5*
  timing of contract   *5*
Bankers Automated Clearing
    Services Ltd *see* BACS
Banker's draft   *112, 114*
  crossings on   *114*
Banker's lien   *31–3*
  on cheques   *150*
  limitations on operation of
    32–3
  property subject to   *32*
  safe custody and   *32, 34*
Banker's opinions   *19, 21–4*
  breach of secrecy   *23*
  credit reference agencies   *23–4*
  fraudulent misrepresentation
    22
  liability to customer   *23*
  liability to ultimate recipient
    22
  libel   *23*
  negligence   *22–3*
Banking Services: Law and Practice
    (White Paper)   *3, 111–12*
  extract from   *349–50*
Bankruptcy
  of guarantor   *238*
  of individual *see* Bankruptcy of
    individual
  termination of contract   *35*
  of trustee   *45*
Bankruptcy of individual   *40–1*
  account after bankruptcy order
    41
  account after presentation of
    petition   *40–1*

Bankruptcy of individual—
    continued
  discharged from bankruptcy
    41
  wages accounts and   *40*
Bankruptcy order   *217*
  see also Insolvency
Bearer bonds   *112*
Bearer cheques   *113, 114, 133*
'Best advice' rule   *106*
'Best execution' rule   *106*
Bills of exchange   *112*
  definition   *113*
  indorsements required before
    paying   *133*
Bills of Exchange Act   *113–14,*
    311–17
Bonds   *98*
Book debts, charges over   *303–5*
Book tokens   *66*
British Eagle principle   *30, 31*
Brokerage, credit   *94–5*

Cancellation rights
  cooling-off period   *86*
  notices of   *84*
  procedures   *86*
Canvassing   *59, 63, 89–90*
Capacity of company   *48, 283–4*
Cash cards   *66–7*
  agreed overdrafts   *190–1*
  as credit-tokens   *66–7,*
    189–94
  fraudulent duplication
    199–200
  lost   *200*
  overdrafts without bank's
    agreement   *191–2*
  unauthorised use   *199–201*
  unsolicited credit tokens   *194*

Cash cards—*continued*
  used in card issuers' own ATMs
    190–2
  used in third party's ATMs
    192–4
  see also Automatic teller
    machines (ATMs): Personal
    Identification Number (PIN)
Cash dispensing machines *see*
  Automatic teller machines
  (ATMs)
Certificates of deposit *32, 98, 112*
CHAPS *172–3, 174*
  direct remitter to *180*
  gateways *172*
  logical acknowledgement
    (LAK) *175–6, 179*
  payee bank's duty *183*
  unconditional and irrevocable
    payment *172–3, 179*
Charge cards *58, 68*
Charge Certificate *247*
Charges
  bank's right to *15*
  over bank balance *see* Bank
    balance charges
  over book debts *303–5*
  see also Agricultural, Fixed *and*
    Floating charges: Registration
    of charges: Security
Charitable trusts *44–5*
Cheque cards *151–3*
  standard conditions *151*
  stopping cheques backed by
    127
  unauthorised overdrafts *152*
Cheque clearing *160–2*
  clearing cycle *161*
  EFT clearing cycles *173*
  settlement day *161*

Cheque clearing—*continued*
  town clearing *162*
  truncation *160, 162–5*
  see also Credit clearing:
    Electronic *and* Paper
    payment systems
Cheque guarantee cards *66*
Cheques *111–58*
  backed by cheque card *127*
  bank not obliged to pay *129*
  banker's lien on *150*
  bearer *113, 114, 133*
  Bills of Exchange Act *113–14*
  clearing *see* Cheque clearing
  collecting bank and *see*
    Collecting bank
  collection of *5, 168*
  company cheques *49–50*
  contributory negligence *147*
  conversion *131–2, 136–7,
    143*
  countermand *126–9*
  crossings *114–16*
  dates *120–1*
  definition *113*
  discrepancy between words and
    figures *121*
  drawee *113, 114*
  drawer *113, 114*
  estoppel defence *148*
  forged *see* Forged cheques
  form of *120–1*
  fraudulent alteration *see* Forged
    cheques
  'good faith' *133*
  holders of *117–19, 125, 126,
    148–51*
  inchoate *125*
  indorsements on *116–17,
    132–3*

Cheques—*continued*
  instruments requiring indorsement   146
  legal relationships involving paying bank   120
  mistaken crediting of account   155–6
  negligence in collection   141–6
  negotiable instruments and   112–13
  not paid to account holding branch   137–8
  'pay cash'   114
  'pay wages'   114
  payee or bearer   113, 114
  paying bank statutory protection   131–4, 164
  paying bank subrogation   134–5
  payment of   119–20
  post-dated   120–1
  recovery of money paid by mistake   153–5
  signature   120, 121–3
  stale   121
  statutory protection for collecting bank   136–9
  statutory protection for paying bank   131–4, 164
  suspicious matters and existing information   141–4
  tracing   155
  wrongful dishonour   129–31, 179
  see also Electronic *and* Paper payment systems
Cheques Act   318
Chinese walls   104
Clayton's case rule   26–8, 43, 52, 53

Clearing *see* Cheque clearing: Credit clearing
Clearing bank   160
Clearing House Automated Payment System *see* CHAPS
Code of Practice   3–4
'Cold calling'   105
Collecting bank
  cheques not paid to account holding branch   137–8
  contributory negligence defence   147
  conversion   136–7, 143
  customer and   135–6
  dishonoured cheque and   136
  estoppel defence   148
  ex turpi causa non oritur acto defence   147–8
  as holder in due course   148–51
  as holder for value   149–51
  indemnity right   148
  instruments requiring indorsement   146
  'lulling to sleep' doctrine   143
  negligence   141–6
  statutory protection for   136–9
  suspicious matters and existing information   141–4
Collection of cheques   4, 168
  negligence in   141–6
  see also Electronic *and* Paper payment systems
Combination of accounts   28–9, 53
  banker's right to combine   28
  company accounts   53
  express agreement not to combine   29
  limits to right to combine   28–9
Commercial paper   32, 112

355

Committee of London Clearing
    Banks *132*
Companies, loans to *56*
Companies Act (1989) *321–5*
Company accounts *48–53*
    agency law and *48*
    appropriation right *53*
    combination of accounts *53*
    company cheques *49–50*
    corporate capacity *48, 283–4*
    criminal offences *48*
    disposition of company
        property *51*
    duty of care to company *48*
    financial assistance for
        purchase of own shares *48*
    insolvency *see* Company
        insolvency
    lending to own directors *48*
    liability of bank as shadow
        director *51–2*
    limited *48*
    plc *48*
    wage accounts *40, 47, 52–3,
        218, 291*
Company insolvency *50–1*
    administration orders *50, 220,
        293–5*
    administrative receivers *see*
        Administrative receivers
    priorities *218–19*
    voluntary arrangements *50*
    winding-up *see* Winding-up
Company security *283–97*
    administration orders *50, 220,
        293–5*
    administrative receivers *see*
        Administrative receivers
    charges over book debts
        303–5

Company security—*continued*
    corporate capacity *283–4*
    crystallisation of floating charge
        288–9
    crystallising event *285*
    debentures *283*
    execution of documents by
        company *284*
    fixed charge *285, 287–8*
    floating charge *284–5, 287–8*
    receiver appointment *see*
        Administrative receivers
    registration of charges *see*
        Registration of charges
    retention of title clauses *288,
        292–3*
    Romalpa clauses *288, 292–3*
    standard debenture terms
        286
    ultra vires *284*
Compensation fund, SIB *104*
Compositions *220*
Compulsory winding-up *50–1*
    disposition of company
        property *51*
    petition *51*
Conclusive evidence clause *9*
Confidentiality *see* Duty of
    confidentiality
Connected lender liability *59,
    72–4*
    claim against supplier *73–4*
    concept of *72–3*
    creditor's indemnity *74*
    limits *73*
    scope *73*
'Connected persons' *221*
Consideration
    guarantees and *234–5, 237*
    past consideration *234*

INDEX

Constructive trusts   *12–13, 120*
  test for liability as trustee   *13*
Consumer Credit Act   *340–8*
Consumer Credit Act lending
      55–95
  advertising *see* Advertising of
      credit
  APR   *83, 84–5*
  cancellation procedures   *86*
  cancellation rights   *76–7, 84,*
      85–6
  canvassing   *59, 63, 89–90*
  charge cards   *58, 68*
  connected lender liability *see*
      Connected lender liability
  contents of regulated
      agreements   *82–4*
  credit brokerage   *94–5*
  credit cards   *58–9, 60, 62,*
      68–9, 73
  credit limits   *57*
  credit token agreements   *61*
  credit tokens *see* Credit tokens
  debit cards   *67–8*
  debtor must be individual   *56*
  debtor–creditor agreements
      59, 60, 62, 63, 192
  debtor–creditor–supplier
      agreements   *59–60, 62, 68,*
      73, 75–6, 193–4
  definition of credit   *55*
  execution procedures   *85–6*
  exempt credit *see* Exempt
      credit agreements
  fixed-sum credit   *57, 58, 193–4*
  foreign currency   *55*
  forms and formalities   *81–9*
  'holy ground'   *83, 84*
  land as security *see* Land:
      Secured lending

Consumer Credit Act lending—
    continued
  linked transactions   *62*
  modifying agreement   *87*
  multiple agreements   *59, 61, 68*
  non-commercial agreements
      62, 73
  overdrafts *see* Overdrafts
  quotations   *92, 93–4*
  regulated agreements definition
      56
  restricted-use credit   *58–9, 60,*
      68
  running-account credit   *57–8,*
      62, 63, 193, 194
  secured lending *see* Secured
      lending
  small agreements   *61, 66, 69,*
      73
  supplier credit   *58–9*
  supplier finance   *59–60*
  termination   *87–8*
  total charge for credit   *84–5*
  unregulated arrangements   *55,*
      56
  unrestricted-use credit   *58–9,*
      60, 62, 63
  variation of regulated
      agreement   *87*
  voluntary early repayment
      88–9
Contract, privity of   *187*
Contracts for differences   *98*
Contributory negligence
  ATMs and   *197*
  cheques and   *7, 8, 9, 122–3*
      142, 147
  collecting bank defence   *147*
  EFT   *178*
  Conversion   *131–2, 136–7, 143*

357

'Cooling-off' period   86, 106
Cork Committee Report   222
Corporate capacity   48, 283–4
Countermanded cheques   126–9
  backed by cheque card   127
  cancellation of stop notice   128
  stop orders   126–9
Countermanding EFT payments   179–80
Credit brokerage   94–5
Credit cards   58–9, 60, 62, 68–9, 73
  connected lender liability   73
Credit clearing   165–70
  agency   168–9
  assignment   167
  completion of payment   169–70
  contractual duty   168
  credit transfers   165–6
  direct debits   166–7
  forgery and fraudulent alteration   169
  legal principles   167–9
  payment by mistake   170
  trust   167–8
Credit reference agencies   23–4
  definition   24
Credit standing status enquiry   19
Credit-tokens   65–72, 153
  agreements   61, 69
  cash cards as *see* Cash cards
  charge cards   68
  cheque guarantee cards   66
  credit cards   68–9
  debit cards   67–8
  definition of   189–90
  definition and scope   65–6

Credit-tokens—*continued*
  dishonest fabrication and duplication   72
  unsolicited   69–70, 194
  use by third parties   70–2
Credit transfers, BACS   171–2
Crediting by mistake   155–6
Creditor priority   217–20
Crossings on cheques   114–16
  'A/C Payee'   115
  'A/C Payee' where no account   142
  deletion of crossing   115
  general   115
  'not negotiable'   115
  'not transferable'   115
  special   115
Crowther Committee   55
Crystallisation   285, 288–9
Currency of the realm   112
Customers
  of bank or individual branch   5, 138
  of collecting bank   135–6
  companies *see* Company accounts
  death of   35, 39–40
  definition of   4–5
  disclosure with consent of   18–19
  employer   37, 141
  individuals *see* Individual customers
  joint accounts *see* Joint accounts
  liability of banker's opinions to   23
  mental incapacity of   35, 39–40
  minors   43–4

INDEX

Customers—*continued*
  opening accounts *see* Opening account
  partnerships *see* Partnership accounts
  paying bank and   *120*
  trustee accounts   *44–5*
  see also Banker–customer relationship: Individual customers

Data Protection Act   *19–21*
  access to information   *4*
  contents of register   *19–20*
  information fairly and lawfully processed   *20*
  information held for lawful process   *20*
  information not obtained by deception   *20*
  Office of Data Protection Registrar   *19*
  'personal data' definition   *21*
Dates, on cheques   *120–1*
Death
  of customer   *35, 39–40*
  of guarantor   *238*
  of one account-holder of joint account   *42–3*
  of trustee   *45*
Debentures *see* Company security
Debit transfers, BACS   *172*
Debtor–creditor agreements   *59, 60, 62, 63*
  cash cards and   *192*
Debtor–creditor–supplier agreements   *59–60, 62, 68*
  cash cards and   *193–4*
  connected lender liability   *73*

Debtor–creditor–supplier agreements—*continued*
  secured on land purchased with loan   *75–6*
Debtors *see* Consumer Credit Act lending
Debts, due on insolvency   *30*
Direct debits
  agency   *168–9*
  assignment   *167*
  contractual duty   *168*
  legal principles   *167–9*
  paper-based   *166–7*
  trust   *167–8*
Duty of care as agent   *10–12*
  tortious negligent misstatement   *11*
Duty of care to company customer   *48*
Duty of care as trustee   *12–14*
  constructive trusts   *12–13, 120*
  liability under express trust   *14*
  Quistclose trusts   *13–14*
  want of probity   *13, 45, 120*
Duty of confidentiality   *4, 15–19*
  after termination of contract   *19, 34, 35*
  ATMs and   *202*
  banker's opinions and secrecy   *23*
  disclosure in bank's interest   *18*
  disclosure with customer's consent   *18–19*
  disclosure under compulsion of law   *15–18*
    court order   *16, 17*
    offence committed by non-disclosure   *16–17, 18*
    valid request from official   *16, 17–18*

359

Duty of confidentiality—*continued*
 duty to public to disclose   18

Early repayment   88–9
Easements   246, 265
Electronic cash dispensing machines *see* Automatic teller machines (ATMs)
Electronic funds transfer *see* Electronic funds transfer at point of sale (EFTOS):
Electronic payment systems
Electronic funds transfer at point of sale (EFTOS)   203–14
 authorisation   204
 bank's own scheme   206, 208
 breakdown or defect in terminal   211–12, 213–14
 cardholder   212–14
 chargeback   211, 212
 consumer-activated equipment   213
 defamation   213
 electronic signature or PIN   205
 floor limit   204, 211
 fraud or forgery   211
 interchange limit   204
 legal implication of contractual relationships   208–9
 polling   205, 206, 212
 refusal of authorisation   213
 retailer   203, 209–12
 retailer acquirer   211–12
 settlement and payment   206, 207
Electronic payment systems   136, 171–87
 BACS   171–2, 180

Electronic payment systems—*continued*
 CHAPS   172–3, 174, 175–6, 179, 180, 183
 clearing cycles   173
 completion of payment   175–6, 183
 contributory negligence   178
 countermanding payment   179–80
 discharge of debt by EFT   173, 175
 electronic signatures   177
 equipment and systems failure   181–2
 payee and payee bank   185–7
 payee and paying bank   184–5
 payee right to payment   186–7
 payee bank and payee   185–7
 payee bank and payer   187
 payee bank's duty   182–3, 185–6
 payee bank's mandate   185
 payer as direct remitter   180
 payer and payee   173, 175–7
 payer and payee bank   187
 payer and paying bank   177–82
 paying bank and payee   184–5
 paying bank and payee bank   182–4
 paying bank's duty   184–5
 payment by mistake   176–7, 180, 184, 185, 187
 PINs   177
 privity of contract   187
 truncation   136
 wrongful dishonour   179
Enduring power of attorney   39
 joint accounts and   43

Entry codes *177*
Equitable assignments *277*
Equitable mortgage
  over land *255*
  over shares *270, 272*
Eurobonds *32, 112*
Ex turpi causa non oritur acto
  defence *147–8*
'Execution only' customers *105, 106*
Executors *45*
Exempt credit agreements *55, 61, 77–80*
  foreign elements *80*
  maximum number of repayments *78–9*
  maximum rate of total charge *79–80*
  property lending *78–80*
Extortionate credit transactions *224*

FIMBRA *100*
Finance Houses Association Base Rate *80*
Financial Intermediaries, Managers and Brokers Regulatory Association (FIMBRA) *100*
Financial services regulation *97–107*
  appointed representatives *103*
  'best advice' rule *106*
  'best execution' rule *106*
  'Chinese walls' *104*
  'cold calling' *105*
  compensation fund *104*
  complaints procedures *103*
  control of advertising *104–5*
  cooling-off period *106*

Financial services regulation—*continued*
  employee investment dealing rules *104*
  'execution only' customers *105, 106*
  exempt bodies *102–3*
  fair allocation of stock *106*
  fair charges *106*
  friendly societies *102*
  full disclosure of interest *105*
  independent advice *104*
  insider dealing *104*
  insurance companies *102*
  investment business *99*
  investments *98*
  'know your customer' rule *105*
  'market counterparty' *106*
  Recognised Professional Bodies *97, 101–2*
  records maintenance and retention *107*
  safe custody of investments *106*
  Securities and Investments Board *97, 99–100*
  segregation of clients' money *107*
  Self-Regulatory Organisations *97, 100–1*
  solvency *103*
  tied agents *103*
  written customer agreements *105–6*
Fixed charges *285*
  agricultural *307–8*
  comparison with floating *287–8*
  see also Registration of charges

361

Fixed-sum credit 57, 58
　cash cards and 193–4
Flawed assets 302
Floating charges 284–5
　agricultural 308
　comparison with fixed 287–8
　crystallisation 285, 288–9
　see also Registration of
　　charges
Foreclosure 262, 264
Foreign currency, credit in 55
Forfeiture of lease 264
Forged cheques
　checking statements 7, 8, 9,
　　122–3
　contributory negligence 9, 147
　duty to inform if aware of
　　forgery 122
　estoppel 122–3, 148
　forged signature 121–3
　forged and unauthorised
　　indorsements 132
　fraudulent alteration 124–6
　inchoate cheques 125
　material alterations 125
　reasonable precautions 7, 124
　signing alterations 124–5
　truncation and 163–4
　unauthorised debits 8, 9
Fraudulent conversion, safe
　　custody and 34
Freehold land 245
　flying freehold 246
Friendly societies 102
Futures 98

Gift tokens 66
'Gold' cards 68
Government bonds 98
Government stock 32

Government warrants, crossings
　　on 114
Gower Report 97
Guarantees 233–43
　'all monies' 237–8, 238–9
　avoided payments 241
　cheque guarantee cards 66
　compounding 239
　conclusive evidence 240–1
　consideration 234–5, 237
　contingent liability 235–6
　continuation of principal
　　debtor's account 240
　continuing security 238
　demand 235–6, 237
　determination 235–6, 238
　estoppel by convention 242–3
　from adult for minor 44
　granting time 239
　indemnities compared with
　　233–4
　independent security 240
　joint 236–7
　letters of comfort 243
　Limitation Act and 236
　notice to determine 238
　parties 240
　partnerships and 46, 240
　past consideration 234
　preference and 241
　release 239
　security from principal debtor
　　240
　standard bank terms 237–41
　third party, bankruptcy and
　　220
　undue influence and 226–8
　variation 239
　whole debt 238–9
　see also Guarantor

Guarantor *260*
　death, mental incapacity or bankruptcy *238*
　duty before guarantee signed *235*
　right of set-off *242*
　right of subrogation and contribution *242*
　right to be indemnified *242*
　right to know extent of liability *241–2*
　security from principal debtor *240*
　see also Guarantees

Holder of cheques *117–19*
　collecting bank as *148–51*
　holder in due course *117–19, 125–6, 148–51*
　mere holders *117*
　valuable consideration *118, 149–51*
Holiday remuneration *52*
'Holy ground' *83, 84*
House credits *135*

Implied pledge *32*
IMRO *101*
Indemnities, guarantees compared with *233–4*
Individual customers *37–41*
　account operation by third parties *37–8*
　bankruptcy see Bankruptcy of individual
　death *35, 39–40*
　employer identity *37, 141*
　opening accounts see Opening account

Individual customers—*continued*
　powers of attorney see Power of attorney
Indorsements on cheques *116–17*
Information, access to see Data Protection Act
Inland Revenue *218*
Insider dealing *104*
Insolvency *217–24*
　administration orders *50, 220, 293–5*
　'associates' *221*
　bankruptcy expenses *219*
　bankruptcy order *217*
　of company see Company insolvency
　'connected persons' *221*
　debits after notice of petition *30*
　debts become due *30*
　extortionate credit transactions *224*
　individual, priorities *219–20*
　liquidation expenses *218*
　'nominee' *220*
　of partnership *48*
　preferences *220–3, 241*
　priority of claims *217–20*
　proving *217*
　of recognised investment exchanges *31*
　set-off following *30–1*
　termination of contract *35*
　transactions at undervalue *220–1, 223–4*
　transactions defrauding creditors *224*
　voluntary arrangements *220*
　wages accounts *218, 291*
　winding-up *217*

363

Insolvency—*continued*
  see also Administrative
    receivers
  Insolvency Act *326–39*
  Institute of Actuaries *102*
  Institute of Chartered Accountants
    in England and Wales *102*
  Insurance companies *102*
  Insurance contracts, as
    investments *98*
  Interest, bank's right to *14–15*
  International trade credit *80*
  Investment business *99*
  Investment Management
    Regulatory Organisation
    (IMRO) *101*
  Investments, definitions *98*
  Irrevocable power of attorney
    39

Jack Report *112, 163, 213*
Jack Report White Paper *70, 72, 182, 194, 196, 200, 203, 213*
Joint accounts *42–3*
  death of one account holder
    42–3
  mental incapacity of one
    account–holder *43*
  stop orders and *128*
  survivorship right *42*
Joint guarantees *236–7*
Joint and several liability *47, 84*
Joint tenancy *249*

'Know your customer' rule *105*

Land
  agricultural *see* Agricultural
    charges
  beneficial interest *249*

Land—*continued*
  Charge Certificate *247*
  Charges Register *247*
  classification of *245*
  Companies register search
    248
  conveyancing of registered land
    247–8
  conveyancing of unregistered
    land *248*
  easements *246, 265*
  equitable interest *249, 250*
  flying freehold *246*
  freehold *245, 246*
  'good leasehold' *247*
  interests in *245–6*
  interests in registered land
    250–1
  interests in unregistered land
    251–2
  joint tenancy *249*
  Land Certificate *247*
  Land Charges Register *251*
  Land Charges Registry *256*
  leasehold *see* Leasehold
    property
  legal and equitable mortgages
    see Mortgages
  legal estates *245–6*
  legal title *249*
  loans secured by *see* Secured
    lending
  local land charges search *248*
  Matrimonial Homes Act *254*
  minor interests *247*
  mortgagee *see* Mortgagees
  mortgages *see* Mortgages
  occupation *252, 254*
  overreaching principle *251, 254*

Land—*continued*
  overriding interest *250–1, 252*
  'possessory title' *247*
  Property Register *246*
  Proprietorship Register *246–7*
  'qualified title' *247*
  registered *246–8, 247–8, 250–1, 252–4*
  registering a caution *256*
  restrictive covenants *246*
  risks to lender *267*
  searches *247–8, 251*
  state guaranteed title *247*
  survivorship right *249*
  tenancy in common *249*
  'title absolute' *247*
  types of ownership *248–50*
  unregistered *246–8, 248, 251–2, 254*
  see also Registered *and* Unregistered land: Secured lending
Land Certificate *247*
Land Charges Register *251*
Land Charges Registry *256*
Land Registry, Agricultural Credits Department *308*
LAUTRO *100*
Law of Property (Miscellaneous Provisions) Act *319–20*
Law Society of England and Wales *101*
Law Society of Scotland *101*
Leasehold land *245–6*
  'good leasehold' *247*
Leasehold property *245–6, 264–5*
  easements *265*
  forfeiture of lease *264*
  mortgages of *264–5*

Leasehold property—*continued*
  repair covenants *265*
  restrictions *265*
Legal assignments *276–7*
Legal mortgage
  over land *255*
  over shares *269–70, 271–2*
Lending *see* Consumer Credit Act lending *and various Credit headings*
Letters of comfort *243*
Liability, joint and several *47, 84*
Libel
  in banker's opinions *23*
  'refer to drawer' *131*
  wrongful dishonour *130–1*
Life assurance policies *275–81*
  basis of lending *275*
  beneficiaries, risks involving *278–9*
  constructive notice of prior assignment *277*
  endowment *275*
  equitable assignments *277*
  insurable interest *279*
  legal assignments *276–7*
  misrepresentation *279–80*
  murder and *280–1*
  non-disclosure *279–80*
  non-payment of premiums *281*
  parties involved in contract *275–6*
  potential risks for lender *278–81*
  priorities between assignees *277*
  remedies of assignee *278*
  standard assignment terms *278*

Life assurance policies—*continued*
  suicide and 280
  term 275
  undue influence 279
  unlawful killing and 280-1
  whole life 275
Life Assurance and Unit Trust Regulatory Organisation (LAUTRO) 100
Linked credit transactions 62
Lloyd's and Lloyd's underwriters 102
Local authority bonds 98
Logical acknowledgement (LAK) 175-6, 179
London Gazette 51
'Lulling to sleep' doctrine 143
Luncheon vouchers 66

Mandate 120
  of payee bank 185
  of paying bank 185
Mareva injunction 16
'Market counterparty' 106
Mastercard 68-9, 73, 95
Matrimonial Homes Act, land and 254
Memorandum of deposit
  mortgage over land 258
  mortgage over shares 270-1
Mental incapacity 39-40
  customer's account and 39-40
  enduring power of attorney 39
  of guarantor 238
  of one account-holder of joint account 43
  of partner 47
  termination of contract 35

Minor account holders 43-4
  guarantors and 44, 234
  'necessaries' 44
  subrogation principle 44
Misrepresentation, security and 228-30
Mistaken crediting 155-6
Mistaken payment
  EFT and 176-7, 180, 184, 185, 187
  recovery of money 153-5
Mortgagee
  applying proceeds of sale 261
  appointment of receiver 261-2, 263
  duty to obtain proper price 259-61
  entering into possession 262-3
  foreclosure 262, 264
  position of 252-4
  power of sale 259-61, 263
  registered land 252-4
  remedies for equitable mortgagee 263-4
  sale by junior mortgagee 261
  suing for covenant to repay 263, 264
  unregistered land 254
Mortgages, over land
  discharge of 265-7
  equitable 246, 255
  leasehold property 264-5
  legal 246, 255
  memorandum of deposit 258
  realisation of 258-9
  registered land 256, 266
  registering a caution 256
  registration and priority 256-7

Mortgages, over land—*continued*
  risk to lender   267
  second mortgages   256
  standard bank terms   257–8
  unregistered land   256–7, 266–7
Mortgages, over shares
  equitable   270, 272
  legal   269–70, 271–2
  memorandum of deposit   270–1
  realisation of   271
  risks for lender   271–3
Multiple credit agreements   59, 61, 68

National Savings Certificates, index-linked   98
Negligence
  in collection of cheque   141–6
  contributory   7, 8, 9, 122–3 147, 197

  in opening account   139–41
  safe custody items and   34
Negotiable instruments, cheques and   112–13
Non est factum defence   230–1, 267
Non-commercial credit agreements   62, 73

Occupation   252, 254
Occupational pension schemes   218
Office of Data Protection Registrar   19
Opening account
  employer   37, 141

Opening account—*continued*
  false name   140
  identity proof   140–1
  negligence in   139–41
  references   140, 141
Opinions *see* Banker's opinions
Options   98
Overdrafts   58, 62–5
  accepted facility letter   64
  advertising   91
  agreed and unagreed   64
  canvassing   63, 89–90
  cash cards and   190–2
  Determination in respect of   63
  EC disclosure proposals   64
  secured lending   76
  temporary excesses   63
  termination of   65, 88
Overreaching principle   251, 254

Paper payment systems   159–70
  cheque clearing   160–2
  credit clearing *see* Credit clearing
  direct debits   166–7
  town clearing   162
Partnership accounts   45–8
  articles or deeds of partnership   46
  countermanded payment   47
  dissolution of partnership   47–8
  guarantees on behalf of   46, 240
  implied powers   46
  insolvency of partnership   48
  joint and several liability   47
  mental incapacity of partner   47

367

Partnership accounts—*continued*
  opening account   47
  partnership definition   45–6
  reformation of dissolved
    partnership   48
  wages account   47
Payee bank
  agent for   169
  EFT and payee   185–7
  EFT and payer   187
  EFT and paying bank   182–4
Paying bank
  cheques and legal relationships
    involving   120
  customer and   120
  EFT and payee   184–5
  EFT and payee bank   182–4
  EFT and payer   177–82
  mandate of   177–9
  statutory protection   131–4, 164
  subrogation   134–5
Payment by mistake *see* Mistaken payment
Payment systems *see* Electronic payment systems: Paper payment systems
Pension schemes, insolvency and   218
Personal Identification Number (PIN)   70, 71, 177, 195, 199–200, 205
  erroneous duplication   200
  fraudulent duplication   199–200
Pledge   31–2
'Possessory title'   247
Post-dated cheques   120–1
Power of attorney   38–9
  enduring   39, 43

Power of attorney—*continued*
  irrevocable   39
Power of sale   31–2, 39
  of mortgagee   259–61, 263
Preferences   220–3
  guarantees and   241
Privity of contract   187
Promissory notes   133
Property Register   246
Proprietorship Register   246–7

'Qualified title'   247
Quistclose trusts   13–14
Quotations   92, 93–4

Receiver
  appointment by mortgagee   261–2, 263
  see also Administrative receivers
Recognised Investment Exchanges   102
  insolvency of   31
Recognised Professional Bodies   97, 101–2
  compensation fund   104
Recovery of money paid by mistake   153–5
  tracing   155
References   140, 141
Registered land   246–8
  conveyancing   247–8
  discharge of mortgage   266
  interests in   250–1
  mortgagee and   252–4
Registration of charges
  agricultural   308–9
  charges requiring registration   295–6

INDEX

Registration of charges—*continued*
  consequences of failure to register 296–7
  errors and omissions 297
  late registration 297
  meaning of 295
  over credit balance 301
  release of charges 297
Regulated agreements *see* Consumer Credit Act lending
Repair covenants 265
Repayment on demand 24
  limitation 24–5
Restricted-use credit 58–9, 60, 68
Retailer 209–12
  legal effect between customer and 210
Retention of title clauses 288, 292–3
Romalpa clauses 288, 292–3
Running-account credit 57–8, 62, 63
  cash cards and 193, 194

Safe custody
  bailment for reward 33
  delivery on authority of all bailors 33
  doubt as to title owner 34
  fraudulent conversion 34
  gratuitous bailment 33
  investments, FSA and 106
  items stolen by bank employee 34
  liability of bank as bailee 33
  negligence and 34
  no banker's lien on 32, 34
  voluntary bailment 33

Secured lending 74–7
  cancellation rights 76–7
  exempt transactions 75–6
  institutional lenders 75
  overdrafts 76
  property lending 75–6
  rights of withdrawal 76–7
  see also Land
Securities 98
Securities Association, The (TSA) 101
Securities and Investments Board 97, 99–100
  compensation fund 104
Security
  charges over book debts 303–5
  duty to advise provider 230
  from companies *see* Company security
  from individuals 225–31
  guarantees *see* Guarantees: Guarantor
  insolvency *see* Insolvency
  land as *see* Land: Mortgagees: Mortgages
  letters of comfort 243
  life assurance policies *see* Life assurance policies
  misrepresentation 228–30
  negligent misstatement 229–30
  non est factum defence 230–1, 267
  over bank balances *see* Bank balance charges
  shares as *see* Mortgages, over shares: Shares
  undue influence 225–8
  see also Mortgagees: Mortgages

369

Self-Regulatory Organisations
    97, 100–1
  AFBD *101*
  FIMBRA *100*
  IMRO *101*
  LAUTRO *100*
  TSA *101*
Set-off
  charges over bank balances and
    299–300
  equitable right of *29–30*
  following insolvency *30–1*
  guarantor and right of *242*
  right of *84*
Shadow director *51–2*
Shares *98*
  basis of lending *269*
  mortgage over see Mortgages,
    over shares
  types of stocks and shares *269*
Signature
  on cheque *120, 121–3*
  electronic *177, 205*
  forged *121–3*
Small credit agreements *61, 66,
  69, 73*
Stamp Duty *270*
State guaranteed title *247*
Status enquiry *19, 23–4*
Stocks *98*
Stop orders *126–9*
  cancellation of *128*
Subrogation principle *44, 46–7*
  guarantors and *242*
  insolvency and *218*
  paying bank and *134–5*
Survivorship
  joint accounts *42*
  legal title to land and *249*
Swaps *98*

SWIFT payment system *176*
Switch cards *67–8, 95*

Tenancy in common *249*
Termination of contract *34–5*
  by bank *35*
  by customer *35*
  by operation of law *35*
Termination of regulated
    agreement *87–8*
  default notice *88*
  written notice *87, 88*
Third parties
  individual account operation by
    37–8
  use of credit tokens *70–2*
Tied agents *103*
'Title absolute' *247*
Title to land *247*
  see also Land
Town clearing *162*
Tracing *155*
Transactions
  at undervalue *220–1, 223–4*
  defrauding creditors *224*
  extortionate credit *224*
Travellers' cheques *132*
Truncation *160*
  cheque clearing *160, 162–5*
  forgery risk *163–4*
  presentation for second time
    164
Trustee accounts *44–5*
  appointment of new trustee
    45
  bankruptcy of trustee *45*
  breach of trust and *45*
  charitable trusts *44–5*
  death of trustee *45*
  executors *45*

Trusts
 constructive trusts *12-13, 120*
 credit and debit transfer and
  167-8
 Quistclose trusts *13-14*
 want of probity *13, 45, 120*
TSA *101*

Ultra vires *284*
Undervalue transactions *220-1, 223-4*
Undue influence *225-8, 267, 279*
Unit trusts *98*
Unregistered land *246-8*
 conveyancing *248*
 discharge of mortgage *266-7*
 interests in *251-2*
 mortgagee and *254*
Unrestricted-use credit *58-9, 60, 62, 63*

Value added tax *218*
VISA cards *68-9, 73, 95*
Voluntary arrangements *50, 220*
Voluntary early repayment of
 credit *88-9*
Voluntary winding-up *50*

Wages accounts
 advantage of *53*
 bankruptcy and *40*
 of company *52-3*
 partnerships *47*
 preferential creditors and *218, 291*
Winding-up *217*
 compulsory *50-1*
 voluntary *50*
 see also Insolvency
Wrongful dishonour *129-31*
 EFT and *179*
 as libel *130-1*
Wrongful trading *51-2*

371